GERMAN DRAMA
BETWEEN THE WARS

By George E. Wellwarth

GERMAN DRAMA BETWEEN THE WARS
THE THEATRE OF PROTEST AND PARADOX
THE NEW WAVE SPANISH DRAMA
THE SPANISH UNDERGROUND DRAMA
THE THEMES OF DRAMA

By Michael Benedikt and George E. Wellwarth

MODERN FRENCH THEATRE
POSTWAR GERMAN THEATRE
MODERN SPANISH THEATRE

GERMAN DRAMA BETWEEN THE WARS

AN ANTHOLOGY OF PLAYS

edited by George E. Wellwarth

E. P. DUTTON & CO., INC., NEW YORK

1972

Published simultaneously in Canada by
Clarke, Irwin & Company Limited, Toronto and Vancouver

Library of Congress Catalog Card Number: 77–95498

SBN 0-525-11291-X

First Edition

INDIVIDUAL COPYRIGHTS AND ACKNOWLEDGMENTS

Oscar Kokoschka: *Job*. Copyright 1917 by Paul Cassirer, Berlin. English translation copyright © 1971 by Michael Benedikt. Published by permission of Oscar Kokoschka.

Hermann Broch: *The Atonement*. Copyright © Rhein Verlag AG, Zürich 1961. All rights reserved by Suhrkamp Verlag, Frankfurt am Main. English translation copyright © 1971 by George E. Wellwarth and H. F. Broch de Rothermann. MS deposited in the Beinecke Rare Book and Manuscript Library of Yale University. Published by permission of the Yale University Library and Suhrkamp Verlag.

Kurt Tucholsky (Peter Panter) and Walter Hasenclever: *Christopher Columbus*. Copyright © 1971 by Felix Bloch Erben, Berlin. English translation copyright © 1971 by Max Spalter and George E. Wellwarth. Published by permission of Felix Bloch Erben.

Carl Zuckmayer: *The Captain of Köpenick*. Copyright © 1960 by Carl Zuckmayer. Originally published in German under the title *Der Hauptmann von Köpenick: Ein deutsches Märchen in drei Akten*. Aus Carl Zuckmayer: *Gesammelte Werke III: Dramen*. English translation copyright © 1971 by Carl R. Mueller. Published by permission of S. Fischer Associates, Inc., New York.

Ernst Toller: *No More Peace!*. English translation by Edward Crankshaw and W. H. Auden. Copyright © 1971 by Sidney Kaufman. Published by arrangement with Sidney Kaufman on behalf of the estate of Ernst Toller.

Karl Kraus: Excerpt from *The Last Days of Mankind*. Copyright © 1957 by Kösel-Verlag, München. English translation copyright © 1971 by Max Spalter. Published by permission of Kösel-Verlag.

I should like to thank Professors John Spalek and Joseph P. Strelka of the State University of New York at Albany for their assistance.

CONTENTS

CONTENTS

INTRODUCTION
to *German Drama Between the Wars*

THIS BOOK is a literary postmortem. Whenever a violent and untimely death occurs, an overpowering morbid curiosity springs up in the minds of the survivors. Belatedly and ineffectually (for the knowledge will surely do them no good in the future), they wish to know why it happened, how it could have been prevented, who was responsible. In 1933 Germany died a violent and untimely—though not, as we shall see, an entirely unpredictable—death, and in 1939 the corpse began slowly to be buried. The plays in this book are the record of that demise.

Although Oskar Kokoschka wrote *Job* (1917) while World War I was still in progress, it has been included here because it is representative of the trend in German art caused by the war. Expressionism had begun before the war but did not achieve its full development until just after it. It had started as a symptom of the intense unrest and dissatisfaction among the younger generation of German writers in the first decade and a half of the twentieth century. The German society that World War I destroyed had been a stifling and stultifying one, based on a narrow-minded patriarchal concept of the family with strongly pietistic overtones, which, in the larger sphere, manifested itself in a rigid political authoritarianism. With the breakdown of faith in this political system, with the refusal to accept any longer the proffered values and make obeisance to the received ideas, there came a whole series of literary movements (of which Expressionism was the first) whose tendency was disintegrative. Instead of attempting to integrate the elements of life as they saw them into a cohesive system of conduct or into a philosophy cemented finally by faith in a priori assumptions, these new writers believed nothing. They knew only that what had been and what was, was no good. Their work was, therefore, largely an attack on or a mockery of existing social forms, usually as embodied in family relationships, or, as in *Job*, in the sexual relationship. *Job* is essentially playful in contrast to the almost unalloyed bitterness of other Expressionistic dramas, but Kokoschka's satire of the "perfect" union with a woman who becomes as one's "soul" is frequently mordant, not least in his choice of the protagonist's name.

The difficulty in understanding a play like *Job*—or any Expressionistic play—stems from the primacy of the language over the form. Rather than theatre pieces these plays are largely lyric poems in dramatic form. All of the Expressionistic dramatists were also poets, and their interest in language took precedence in their minds over their interest in stage technique. The Expressionists were poets who turned to the theatre as the most convenient medium for the dissemination of their ideas. Only through the theatre could they hope to transmit their message to the people as a whole. Poetry rarely shocks: it is read almost exclusively by people who empathize with the poet to begin with. Through the theatre, then, and the animation of their lyric scream of protest against the bonds imposed by the family and society, the Expressionist playwrights could hope to shock and impress greater numbers by striking a responsive feeling in them.

After the war, Expressionistic drama held the stage for only a very few years. The war did the job of demolishing the hierarchical family system well enough. The hopelessness and bewilderment engendered by the war, with its destruction of the old social values that had been accepted on faith and followed automatically, produced a condition in which the family was no longer the important unit. The greater freedom of the Weimar Republic had also done away with the necessity of a microcosmic approach to the artistic treatment of social problems. As both family and national discipline slackened, social and political problems could be dealt with directly.

The society depicted in Hermann Broch's *The Atonement* (1934) is a society on a suicide course. There is a really extraordinary similarity between the Weimar Republic rushing toward its willful self-destruction and the Second Spanish Republic. The rhetoric of the Nazi Party and of the Falange, their aims,

beginnings, rank and file, and rise to power from ludicrous
insignificance are all virtually parallel. What enabled them to
become powerful was the internecine strife of the numerous
political groups active in the country, most of them divided by the
barest ideological differences. Had they been able to resolve those
insignificant differences, they would have been able to combine
against the menace and easily defeat it. As it was, society became
completely polarized, as shown in Broch's play for Germany, or
in a work like Gironella's *The Cypresses Believe in God* (1958) for
Spain. The strength of the German society clearly lay in the solid
rank and file of the workers, in men like Rychner, who is killed
early in the action, leaving the field clear for the remaining collection of cynics, wild-eyed fanatics, and impotent intellectuals. Not
even the faintest ray of mutual respect or understanding illumines
the thoughts of the opposing parties in the paradigmatic conflicts
of the play. In view of later events the barely held-in ferocity of
men like Herbert Filsmann, Rosshaupt, and Lauck becomes
disturbingly prophetic. Young Filsmann's remark, "Revolution?
What we need is a properly run police force—that's all!" demonstrates the bull-headed attitude of the moneyed classes, which had
caused the fanaticism of the Laucks in the first place—and which
remains uncannily contemporary. It was attitudes like this one
or like that implied in Rosshaupt's babble about "community of
the blood" that made it possible for the Nazis to step into the
chaos with their precise program and unified organization. The
real villains, however, are the superficially attractive unscrupulous
cynics like Menck (or his lower-class avatar Jeckel), who says
quite frankly, "If the Communists guaranteed my job, I'd become
a Communist."—or a Nazi, of course.

The chaotic strife and lack of even the will for mutual understanding portrayed in Broch's play is balanced by Kurt Tucholsky's
and Walter Hasenclever's picture of graft and greed in *Christopher
Columbus* (1932). This allegorical parable, in which the Ameri-
can Indian "savages" are shown as urbane and civilized gentlemen enslaved and corrupted by the Europeans, seems clearly
marked by Tucholsky's characteristic cabaret satire style rather
than by Hasenclever's Expressionistic intensity. For Tucholsky
and Hasenclever, both of whom later fled from Nazism, the
archetypical German figure of their time is contained in the aptly
named Vendrino, the utterly unscrupulous and unprincipled op-

portunist.[1] The opportunists Menck and Vendrino, however, represent a universal type. They are not unusual; we all recognize them. It is only in an amorphous and unstable society where the strata of power are shifting rapidly and randomly that the unscrupulous opportunist comes into his own. The Weimar Republic was a veritable *Schlaraffenland* for cynical climbers. One of the things that made their progress easier was the exaggerated respect for authority and capacity for hero-worship exhibited by the Germans. In a milieu consisting of people who cringe instinctively before the trappings of power, whose individuality is spurious and instantly becomes subordinated to the mere appearance of authority, the man without scruples or illusions rises to the top like scum in a stagnant pool.

Carl Zuckmayer's *The Captain of Köpenick* (1931) is a straight dramatization of an event that actually occurred in the early part of the century. Neither the name of the "captain" nor that of his town has been changed. There is a distinctly German flavor in this story; indeed, one doubts that it could have happened anywhere else. Zuckmayer, who later had to flee from the Nazis, perceived clearly that the slavish craving for authority (which is the same as abdication of moral responsibility) was so great in his countrymen that the mere sight of a uniform and the mere sound of an arrogantly assertive voice was enough to transform them into robots.[2] In its ultimate manifestation, the spirit displayed by the town officials of Köpenick became the goose-stepping, brown-shirted thugs of the Nazi era with their "Sieg Heils" and their numbed, glazed, brutalized mindlessness. Zuckmayer makes his play all the stronger, of course, by taking pains to establish the complete insignificance and innocuousness of Voigt. The uniform

---

[1] There is a curious parallel between this play and the somewhat later *Christopher Columbus* by Jura Soyfer, which has a virtually identical final scene. Cf. my "Jura Soyfer: An Attempt at Rehabilitation," *American-German Review*, XXXV, iii (1969), pp. 22–26.

[2] An amusing complementary story from real life is related by Ernst Josef Aufricht, the producer at the Theater am Schiffbauerdamm. During the struggle to stage Peter Martin Lampel's *Giftgas über Berlin* two police officers showed up at the theatre to check the ticket distribution for the single performance permitted this violently anti-militaristic play. They never got the list they were after, however, because an actor who played a colonel in the play happened to stroll by in costume, and they jumped to attention and saluted. Their feeling of authority gone, they were easily persuaded to leave. (Ernst Josef Aufricht, *Erzähle damit Du dein Recht erweist* [Berlin: Propyläen Verlag; Ullstein, 1966], p. 89.)

is enough: authority does not reside in the individual; it resides in the façade. And people who will cringe before Wilhelm Voigt and his shabby uniform will cringe before anything.

In the plays of Ernst Toller and Karl Kraus the tone is one of apocalyptic prophecy. Toller's *No More Peace!* (1936) has some of the gaiety of a W. S. Gilbert satire in W. H. Auden's translation of the verse sections, but Toller, who committed suicide in exile in 1939, is cynical rather than gay in this work. The love of war, the xenophobia, the patriotic mania, and the instantaneous perversion of values under the influence of slogans that characterizes the Dunkelsteiners is something that Toller sensed in the Germans of the 1920's, just as Kraus saw it in the Austrians during World War I. As the artist George Grosz put it, "The world of the 1920's was like a boiling caldron. We did not see those who fed the flames. However, we did feel the growing heat and watched the violent seething. There were speakers and preachers on every street corner. Sounds of hate could be heard everywhere. There was universal hatred: hatred of Jews, Junkers, capitalists, Communists, militarists, homeowners, workers, the Reichswehr, the Allied Control Commission, corporations, and politicians. A real orgy of hate was brewing, and behind it all the weak Republic was scarcely discernible. An explosion was imminent." [3] Although he felt this ferment as much as Grosz did, Toller (like Kaiser) saw the characteristics of his Dunkelsteiner Germans as basic to humanity and set his play in a perspective that was at once historical, biblical, and allegorical. The wistful ending based on the angel's human longing for better wings need not be taken too seriously: Toller's suicide in a New York hotel room is sufficient evidence that he found no Utopia of peace outside Germany.

The brief scene from Karl Kraus's *The Last Days of Mankind* (1919–21) included in this book expresses his apocalyptically pessimistic vision of the disintegration of Austrian society. To understand fully the complexity of Kraus's vision it is necessary to set him in the context of Viennese culture, of which he was so integral a part (a large part of the play is written in the Viennese dialect) at the same time that he represented the satiric counter-

[3] George Grosz, *A Little Yes and a Big No* (New York: Dial Press, 1946), p. 201.

weight to the self-indulgent preening in which the Viennese and their less serious artists love to wallow.

To understand the satiric drama of Austria it is first necessary to say a few words about the literary influence of the city of Vienna, which in a very real sense *is* Austria, and which has dictated the nature of its literature for centuries. Every great city may be said to have a "personality" of its own; and there is usually some key word that is supposed to characterize its essence. Sometimes the word is appropriate, more often it is not. When it is not, the city simply has to throw up a façade in order to live up to its mysteriously earned reputation. This appears to be the case with Vienna. Vienna is the city of romance par excellence. Not the gay, sensual, immediate romance of Paris, but a quiet, nostalgic, sentimental romance. In Vienna one thinks of the nineteenth century, of coffeehouses and wine gardens, of the waltzes of Lanner, Schrammel, and Strauss, of beautiful and graceful women, and of men who somehow manage to combine the sleekness of a gigolo with the debonair gentility of an *homme du monde*, vintage 1852.

Alas, it is all a façade. The popular conception of Vienna is that its glory ended in 1918, and that it has quietly and graciously been living on its reputation ever since. It is a city that capitalizes on being dead; and people come from all over the world to worship the perfumed corpse. But what makes it even stranger is that the "corpse" was probably never alive. Vienna seems always to have been hypocrisy covered with gaiety; stench muffled with rose water. Perhaps this was not true when Vienna was still the Vindobona of the Romans, but certainly in Joseph II's day when Mozart starved there; and in Franz Joseph's day when Mayerling was in the news and the municipal workers dropped in the streets from overwork and starvation; and in the days of Dr. Karl Lueger, Msgr. Ignaz Seipel, and Engelbert Dollfuss, whose "canonization" by a Nazi bullet obscured the fact that he and his two predecessors prepared the way for the Nazis in Vienna as surely as if they had been in their pay. No, Vienna has indeed never been gay; it has only produced gaiety.

Vienna's reputation for gaiety has always been based on its music. But Vienna produced Freud as well as Strauss; and its serious drama has followed the cold realism of the former rather than the sugar-glacé illusionism of the latter. At the same time, it must be admitted that there is very little serious Viennese drama. Most Viennese drama is characterized by the spinelessness that Viennese and non-Viennese alike always disguise under the amiable label of *Schlamperei*. The word *Schlamperei* literally means "sloppiness," which describes very well the *moral* sloppiness that made Vienna the logical breeding ground for Freudian psychology, and that is so precisely found in lighter Viennese drama with its emphasis on erotica *à la papillon* and its deliberate burial of real moral problems under a soothing balm of lachrymosity. Tears, however, are rarely sincere. They are usually a form of exhibitionistic self-indulgence. Such are the tears of the virtuous Viennese burgher when his native city is mentioned, or when he contemplates the vista of the Schwarzenberg Platz with its *Kaffeehäuser*, or when he hears from afar the strains of the Radetzky March or the *Heurigen* songs from Grinzing. Nostalgic tears are both Vienna's stock-in-trade and its heaviest industry. But it is a *nostalgie de la boue*. The tears are phony, the emotion is fake. For there is little or nothing to be nostalgic *about*. Vienna, glittering city of romance, evocative siren of imagined joys, is no more than an objective correlative, a catalyst for the formation of a false emotion born of imagined ingredients. Like the mirror castles of mythology, it is all façade, reflecting itself when looked at from the rear and disappearing altogether when looked at from the side (i.e., analytically). It is a chocolate-icing and whipped-cream covered garbage heap.

No one saw Vienna and the Viennese more clearly than Karl Kraus. As dramatist and as political pamphleteer he served Vienna as its conscience. Kraus is usually billed as "the great Viennese satirist," but that is an entirely inadequate description. Kraus was no satirist, for one thing. A satirist is an equally tempered and mild-mannered man compared to what Karl Kraus was. The satirist's weapon is the long, thin, graceful rapier insinuated between the ribs from behind and perhaps given a slight, subtly sadistic twist or two. Kraus's weapons, on the other hand, were the nail-studded war club, the two-handed battle-axe, the sledgehammer, the caldron of boiling oil, the steamroller, and the battering ram. There was no subtle twist; when he had his man down, Kraus jumped on him and pounded him until he was exhausted.

Kraus is known today chiefly for *The Last Days of Mankind* a tremendous epic in dramatic form about World War I. Kraus's grandiose title may seem somewhat naïve in the light of later events he did not live to see (he died in 1936), but that is how things appeared to his essentially realistic mind at the time. *The Last Days of Mankind* is a day-by-day chronicle of life in Vienna during World War I. It is almost as long as a day-by-day diary of the war would have been, for it runs to 792 pages in the printed text.

The drama is a triumphant vindication of the technique of realism. It is as if Kraus had been flitting invisibly about Vienna listening over peoples' shoulders in cafés, hiding under ministers' chairs during state conferences, or hovering behind strolling pedestrians on the streets. And all of it added up to a furious denunciation of the war and the people that wanted it. The epic begins with a series of scenes showing the jubilant or complacent reactions of various levels of the populace to the news of the war. These scenes are made all the more fiercely ironic by the dispassionate reportorial matter-of-factness with which they are recorded. Particularly effective are the scenes in which Kraus depicts the real culprits, the monumentally inefficient and effete aristocrats who were running the country and who welcomed the war as a relief from boredom. There is a macabre, sarcastic quality in Kraus's Graf Karl Maria Leopold Ludwig Rudolf Franz Wilhelm Josef Ferdinand comfortably planning to take a vacation in Nice after Serbia is crushed "in three weeks." Later on Kraus has a scene in which a group of hoodlums go around repainting all foreign-looking signs; their ultimate triumph comes when they succeed in persuading the owner of the Westminster Café to change the name to Westmünster Café. It seems the other side had its "anti-Wagner" morons too. As he goes on, Kraus becomes more and more bitter until toward the end his fury is so intense that he tends to lose control. When a brilliant and sensitive intellect like Kraus smashes up against the unconscious and impenetrable stupidity of a force such as a pro-war party, the step over the line into the imagery of insanity is easily made. This can be seen in the scene included here in which The Carper raves on and on in an almost delirious ecstasy of baffled fury about the bestial idiocy of the men who run the war and the transformation into mindless brutes of the men on whom they force their uniforms. The Carper is an alter ego for Kraus and appears in several scenes interspersed throughout the play. He is essentially the mouthpiece for Kraus's own mordant comments on the insanity he depicts in the main body of the play. That the The Carper's comments in this scene are framed between the cries of a newspaper vendor and begin with a statement that only three hours and twenty-five minutes are required to convert a living tree into a piece of newsprint is in itself significant. This is because Kraus, a working journalist who edited and published his own paper, attributed much of the evil of the war to the jingoistic and servile pro-government press and its deliberate falsification of the news for propagandistic purposes.

The Last Days of Mankind ends with a tremendous scene in which a group of carousing Austrian and German officers receives news of defeat after defeat and sees a series of visions of the horrors of the war. As this fades out, we see a chorus of hyenas with human faces commenting on the action. At the very end, the voice of God rolls down from on high, saying, "Ich habe es nicht gewollt." ("I did not desire it.") That, by the way, was reputedly the immortally ineffective comment of the Emperor Franz Josef on the mess.

From the Expressionistic intensity and emotional incoherence of Kokoschka's Job in 1917 to the cynical pessimism of Toller's No More Peace! in 1936 the theme of all of the plays in this book is disintegration. German art between the wars was a chronicle of foreboding. The artists saw the morally nihilistic effects of World War I and the approaching disaster far more clearly than the politicians did and certainly more clearly than the oblivious masses who only sought security in ideologies that led to slavery. Emotionalism, class oppression, and misplaced hero-worship were the main factors in the decline of Germany between the wars, a process that was later to be summed up by Eugène Ionesco in his play The Lesson, when he has his prototypically totalitarian professor say, "It's not enough to integrate, you must also disintegrate. That's the way life is. That's philosophy. That's science. That's progress, civilization." [4]

GEORGE E. WELLWARTH

[4] Eugène Ionesco, Four Plays, trans. by Donald M. Allen (New York: Grove Press, 1958), p. 55.

JOB

by OSCAR KOKOSCHKA

TRANSLATED BY MICHAEL BENEDIKT

A Rib Bone Equals a Big Groan

While Adam was sleeping upon the green lawn
God relented, the sun poised high up in the sky
And Adam, out of sheer boredom, began to nod and yawn.
Awakened by a swift kick in the ribs, Adam cried out "HEY!!!"
And discovered his and Eve's matrimony.
"Oh my God, had he only left my bones alone."

CHARACTERS

JOB
ANIMA, his wife
MR. RUBBERMAN
ADAM, the gardener
EROS
CHAMBERMAID
YOUNG LADIES
GENTLEMEN
A PARROT

ACT I

JOB, *in nightcap and dressing gown, knocks at the door of his
wife's room.*

CHAMBERMAID (*sticking her head cautiously out the door opposite,
   while hiding something behind her back*):
   I've been knocking and knocking because I'd like to know
   Whether you, good sir, couldn't remove
   Something that's been a big load on my back.
   Your good wife bestowed it upon me
   With two good kicks in the behind; claws and feathers
   Are its chief features, and a sharp tongue and a beak.
   As for your honored wife, she's gone away
   And since this morning has been with a man,
   A gentleman, neat as a pin, tidy and trim.
   —This feathered thing is what's been left for you,
   For your pleasure and your delight, sir.
   (*She launches a* PARROT *from a basket. The* PARROT *flies
   straight up to* JOB's *shoulder. The* CHAMBERMAID *exits, sing-
   ing*):
   Oh, 'tis a balmy summer night tonight—
   Quietly sighing, quietly sighing
   Within some deep abyss.
   Watering all tongues, salting all tears,
   Behind the little light that goes flickering through the night
   A little lock of golden, gleaming hair
   Is weaving its web, is weaving—
   And even heroes
               who are experienced heroes
                              fall in . . .
JOB: And I could have sworn she was here just a moment ago!
   (*Pointing to the door.*)
   Virginity has been traded for the mere hope of a Soul
   And has slipped from one man to another,
   Leaving the skull after picking it clean.
   (*Pointing to his forehead.*)
   Here, where once she nested, in mid-
   Flight, even, she has hastily laid her egg,
   Egg from which she herself leaps out again,
   Phoenix-like, reborn in a hop.
   As for me, I'll have no sun rising
   No skies looming and towering
   With their castles of air, before which sphinxes

3

Gossip!
(*While* JOB *is pacing around the* PARROT *suddenly flies onto
his head.*)
Woe to any young man she tries to enrapture anew
Until he starts to feel just the way I do!
(*He falls into a chair.*)
Once from the head of our Creator
The Mother of Creation leapt out—long ago—
And inside her womb his whole world was hiding.
(PARROT *tears at his hair.*)
Ouch, ouch, ouch, my head!
It's disappeared, destroyed!
This horror is the horror of the void!
(*Sings.*)
How love has entwined and twisted me
Since in this empty house
From a lady's room a gentle voice
Called me in to search for her—
Tricked me into a labyrinth.
From it tempting echoes call
And I'm drawn on by each little puff of the air
Chasing everywhere in search of her.
"What's in the wood when you call is what will come out."
I denounce her, and so she deceives me,
And never comes honestly out.
For in the briefest blink of an eye
She suffers metamorphosis
At any open back exit that happens to be open
Into a creature I see
Is once again, me!

(*Behind the door* ANIMA *quietly begins to sing.* JOB *hears
nothing, but plays with the bird, enticing it to his finger.*)

JOB: Tell me: what is all mankind's favorite pastime?
PARROT (*imitating the voice of his spouse*):
  It's Anima—your own soul—your wife.
JOB: My own soul!
  Her continual naughtiness or flightiness,
  Or whatever I finally decide to call it
  Her absence, maybe, gives me time to think
  That . . . Um . . .
  Aha! what name can any man call his own, anyway?
PARROT: Amen and oh—mankind's personal woe!

(*The* PARROT *leaps back onto* JOB's *head, and scratches him in a friendly way.*)

JOB: That treacherous woman has gone to my head—
Sees with my eyes,
Talks with my mouth,
Draws me out and turns me inside out.
(*Shaking the impudent guest on his head, who hangs onto his ears.*)
All in all, what I am is a blockhead
Who in some ditch with his pretty, mystical halo
Must rot.

(*The bird puffs itself up, covering* JOB's *head with feathers.*)

Whether what you are is hopefulness
Or whether you really represent treachery
You're getting too heavy!
Leave me, at least, my mentality
So I can comprehend you a little!
And endure! (*Pauses to think.*) Yes, I do understand you!
And now
HELP!
(*Softly.*)
Wait—didn't I hear her just then? How . . . ?

ANIMA (*equally softly*): I cannot relieve you, Job.
We are together forever,
Eternally we are one.

JOB: But by heaven or hell then tell me—
Who are you?

ANIMA: Who I am is Anima,
Anima, your wife,
And what I am is your soul.

JOB: You say "I am, I am,"
But that's all done, now it's all done
And what remains is "I! I!! I!!!"
(*Once more frantically shaking the doorknob.*)
Once I had a wife
And that wife was once my world! (*Tearfully.*)
I thought these feet encompassed
The very horizons of the globe!
Then the ground vanished
And now all my mastery hangs high in the air
Like a puffed-up big pig bladder, suspended there.
This horror is the horror of the void! (*More calmly.*)

Only half mapped out though it may have been
It was still my world!
(*Dizzy, he stumbles.*)
ANIMA (*softly, behind the door*): He who does not take care
He who does not beware
May find he has lost his head!
JOB (*in a frenzy*): Head or world! They're exactly the same!
Oh look how my very own words
Are torn out of my mouth!
If only I could completely forget
I'd ever heard them before . . .
As a sponge sponges away the harshest of vinegar,
Absorbing, then releasing without retaining a thing . . .
(*His efforts to gain admission having failed,* JOB *turns away from the door.*)
ANIMA (*softly*): Such a man was surely not meant
To be my only entertainment—
A provider of so, so much vinegar
Who expected pure wine in return.

ACT II

JOB, *in order to be alone, flees to the bathroom where the wash— various articles of men's and women's clothing—is hung up to dry. He hoists himself up to the little window there. Outside, thunder and lightning. He seems to be about to throw himself out, but then he notices something down in the street.*

JOB: Oh elements! Drain yourselves dry, you heavens!
Floods, rush over my hurting heart!
Wait—what's this—a dog? Here, boy!
A faithful dog—
Final solace for a man
In whom mankind inspires only hate.

(*The poodle, having run into the building, bursts through the door and jumps up on* JOB, *wagging his tail.*)

Woof woof woof!
This dog's got a keen nose.
I'm a psychologist is what he seems to me to say!
Look look look!
Observe how Sir Species smells the clothes

Of Madame Species!

MR. RUBBERMAN (*wriggles his way out of the dog's skin*):
Forgive me this foolish masquerade.
I am this poodle's nucleus!
And I see *you* have become a misanthrope.
(*Points out the door.*)
That sweet lady there would surely never
Turn a poor dog out in a weather
Raining cats and dogs!
My hat's off to that member of mankind
Who harbors true feeling in his heart and in his liver!
And should it slacken ever—off with his head!
After all, research has made the discovery
That after the decapitations of poor, unfortunate sinners
The heart goes on
Beating a while, still full of feeling.
Unfortunately we cannot prove just whether it might,
In that condition, feel pleasure and delight.
Despite all our winding all clocks run down some day!
As I have already had occasion to suggest
In another context
I am a Psychologist! And I stand absolutely ready
To offer much, much profitable advice.
A Defense Attorney, of course, for the cause
Of Life, I'm not. That might kill the patient!
If he simply trusts in me, then
I have sufficient claims on him . . .
Isn't it the truth, though—
"An exchange of opinions
May not be at all an exchange of good reasons
But an exposure too precipitous of one's precious prognostica-
    tions"?

(*Through the window* RUBBERMAN *sees the lady of the house
returning. She busies herself in the adjoining room. He begins sniffing curiously at the keyhole.* JOB, *hearing her movements next door, turns away uncomfortably.*)

What a lovely lady!
Taking it off—she's turning me on!
(*To* JOB, *who with great effort is directing his attention away
from the ominous door.*)
Besides, in case it should fall out some day
That some crisis,
Some tight squeeze

Should call for my professional assistance . . .
(*Peering harder and harder into the keyhole, nearly crawling into it.*)
In short, I am observing the kind of woman
Who can turn a man's head!

JOB (*distressed, still standing away from the door*):
And you, a doctor,
The friend of the ill and weak
Have no wish to prevent this outrage?

MR. RUBBERMAN: Only the private joy of my personal research
Interests me—I am no mere doctor. (*Peering.*)
Experiment alone interests me . . . (*Overjoyed.*)
Eureka! I have it now!
Her secret technique! It's revealed!
—Eroditis, jealousy! The germs of which
Are incubated by a famous bacillus
Called Erotococcus. It's nothing less than lumbago itself!
Commonly known as witches' curse
And, unfortunately, the only discovery
My colleagues have left for me! It most frequently occurs
In cases precisely like yours
In which the patient, weakened
By marital misery after marital misery
Retains no resistance
Or immunity.

ANIMA (*from the adjoining room*): Beheaded with ease by science
is any man
Who does not fit into its tight little compartments.
It severs the head from any man twisted
By ideas, head turned by the power of love,
Who is briefly reflective too long, who forgets
His little self, and wanders.

(JOB sees RUBBERMAN, *all drooling mouth and greedy eye, pressed against the keyhole. The door opens slowly and* ANIMA *steps through, and then stops.* JOB, *dazzled by the sight, turns his eyes abruptly away; then, finding that he is no longer able to get his head back into the traditional position, he clutches his ears in horror, pulling out his hair by the handfuls.*)

MR. RUBBERMAN (*running up to* JOB, *astonished*):
Let me feel your pulse!
This man's dying of Anxiety under my very eyes!
You're choking! Open your collar!

This is the result of your crooked, contrary view
Of things that can't
Be set to rights:
You're always getting everything backward!

JOB (*bellowing*): They've turned my head!
They've turned my head! (*Whimpering.*)
Turned it . . .

MR. RUBBERMAN (*tapping JOB's chest*): Aha! The heart is still in-
tact! The reversed
Circulation must be corrected! (*Brandishing a surgical saw.*)
The infection must not be allowed to reach
His heart! Here goes the head—take heart!
If you live without a head the trouble
Won't be half so bad . . .

ANIMA: If only I could help!
But nobody ever pays any attention to me!

JOB (*dances around in circles and roars at* RUBBERMAN, *who is
winnowing the air with his saw*):
I can't locate my head anymore!
Does this one belong to me—or that?
You are next to me now . . . and that means
. . . I must get at your throat!
I reach for it—I catch it!
I drop it—I look for it! (*Shaken.*)
Only one more mirage just pretending to be a shape . . .
(*To* RUBBERMAN.)
Why do you look at me so calmly?
Wait and see! Against a madman
Rational man is nothing!
(*Trying to tear his head from his shoulders, beating his fists
against his forehead.*)
World no sooner designed—than resigned!
The world when it turns
Is rolling away!
A woman has twisted my head around . . .
Completely bewitched and possessed it!

MR. RUBBERMAN (*motioning for* ANIMA *to come a little closer,
while he inspects* JOB's *head*):
Once a wife takes possession of her husband's head
She invariably looks for another lover
For *it*.
And since I take an interest in yours . . .
Here she comes now . . .
Please do introduce me!

ANIMA (*innocent, bourgeois, gentle, and blonde*):
You bad bad husband you! That's just your way
Of trying to make me feel guilty.
Me—Anima! Your own wife!
Born of the breath that blew Creation into being—
From which Anima was finally driven by impatience
Before she was really, to tell the truth, perfectly ready.

JOB (*with imploring gestures*): Anima! My soul!

PARROT (*flying into the room, screeching*):
Anima! My soul!

JOB (*reaching out for* ANIMA, *who has turned toward* MR. RUBBER-MAN):
You! who confused my poor head, with him!
You! Who stole the soul from the dozing Adam!

MR. RUBBERMAN (*clasping* ANIMA *to his breast*):
What! That old Bible story, that old potter's tale?
Woman came out of no clay of yours.

EROS (*comes hopping through the door, looking very impish*):
Papa's tears
Did deploy
In Mama's womb
A little boy . . .
(ANIMA *winces;* EROS *trips, and, as he furiously rubs his leg, shouts.*)
The mother of grief
Expected pure joy!

MR. RUBBERMAN: I don't understand a single syllable!
Oh, what ecstasy just to exist!

(*From here on all raise a general and total pandemonium, screaming at the tops of their lungs; the* PARROT *rushes about, screeching;* EROS *weeps.*)

JOB (*pacifies the child. To* RUBBERMAN):
You opportunist!
What she thought was a springboard which would keep her
leaping
From ecstasy to ecstasy
Is only vulgarity. And all her heavens even to the seventh—
Hell!
The birth of a baby is a descent to the earth;
He weeps immediately, at the very gateway.

MR. RUBBERMAN (*to* JOB): He's the spitting image of you.
Now; stop him from slobbering like that.
This whole house is spooked and cursed!

(*Pointing at the* PARROT *and speaking to the* CHAMBERMAID.)
So the thing to do I tell you
Is to show this absolute *animal* the door!
JOB (*wearily*): Back to Hell with him, then.
ANIMA (*taking* EROS *by the hand and dancing in circles out the*
    door):
Heaven or Hell, Hell or Heaven!
I love my holy lord Eros.
I have borne him out of imagination—
He whom I dreamed of even as a girl,
One feature borrowed from this man
One feature borrowed from that.
To my lover I brought lips of resignation
To my husband mocking melancholy only
And I traveled from one to the other! Like a bee
Faithlessly gathering! Until holy lord Eros
Came. And came! And came!!
MR. RUBBERMAN (*babbling after the two fugitives, while the gen-*
    eral clamor dies down):
Adored lady . . . Stay!
Your Erotology inspires me as much as you!
However—purely objectively—I would like to remark
That the likely genetic history
Of your so-called mythological son
Makes me think we'd be left less in the dark
By a somewhat more naturalistic explanation.

ACT III

JOB, *out of grief, has fallen asleep on a bench before his house.*
The little garden there is filled with many small flowering trees.

FIRST YOUNG LADY (*slowly emerging with her head of curly hair*
    from the bed of roses; trying to awaken JOB *and to take his*
    dangling hand):
It works just the way you wanted,
Oh dear God! In the wilderness
The strong eat the weak.
But back home it's not in the least like that.
And that is why, there, one displays
The face of a l'il lambkin, the spleen of a capon, and . . .
JOB (*softly, in his sleep*):

. . . also you show about half the brains of a chicken.

SECOND YOUNG LADY (*snickering softly behind a tree*):
    Ah yes; whenever a passionate young man
    Comes to pay a call,
    She immediately roosts in her bed.
    And she must apologize but she just *must* ask—
    Does he happen to have his big red comb with him?

THIRD YOUNG LADY (*who has been quietly crouching under the bench, gazing up at* JOB):
    You'll never be able to knock him
    Off his balance again!
    There he is! Homo anthropos!
    Let's begin by feeling those calves!

(JOB, *tickled, kicks out in his sleep; the* YOUNG LADY *falls over backward.*)

THIRD YOUNG LADY: Damned frog's-eye view!
    I'll probably be crippled for the rest of my life!

FOURTH YOUNG LADY (*who has been hiding behind a bush in back of him, tickling his ear with a flower stem, drops an apple onto* JOB):
    Adam was handed down to posterity only
    Because in Paradise once, he bowed down
    Before Eve!

JOB (*still in dreams*): When you think how
    Posterity is produced
    By such ridiculous means,
    You lose all faith
    In a better future!

FIFTH YOUNG LADY (*reaching out from the façade of the house's doorway for* JOB's *hair, softly*):
    It's Dame Fortune here! Grab hold of her
    Or else she'll be the one to drag *you* around
    By the hair!

SIXTH YOUNG LADY (*tapping him gently on the back*):
    A man of the world! Therefore let him decide
    Which hemisphere of himself
    He wants to show!

JOB (*sleepily*): Dame Fortune is just a gypsy girl
    Who leads us around by the nose,
    Who would like to have her posterior
    Run after.
    And since she exposes it so sweetly
    You may fail to see

That great horn of plenty
She was supposed to overwhelm you with.
SEVENTH YOUNG LADY (*mockingly, from a tree*):
Oh, to drift in the atmosphere
Of secret confessions! Oh, for floating
Upon the rainbow of reconciliation
Far above all these sexual battles!
JOB (*overwhelmed with melancholy, still dreaming*):
My feelings are falling meteorites
Coming down in the night of my heart,
Burning down in the darkness there!
And my words, which rise to try and transcend me,
Like gestures of some invisible hand,
Are just another cheap stage effect for you!
ALL THE YOUNG LADIES (*singing softly in ensemble*):
Oh how we all adore theatrical tricks,
Farces and tragedies played out at midnight,
Softly suspending our slumbering . . .
JOB (*murmuring*):
Is this really no demon enthroned in heaven
Coming to stamp upon me as I lie here in mud?
But actually a kindly angel who comes
To fan my head, to cool my brow?
EIGHTH YOUNG LADY: Look around you now, Sunday's child!
When did you ever hear of ghosts donning clothing?
What then would be left
For flesh and blood to wear?
(*She comes down the path of the now dimly illuminated garden; and, as the sun rises, she kisses him upon the forehead.*)
Good morning, dear friend!
Life is smiling on you!
JOB (*snaps at her, wiping away the kiss*):
I have witches' curse! Lumbago!
EIGHTH YOUNG LADY (*giving up*): That kind of cold reaction
Freezes love to petrifaction.

(JOB, *feeling himself fore and aft as if to locate some fresh physical disaster, totters toward the sunlight to see a little better.*)

NINTH YOUNG LADY: Uprooted plants wither
Equally well in sun or shade.
JOB (*peevishly*): I drink your health, Dame Fortune!
Morning itself crows instead of the cock!

The prey all shoot the hunter down!
Now he curses the whole carnival, now he shuts up shop—a
   very weary man.
(*He goes into the house. He appears at the window with a
bottle of poison, a skull, and a couple of old bones; he contemplates the skull, then lifts the bottle to his lips. The*
TENTH YOUNG LADY *reaches down from her tree and begins
drumming merrily with the bones on the skull.* JOB *flings
the bottle of poison at the young lady; she retaliates with
both skull and bones, which* JOB *grabs and wraps up quickly
in some paper.*)
All you women—get out of here!

ALL THE YOUNG LADIES (*softly singing in a folk-song-like way,
   depart*):
      "Now I lay me down to sleep
      I pray the Lord my soul to keep . . ."

(*Slamming the shutters closed,* JOB *shuts up shop. Short
pause.*)

JOB (*behind the closed shutters*):
The Soul of Man; or, The Magic Lantern . . .
Once it projected God and Devil into the world;
Today it projects Women, wriggling on my walls.
(*Humiliated.*)
Oh, to laugh a little, to laugh . . .
And to stop for all time this perpetual pursuit
Of these wet nurses teasing and tickling us like children . . .
But from out there the Witch keeps staring in at me
And cannot be overlooked . . .
(*He laughs wistfully; a silvery, many-voiced choir echoes him
—then, cascades of laughter, a hurricane—an inundation of
laughter.* JOB *leaps out of the window, holding his pants up—
and then stops short. In the upper story, just above* JOB, *a
window lights up rosily. The* PARROT *flies down from the
opened window, flutters after the fugitive, takes careful aim,
assails him, and, during the scene to follow, refuses to allow
him to leave the shelter afforded by the side of the house,
where* JOB *runs constantly back and forth.* JOB *sprouts horns
—then these horns turn into antlers. Every time he dashes
past the lit window two shadows there toss articles of
clothing upon them, so that they are soon transformed into
clothes trees. Cuffs, collar, jacket, nightgowns, and under-
garments of a gentleman and a lady.* JOB *jabs at the doorbell
and shouts in terror into the house telephone.*)

Help! Mercy! They're frightening me!
Anima, help! Salvation!
What are they trying to do to me?
ANIMA (*calmly, at the window*):
These are the Exorcising Spirits, and I hope you can tell
That what they are doing is quite, quite usual.
ADAM (*the gardener, coming out of the garden*):
I see that, having sufficiently turned his head,
A woman is making a complete fool of him now.
ANIMA: It's the result of an attack of Mother Wit!
An enlightened spirit has made me his mate today,
Has thoroughly disenchanted me,
And now I am aiding him in his work!
JOB: That devil! He really *is* a magician!
So is any man with only kisses and promises
Who can capture Anima for his own purposes. Oh, bottom-
less pit!
Trickiest of all the witches! Signs all agreements
If only they will agree to betray her; dazzled,
Blushes all over her bosom
And offers her heart, lifting skirts, exposing all secrets!
And then, in bed, in a more housewifely way
She submits herself to masculine authority . . .
And how do I feel in the meantime? At least, I'm glad not
to be impossible as my Opposite,
The man who begets the second he sits down . . .

(ANIMA, *half-naked, drops like a ripe apple from the window.
Her bottom lands on* JOB's *head.* JOB *dies of concussion.
From the window* MR. RUBBERMAN *continues launching his
shameless assaults against* ANIMA's *morals.*)

ANIMA (*reproachfully*): My dear, dear Mr. Rubberman—never!
PARROT: My dear, dear Mr. Rubberman . . . my dear, dear Mr.
Rubberman . . .
ADAM (*sympathetically*):
You have placed your wife
Too high in the heavens, Job.
Only now, after the fall
Can you truly get down to the very bottom of her.
(ADAM *draws a curtain across the house, the garden,* JOB, *and*
ANIMA.)

(*Ten gentlemen in mourning dress are painted on the cur-*

tain. Instead of faces there are holes through which each actor thrusts his head when he is supposed to speak.)

(PARROT *explodes and drifts upward as a pinkish cloud.*)

ADAM (*looking up after it*):
In paradise once this same little birdie
Sang out its warning to me.
But I was busy studying apples
And didn't hear a thing. (*Sighs.*)

ANIMA (*appears, gnawing on an apple*):
My husband, God rest his soul,
Was eager for the Apple of Knowledge, also.

FIRST GENTLEMAN (*impudently*):
The reason that Eve offered her husband the very first bite
Was because a little worm in it had attracted her sight.

ADAM: Quiet! Quiet! Stay in line!
Everybody will have his turn!
First stick your head through this hole
Exercising great care and great control
So as not to kick. Otherwise, I think,
This whole wall will fall.

(*As a result of all this commotion* JOB's *head rolls out in front.* ANIMA, *horrified, bends over it, and nearly goes out of her mind.*)

SECOND GENTLEMAN: Madame Sphinx received but small reward
For introducing philosophic man to the world—
Especially his problem-concocting head.
Today Madame Anima is her brand-new name
But her own imagination has become so poor
She can't even understand herself anymore!

THIRD GENTLEMAN: And divine insanity was the cause of it all!

FOURTH GENTLEMAN: Seduction's pathetic victim
Should be persuaded to withdraw
This abortion. And let us pray then
That she may become pregnant all over again.

MR. RUBBERMAN (*stepping forth a bit bashfully*):
Modern science will be glad
To help!

FIFTH GENTLEMAN: Having become ashamed in nursery school
Of its own descents and origins
Science limits itself to the analyzation of everything
And the question of whether it was all *really* necessary.

ADAM (*drags* JOB's *body out from under the house façade and*

neatly restores JOB's *head. With a black look in the direction of* MR. RUBBERMAN):
The doctor invents the disease
While the patient foots the bill.
SIXTH GENTLEMAN (*to* JOB, *who lies at the front of the stage, arms outspread*):
Death, who hit you with woman
Right at that cross of your arms and legs,
Otherwise known as your spine,
Will open no more hell holes for you
No matter how hard you strain.
SEVENTH GENTLEMAN (*to the* SIXTH): Even in hell holes a single ray
Is broken down into thousands of colors!
Now after darkness
We can only look forward
To the so-called bright lights of these enlightened times.
EIGHTH GENTLEMAN: A too total daylight
May never again become night!
Swallow, Oh Phoenix, mankind,
Swallow all this and then die!
ADAM (*who has been standing as if guarding* JOB, *now places a handful of earth on his chest; and says softly*):
So many flowers may emerge
From a single spadeful of earth.
Let earth lie lightly upon him.
ANIMA: Is he dead?
ADAM (*quietly*):
No: his head and his heart and the various other vitals
Are gone—but that's all.
MR. RUBBERMAN (*blubbering*):
Mankind must be cultivated
Upward to the heights!
Marriage reform, marriage reform!
And may all intercourse henceforth proceed
Before the eyes of technical committees!
NINTH GENTLEMAN: Science, unrefined by any spiritual filtering
Dances above both death and life
Leaving them untouched still, but unclean!
TENTH GENTLEMAN (*firmly*):
I believe that the Genius of Mankind will triumph!
Oh Anima—Amen!
ADAM (*quietly walking about and turning off all the stage lights*):
Good faith is much like a green eyeshade:

It screens out the light of earthly truth
From injured eyes. And so the only decent thing left for me
    to do
Is to put out these lights now
So that they need not go on shining in here anymore.
(He exits—with ANIMA.*)*
ANIMA *(from the darkness)* :
Perhaps Job could not help but bear that enormous cross of
    his!
I've seen with my own eyes here tonight
How they all go around saying nasty things about little me.
And then again, perhaps I alone am to blame
And Anima—this Anima
Who places the heavy cross on Job's aching shoulders—
Is really
Eve!

THE ATONEMENT

by HERMANN BROCH

TRANSLATED BY GEORGE E. WELLWARTH AND
H. F. BROCH DE ROTHERMANN

CHARACTERS

COUNT SAGDORFF, retired diplomat; Chairman of the Board of Directors of the Filsmann Works. Well-bred aristocratic type, sharp, alert, accustomed to command, around fifty years old.

ALBERT MENCK, industrialist, member of the Board of Directors of the Filsmann Works; "Councillor of Commerce"; holds an honorary doctorate. He is about fifty-five, of medium height, his hair sprinkled with gray, portly in appearance though youthful in his movements.

FRIEDRICH JOHANN FILSMANN, Vice-Chairman of the Board of Directors of the Filsmann Works, eighty years old.

MRS. FILSMANN, his wife, in her seventies, a woman of a markedly motherly appearance.

DR. HERBERT FILSMANN, lawyer, Executive Vice-President and member of the Board of Directors of the Filsmann Works. Son of F. J. Filsmann, forty years old, nervous, fidgety, and aggressive.

GLADYS, his wife, a fashionable woman in her early thirties.

ERNST HÜGLI, engineer and General Manager of the Filsmann Works. A thick-set man, forty-four years old, prototype of the stolid, reliable Swiss.

MRS. HÜGLI, his wife, a blonde provincial woman of twenty-five.

THEA VON WOLTAU, a writer, twenty-eight years old.

DR. VIKTOR HASSEL, a scholar and editor of an economic review, thirty years old.

EUGEN, BARON VON ROSSHAUPT, thirty years old, military and yet exalted in his bearing, prototype of the militant liberal.

MARTIN DURIG, engineer, industrialist of the wheeler-dealer type, massive, portly, jovial, he is about fifty years old.

EVA GRÖNER, executive secretary at the Filsmann Works, about twenty-four years old.

KARL LAUCK, secretary of the labor union and editor, about twenty-eight, slightly humpbacked and sickly looking. A fanatic type.

GEORG RYCHNER, head of the Workers' Executive Council at the Filsmann Works; a big blond man in his thirties, good-humored and self-assured, the type of the intelligent worker.

MRS. RYCHNER, his mother, in her fifties, quiet and self-assured like her son.

FRANZ GIESLING, member of the Workers' Executive Council at the Filsmann Works, in his forties.

RUDOLF KRAITSZAK, a worker at the Filsmann Works; sharp, alert, and argumentative, about thirty-five.

HEINRICH BEREND, a worker at the Filsmann Works, member of the Christian Workers Union, a quiet man in his thirties.

KÖNIGER, a foreman at the Filsmann Works, member of the National Workers Union.

HOFBERG, office employee at the Filsmann Works.

ANTON SEBALD, an amiable unemployed young man of twenty-five.

GUSTAV WORITZKI, a very run-down unemployed man of about thirty-five.

MRS. WORITZKI, his wife, a working-class woman of undetermined age.

OLD MRS. WORITZKI, his mother, about sixty years old, much worn by work.

BERTA, a young working girl.

RICHARD JECKEL, a traveling salesman for the Peda Shoe Company, about forty years old, a fluent talker; so stereotyped in his mechanical behavior pattern as to appear almost demented.

A PROSTITUTE.

OTHERS: guests at Filsmann's home, the canteen waiter, street orator, First Worker, Second Worker, First Working Girl, Second Working Girl, a policeman, a café waiter, Menck's chauffeur, hotel maids, maids at the Filsmann residence, several office employees, workers in a demonstration, café customers, passers-by at the railway station.

CHARACTERS IN THE EPILOGUE

SAGDORFF, MENCK, DURIG, HÜGLI, a notary, MEMBERS OF THE BOARD OF DIRECTORS, KRAITSZAK, ERHARDT, KÖHLER, BEREND, and RECORDING SECRETARY WENGER. The VOICES OF THE WOMEN.

PLACE

A large industrial town in southwest Germany.

TIME

1930.

Each of the three acts takes place on a single day: the first at the beginning of September, the second two weeks later, and the third at the end of October.

SUGGESTIONS FOR STAGE PRODUCTION

SCENERY: Should be as simple as possible and can be kept down to two main sets: (1) conference room; plant canteen; worker's one-room apartment with kitchen; (2) Filsmann's living room; Menck's office; coffeehouse. Change of scene within the main sets can be indicated by merely changing some of the furniture and the lighting. Only one small set is necessary for the interlude scenes inserted between the principal ones; this set can be transformed into Gladys' bedroom, the prostitute's room, Thea's living room, Hassel's work-room, or Eva's room by a simple change of furnishings. Finally, two simple background scrims are needed for the closing off of the pro-scenium stage aprons: (1) factory wall; (2) open fields.

The scenes have been arranged to alternate between the main sets and the sets for the interludes, or the scenes taking place in the proscenium stage aprons, in order to facilitate rapid scene changes without necessitating a turntable.

STYLE: The play begins in a naturalistic style and ends with the Epilogue as a rigidly stylized drama. This shift in style to abstract theatre is reflected by the play's gradually changing structure (through the use of monologues, for example). The direction is to be geared to this gradually increasing abstract quality, which first appears in the coffeehouse scene of Act I. It would also be advantageous if the scenery could be "denaturalized" somewhat as the play progresses.

INTRODUCTIONS TO THE SCENES: The "surrealistic naturalism" of the play requires these introductions, particularly the sound introduc-tions (which are also useful for bridging the scene changes and, incidentally, will be especially appropriate in any eventual radio production). The film introductions can, of course, be omitted.

ACT I

SCENE 1

SOUND EFFECT: *Factory sirens.*

FILM: *Factory smokestacks.*

The scene is a factory canteen. There is a large table in the middle with several men eating at it. A couple of smaller tables on the side. Timetables on the wall; labor union announcements; factory work rules; brewery posters.

KRAITSZAK: First they put through their so-called rationalization—and now they'll start cutting our pay. Just you wait and see—that's what's going to happen or my name isn't Kraitszak.

WORITZKI (*looking dully into his beer glass*): Bloody swindle, this "rationalization." Those bastards wanted to get rid of me—that's all it was!

RYCHNER: Come on now, Woritzki, you can't really think they let over four hundred men go just to get rid of you . . .

WORITZKI (*bitter*): I was number one on the list . . . I saw it . . . and you signed it . . . we sure were lucky to have a union representative like you.

GIESLING: If they're really going to get serious about cutting our pay—I mean *really* serious—I'll quit as a member of the workers' committee . . .

KRAITSZAK (*laughing*): Maybe it's high time it happened . . . you're all scared stiff of them anyway, always talking about being sensible and making concessions . . . the hell with being sensible, and you can't make concessions to the capitalists.

BEREND: There wasn't anything you could have done to prevent the Gelshausen Works from being shut down—you want to have the same thing happen here?

RYCHNER: That's the way it is, I'm afraid.

KRAITSZAK: You and Berend make a fine pair . . . how about signing him up for your Christian party, Berend? He still goes around saying he's a Socialist, sure, but he'll be giving that up pretty soon now.

WORITZKI: Them and the Board of Directors—they're all in it together . . .

SEBALD (*entering*): Morning, everybody—what's the word on the pay cut?

HOFBERG (*looking out of the window*): They're still at it up there
—all their cars are still here.

SEBALD: Still here? All of them? Wonderful! It's really too bad I
was laid off, you know—I was so proud to be working in a
place that had a count as president. Right, Mr. Hofberg?

HOFBERG: Count Sagdorff? . . . he doesn't have anything to say—
Menck's the one who gives all the orders.

KRAITSZAK: You guys that work in the office have got it easy . . .
you don't get laid off. You don't have anyone like Hügli to
worry about.

HOFBERG: Don't say that.

WORITZKI: Rychner decides who gets laid off together with his pal
Hügli of the Board of Directors.

GIESLING: Hügli isn't as bad as some of the others. Young Filsmann—Doctor Filsmann, if you please—you gotta watch out
for him.

HOFBERG: They sent for Miss Gröner a short while ago.

SEBALD (*looking out of the window*): Nice cars they got out
there . . . Gröner's a nice girl.

RYCHNER: She's a decent kid, Eva is—her family would starve
without her. Her mother just gets a widow's pension, and you
know what that's like.

KRAITSZAK: Eva Gröner must know something about what's going
on, come to think of it.

HOFBERG: You can't wheedle anything out of her.

KRAITSZAK: Of course not—her father was a privy councillor . . .
once a bourgeois, always a bourgeois, even if she has got
something going with Lauck. As far as I'm concerned, anyone who sits up there in the office is a bourgeois. (*To* HOF-
BERG.) You hear that, Mr. Hofberg?

SEBALD: What's she see in that Lauck? Ah—what's it to me?

GIESLING: Lauck's coming here today.

EVA GRÖNER (*enters*): Good morning.

SEBALD: Well, really now, Miss Gröner, aren't you scared to come
in here?

EVA: Why should I be?

SEBALD: Well, there's nothing but men here.

KRAITSZAK: You been working overtime, Miss Gröner?

EVA: Yes, and without pay too, Mr. Kraitszak . . . I've got to
hurry, lunch hour's almost over. (*She sits at one of the side
tables.*)

RYCHNER (*going over to her*): Good morning, Miss Gröner.

EVA (*shaking hands*): Good morning, Mr. Rychner.

RYCHNER: Nice of you to come and visit us for a change—but they might just chalk it up against you up there, mightn't they?

EVA: Oh, they don't know about it . . . and anyway, I have to eat somewhere if they insist on keeping me up there for so long.

(*The waiter brings her a glass of milk and some bread and butter.*)

RYCHNER: Did you know that Lauck's coming here too?

EVA (*startled*): No, I didn't know that.

HOFBERG: They still in conference up there?

EVA: Yes, they're still all up there—even old Filsmann; but they'll soon be through. Mr. Hügli . . .

WORITZKI (*shouting*): Down with Hügli!

LAUCK (*enters*): Well, well! Has the revolution started already? (*He notices Eva and nods to her.*) Eva! (*She wants to shake hands, but he has already crossed over to the workers' table.*) What's new?

KRAITSZAK (*pointedly*): How the hell should we know—you'd better ask someone from the office or from the Christian club.

BEREND: I'm getting fed up with this . . . I think I'll take off . . . so long!

KRAITSZAK (*laughing*): So long, Comrade Berend!

GIESLING: They'll try to push the pay cut through, don't you worry . . . (*Gloomy.*) . . . or they'll try to shut the works down, the same way they did in Gelshausen.

LAUCK: It's the last gasp of the capitalists trying to save themselves—they can't save the economy anymore. As far as we're concerned, the more things get fouled up, the better.

RYCHNER (*coming over from EVA's table*): I can't believe that everyone's going to have to suffer so much first.

WORITZKI: What the hell are you worrying about—Hügli's paying you anyway, you bribe-taking swine!

LAUCK: It's a question of principle: our generation will have to suffer so things will be better in the future. Unemployment is capitalism's admission of bankruptcy.[1]

KRAITSZAK: Capitalism's getting ready for another war to save itself.

WORITZKI (*waking up momentarily from his brooding*): A war wouldn't be such a bad idea at that.

GIESLING: What's that supposed to mean?

WORITZKI: All of you should be shot . . . (*Screaming.*) . . . everyone who's collaborating with the bosses should be shot!

[1] These are literal quotations of political slogans of the thirties.—B. de R.

RYCHNER: One can only pity you, fellow.

WORITZKI: You can shove your pity! (*He runs out.*)

RYCHNER: Poor fellow . . . something ought to be done about helping people like that.

EVA (*getting up from the sidetable*): It's nice of you to say that, Mr. Rychner.

LAUCK (*sharply, looking at* EVA): We'll never get anywhere by babbling about humanitarianism.

RYCHNER: It's our duty to help.

LAUCK: There's only one sacred duty: serving the idea.

SEBALD: Getting your welfare payments isn't a bad duty either.

LAUCK (*fanatically*): There isn't any way to stop misery and starvation—there isn't any way at all. We ourselves don't matter a damn anymore . . . but one day . . .

(*The factory siren sounds.*)

EVA (*looking at him, startled*): I've got to go now.

LAUCK (*absently*): Yes.

GIESLING: Yes, it's high time. Check please.

(*They all pay the waiter.*)

RYCHNER (*at the window*): They're driving off now, Miss Gröner —nobody'll see you going across from here now.

LAUCK (*sharply*): I didn't know she had anything to hide.

EVA (*timidly*): Well, I'm supposed to be secretary to the Board of Directors, after all . . .

(*The sirens blow again.*)

RYCHNER: Let's go, let's go. So long, Miss Gröner, Lauck.

GIESLING (*at the door*): Good-bye.

KRAITSZAK: Good-bye, gentlemen.

EVA: Good-bye, good-bye.

SEBALD: Well, I'm scared to be left alone, so I think I'll go too . . . so long, miss.

(EVA *nods to* SEBALD *and gets ready to follow him out.*)

LAUCK: One moment, Eva.

EVA: All right, Karl, but I'm late.

LAUCK: What's all this secrecy? What are you feeling guilty about?

EVA: That was just because I was here in the canteen . . . after all, I'm secretary to the Board of Directors.

LAUCK: It's high time that stopped . . . that's no job for you— you're a Socialist.

(*Eva remains silent.*)

What's Rychner hanging around your table for, anyway?

EVA (*humbly, but with a certain stubbornness*): He's a good man.

LAUCK: You can't afford to let every good man sit next to you.

EVA: He has to support his mother and the younger children.

LAUCK: So do you—I know . . . besides, I've told you often
  enough that you can have a job at the newspaper anytime
  . . .

EVA: Come on, let's go . . .

(*The factory sirens sound for the third time.*)

CURTAIN

SCENE 2

SOUND EFFECT: *Factory sirens changing to muted jazz music.*

FILM: *Cars driving up to a brightly-lit town house.*

*The living room of the Filsmann residence. The rear of the room
is cut off by a large sliding door.* COUNT SAGDORFF, OLD FILSMANN,
HERBERT FILSMANN, MENCK, *and* HÜGLI *are sitting down front.* OLD
FILSMANN *wears a black cutaway,* HÜGLI *a tuxedo, the rest wear
tails. They are smoking. From time to time* HERBERT FILSMANN
replenishes the drinks.

HERBERT: I still think that if we must cut the workers' pay, the
  only way to do it is through a lockout. I realize you don't
  think much of that idea, Mr. Hügli.

HÜGLI: I simply wish to observe that you're not going to get anywhere against Durig's constant undercutting of your prices
  by reducing the workers' wages. Durig's paying the same
  wages as we right now, Mr. Filsmann.

MENCK: A general lockout would cause a drop not only in Filsmann stocks but in those of the whole combine. It's my
  business to keep those stocks up; if I don't, your fight with
  Durig is irrevocably lost. Stocks have a life of their own, and
  you'll find that industrial fights ultimately are won and lost
  on the stock exchange, not with the rise and fall of sales and
  prices.

SAGDORFF: A complex and diabolic theory, Mr. Menck.

MENCK: To be sure it is, Count Sagdorff. This is a pretty diabolic business we're involved in here, but in the last analysis a simple one. I remember seeing a bunch of fishermen dragging a net full of fish out of the water once and noticing a large fish swallowing a smaller one with what was practically his last breath. That's the way it is in business nowadays. The only difference is that the swallowing is a little more complicated. We're all in the same net, gasping for air. That's the way things are in business nowadays.

HERBERT: For the time being I'll be quite satisfied if I'm the last big fish around. And that's why wages have to be cut.

MENCK: The trouble is I've got no taste for the Durig fish at all, but circumstances force me to swallow it.

OLD FILSMANN: Gentlemen, I'm a German merchant of the old school who started small and worked hard for half a century. Five years ago you promised me that the merger of all our works would result in an increase in profits. My son gave me his word on it.

HERBERT: The necessity of that merger has been justified all over again by the present crisis.

OLD FILSMANN (*paying no attention to him*): Today my Gelshausen Works were shut down, and your statements show losses, not profits. There were never any losses on the books when I was in charge of things.

HÜGLI: As you will remember, I pointed to the large overhead expenses of the whole combine this morning.

OLD FILSMANN: Quite right.

SAGDORFF: First and foremost, we need a little more discipline. Once we reestablish some real German order and discipline, the economy will improve again too. That's your way of thinking too, isn't it, Mr. Menck?

MENCK: To put it as cynically as possible, all I'm doing is protecting my job. I've had it for thirty years, and I'm rather fond of it. If the Communists guaranteed my job, I'd become a Communist. But since they're hardly likely to do that, I'm sticking with your side, Count Sagdorff. Forgive the cynicism!

SAGDORFF: Every love needs a little bit of cynicism. As for me, I love Germany.

HÜGLI: Back home in Switzerland things are much more firm and solid . . . to be sure, I'm just a technician . . .

HERBERT: Yes, order and discipline, that's what we need above all. And the first step in that direction is getting this question of wages settled once and for all.

MENCK: Oh well, we'll manage that, all right . . . (*Raising his glass to* HÜGLI *in a friendly gesture.*) . . . right, Hügli?

HÜGLI: If that's your decision—but it's a thankless task any way you look at it. I can't afford to lose the confidence of the workers since, ultimately, you want me to get the whole combine into operation again.

OLD FILSMANN: Gelshausen must be reopened.

MENCK: Nothing's impossible for you, Hügli—I know you. We'll get the matter through by negotiating.

MRS. FILSMANN (enters): Are you gentlemen still talking business?

HERBERT: No, we're just finished, mother. (He gets up and opens the sliding door. The jazz music becomes louder; dancing couples are seen in the next room.)

MRS. FILSMANN (to HÜGLI): Even you are neglecting your young wife. (To SAGDORFF.) Mr. Hügli is a recent bridegroom, Count Sagdorff.

HÜGLI (embarrassed): Yes, despite my forty-four years . . . you see, I thought I'd get where I was going before I could settle down.

MRS. FILSMANN: And now he's got a son and heir . . . we'll celebrate his first anniversary soon.

SAGDORFF: My heartiest congratulations, sir.

(Enter THEA and ROSSHAUPT.)

MRS. FILSMANN (seated next to her husband): Well, Thea, my little poetess, and how are you? How's the new novel going?

THEA: Oh, it's really a terrible way to earn a living, Mother Filsmann, but thanks anyway.

SAGDORFF (standing beside ROSSHAUPT): You wouldn't by any chance be related to the Rosshaupt who was involved in that thing in East Prussia and Upper Silesia . . .

ROSSHAUPT (after a reluctant pause): Yes.

SAGDORFF: My brother was involved there too.

GLADYS (enters): Well, even father's still here.

OLD FILSMANN (proudly): What's so remarkable about that?

MENCK: We must ask you to accept our apologies for having dragged our business affairs into this convivial company, Mrs. Filsmann . . . but that's the way men are, and your father-in-law is absolutely indefatigable.

MRS. FILSMANN (giving her husband a gentle glance): Well, well! (The jazz music has stopped. MRS. HÜGLI and HASSEL enter through the center door.)

HÜGLI (pleased): Ah, here comes my wife from the dance.

HASSEL (to MRS. HÜGLI): Our whole situation somehow reminds me of the eighteenth century. We're dancing right through the revolution. They might be shooting at each other two

blocks from here, and here we are dancing. . . . (*They join
the others.*) Actually, we're quite heroic.

MRS. HÜGLI: Don't talk about shooting—that's terrible; I've got
my baby at home.

MRS. FILSMANN: Aren't you the cheerful one tonight, Dr. Hassel!

HERBERT: Revolution? What we need is a properly run police
force—that's all.

MRS. HÜGLI (*to* HASSEL): I'd like to show you a picture of my little
baby. . . . (*She pulls out a locket.*) . . . Isn't that sweet?

MRS. FILSMANN: Let me see, my dear . . . oh, that's really darling.

MRS. HÜGLI: And this terrible man says that they could be shooting out there.

MRS. FILSMANN: You're quite right, my dear . . .

(*The jazz music swells up again.*)

CURTAIN

SCENE 3

This scene may be mimed.

*The jazz music breaks off. The proscenium apron is closed off by
a factory wall. Gas lantern. The stage is empty.*

RYCHNER (*enters and stops under the lantern to examine some
papers; hearing steps he turns round and recognizes* WORIT-
ZKI): Hello there, Woritzki.

WORITZKI (*looking at him distractedly*): Running scared, eh?

RYCHNER: You're out of your mind . . . I didn't even see you.
(*Pause.* RYCHNER *goes back to his papers.*)

WORITZKI: Those the new lists? . . . (*Looking at him furtively.*)
Where'd you come from?

RYCHNER (*curtly*): From the office.

WORITZKI: Yeah, Hügli's office.

RYCHNER: From the union office.

WORITZKI: Don't lie to me—you've been making up lists with
Hügli again.

RYCHNER: Play another tune, will you?

WORITZKI: You put me right at the head of that list . . . don't
try to deny it.

RYCHNER: Oh, go to the devil with your everlasting nonsense. (*He
turns away and walks on.*)

WORITZKI: Go to the devil yourself—you'll go to the devil, all

right, you swine. (*He pulls a gun and shoots* RYCHNER *from
behind.* RYCHNER *falls and lies without moving.*) You swine.
(*He goes over to the body.*) You've had it, swine. (*He shoves
the body with his foot and spits on it.*) Ugh. (*He walks
away slowly, stops several times to look back, then returns to
the body.*) Give me those lists, you bastard. (*He takes*
RYCHNER'*s notebook, picks up several banknotes that flutter
out of it, and pockets them.*) The swine had money too . . .
others starve . . . (*He spits on the body again, finds a cigarette in his pocket, and lights it.*) Ugh! (*Exit.*)

SCENE 4

*The jazz music swells up again. Filsmann's living room, as in the
second scene.*

THEA (*entering through the center doors with* HASSEL): Well,
    Hassel, will you be my slave . . . are you going to do what-
    ever I want, with zest and spirit?
HASSEL: Oh yes, with zest and ghostly spirit, the way it ought to
    be.
THEA: That implies a homosexual relationship, my dear Hassel—
    we too are just pals. But afterward I'll go to a coffeehouse
    with you, if you like—I'll even go to that journalists' hangout
    of yours. We might even take Rosshaupt with us, bad temper
    and all; I've always wanted to see a conspirator up close. You
    two are quite good friends, aren't you?
HASSEL: Sporadically—you never know with him. But that busi-
    ness with Gladys is really unbelievable.
THEA: Hold your tongue . . . ah, here's Mr. Menck.
MENCK (*coming over from the left*): And here's Miss Thea von
    Woltau.
HASSEL: I'll go and get hold of Rosshaupt before he runs off.
    Excuse me. (*Exits.*)
THEA: So you managed to escape the bridge table?
MENCK: Thank God, yes!

    (*The jazz music dies down.*)

THEA: The party's ending . . . come on, sit down with me . . .
    the spooks and ghouls are starting to leave (*She looks
    around.*) . . . they're all gone.
MENCK: All except me.

THEA: You're not one of them. You're a person.

MENCK: Notwithstanding some spooky remnants.

THEA: When one gets to be quite old, one either becomes one hundred percent zombie or one hundred percent human, like old Mrs. Filsmann . . . but as long as you are still haunted by a few spooky remnants, you're still young.

MENCK: That's nice to hear, though I'd prefer to talk with you about something other than my age.

THEA: It's not so easy to talk with you—you're practically never around. I hear you're off again tomorrow.

MENCK: Yes, I'm going to Berlin with Sagdorff. May I call you when I come back, though?

THEA: Of course.

(*Enter* HERBERT *and* SAGDORFF.)

HERBERT: So you're really going to leave us already, Count Sagdorff?

SAGDORFF: Mr. Menck and I are taking the early train tomorrow. (*To* MENCK.) Not that I want to drag you away from such charming company.

MENCK: No, no, I'm afraid I have to go anyway . . . let's go and look for our hostess.

THEA: You stay here—I'll get Gladys . . . I have to speak to her anyway. I'm sure you men still have something to discuss, don't you? (*Exits.*)

HERBERT: I really would like another word with you, Menck; I don't really think we should stand for someone like Hügli sticking his nose into the financial transactions of the combine.

MENCK: He only criticized some of the overhead cost items.

HERBERT: Yes, well, we know what that means: the fellow's a Socialist.

MENCK (*ambiguously*): No more so than I am.

SAGDORFF: He seems all right to me.

HERBERT: Basically, he's on the side of the workers. He's a production man and feels loyalty to the plant but not to the company. He'll always be ready to oppose us.

MENCK: He'll always do the job he's been given to do—no more and no less. If I were to take him into the combine—and I'd do it if you let him go—he'd work for the combine as efficiently as he's working for your company right now.

HERBERT: Don't deceive yourself. The fellow worked his way up from the bottom.

GLADYS (*entering with* ROSSHAUPT): I hear you want to leave already, gentlemen. Is there no way I can dissuade you?

MENCK: No, I'm afraid it's high time for an elderly party like myself to be off.

SAGDORFF: This is really aimed at me, I'm afraid . . . Many thanks for a lovely evening, dear lady.

GLADYS: I trust we'll see you again soon, Count.

MENCK: You'll have to put up with me again soon, I'm afraid.

SAGDORFF (*to* ROSSHAUPT): Good-bye, my dear Rosshaupt . . . do drop in and see me when you come to Berlin.

ROSSHAUPT (*clicks his heels in the military manner*): Thank you, your Excellency, at your orders.

HERBERT: I'll take you to the door.

GLADYS: You'll stay a little longer, Rosshaupt, won't you?

(*Everyone leaves except* ROSSHAUPT *and* GLADYS.)

ROSSHAUPT (*glancing at the departing figures, and once they are out of the room, tensely desperate*): I can't take it anymore . . . I can't take this filthy situation anymore.

GLADYS: You're always saying the same thing over and over again. What do you want? D'you want me to drop everything and run away with you? D'you want me to cause a scandal? I thought you were such a conservative.

ROSSHAUPT: I can't let things go on like this—I just can't. I can't stand to see you close to this man anymore. (*He sinks into a chair, his face in his hands.*)

GLADYS: Darling . . . (ROSSHAUPT *looks up.*) how many times must I tell you that I've got nothing to do with him anymore, that your jealousy is insulting. (*She strokes his hair.*)

ROSSHAUPT: Oh, I believe you . . . (*Rather pathetically.*) . . . I believe in you. But I can't stand to think of you among these people, in this atmosphere of money . . . it's just too revolting.

GLADYS (*pensively*): Sagdorff seems to like it all right, though . . . someone's coming . . . (THEA *and* HASSEL *enter.*)

THEA: We've come to say good-bye, Gladys . . .

GLADYS: No, no, you can't go yet . . .

CURTAIN

SCENE 5

SOUND EFFECT: *Street noises increasing slowly, automobile horns, streetcar bells, etc.*

FILM: *Aerial view of a large city at night. Only a small section of the stage is illuminated.*

The scene is a street by night. The street noises continue throughout, although somewhat toned down. After a short pause SEBALD *enters with* BERTA.

SEBALD: See, Kitten, that's where Filsmann lives, over there where they're just turning the lights off; now in the other room just because we're watching—that's how stingy he is!

BERTA: Why do you call me Kitten?—my name's Berta.

SEBALD: Never mind, I'm gonna call you Kitten—it's a sort of pet name.

BERTA (*nestling against him*): Anton.

SEBALD: I'm showing you all the greatest sights, Kitten, and you're still not satisfied. Now, of course, if I had money, we'd go to a top-notch restaurant and then to a theatre and then to a movie and then we'd go and eat and then we'd go to another movie or to a football game and then we'd go to a restaurant. And then afterward you'd go to bed in a four-poster with silk sheets and you'd be so grand I wouldn't dare come near you —I'd just stand there and look at you . . . boy, am I glad I don't have money! (*Long embrace.*) . . . and now you go home with me, Kitten. (*They go off in each other's arms. Street noises well up.*)

CURTAIN

SCENE 6

Street noises fade away. Pause. Curtain goes up. GLADYS' *bedroom. She wears a kimono over her nightgown and stands before a mirror, looking at herself very carefully. The door opens quietly, and* HERBERT, *dressed in pajamas and wearing a monocle, comes in. Obviously accustomed to these visits, she takes very little notice and continues powdering her face. He sits down on the bed and lights a cigarette, a stiff and rather forced smile on his face when she turns around to look at him. He gets up and kisses the nape of her neck. She takes no notice, continuing to rub cream into her hands. He puts one arm around her, holding his cigarette in the other hand. She protests weakly and only for a moment. Then she lets him pull her onto his lap. The kimono slides off her shoulders. He carefully extinguishes his cigarette in the ashtray on the night table, reaches for the light, and plunges the room into darkness.*

CURTAIN

SCENE 7

The same basic set as the previous scene, but with all the luxurious furnishings removed so that the room is transformed into a prostitute's bedroom. The bed is in the same place, but this time it is covered with cheap, colored sheets; the mirror is also in the same place, but has picture postcards stuck into its frame. RICHARD JECKEL *and the girl are dressing. His suspenders are hanging down in back. She is fixing her makeup at the mirror with much the same gestures as those used by* GLADYS *in the previous scene.*

JECKEL: . . . next time I come, I'll bring you a pair of shoes. You like suede or fake snakeskin? You see, that's my business —I travel in shoes. I'll have to get going early tomorrow again. First thing tomorrow morning, I'll have a man come to carry my cases—that's cheaper than hiring a car. Always keep expenses down—that's the main thing. I go on the principle that anything anyone else can do, I can do better. The people I work for know that, too. You can imagine what selling is like these days. Everyone wants everything cheap, they practically want it as a gift—and *then* they don't want to pay. It's got so I only go to customers I'm sure of. Of course, you've got to know who they are. If there's only two really solid businesses in a town—say, a town like Fürth— why, then that's all I go to. I don't take any notice of the others at all. I just let them lie. That's the only way I manage to get through all of central and southern Germany in three weeks, see? Say, where do you buy your shoes, anyway? I'll give you a good tip—you go to Perlmann's, use my name if you like; or better still, just ask for Peda shoes made by the Peda Company. Don't ever buy any other brand! That's my company, you see. You can just imagine how many pairs of shoes they put out every day . . . no, come to think of it, you can't imagine that, no one can—ten thousand pairs every day! Enough for a whole town—what am I saying?—for a whole country. I can't even imagine it myself. And it all has to be sold. You know what you need for that? You need top-notch, cannonball salesmen, that's what you need. (*He takes an order book from his pocket.*) Here, take a look. This is from this afternoon: 18 pairs, 25 pairs, 16, 10—that's not much but 10 pairs isn't bad for a first sale—well then, 18 and 25 makes 43 and 16 is 59—69 altogether. But then comes the clincher: Perlmann's, 48 pairs. That's 117 pairs in one afternoon. A first! Sometimes I'm sorry I don't work on commission. I'd be rich if it always went as well as this. Still, it's better to have a steady salary . . .

THE GIRL: I'm ready. Let's go.

JECKEL (*disappointed*): You're cold as a fish!

(*She opens the window. Street noises become louder.*)

CURTAIN

SCENE 8

SOUND EFFECT: *Street noises continued from the previous scene come up strongly, but break off suddenly as the curtain rises.*

FILM: *A street at night; prostitutes walk up and down.*

Curtain rises on the interior of a coffeehouse. A few customers. A buffet at left. Only the occupied tables are lighted. A waiter leans on the buffet. LAUCK *is reading at a table.*

THEA (*entering with* HASSEL *and* ROSSHAUPT): Well, that was a nice brisk walk . . . are you satisfied now, Baron Rosshaupt?

ROSSHAUPT (*after a pause*): Yes, I feel better now.

HASSEL: Not that the air here is anything to write home about . . .

THEA (*sniffing the air*): But it has the smell of home. (*They sit.*)

HASSEL (*to the waiter*): Three mochas . . . that's all right with you, isn't it? (*He looks around.*) Well, well, there's Lauck . . . do you know him? He's with the workers' newspaper—smart fellow.

THEA: Well, then, ask him over.

HASSEL: Okay, I'll go and say hello to him first. (*He goes over.*)

ROSSHAUPT: Yes . . . (*He stops.*)

THEA: I suppose you feel pretty put upon because I've dragged you here.

ROSSHAUPT: How can you say such a thing?

THEA: Easily enough . . . but the fact is that when I noticed the way you looked tonight—and you must admit you weren't looking overjoyed—it struck me we have some things in common, and so Hassel and I thought we ought to get together.

ROSSHAUPT: I must apologize for having acted so out of place—it's most embarrassing.

THEA: Apology accepted . . .

JECKEL (*enters*): A dark beer . . . sausages and eggs, bread and butter . . . oh, and bring me some cheese as well. (*He sits down, takes his order books from his briefcase, and starts transcribing; he continues his work while he eats.*)

ROSSHAUPT: I think I should say in extenuation that . . . I come from the Baltic area.

THEA: You really come up with some extraordinary grounds for apology, Baron.

ROSSHAUPT: No, excuse me, that's not so . . . actually I wanted to say something else . . . but it would just bore you!

THEA: I wish you wouldn't apologize all the time!

ROSSHAUPT: I only wanted to say that those of us who grew up in the border provinces have had a certain sensitivity bred into us about Germany and what it means to be German. So we tend to become excessively irritable when we see all this cynicism and wheeling and dealing and money-grabbing while the rest of the country is practically starving.

THEA: I understand that all right . . . even though I grew up right here.

ROSSHAUPT (*emphatically*): Really?

THEA: Of course.

HASSEL (*coming back with* LAUCK): May I introduce Mr. Lauck . . .

THEA (*offering her hand*): How very nice . . . do you know we've already penetrated the enemy's camp this evening?

LAUCK: Yes, I heard.

HASSEL: I'm terribly unethical: I cater to both sides.

THEA: Don't make yourself out worse than you are already, Hassel.

HASSEL: All right, if you like, I irk both sides. That's the way it should be, too; people like us don't belong to the left or to the right—people like us make both sides uncomfortable since they both feel that we see through them.

LAUCK: At least you have kept an enviable degree of conceit, Dr. Hassel.

HASSEL: You don't really think I take my ability to see through people seriously, do you? Everyone sees through everyone else—and comes to whatever conclusion suits his own conceit best. You, for example, you think you know all about the so-called bourgeoisie because you believe that all they care about is money; and the bourgeoisie, in delightful symmetry, assume precisely the same thing about the proletariat. And since they're both right to some degree, both sides understand each other basically very well.

THEA: And what is your conceit, Rosshaupt?

ROSSHAUPT: There's something above right and left, something above anything that can be put into words: the sense of national unity. It's not a concept—it's just a feeling, but it has its roots in the community of the blood.

THEA: What do you say to that, Hassel?

PROSTITUTE (enters): A glass of bitters, please, quickly.

(JECKEL looks up from his writing, recognizes the girl, grabs a newspaper, and hides behind it.)

WAITER: Sorry, we don't serve single ladies.

PROSTITUTE: You bastards!

HASSEL (pointing out the exchange to THEA): That's disgraceful.

THEA (listens, grasps the situation; to the WAITER): The lady belongs to our party. Be so good as to bring her what she ordered. Do come and join us, miss.

PROSTITUTE (comes over reluctantly): But don't you try and make fun of me!

THEA: We wouldn't be so silly as to do that. Do come over.

PROSTITUTE: Good evening. (She shakes hands with everyone, sits down on the edge of a chair, but then moves closer when THEA offers her a cigarette.)

LAUCK (fanatically): It's not true to say we're fighting for money. We're fighting against money, we're fighting to conquer it and to destroy it. We hate money. So long as mankind is tied down to the need for money, we'll have hunger, and we'll have killing because of hunger, which is money, and blood will flow for the sake of a life which isn't worth living because all it is is money. Those of us who can see into the future hate money.

(Most of the customers have drifted out by this time. The waiter has turned most of the lights out. Only JECKEL remains, feebly lighted by a lamp from the buffet. The table at which the four speakers are gathered is directly under a strong lamp so that they seem to be in a spotlight. The scene takes on a surrealistic character.)

ROSSHAUPT (with unrestrained vehemence): I too hate money! Oh

God, how I hate it! I hate all the faces around me, those faces scarred by money! What's left for them to believe in? Just money and more deals for the sake of more money! They're not a nation anymore—no, there are no nations anywhere anymore—there are only hordes of people intent on swindling one another. They no longer have a feeling of communion because no longer are they a community. We need to visit them with fire and sword, yes, with death and destruction shall they be visited so as to become a nation once more and once more be united in true communion. Their blood has been clotted by money and need be rinsed and taught to flow freely once more. Infamous is this world, infamous a Germany that no longer is Germany but a land of loan sharks and profiteers. Unclean and filthy it is, this land of mine, and oh, how much I need hate it so that one day I may be able to love it once more.

(JECKEL *has crept over to the table. He stands in the half-light, grinning at the speakers. He now gestures to the* WAITER *leaning on the buffet, intimating that these people are lunatics. The* WAITER *shrugs his shoulders.*)

PROSTITUTE (*quietly*): The men have the money, and that is why I must sleep with them and many are the things I have to do for their money. And their breath stinks—it stinks of money. I hate the men, and the men and the money are but one. Even my lover, my sweetly beloved, even he screams for the money, and it is I who have to procure it for him. Oh, how sweet and tender is the postcard in my mirror whereon the fair maiden in the beautiful dress, sitting calmly in the tree-held swing, is gently rocked by the handsome hunter, and far removed from money are their lofty thoughts. But the world is money and nothing but money, and that is why I hate this world and why one need hate all and everything in it.

THEA: To us who are young, us who are lonely because we need search for love, to us money is an object of hate for we hate those empty forms which are meant to constrain us. We who are young and lonely know that life should have meaning, and that we need fulfill this meaning because each one of us has but a single life to live. We behold our elders and find them seared by money and empty, and we behold a world peopled by ghosts and the living dead, and great is our fear that one day we too shall be as they are now.

ROSSHAUPT: No longer shall we be lonely once we are a nation again, and once we hark again to the voice of the blood within us.

LAUCK: Not until the worker no longer shall have to slave for the rich, and not until the money buried in vaults no longer rules the world, not until then shall the meaning of life be permitted to be fulfilled in truth.

HASSEL: Not until the spiritual and not the commercial is recognized as truth, not until then shall we be filled once more by life, for we who do not believe in empty forms, we know that only the spiritual contains truth. We who are lonely and cherish that loneliness because we know that only out of loneliness knowledge and life can grow, we recognize the world as a ghostly illusion. We repudiate commerce because we are aware that money has grown into a gigantic machine that threatens to strangle everything alive but neither do we embrace a community of blood from which nothing can arise but war and death. We hold no faith in concepts which are to derive from commerce, nor in those that are to grow from a union of blood. To us, intent on knowledge and on living truth, the reality of this world appears ghostly and sterile. We turn aside and we shall wait, wait until the spiritual and divine in which we hold faith will be carried forth once again by the tide of perception-endowed feeling wherein all life rests.

LAUCK: I'm afraid you'll have to wait forever.

(*Pause. The* WAITER *has turned off the light over the buffet so that he and* JECKEL *are now in complete darkness. The people at the table remain immovable.*)

EVA (*bursting in, out of breath*): Karl . . . thank God I . . . (*She notices the others and hesitates.*) . . . thank God I found you, Mr. Lauck . . . Rychner is dead . . . shot . . . nobody knows who did it.

ROSSHAUPT (*quietly*): Money.

CURTAIN

ACT II

SCENE 1

SOUND EFFECT: *Many typewriters.*

FILM: *A large office with several girls typing, etc.*

Curtain rises on MENCK'*s office. The set used for* FILSMANN'*s living room could be used here, the large sliding door at the back being covered in subsequent scenes by a bookcase.* MENCK'*s desk stands downstage right with telephones on it. It is flanked by two chairs for visitors. Downstage left a set of armchairs with table.* MENCK *sits at his desk;* HERBERT FILSMANN *is next to him.*

HERBERT: You came by the night train?

MENCK: Yes, I arrived this morning . . . did you call the meeting?

HERBERT: Yes, for four this afternoon.

MENCK: Excellent. As soon as I got here I found something rather interesting . . . (*He indicates a letter that he is holding.*) What do you suppose this is?

HERBERT: Well?

MENCK: Durig wants to meet us—in person . . . naturally I called him up right away and arranged to meet him here this morning.

HERBERT: That *is* rather interesting. Meanwhile he's lowered his prices again.

MENCK: He's got to go for broke. I didn't exactly waste my two weeks in Berlin, and so I managed to discover a few things I'm pretty sure of. For instance, he owes the Farmers Trade Bank two million.

HERBERT: Hmm, that's more than I thought.

MENCK: Naturally the bank would like him to merge with us so that they can have a somewhat better debtor . . . since they're perfectly well aware I'd have to take over responsibility for his liabilities. Nonetheless, Durig will agree to a merger only if he is permitted to retain his executive positions in the new organization. At the same time it's obvious that the merger and exchange of shares with us becomes all the more desirable the more his shares go up and ours go down. And that's how he's got everyone to finance the current dumping of his goods on the market. It's the price they're paying him for his willingness to merge. I must say I really admire the man's shrewdness.

HERBERT: A merger with Durig is out of the question. I can't spare one single share from my fifty-one percent.

MENCK: We could get around that by agreeing to form a syndicate.

HERBERT: A syndicate? Listen, on the day I'm forced to share or give up my supremacy in the Filsmann Works I'll hang myself.

MENCK (*laughing*): Come, come now . . . let's keep it cool, Dr. Filsmann.

HERBERT: It's no joke . . . nobody can go against his own nature. That's the way we Filsmanns are made: look at my father.

MENCK: Well, for the time being there's no argument. For my part, I could not agree to a merger with Durig which would burden us with his liabilities.

HERBERT: Well then, there's no problem—we're agreed.

MENCK: For a change.

HERBERT: All right, for a change. The only thing that remains is to decide how to deal with his dumping policy.

MENCK: Let's wait and see what Durig has to say . . . how's the situation regarding the wage reductions?

HERBERT: We've got nowhere . . . I knew Hügli wouldn't be able to do anything. On top of everything they're starting to shoot one another, though unfortunately only one at a time. We'll talk about it this afternoon at the meeting.

MENCK: Terrible times. What happened exactly?

HERBERT: Oh, the union representative at the works, a certain . . . oh well, his name's not important . . . was shot. Obviously the Communists trying to use the wage reductions to start trouble. They'll get nowhere, though. They're using some editor named Lauck as their spokesman now.

MENCK (*the telephone rings*): Hello? Yes, I'll be ready in a moment. (*To* HERBERT.) Durig's here.

HERBERT: It's your appointment. I'll leave. (*Exits.*)

MENCK: I'll see you later. (*Into the telephone.*) Show Mr. Durig in. (DURIG *enters left;* MENCK *greets him with outstretched hand.*) This is a pleasure, my dear Mr. Durig, a real pleasure. (*He shows him to one of the armchairs downstage left.*)

DURIG: I've been wanting to meet with you again for a long time.

MENCK: Ah, dear God, we live in the same town and yet we might as well be as far apart as China and Bolivia! We just aren't free men . . . we've become slaves and we don't know why. (*They sit.*)

DURIG: You're quite right there . . . the senselessness of it all strikes one anew every single day.

MENCK: You at least have a family to work for, but a bachelor like me . . .

DURIG: Anything can happen, my dear sir, you look younger every day.

MENCK: Staid businessman on the lookout for a wife? No, no,

that just won't do. But tell me, how's your family? According to my calculations, you must have some grown children by now.

DURIG: My oldest boy is about to take his college entrance examinations.

MENCK: You don't say! . . . then he'll be a junior executive in a couple of years.

DURIG: He's still got quite a bit to learn . . . I want to send him to America.

MENCK: Quite right . . . the younger generation isn't going to have anything easy, it'll have to show its worth . . . though your boy, to be sure, has the best of examples.

DURIG: Not as good a one as you would make, Mr. Menck.

MENCK: Do you think so, really? (*He leans back in his armchair, takes a puff on his cigar, and laughs.*) I can take a hint, Mr. Durig. So we've got to the point, have we?

DURIG: I'd like to be sure you understand me correctly, Mr. Menck. I haven't come here to beg. Durig is on precisely the same footing as five years ago.

MENCK: I know what the Durig position is. But I know, too, that whatever footing we're on, none of us any longer have stable ground under our feet. And I'm sorry if I blow my own horn by pointing out that I played the part of the prophet in the desert already five years ago.

DURIG: I admit it. But, since we're both prepared to speak openly, I must say that any collaboration with Filsmann was impossible for me at that time and that's why your great merger idea came to nothing.

MENCK: And today?

DURIG: Now, as then, my connection with Filsmann can only be one that allows me freedom of decision.

MENCK (*thinks for a moment*): Just a minute—this is something new altogether . . . if I understand you correctly, you're thinking of an agreement to fix prices with corresponding production quota allocations among members of the trust. Right?

DURIG: Given certain reservations, yes.

MENCK (*gets up and paces back and forth*): Listen here, Durig, this is all very well and good, but you must be perfectly well aware, probably better than I am, that it won't do. You're operating at full capacity right now while our Plant A is down. Are you suggesting quota allocations on the basis of current production? That's something we could only agree to if you agree to compensate us for that plant's stoppage

. . . (*Pause.*) . . . though perhaps even that might be
cheaper for you than this insane price-cutting policy of yours.
You don't mind my putting it that way, do you?

DURIG: You're speaking as manager of the Filsmann Works. If
you will permit me to speak as openly as you, you'd think
differently if you held an interest in the Durig Works. In
other words, I'm still not willing to enter into a general
merger, but I am prepared to work out a personal merger between our two concerns with you; that is to say, offer you
personally the same interest and authority that you have with
Filsmann.

MENCK: You have an extremely limber mind, Mr. Durig, and
I'm afraid I'm a slow thinker . . .

DURIG: . . . but the advantages I'm offering are quite clear. Your
own industrial theories are in favor of expansion . . . and
you can't just stop half-way.

MENCK: So you're hoping to get a favorable quota allocation
through combining forces with me . . . since I presume
you're hardly counting on my simply buying your shares.
It was different five years ago, but Filsmann hasn't done
so badly with me in the meantime . . . (*Stopping in front
of* DURIG.) . . . besides, I can't underwrite your liabilities.

DURIG: My liabilities are covered by liquid assets; and the factory
is valued at close to ten million.

MENCK: Let's talk plainly. In truth none of our factories are
worth anything today, and your shares could drop by half
tomorrow.

DURIG: Any time you've thought the matter through and want
to give it a closer look, my books are at your disposal.

MENCK: I have an extremely high regard for you, Mr. Durig, both
as a person and as a businessman, believe me, and I'd like
nothing better than to be able to work with you. But, without trying to anticipate anything, I keep seeing the same
thing: that the blanket of industry has become too small to
cover all of us. Five years ago I already had the feeling that
if times got bad, the way they are today, only one of our
three plants would be able to remain in operation. And that's
the way it's going to be, whether we merge or not—and I'm
afraid that even that one plant won't be able to pay its way.
So?

DURIG: You're very pessimistic.

MENCK: The upshot of the matter, then, is this: you're offering
me the same share in the Durig Works that I've got in the
Filsmann Works. Quite apart from the ethics of the matter,

which aren't quite clear to me as yet, and the fact that I wouldn't do anything behind the back of my present partners, I might have been able to ride both horses together under normal circumstances. At the present time, however, there's no doubt that one of them is going to collapse.

DURIG: It won't be the Durig horse.

MENCK: Be that as it may, for the time being I'm sitting on the Filsmann horse.

DURIG: You know how it was meant.

MENCK: Besides, you're playing a pretty risky game.

DURIG (*smiling*): Oh, I'm pretty sure of myself.

MENCK: Nobody in Germany today is strong enough to carry off a dumping policy. Not even a Durig. If you continue to lower your prices, we'll close our works down completely and use that as an excuse to lower wages drastically. We'll leave the market entirely to you for a while, thus forcing you to keep on paying your present high level of wages. Then when you're forced to raise prices again, we resume operations with our lowered pay scale. You can predict the rest yourself.

DURIG: Among other things I can predict the effect your closing down is going to have on the price of your shares.

MENCK: There's practically no connection between shares and production anymore, and an old stock exchange man like myself should be able to prevent the shares from falling anyway. Besides that, my nerves are quite strong enough to weather a depression.

DURIG: War to the death, then.

MENCK (*smiling*): Not yet, Mr. Durig—we're merely mapping out the battleground. One of the things we've found out, after all, is that basically you wish me well, at least up to a point, and I feel the same way toward you. Let's not kid ourselves—that's the way it is. Besides, we're not gladiators entering the lists against each other—we're merely puppets acting out something called The Economy.

DURIG: And the whole thing emanates from a machine that doesn't work anymore.

MENCK (*jovially*): It would be rather amusing at that . . . if the puppets that get broken in the process were not, after all, also human beings. Oh well, we'll both think it over a bit yet, but for today let's close with a glass of sherry. (*He goes to a cupboard and takes out a bottle and glasses.*) You will have one, won't you?

DURIG (*also getting up*): To be sure. (MENCK *pours; they stand next to each other, glasses in hand.*) By the way, in all seriousness, why don't you just simply let the Filsmann shares drop? With the money you'll make on the difference between the fall of the Filsmann shares and the rise of the Durig shares you can easily finance my little project . . . and then when the whole thing is fixed up, we can easily push the Filsmann shares up again. That's another way of getting there, and Filsmann wouldn't even be hurt by it.

MENCK (*laughing*): I knew you were keeping your trump card for the end. . . . You really are a man of the times, Durig.

DURIG (*earnestly*): Maybe . . . but perhaps the times have left us behind, and we're nothing but well-trained puppets, to borrow your expression.

MENCK: Well, if that's the way it is, let's drink to the hope that the machinery that runs us will get fixed some time.

(*They clink glasses.*)

SCENE 2

SOUND EFFECT: *Soft, gentle music.*

FILM: *Fields and meadows in a gentle breeze.*

Curtain rises on interior stage. THEA WOLTAU's *living room. Ultramodern couch, end table with coffee service.* THEA *and* EVA.

THEA: But, child, that's no reason to be in such a state!

EVA (*hunched up, her face hidden in her hands*): It's such a terrible disgrace . . .

THEA: My God, it's no disgrace to be fired . . . and you could hardly have expected to keep your job once you got engaged to a labor leader like Lauck.

EVA: I know, I should have admitted it long ago . . . that's what Mr. Hügli reproached me with . . . he was quite right to throw me out.

THEA: Did he really throw you out, then?

EVA: He wanted to transfer me to wage accounting . . . naturally, I couldn't go there.

THEA: I still don't see what's so disgraceful about the whole thing.

EVA: They found out about it from the police files.

THEA: Well, it certainly wasn't very bright of Lauck to report you as his fiancée after you'd kept it secret for so long. I really don't understand him.

EVA: We were all so upset at that time . . . (*Pause.*) . . . and maybe he had another reason, too . . .

THEA: What?

(EVA *starts to say something and then stops herself. A silence.*)

Lauck told me that you could have a job at the newspaper any time.

EVA (*quickly*): I don't want it.

THEA: But after all . . . sooner or later you two would have married anyway . . . (*With sudden understanding, after a short pause in which* EVA *stares fixedly before her.*) You don't love him? I'm sorry, I shouldn't have asked that . . . forget it, don't answer.

EVA (*after a pause*): So much happened all at once . . . you're very good to me, Miss Woltau.

THEA (*goes over and kisses her on the forehead*): I'm older than you are . . . let's call each other by our first names—that makes talking easier . . . people who have got to know each other under such tragic circumstances, belong together.

EVA: Yes. (*They sit hand in hand for a few moments.*)

THEA: Rychner?

EVA: I don't know, I don't know anything . . . I just feel so terrible that he's dead.

THEA: And before? . . . don't answer if you don't want to.

EVA (*hesitating*): Lauck was jealous of Rychner . . . I don't know why . . . maybe that's it . . . it's as if Rychner's death were Lauck's fault.

THEA: But that's ridiculous.

EVA: I know it's ridiculous . . . and I can't stop thinking it. Somehow or other he must be glad it happened, and I can't stop thinking that he must be glad it happened because Rychner was big and strong and young while he's . . . oh, it's unbearable to have to think like that!

THEA: And you shouldn't! (*Cheerfully.*) One shouldn't think about men at all.

EVA: Lauck's different.

THEA: That's far from being a reason for being in love with him.

EVA: Lauck knows what life's all about . . . and the others don't know . . . that's why he has so much influence on them— even if . . . even if he does have that thing wrong with his shoulder.

THEA: Nobody knows what life's all about, my child—remember that.

EVA: He's always terribly tense . . . (*Fearfully.*) . . . I'm sure he doesn't love me at all . . . and he only got engaged to me so he couldn't go back, so he'd be absolutely certain of his way.

THEA (*still cheerful*): Obviously we women exist only to console men for not knowing what life is all about.

EVA: Oh, how I wish everything were clear and simple!

THEA: Nothing can be clear and simple the way men have messed the world up. (*She strokes* EVA's *hand*.) Feel better?

EVA: Yes.

THEA: You've got to get rid of Lauck . . . you can't slee . . . live with a man you're not in love with.

EVA (*hesitating*): It would be much . . . it would be much nicer to live with another woman in some lovely place . . . away, away from it all.

THEA (*gently but marking her distance*): I'm afraid we'll just have to learn to live alone.

EVA (*hysterically, hiding her face on* THEA's *shoulder*): Oh, I'm so scared of him . . . don't let him come . . . I'm so scared of him.

THEA (*holding* EVA's *head*): What can I do, my dear? And here I thought I was inviting a pair of happy lovers . . . and the coffee's got cold . . . (*She kisses* EVA's *hair*.) . . . and now the fellow will be here any moment . . .

EVA (*still holding on to* THEA): I'm scared . . . he's so odd!

(*The doorbell rings*.)

THEA: And there he is . . . (*She frees herself from* EVA's *embrace*.) You really look like you've been crying . . . do wipe your eyes. (*She goes out and comes back with* LAUCK.)

LAUCK: Hello, Eva.

EVA: Hello . . . Karl.

LAUCK: I'm afraid I'm late, but I had to go to a meeting at your place. Ha, there I go still saying "your place"—silly! Thank goodness, you're out of it.

(EVA *makes no answer*.)

THEA (*quickly*): What happened at the meeting?

LAUCK: The same nonsense about the wage reduction and the murder all over again.

EVA (*distressed*): All over again . . .

(THEA *strokes her to calm her*.)

LAUCK: The whole thing was stupid, of course, and as usual without result.

THEA: You sound rather bitter about your fellow party members.

LAUCK: I don't know any fellow party members; I only know an idea.

THEA: That sounds almost fascistic.

LAUCK: Everyone who's trying to attain a goal is dictatorial . . . that's the essence of politics. . . . I'm just not one of those who are capable of sitting around and waiting. . . . Our idea is the goal; the party must take second place.

THEA: Aren't you afraid to talk that way openly?

LAUCK: You can say anything quite openly. . . . You can say it in Botocudian or in Chinese; it all depends entirely on the tone of voice you're using, whether you have any effect or not.

EVA: All this is horrible.

LAUCK: Of course it's horrible . . . everything's horrible, like humanity that's enslaved without noticing it and that has to have the idea planted in it so it can wake up.

THEA: What did you accomplish today?

LAUCK: Nothing. I just let them talk so that they'll work themselves up. You've got to wait until a crowd starts acting like a bunch of chickens with their heads cut off because they don't have a leader. You'd just waste your energy trying to step in earlier.

EVA: This is all so horrible—I wish you'd stop talking about it!

LAUCK: And what the management at your works did—did that strike you as any less horrible, to take only one example? (*He gets up and paces up and down.*) How about the business deals? The buying and selling? Isn't that horrible too? (*He comes down to the apron of the stage and directly addresses the audience.*) Isn't it horrible when you leave your offices and walk the streets . . . when men look for women and women for men . . . and when you lie together in bed, isn't it terrifying? . . . (*His voice has gradually become louder until he is actually screaming at the audience.*) It's all horrible . . . everything that you do is horrible . . . everything, everything! . . . and you know it! (*Pause.*)

THEA (*quietly*): That's life, though.

EVA (*screaming*): No, that's death!

LAUCK (*still on the apron, slowly and with meaning*): Yes, that's death . . . it's death that will emerge from all your wheeling and dealing, out of the poison gases that you manufacture and that will rot you. The horror of your non-lives will be surpassed only by the horror of your mechanical deaths.

EVA (*hysterically*): Rychner was murdered.

LAUCK (*turning toward the stage again*): Yes, that's right, Rychner was murdered, and it doesn't matter a damn who murdered him or who was murdered—whether he was murdered

by the Communists or by the Fascists. He was caught up in
the machinery of this non-life, and it ground him up—a
sacrifice for what has been and a sacrifice for what is to
come.

EVA (*hysterically*): The machinery of non-life . . . you're a machine yourself—you feel good because things are like this!

LAUCK (*sharply*): What's that supposed to mean?

EVA: It's your fault—yours too! (*Clinging to* THEA.) Tell him, go
on, tell him how it is—tell him it's his fault!

THEA: They're all at fault, all of them . . . come, child . . .
(*She leads her to the door of the adjoining room.*) . . .
Come on now, everything will work out all right . . . I don't
want you to hear any more about this now. (*Exits.*)

LAUCK (*alone*): Of course, it's my fault too. Of course, we're all
at fault as long as the goal hasn't been attained. As long as
things are like this, we're all at fault for every murder that's
committed anywhere. Caught up in the horrible machinery
of murder which we would not stop! Horrible machinery that
we've set up and now can't escape! We're tools, all of us,
repellent to each other, nothing but tools of a fate that isn't
God's and isn't the Devil's but that we have to believe in so
that we do not die of hopelessness.

CURTAIN

SCENE 3

SOUND EFFECT: *Machines humming and clattering.*

FILM: *A room full of machines; then moving parts of machines
with a revolver and finally a guillotine occasionally appearing
in their midst.*

*Curtain rises on stage set on proscenium apron closed by a scrim
showing a factory wall. Lantern. A hand-made sign with "A swine
was slaughtered here" written on it is fastened to the lantern.*
WORITZKI *alone.* WORITZKI *walks up and down with his hands in
his pockets. Each time he comes to the sign, he stops and reads
it. Then he leans on the wall and impatiently rolls himself a
cigarette.* SEBALD *enters, nods to* WORITZKI *without noticing the
sign, and is about to walk on.*

WORITZKI: Here, read that.

SEBALD (*reads*): Who put that there?

WORITZKI (*laughs*): The Black Hand.

SEBALD: Idiot. (*Moves to remove the sign. The factory sirens wail.*)

WORITZKI (*agitated*): Leave that alone! Everyone has to see that . . . now, when they're all going in to work . . .

KRAITSZAK (*enters*): Good day.

SEBALD: Good day, comrade.

KRAITSZAK (*reading the sign*): Looks like management put it there. . . . I'm getting sick and tired of it; the police interrogated me for four hours yesterday . . .

WORITZKI: You don't know nothing . . . (*Proudly.*) They've called me in for tomorrow again.

SEBALD: Well, they've got the right one in you, all right.

KRAITSZAK: This snooping around for Communists is getting disgusting . . . I don't see them calling Filsmann in for questioning . . . (*Looks at the sign again.*) . . . which, of course, doesn't mean that Rychner wasn't really—ah, forget it, I ain't saying nothing.

WORITZKI: You're damn right Rychner was a swine . . . a filthy swine, and he was shot down like one—pow!

GIESLING (*enters*): What's going on here?

WORITZKI: Shot down—pow!

SEBALD: Shut up, you!

GIESLING (*reading the sign*): Who's the bastard who put this up?

WORITZKI: The Black Hand.

GIESLING: You, eh? . . . be just like you . . . take it down before the police see it—they're looking for someone to arrest as it is.

WORITZKI: I told the Inspector down at the police station what kind of a guy Rychner was, and he agreed with me, too. . . .

GIESLING: Keep talking like that and it'll cost you your neck.

SEBALD: They'll chop your head off, Woritzki.

WORITZKI (*feeling the nape of his neck*): They're pals of mine down at the police station . . . fine fellows . . . they offered me cigarettes.

KRAITSZAK: Why don't you get *real* pally with them like the Social Democrats?

GIESLING: Ah, shut up and lay off us—where would you be today if it hadn't been for us?

KRAITSZAK: You had to go get Lauck because you couldn't make it without his help.

POLICEMAN (*enters*): What's all this loitering?

GIESLING: I didn't know there was a law against it.

(WORITZKI *taps the* POLICEMAN *familiarly on the shoulder and points at the sign.*)

POLICEMAN: Keep your hands off me. (WORITZKI *laughs and points at the sign again. The* POLICEMAN *reads the sign, takes it down, and pockets it.*) Who put that up?

KRAITSZAK: Persons unknown.

WORITZKI (*laughing slyly*): Unknown person.

POLICEMAN: I'd better take down your names, just in case . . . Who are you?

KRAITSZAK (*offhandedly*): Rudolf Kraitszak, 4 School Street.

SEBALD: Name's Anton Sebald and I'm a moderately satisfied tenant at Mrs. Henrietta Walter's, 37 Broad Street; I'm unemployed, and I don't have my identification papers with me at the moment either. You'll be good enough not to make too much of that since I can produce them at any time.

POLICEMAN: Nobody asked you for them. . . . And you?

GIESLING: Franz Giesling, 12 Factory Street—I'm the chairman of the Workers' Committee at the Filsmann Works.

POLICEMAN: And you?

WORITZKI: Person unknown.

POLICEMAN: I asked what your name is.

WORITZKI: The police know me . . . (*Becoming sly again.*) . . . I've been called in for ten o'clock tomorrow morning again.

POLICEMAN: Are you going to tell me your name or not?

WORITZKI (*uncomprehendingly*): Gustav Woritzki.

POLICEMAN: Well, finally! Where do you live?

WORITZKI: Unknown.

POLICEMAN: What's *that* supposed to mean now? Any more of that and I'll arrest you. (WORITZKI *feels the back of his neck.*)

SEBALD: He lives at 8 Filsmann Street.

POLICEMAN (*to* WORITZKI): That right?

WORITZKI (*absently*): Yes . . . yes . . . that's right.

POLICEMAN: OK, next time you can cut out the clowning. (*Exits.*)

KRAITSZAK (*at the policeman's back*): Big shot!

WORITZKI (*chiming in*): Yeah—big shot! But he doesn't know that he was found lying right here. (*He points at the spot where* RYCHNER *fell.*)

GIESLING: Yeah, that's where he was lying.

(*They all stare at the spot.*)

WORITZKI: There'll be plenty more lying there yet.

GIESLING: Don't talk rot.

WORITZKI: Here, step over here . . . go on, go on, what are you

—scared? . . . and back here stands the guy with the gun and shoots—pow!

SEBALD: This is where he died . . .

WORITZKI (*bending over the spot*): I'll show you the bloodstain . . . here.

KRAITSZAK: You can't see a bloodstain after two weeks.

WORITZKI (*furious*): If I tell you it's there, it's there!

KRAITSZAK: There'll be blood running in the streets yet . . . more than you bargained for!

WORITZKI (*eager and pleased*): Yeah . . . here?

KRAITSZAK: Just let them try to cut our wages . . . then you'll see plenty—I promise you that!

GIESLING: Anyone would think you're looking forward to it, Kraitszak.

KRAITSZAK: If it's got to come, it'll come . . . you're not going to prevent anything with your appeasement tactics . . . things won't stop at one killing—this guy was just number one.

WORITZKI (*eagerly*): Another one . . . another one.

SEBALD: I've had enough of this . . . I'm going.

(*They all leave. After a few moments* WORITZKI *returns. He takes another look at the spot where* RYCHNER *fell and at the lamppost. He takes a piece of paper and a pencil out of his pocket, puts the paper on a projecting piece of wall and writes. Then he fastens the paper to the lamppost. He has written "Yet another one." He looks at his work with satisfaction, lights a cigarette, and exits.*)

CURTAIN

SCENE 4

SOUND EFFECT: *The sound of typewriters.*

FILM: *Account books, typewriters, and adding machines in whole and in part. Finally, a forget-me-not springs forth from the machine parts and merges into forget-me-nots in a field.*

MENCK'S *office.* THEA *and* MENCK *are seated in the armchairs at left.*

THEA: I realize it's highly unbecoming of me to descend on you like this on the very first day you're back.

MENCK: Spreading sweetness and light has never been considered particularly unbecoming.

THEA: I've been very impatient for you to get back . . . terrible things have been going on here . . . and I've had the feeling that you're absolutely the only one who could do something about the situation. But now . .

MENCK: . . . your confidence has been dispelled. It's understandable.

THEA: No, it's just that I feel a little superfluous now.

MENCK: Well now, since you insist on feeling superfluous, supposing you tell me what's happened to upset a pretty young woman like yourself so much.

THEA: You've heard about the murder, I take it?

MENCK: More or less.

THEA: One side says the Communists did it, the other says the Fascists are behind it.

MENCK: The usual theories.

THEA: Rosshaupt . .

MENCK: What about Rosshaupt?

THEA: He's disappeared.

MENCK: There's nothing remarkable about that . . . it's a way of life with him.

THEA: But the workers claim that he's the murderer, directly or indirectly . . . and they claim that ultimately Filsmann's behind it because of the wage reduction.

MENCK: May I ask what your source for all this is?

THEA: An editor named Lauck, but he doesn't really take it seriously himself.

MENCK: Well, and what's your opinion of all this balderdash?

THEA: I think that passions make people capable of doing things which they otherwise . . . you know what I mean?

MENCK (*laughs*): Gladys Filsmann? God in Heaven, there's no one in this wide world who cares less about the wage cuts than Gladys.

THEA (*also laughing*): No, Gladys would be the last to arrange a killing. (*Becoming serious again.*) But even a vague rumor is quite enough—not even you could stand up against that, Mr. Menck. Everyone knows that you're the real brains behind the concern, and that you have certain political connections—and the spirit of blood feuds is in the air.

MENCK (*cheerfully*): Corsica in full swing, eh? . . . (*Turning suddenly to* THEA.) . . . Thea, are you afraid for me?

THEA (*almost gloomily*): I'm beginning to think that that's why I came.

MENCK: That is remarkable.

THEA (*pondering*): You think that's remarkable?

MENCK: Thea . . . ?

THEA (*rubs her eyes, shakes her head, smiles at Menck, shakes her head again. Short pause, then very gently*): No . . . I just want to know what you're going to do.

(MENCK *gets up and walks back and forth without speaking. Then he stops, also smiles, and nods to* THEA.)

THEA: What are you going to do?

MENCK: Do you really think I should do anything about it?

THEA: Yes, for my sake . . . anything is possible, after all.

MENCK (*cheerfully*): Thank God, yes, anything is possible in this senseless world we live in! Well now, let's find out what Hügli has to say to all this—all right? He's sure to know all about these things. (THEA *nods;* MENCK *goes to the telephone.*) Hello! Hügli? . . . Yes, yes, I'm back all right . . . no, no, it's OK, it's not four yet . . . yes, I know the meeting isn't till four, but I'd like you to drop over before then about another matter . . . yes, right away, if that's all right with you. Excellent . . . (*To* THEA.) he'll be here right away.

THEA: Perhaps you'd like to talk to him alone?

MENCK: No, no, no . . . I wouldn't dream of throwing my guardian angel out—that would be sacrilege.

HÜGLI (*enters*): Mr. Menck . . . (*He sees* THEA *and makes a stiff bow.*) . . . Madam . . . (THEA *nods amiably.*)

MENCK: Come in, come in, my dear Hügli, nice to see you. Have a seat. We're having a little private conference here.

HÜGLI (*not grasping the situation as yet*): Oh? . . .

MENCK: To cut a long story short, Miss von Woltau here has been giving me some private information that's come to her ears to the effect that the murder of the union representative is being blamed on the Fascists by the workers. Furthermore, that they're blaming the management for it. Do you know anything more about all this?

HÜGLI: The negotiations about the pay cut have come to a standstill as a result of this matter. The workers really are restive, and I'm afraid there might be disturbances in the works. I've spent as much time over there myself as possible. So far there hasn't been any decrease in production.

MENCK: Good . . . but what about the rumors that are going round?

HÜGLI (*hesitating*): The mood of the workers was quite calm at first . . . later on it changed.

MENCK: When, specifically?

HÜGLI (*casting his hesitation aside*): Well now, Mr. Menck, that touches upon certain internal matters that have to do with the works.

THEA: Aha, I knew I should have made myself scarce.

MENCK: What on earth are you thinking of? One confidence deserves another . . . but I'll make things easier for all of us by simply putting a question. Mr. Hügli can answer with a simple yes or no. It has to do with Dr. Filsmann, doesn't it?

HÜGLI (*hesitating*): Yes.

MENCK: Never mind the hesitation, Mr. Hügli, come right out with it—yes or no. Just like in the army. Did Dr. Filsmann rub the workers the wrong way?

HÜGLI (*promptly*): Yes.

MENCK: And as a result the rumor that Filsmann or the management had organized the murder sprang up?

HÜGLI: Yes.

MENCK: And did the name of Lauck play a part in all this?

HÜGLI: Yes.

MENCK: Wouldn't I make a fine police detective, Miss Woltau?

HÜGLI: Yes.

THEA: There's certainly no need to worry about you.

MENCK: Well, now that we have defined the limits of the problem, perhaps Mr. Hügli will be so good as to tell us precisely how Dr. Filsmann irritated the workers so much.

HÜGLI: Certainly. It was like this: Dr. Filsmann was annoyed at the slowness with which the wage negotiations were proceeding; but the fact was that the workers really didn't have any suitable substitute for Rychner in the talks. The second in command of the Workers' Committee quite obviously felt that he was too weak to handle the situation and asked for permission to call in Lauck to help him. It's possible that he was put up to doing that by the Communists on the committee since Lauck's views are known to be far over to the left. In any case, it was quite enough to knock the bottom out of the barrel. Dr. Filsmann stated categorically that he would not have anything to do with Lauck. Fortunately he refrained from putting his statement into the form of an ultimatum with a time limit, but the workers have not so far sent anyone else to handle the negotiations. I'm sure things will straighten themselves out one way or another, though.

MENCK: Did Filsmann consult you before making his move and did you agree with him? Yes or no again, Mr. Hügli, if you please.

HÜGLI: The whole thing took me by surprise—I wasn't even there when it happened . . . (*Hesitating.*) . . . I wanted to bring that up at the meeting.

MENCK: Now that it's happened, though, you've announced your support of his position—right?

HÜGLI: Publicly, yes—it was a *fait accompli*, after all.

MENCK: Excellent . . . don't look so surprised, Hügli . . . one more question for the sake of our friend's peace of mind here —do you consider either yourself or Filsmann to be in personal danger?

HÜGLI: Naturally I'm very upset over the fact that the workers will question my good faith in the matter . . . but as far as danger is concerned, everyone's in danger these days. No one would have supposed that Rychner had any enemies, either.

MENCK: Yes, well, in other words, all you're saying is that we're all in God's hands.

HÜGLI (*earnestly*): What do you mean by that, Mr. Menck?

THEA (*laughing*): I suppose that Mr. Menck means that nowadays not even a guardian angel is worth her powder. (*She gets up.*) Don't be too surprised at my stepping into this affair, Mr. Hügli, and give your wife my best regards . . . All right? (*She offers* HÜGLI *her hand.*)

HÜGLI: Of course, of course.

THEA: Give me a ring some time soon, Mr. Menck, I want to be sure you're still alive.

MENCK (*accompanying her to the door*): Many thanks, my dear . . . (*Comes back and sits down again.*) Don't go, Hügli, it's almost four anyway. Now tell me, what about this thing with Filsmann—did he just lose his temper or did you talk the matter over with him beforehand?

HÜGLI: We had a pretty serious disagreement.

MENCK: Now listen, Hügli, and don't get so surprised all over again. For once I happen to agree with Filsmann; before we deal with this Lauck character, we'll close the factory.

HÜGLI: I was planning to tender my resignation at the meeting anyway, Mr. Menck. Dr. Filsmann stabbed me in the back and now they say you're on his side . . .

MENCK: Do you want me to tell you how highly I value you all over again, Hügli? I've got big plans for you yet . . . but once in a while you've got to be able to admit that the other fellow may be right, too. I've got excellent reasons for what I'm doing. So never mind the resignation—think it over for a bit; you'd have to give considerable notice anyway, and by the time you're ready to leave, everything will have changed completely. You understand this is all in confidence, of course.

(HÜGLI *listens with bowed head.*)

We understand each other, we two—right?

(*The sound of the typewriters comes up again.*)

CURTAIN

SCENE 5

SOUND EFFECT: *The typewriters fade into the sound of a boys' choir.*

FILM: *Boy Scout camp with bonfire. Scouts marching in military formation.*

Curtain up on interior stage. HASSEL's *study.* HASSEL *is at his desk.*

HASSEL (*writes and looks at the clock several times. The bell rings; he goes out and comes back with* ROSSHAUPT, *who now has dark glasses and a moustache*): I really wouldn't have recognized you, Baron Rosshaupt.

ROSSHAUPT (*taking the glasses off*): You have every right to be surprised.

(*They sit.*)

HASSEL: Many thanks for your letter . . . and for your trust.

ROSSHAUPT: It's a trust that might become a burden to you under certain circumstances . . . I really must ask you to forgive me.

HASSEL: What can I—or may I—do for you?

ROSSHAUPT: That evening two weeks ago has become extremely significant for me . . . I had to speak to you again.

HASSEL: Why *me?*

ROSSHAUPT: Perhaps . . . perhaps I may never see you again.

HASSEL: It was on the evening of the murder.

ROSSHAUPT: Do you think I committed it?

HASSEL: No . . . even though you don't condemn it.

ROSSHAUPT: Murder is horrible—and yet the decay of the world is even more horrible than death.

HASSEL: That's nothing but an ingenious way of justifying murder.

ROSSHAUPT (*after a pause, abruptly*): I spent two years in prison . . . I paid for my ingenuity.

HASSEL: I'm sorry, but I don't think that proves anything.

ROSSHAUPT: Possibly not—the only thing that proves anything is one's own death.

HASSEL: And now?

ROSSHAUPT: I escaped from prison . . . Rosshaupt isn't my name . . . not directly, in any event . . . it's the name of one of my ancestors in Russia.

HASSEL: Are the police looking for you?

ROSSHAUPT: Yes . . . I've been warned, what with this Rychner affair and all these rumors of a political assassination.

HASSEL: And you came back anyway?

ROSSHAUPT: I had to . . . (*Hesitating.*) . . . for private reasons, since my work here is done really . . . and I wanted to talk to you.

HASSEL: How could I be of any help to you? I'm not in politics, you know.

ROSSHAUPT: But you do believe in the Spiritual—in the Idea . . . you're one of us.

HASSEL: I'm not a member of any political party.

ROSSHAUPT: We aren't a political party: we are a covenant, a communion.

HASSEL: Yes, but with political overtones, nonetheless.

ROSSHAUPT: If you want to convince someone, you've got to speak his language.

HASSEL: The spiritual in life can't have anything to do with that kind of propaganda . . . I know too much about politics not to hate it.

ROSSHAUPT: The spiritual must be converted into action . . . the action must become deed and requires our sacrifice, for we cannot wait for it to realize itself. You, too, are young.

HASSEL: Yes, I'm young . . . and the spirit is timeless.

ROSSHAUPT: The community of the blood is eternally young, and ever anew the spirit is born from it. What you call spirit is foreign to us, and must be to you too, for it is the spirit of Rome and of the West . . . we have put our faith in it for far too long, and it has brought us to the edge of the abyss . . . but the German spirit emerges from the communion—it is the community of the race.

HASSEL: The faith that we await is greater than both West and East. Communion can come only through faith.

ROSSHAUPT: We believe in our national communion, and this

communion is our faith. For beyond the spirit is the conscious feeling of our being

HASSEL: The merely affective consciousness of our being stands at the beginning of our life . . . and whoever clings to that, clings perhaps to the mere illusion of youth, Rosshaupt.

ROSSHAUPT: No, Hassel, we're not immature adolescents.

HASSEL: Perhaps not . . . yes, perhaps the community of feeling is reserved to women . . . perhaps it is the women who will bring forth a renewal of life.

ROSSHAUPT: If you stand apart, you become an enemy of the community and an enemy of the people, Hassel.

HASSEL: I am a man, Rosshaupt, with all the vices of a man and with all the ties and bonds that a man is forced to make on this earth; and I, too, seek friendship and am unhappy without it. But I know that we can attain feeling only through perceptive knowledge. Only the man who has taken upon himself the loneliness of true knowledge, and has followed that path through to the end, will have gained the world.

ROSSHAUPT: We will follow that path together. Do you really reject that? (*Almost pleading.*) Do you really wish to reject that, Hassel?

HASSEL: We have to be thankful if we can be together for a little way . . . and I am thankful to you, Rosshaupt.

ROSSHAUPT: Good-bye, Hassel.

HASSEL: Yes . . . give me your hand.

(ROSSHAUPT *exits quickly.* HASSEL *sits down to his work again.*)

CURTAIN

SCENE 6

SOUND EFFECT: *The boys' choir singing the folk song again. It fades out.*

FILM: *A safe, a coffee table, the Riviera, automobiles, etc. The safe keeps appearing between the other images.*

Curtain up. FILSMANN'S *living room. The table is laid for tea.* MRS. FILSMANN *and* GLADYS *are seated at it.*

MRS. FILSMANN: What time does your train go, Gladys?

GLADYS: Ten past six, Mama.

MRS. FILSMANN: It's almost five-thirty, and Herbert isn't here yet.

GLADYS (*nervously*): He said he'd get here with the car in plenty of time . . . if he doesn't come, I'll have to take a taxi.

MRS. FILSMANN: You wouldn't see Herbert again if you did that.

GLADYS (*absently*): Yes, to be sure . . . (*Recovering her presence of mind.*) . . . but I'll only be gone a couple of days.

MRS. FILSMANN: You could leave tomorrow just as well as today.

GLADYS: But I've already sent Mama a telegram.

MRS. FILSMANN: Well, a second telegram wouldn't be a disaster.

GLADYS: No, no . . . I've made up my mind to go now—who knows how I'll feel tomorrow . . . I might not be able to make up my mind to it then . . . (*Decisively.*) . . . No, I'll stick to my plans.

MRS. FILSMANN (*interrogating*): You certainly made up your mind quickly this time . . . have you got everything packed?

GLADYS: Yes, yes—everything.

MRS. FILSMANN: Things are difficult for Herbert just now.

GLADYS: He complains about Menck—and he isn't too satisfied with Hügli either.

MRS. FILSMANN (*shaking her head*): It isn't Menck's fault, and it isn't Hügli's. It's just that the whole world is out of kilter . . . the whole world's full of unholy confusion . . . men can't manage it anymore . . . that's why it's wrong to forsake a man these days.

GLADYS: The couple of days I'm away won't make any difference . . . (*As if trying to convince herself.*) . . . I have to go and see Mama.

MRS. FILSMANN (*to herself*): A couple of days . . .

GLADYS: You're frightening me . . .

HERBERT (*enters*): Good evening. (*He kisses his mother's and his wife's hands.*) I'm afraid I'm a bit late, but I can still have a cup of tea, can't I? You've still got a little time to spare, Gladys, the car's waiting downstairs.

MRS. FILSMANN: You're looking cheerful, Herbert, has something good happened?

HERBERT: As a matter of fact, yes—even if it doesn't look that way. We're going to close up shop.

MRS. FILSMANN: Good news really does look peculiar these days. You're closing down the whole works?

HERBERT: Yes, I've managed to force it through despite Menck . . . he finally had to admit that I was right . . . he's been forcing his will on me for years, and I've always given in . . . today I finally made him back down . . . that makes up for a lot, I must say.

MRS. FILSMANN: Yes, yes, to be sure, that's very good. And do you think a lot of good will come from this shutdown?

HERBERT: Yes, this is going to decide both the fight against Durig and the fight about the wage levels . . . and once those are over, we'll have peace and quiet at last.

MRS. FILSMANN: I'm surprised that Menck didn't follow your lead sooner than this—he's a very sensible man, after all.

HERBERT: Hügli turned the scale himself—he's the one who brought the wage negotiations onto a completely wrong track . . . well, he's been effectively blocked now.

GLADYS: Thank goodness, he's such a tedious fellow.

HERBERT: He certainly is . . . Menck's pet, that's what he is. Well, as far as I'm concerned he can take him over into the combine with him, but from now on I'll handle things at this end.

MRS. FILSMANN: I'm glad that you're satisfied, my boy. God grant that everything will work out for the best.

HERBERT: Yes, yes, Mama, everything will be all right. Well, Gladys, isn't it time for you to go?

GLADYS (looks at her watch): No, I've still got some time . . . I'm so interested in what you've got to say . . . my bags must have been taken down by now anyway . . .

MRS. FILSMANN: Couldn't Menck have some sort of ulterior motives?

HERBERT: Oh, how could he? I do think it's really time for you to go, Gladys . . . what ulterior motives could he have . . . his own money's involved too, after all.

MRS. FILSMANN: That's precisely the point.

GLADYS: It's always hard for me to leave any place.

MRS. FILSMANN: Well then, don't go, Gladys.

GLADYS (to HERBERT): Shall I stay?

HERBERT (somewhat impatiently): It's almost six . . . you're always changing your plans and then regretting it . . .

GLADYS (reluctantly): Well, then, I guess I'll go . . . I'll be back in three or four days.

MRS. FILSMANN: Good-bye, Gladys . . . don't change your plans.

HERBERT: Oh well, I know my wife—it'll be a week at least, if not more. I'll take you down to the car. (They exit.)

MRS. FILSMANN (alone; she tidies the tea table, then leans back and speaks quietly): Things can't get well again now . . . we old people, who still had a goal in life, we can see that things can't get well again. The young people don't see it— they don't even realize that they don't have a goal in life. Their paths are mapped out for them and they can't branch off them anymore, but they don't have any goal. They live for today and tomorrow, and their love is not true love anymore. They're not less intelligent than we are, perhaps more so even, but with all their intelligence they can't do a thing. It's not that they make mistakes—they're too intelligent to make mistakes; but even so their lives are nothing but confusion and mistakes. They don't love the world and they don't love their lives—but, my God, how could they? . . . and yet, what a wonderful gift we thought we were giving them when we gave them life! They'll never come back to us, who really love life . . . Is it only years that lie between our youth and our old age? Oh my child, you who were once a little boy, the heart beneath which you rested has become heavy . . . and how I love this life and this world, in which a child of mine lives—oh, I want to love it ever more and more, though full of despair I want to love it until my last breath, I want to smile at life, that it, too, may smile and become a gentle world for my child. That is what I, an old woman, want to do. (*She closes her eyes and smiles.*)

(*The curtain comes down slowly.*)

SCENE 7

SOUND EFFECT: *Sounds of a railroad station.*

FILM: *The interior of a railroad station. Trains leaving.*

Curtain goes up on small section of stage. The ticket office of a railroad station. The traveling salesman JECKEL *is idly standing next to his sample cases. Passersby and travelers.*

ROSSHAUPT (*entering with* GLADYS *and wearing dark glasses again*): Thank you, oh thank you for coming, Gladys. (*He kisses her hand.*)
GLADYS: I told them at home I was going to see Mama . . . (*She looks around anxiously.*) . . . I hope the chauffeur's gone.
ROSSHAUPT: Why bother with excuses—why didn't you simply pack up and go? That's not your home anymore.
GLADYS: I've still got to talk all that over with you . . . here's my luggage check . . . (ROSSHAUPT *takes it.*) . . . I'm sure I can stay away two days—nobody'll notice that.
ROSSHAUPT: You mustn't ever go back there again.

GLADYS: No, no, of course not, I don't want to go back there—
oh, I just want to be with you . . . did you buy the tickets?
Everything is so complicated . . . people say you killed
that worker.

ROSSHAUPT: Yes.

GLADYS: It isn't true, is it?

ROSSHAUPT: No, it isn't true.

GLADYS: Thank God, that would have been most embarrassing.
You get into another compartment first, all right? I just
don't understand all these things . . . why did you disappear like that then? And what's the point of all this disguise
now . . . ?

ROSSHAUPT: I'll explain it all to you later. The main thing now
is to get away from here.

GLADYS (*tenderly*): Yes.

ROSSHAUPT: Once I've got you out of this fake society, once you've
had an opportunity to discover what people really can be to
one another . . .

GLADYS (*tenderly*): Yes, darling. (*Uneasy again.*) Why didn't you
get the tickets before?

ROSSHAUPT: I love you, oh I love you so much . . .

GLADYS (*smiling at him*): Oh, you . . .

(JECKEL *has crept up.*)

ROSSHAUPT: . . . and you'll see that life will be beautiful and
serious again and big and happy—because once more it will
be found in the communion of the blood.

GLADYS (*tenderly*): Yes . . . but what about the tickets?

ROSSHAUPT: Right away . . . (*He goes to the ticket window.*)

(JECKEL *gets right behind him so that he can look over his
shoulder as he buys the tickets.* ROSSHAUPT *comes back with
the tickets.*)

There . . . I think we can get on the train.

GLADYS: Yes, darling . . . (*They exit,* GLADYS *looking around
shyly.*) . . . are you sure no one saw us?

ROSSHAUPT (*also looking around*): Not a chance . . . the more
risks you take, the less chance there is of anything going
wrong . . . (*Looks around once more and notices* JECKEL.)
. . . there's someone I've seen before, come to think of it,
probably in the army or some place like that . . . oh well, it
doesn't matter—he didn't recognize me. (*Exit.*)

(*Pause. The ticket office empties.*)

JECKEL (*alone, he remains leaning against a pillar next to his sample cases; at first he does nothing, then begins to gesture with his hands as if he were speaking; finally he speaks*): So that was Mrs. Filsmann. I know her car—nice-looking job. She had her initials on her luggage: G. F. And that fellow was the baron I saw in the coffeehouse. And so they're going to Nördlingen together now. Actually I wouldn't mind taking a trip with them there myself and playing detective. It might rake me in more money than selling shoes here. Me and my idiotic sense of duty! Is my firm going to make it up to me? Damn right they're not! They want to put me on commission now, that's what they want to do! All of the traveling salesmen are supposed to be taken off salary and put on commission. Well, I'll just wait and see if they dare do it. They'll have a pretty hard nut to crack when they try it on me. Still and all, it's interesting. Mrs. Filsmann, rich Mrs. Filsmann, together with the baron from the coffeehouse. Come to think of it, there isn't anything to stop me including Nördlingen in my business itinerary. That's the advantage of being a traveling salesman—you're independent, and you can map out your route any way you like. You don't get much expenses, but at least no one tells you which way to go first. No one can stop me going to Nördlingen before Ingolstadt or from doing it the other way round. The traveling salesman's got his family at home, and he comes back to it; but when he's out on the road, he sleeps anywhere he likes and with anyone he likes. Ah, it's grand to be alive, all right—even if times are hard.

CURTAIN

SCENE 8

SOUND EFFECT: SEBALD's *voice singing a folk song.*

FILM: *A cat playing with two buttons. A prison yard from above.*

A number of men standing around a guillotine. Everything is seen from above; no faces. A short close-up of the knife. Then the cat playing again.

Curtain up on inner stage. The kitchen in RYCHNER's *home.* SEBALD *is alone, doing some work on the gas stove. He continues*

*singing the same folk song heard in the introduction as he works.
He gets up, looks at the stove, scratches his head. His singing
becomes louder. A short pause while he looks for something in his
tool case. Then he continues singing more softly. Finally he finds
the wrench he is looking for and bursts out into loud song.*

EVA (*has entered during the song and has been listening*): Well,
well, Mr. Sebald, you're not going to get any louder than
that, are you?

SEBALD: No, I guess I can't do any better than that.

EVA: What are you doing here, Mr. Sebald?

SEBALD: Oh, all sorts of things . . . (*He checks them off on his
fingers.*) grinding coffee, cleaning windows, sweeping floors,
baby-sitting, if there were any dogs here I'd be walking them,
but there aren't any, hanging up the washing . . .

EVA: Enough, enough, Mr. Sebald, I can imagine the rest.

SEBALD: I'll be through in a moment—yes, I have to peel the
potatoes too.

EVA: That's marvelous . . . are you living here now at Mrs.
Rychner's?

SEBALD: No, no, that wouldn't do—Mrs. Rychner's a very moral
woman and I need a landlady that closes both eyes . . . no,
I just come over to do odd jobs since—well, since what happened. I don't have anything to do anyway . . . and so,
that's the way it goes.

EVA: How is Mrs. Rychner?

SEBALD: She's sent the two little ones to relatives for the time
being, and she hires herself out as a seamstress . . . one way
or another, she'll make out. She'll be back soon, by the way,
so I'll put the potatoes on to cook . . . (*He tightens a
screw.*) . . . there, that's finished.

EVA: And so you sing all day while you're doing all this?

SEBALD: Oh, well, you know, you have to bring a little zest into
the whole thing. (*He wipes off the place he has been re-
pairing on the stove and bursts into the song again; then he
interrupts himself and asks*) Do you like that?

EVA: You know nicer songs than that, don't you, Sebald?

SEBALD: Oh, sure, wait a minute. (*He starts another song.*)

MRS. RYCHNER (*enters*): How nice of you to drop in, Miss
Gröner.

SEBALD: She interrupted my work . . . and now the water still
isn't boiling.

MRS. RYCHNER: Well now, isn't that terrible . . . You'll have a
spoonful of soup with us, won't you, Miss Gröner?

EVA: That's very nice of you, Mrs. Rychner. Actually I just dropped in to see how you were.

MRS. RYCHNER: Dear God, Miss Gröner, life goes on—it has to. If they just wouldn't bother me with the investigation anymore . . . they're very nice to me, of course . . . but I just don't want to hear any more about it.

EVA (*shuddering*): I can certainly sympathize with you there, Mrs. Rychner.

SEBALD (*who has been fiddling around with the stove again*): There!—now it's all fixed up . . . I'll go and open the gas main outside, Mother Rychner, and then all you'll have to do is light up . . . (*He takes the grocery basket.*) . . . and now I'm off to do the shopping. (*Exits.*)

EVA: He's a very good boy.

MRS. RYCHNER (*looking at* EVA): Yes, my dear, that's the way it goes . . . I was once as young as you are now, and life went on, and now it's come to this. It goes by so quickly, you can't really grasp it. Life is terrible, just terrible . . . (*She takes* EVA's *hand.*) . . . People like me would like to protect you from it . . . but it just can't be done.

EVA: Yes, yes, I know—nobody can do anything for anyone else . . . everyone has to work things out for himself.

MRS. RYCHNER (*wiping away a tear*): It's all right, girl . . . (*She goes to the stove.*) . . . I'll warm up a cup of coffee at least —all right?

EVA: There's someone at the door, Mrs. Rychner.

MRS. RYCHNER: Yes—come in!

GIESLING (*enters*): Good evening . . . ah, Miss Gröner, you're here too!

EVA: Hello, Mr. Giesling.

GIESLING (*shakes hands with both women*): I'm here to bring you a little bit of money from a collection we've taken up, Mrs. Rychner . . . it's going pretty slowly, but for the present I've brought you 150 marks. It's not much, but it's better than nothing.

MRS. RYCHNER (*holding the money dubiously*): You're very good to me, Mr. Giesling . . . all of you that contributed are very good . . . but . . . (*She cannot bring herself to say it.*)

GIESLING: Don't hesitate to take it, Mrs. Rychner—it isn't charity . . . it's part of our debt to George.

(*The stage becomes darker.*)

MRS. RYCHNER: It was easier to take the 200 marks I got from the management.

GIESLING: It was little enough . . . how are things with you otherwise?

MRS. RYCHNER: Oh, well . . . Anton Sebald is very good and helps me out a lot . . . (*She goes back to the stove.*) . . . the water'll boil right away. . . . You'll have a cup of coffee with us, won't you, Mr. Giesling? (*She brings out cups and saucers.*)

GIESLING (*sits at the table*): Have you any idea how things are with Woritzki?

MRS. RYCHNER (*going back and forth between table and stove*): Woritzki? . . . yes, I was over there just this morning . . . always the same misery over there . . . they've had him in for interrogation twice already . . . I can't think why they're picking on him.

GIESLING: Because he's always talking such a lot of idiotic nonsense, probably . . . they're convinced that it was a Communist plot anyway.

MRS. RYCHNER: I don't want to talk about it anymore . . . (*To EVA, who is standing at the window.*) Come along, coffee's ready.

EVA: There's something going on over there.

MRS. RYCHNER: Let it go; don't pay any attention . . . it's never anything good.

EVA: It's hard to see anything clearly . . . it's getting dark.

MRS. RYCHNER: That's true, we do need the light on in here . . . and it isn't even seven yet . . . (*She turns on the light.*) oh well, it's September already.

EVA (*leaning out of the window*): They've arrested someone . . . they're leading him away down there.

MRS. RYCHNER: A drunk maybe.

EVA: Everyone's still standing around.

GIESLING (*gets up and goes to the window*): That's . . . that's at Woritzki's . . . I've got to go over there. (*He runs to the door.*)

MRS. RYCHNER: Woritzki . . . for Heaven's sake!

EVA (*still at the window*): Someone's running over this way anyhow.

GIESLING (*back at the window*): That's old Mrs. Woritzki . . . er, why don't you go on over into the next room, Mrs. Rychner.

MRS. RYCHNER (*supporting herself on the table*): I can't . . . there's no point anyway . . .

EVA: What's it all mean . . . Woritzki?

(*The door is thrown wide, and old* MRS. WORITZKI *dashes in. On seeing the people in the room, she recoils, horrified, leans against the doorpost, breathless. Pause.* GIESLING *makes a movement as if to go to the door.*)

MRS. WORITZKI: They've . . . taken him . . . away . . . they've . . . taken him . . . away . . . they've taken him away. They tied his hands . . . like that (*She crosses her hands.*) . . . it can't be true . . . say that it can't be true. (*She holds her hands to her head and screams.*)

GIESLING (*supporting her*): Of course not, everything will be cleared up, Mrs. Woritzki—he'll be back tomorrow morning.

MRS. WORITZKI (*tears herself away from him and approaches* MRS. RYCHNER *with faltering step*): They grabbed him by the jacket . . . tore it apart . . . (*She opens her hand, showing two buttons.*) here are the buttons . . . and then they twisted his arm . . . like that . . . and I had to stand and watch, I had to stand and watch!

(*People who have followed up from the street try to push in at the door.*)

EVA: Come along, Mrs. Woritzki, I'll take you home.

WORITZKI'S WIFE (*pushing her way through the crowd*): Is Mother there? . . . Come along, Mother, come away from here . . . come away from these people . . . (*She grabs the old woman by the arm, spilling the buttons on the floor.*)

MRS. WORITZKI: The buttons . . . (*She shakes her daughter-in-law off, falls to her knees, and starts crawling after the buttons. Panic-stricken.*) Where's the second one . . . where's the second one?

EVA (*finding it*): Here, Mrs. Woritzki . . . come along . . .

(*Together with* GIESLING *she helps her to get up again.*)

MRS. WORITZKI (*grabs the button from* EVA's *hand and continues pursuing* MRS. RYCHNER, *so that both women face each other in the foreground, whereupon she stretches out her hand with the buttons in it again*): . . . let her say that it wasn't him . . . that it wasn't him . . . (*She still holds out the buttons, hopeless and despairing.*) . . . that it wasn't him . . . (*Weakly.*) that . . . it wasn't . . . him . . . that . . .

MRS. RYCHNER (*producing the ghost of a smile with great effort*): No, it wasn't him, Mrs. Woritzki.

CURTAIN

ACT III

Scene 1

Sound effect: *Muffled drums.*

Film: *Idle workers in front of a factory gate.*

Curtain rises. The Filsmann living room, MRS. FILSMANN *and* GLADYS.

GLADYS: I'm frightened, Mother.

MRS. FILSMANN: Do you want to leave us again?

GLADYS (*shaking her head*): No, I'm staying.

MRS. FILSMANN: You mustn't be afraid . . . we women must not be afraid now.

GLADYS: I came back.

MRS. FILSMANN: One forgets how to be afraid as one gets older.

GLADYS: I don't know whether I'm young or not, but I know I'm frightened.

MRS. FILSMANN: Once you have a child, you'll feel more secure.

GLADYS (*uncontrollably*): No . . . no, I don't want to.

MRS. FILSMANN (*looking closely at her*): That is . . . bad.

GLADYS: No . . . I'm afraid . . .

OLD FILSMANN (*enters; he is dressed informally*): Where is Herbert? (*Short pause.*) I asked where Herbert was.

GLADYS: At the plant, Father . . . same as every morning.

OLD FILSMANN: Everything's kept secret from me.

MRS. FILSMANN: What's kept secret from you, Father?

OLD FILSMANN (*taking a newspaper from his pocket*): The Filsmann shares fell fourteen points yesterday . . . that's what's kept secret from me.

MRS. FILSMANN: But you never read the stock market news.

OLD FILSMANN: And I don't want to have anything to do with all that stuff either . . . I shall go to Gelshausen today and open up the plant there.

MRS. FILSMANN (*startled*): You really want to do that?

OLD FILSMANN: I'm waiting for Herbert . . . (*He sits down in an armchair and starts studying the newspaper again.*)

GLADYS: He won't be back for another two hours at least, Father.

OLD FILSMANN (*stubbornly*): I'm waiting for Herbert.

GLADYS (*softly*): They smashed windows and wrecked machines yesterday . . . I'm scared.

MRS. FILSMANN: Aren't they negotiating with the workers today?
GLADYS: In the afternoon, I think . . . they're having a meeting at Menck's now.

(OLD FILSMANN *has fallen asleep.*)

MRS. FILSMANN: Let's hope Herbert is able to stand up to him.
GLADYS: Everything looks so threatening . . . everything . . .

(*The stage becomes dark; the muffled drums are heard again.*)

SCENE 2

A small side stage is lit up on the apron.

A hotel room. ROSSHAUPT *alone. He is writing.*

ROSSHAUPT (*laying his pen aside*): It's pointless: I can't write. She's gone back to the money. Oh, how powerfully it pulled her, and how unwillingly she obeyed . . . if she'd left me easily, it wouldn't hurt so much. But it was overwhelming, and she was helpless against the incomprehensible power that held her fast and crushed her heart . . . and I—I did not have the strength to hold her back, I was powerless against the weakness that blew her away . . . because I loved her weakness, because I loved her so much, I was defeated. What a terrible parting it was and how bitterly we wept—and how wretchedly feeble I am not to be able to rescue a weak woman from the power of money! Or is money more powerful than the powers in which I believe? How could I go on living? But I mustn't let that happen, for it's only a woman that has left me while the idea is alive.

(*A knock on the door.*)

CHAMBERMAID (*enters*): Someone to see you, Mr. Scholtz.
ROSSHAUPT: Please ask him to write to me what he wants.
CHAMBERMAID: He says it's about the Rosshaupt matter.
ROSSHAUPT (*gets up*): Indeed . . . ask him to come in, please.
JECKEL (*enters*): Good morning, Baron Rosshaupt, allow me to introduce myself. My name is Jeckel, and I'm with the Peda Company.
ROSSHAUPT: In what way can I be of service?
JECKEL: I've had the honor to recognize you, Baron.
ROSSHAUPT: Are you a detective?

JECKEL: I have some connections with the police.

ROSSHAUPT: In that case, why haven't you turned me in?

JECKEL: Because it occurred to me that you might place a certain value on Mrs. Filsmann's reputation.

ROSSHAUPT: Oh, so that's the way the wind blows—you just want some money.

JECKEL: I'm not a blackmailer, and I'll thank you not to slander me by calling me one.

ROSSHAUPT: But you are willing to accept money that I might give you of my own free will?

JECKEL: Big turnover, small overhead, that's my motto. But it cost me plenty to track you down here in Berlin, Baron.

ROSSHAUPT: What do you call a big turnover?

JECKEL: I leave the definition of that to your generosity, Baron. But be so good as to remember that I have a family to support.

ROSSHAUPT: You have no shame at all.

JECKEL: I live by the principle that what anyone else can do, I can do too. And everyone does the same thing. We live in a commercial world.

ROSSHAUPT: So that's how you see the world.

JECKEL: I know the world, Baron. If you don't chase the money, you starve. You have to keep moving if you want to keep your head above water. And you have to look sharp, too.

ROSSHAUPT: You're not even aware of your own depravity.

JECKEL: Once you've done a bit of running around from customer to customer with a sample case in your hand, Baron, you won't be calling smartness depravity. The German businessman still has some standing in the country and in the world, thank God.

ROSSHAUPT: That would be a pretty sad kind of standing.

JECKEL: There isn't any other, Baron. Some people do it in a bigger way, some in a smaller—but they all do it. Everyone as best he can. The big shots squeeze out a lot of money; and the little people have to make do with a little. But everyone grabs something off the next man, because everyone's got a belly to fill.

ROSSHAUPT: Even if that's the way it is, that's not the way it's going to be. All that has to be eradicated.

JECKEL: It will never change because that's the way of human nature.

ROSSHAUPT: The nature of the gutter class.

JECKEL: Money rules the world. And you're no exception either, Baron. You're cursing things as if you'd already paid out your money . . . But then, no one likes to shell out dough . . .

ROSSHAUPT (*has taken out his wallet and throws a bundle of bank-notes on the table*): Here . . . and now get out, you gutter-snipe.

JECKEL: I realize that time is money, but I'll have to count this just the same . . . (*He counts deliberately.*) . . . I take pleasure in acknowledging the receipt of 870 marks with my deepest thanks. . . . Your generosity is of medium size, Baron, and I'm sorry you found it so difficult . . . I have the honor to take my leave, Baron.

ROSSHAUPT (*alone; he has sunk down at the table*): If the world really were as that scum sees it, it would be high time to shoot oneself. But even that worm covers up what he does by claiming to do it for his family. Even if the whole nation were corrupted by money, there's still a spark of decency and faithfulness in everyone. No matter how much they haggle and grab among themselves, no matter how much they have forgotten that they belong together, the day will come when the seed will sprout and everything false will wither, the day when everyone will do his work for the sake of his work and for the sake of the people, for that which is truly alive must come into its own again. As long as that hope survives, we must serve it and are not permitted to withdraw . . . no matter how tempting this may appear . . . oh, how tempting! (*He has taken a revolver out of the table drawer and is looking at it. There is a knock on the door; ROSSHAUPT puts the revolver back.*)

CHAMBERMAID: I'm to give this to you . . . the gentleman's waiting. (*She hands him a sealed envelope.*)

ROSSHAUPT (*reading*): Ask the gentleman to come in. (*He tidies the table a bit and glances at himself in the mirror.*)

SAGDORFF (*enters*): Greetings, my dear Rosshaupt—that is to say, my dear Scholtz; things get a little confused with you con-spirators.

ROSSHAUPT: This is an unexpected honor, your Excellency.

SAGDORFF (*sitting and lighting a cigarette*): I wanted to ask you to visit me, but that would have been a little rash, what with the various people I've got coming in and out of my place all the time . . . and since it's convenient for me just now . . . oh, by the way, do you know what I've come for?

ROSSHAUPT: I think I do.

SAGDORFF: Yes, well . . . so you propose to use the disturbances at the Filsmann Works as a justification for mounting an operation in the Southwest . . .

ROSSHAUPT: Pretexts for declarations of war are, to be sure, always immoral, but there's a distinct danger right now that the people might be radically swayed by the Left.

SAGDORFF: Granted . . . I ought to tell you that I put the matter up to Menck immediately . . . he went back again yesterday.

ROSSHAUPT: Do you approve of my plan, Excellency?

SAGDORFF: There's no doubt about it being an excellent plan, but just now it's running into some stiff opposition from Menck.

ROSSHAUPT: Excuse me, but what has Menck to do with it?

SAGDORFF: Well now, the Filsmann Works belong to Menck's combine, after all—and the Durig Works are right now in the process of merging with them . . . You read the papers, surely.

ROSSHAUPT: Rarely . . . and never the commercial news.

SAGDORFF: The commercial news is a good deal more important for anyone involved in politics than the so-called political news.

ROSSHAUPT: The aims of our movement lie beyond politics . . . as well as beyond the confines of commerce and money.

SAGDORFF: At the beginning and at the end there always stands the Platonic idea. But the beginning and the end lie in darkness: the path between leads through reality.

ROSSHAUPT: So Mr. Menck is powerful enough to have a decisive influence on our movement?

SAGDORFF: At the moment we are moving through the sphere of reality.

ROSSHAUPT: The protection of the Filsmann Works is not the purpose of my plan: our aim is to achieve something conclusive.

SAGDORFF: But in reality it's not only going to be a matter of this protection—it's going to involve us in a very unpleasant connection with the proposed action . . . don't forget that I'm Chairman of the Board of the Filsmann Works.

ROSSHAUPT: The man who killed the shop foreman is a Communist.

SAGDORFF: Rumors are stronger than facts—particularly when financial interests are suspected to be behind them.

ROSSHAUPT: That's the way to destroy the purity of our movement!

SAGDORFF: Nobody is prepared to grant pure motives to anyone at all—nobody! Even your best friends won't be able to suppress the suspicion of personal interest completely . . . *your* personal interest, Rosshaupt.

ROSSHAUPT (*faintly*): I think . . . I understand.

SAGDORFF: Therefore, beware of any independent operations.

ROSSHAUPT (*very quietly*): A quarter of an hour ago a man was here trying to convince me that in Germany money was king and that it could never be any other way.

SAGDORFF: The man was uttering only what everyone knows for fact.

ROSSHAUPT (*making a last attempt*): Still, we . . .

SAGDORFF: Platitudes are true and false at one and the same time . . . overcoming them involves one in difficulties . . . I believe we understand each other.

ROSSHAUPT: I have understood you, Excellency.

SAGDORFF: In that case everything is in order and I'll be on my way. (*They shake hands.* SAGDORFF *exits.*)

ROSSHAUPT (*remains standing, alone*): So he belongs to them, too. And they all, all of them, belong to it, to the world of money. The only world there is is the world of money. There's no other way of life; and we, we who believe in other powers, are in the midst of death. That—that is why she had to leave me: conscious of returning to life, conscious of turning away from death. Is the illusion really life? Oh, friends—our shattered union, crumbling into dust. Oh, hand of shadows, stretched out to grasp the shadows . . . oh, when the specters surround you like trees and look into your darkened window . . . oh, when the beloved being becomes transparent and reveals to you the landscape lying behind . . . then, oh, then . . .

(*The remainder should not be read as a poem and, at the discretion of the actor playing* ROSSHAUPT, *may be left out altogether.*)

. . . already the forest has been thinned by the Fall . . . and all that is living stands transfixed in starkly tender poise. . . . But you who have sought, seek no more the path to the earthly abode . . . To you the open doors are shut and you walk through frozen walls. . . . For once more you are thrown and surrendered, thrown into the all-encompassing All . . . and that which you touch is the Heavens . . .

CURTAIN

(*The sound of a shot is heard.*)

SCENE 3

No sound effects or film.

FILSMANN'S *living room.* OLD FILSMANN *is sleeping in the armchair.* MRS. FILSMANN *is doing needlework.*

HERBERT (*comes in hurriedly, deeply upset; he does not greet his parents and does not notice that his father is asleep or that his mother has signaled him to be quiet*): Oh, so you're here, Father . . .

OLD FILSMANN (*waking up*): Yes . . . what's going on at the plant?

HERBERT: At the plant?

OLD FILSMANN: Something's going on over at the plant . . .

HERBERT (*absently*): Oh . . . just a few people kicking up a row again.

OLD FILSMANN: The workers want bread . . . well, let them have it; I'll reopen Gelshausen.

HERBERT (*rousing himself from his abstraction*): Are you serious? Reopen Gelshausen—that's crazy . . . (*He rubs his eyes.*) Besides, everything will turn out all right yet, Father.

OLD FILSMANN: I don't tolerate workers kicking up a row in my place . . . I'll run them out of here . . . anyone who earns his bread from me, had better know who's boss.

GLADYS (*enters*): I heard your car, Herbert . . . you're so early today . . .

HERBERT (*pulling himself together with difficulty*): We might be able to swing it yet . . . Menck has drawn up a price and quota agreement with Durig according to the terms of which we might be able to reopen the works.

OLD FILSMANN: Menck is a very capable man.

HERBERT: I've asked him to come over here for a discussion, so that he may talk things over with you as well.

OLD FILSMANN: The Filsmann stocks fell again . . . I have to get my information from the newspapers.

HERBERT (*exhausted*): You shouldn't concern yourself with those things . . . once we open the works again, the stocks will rise again.

OLD FILSMANN: I'll tell this Mr. Menck a thing or two. (*Leaves abruptly.*)

MRS. FILSMANN: For Heaven's sake, what's happened, Herbert?

Why have you asked Menck to come here?

HERBERT (*tired*): These are decisions for which we need Father's signature . . . the Durig affair.

GLADYS: Is Menck going to lunch with us?

HERBERT: I don't know . . . I didn't think of it.

MRS. FILSMANN: I'm afraid that having lunch with Menck will hardly be appropriate anymore.

HERBERT: What do you mean by that, Mother? (*He has somehow managed to regain his composure.*)

MRS. FILSMANN: Why don't you go up to Father . . . and try and prepare him. I'll call you when Menck arrives.

GLADYS: I don't understand any of this.

MRS. FILSMANN: I'm afraid I think I do.

GLADYS: Just what has happened, anyway?

MRS. FILSMANN: That's what we're going to find out . . . be so good as to leave me alone with Menck . . . I want to try to talk to him privately.

GLADYS: I have to go and attend to the luncheon anyway. (*Exits.*)

(*The Maid enters with a calling card.*)

MRS. FILSMANN: Yes . . . show him in. (*Short pause.*)

MENCK (*entering*): Ah, my dear friend . . .

MRS. FILSMANN: It's nice to see that you still address me that way.

(MENCK *makes a surprised gesture.*)

Very well then, my dear friend . . . sit down . . . there . . . and now, without any beating about the bush, what exactly is going on? You know that I don't understand anything about business . . . but there's something going on here that extends beyond matters of business and, therefore, it is my concern.

MENCK: You're right, as always. To put it as briefly as possible, your son's experiment has not worked out.

MRS. FILSMANN: Why did you agree to the experiment? I'm not trying to saddle you with the responsibility for it . . . but I know your foresight.

MENCK: The source of the whole trouble lies in the Durig-Filsmann fight. Things never work out when an individual is placed above circumstances; things are always stronger than men.

MRS. FILSMANN: And what if the merger had been made in time?

MENCK: You are aware of the tremendous losses that Filsmann has suffered—and Durig has been bled pretty dry too; well, insofar as those losses were due to the competition between the two, they could have been avoided . . . today it's a matter of avoiding any further loss . . .

MRS. FILSMANN: And what about Herbert's experiment in this connection?

MENCK: If I had opposed him, I would have been blamed for capitulating to Durig, even though it would not have been a capitulation—any more than it is one now. The merger had to come one way or another.

MRS. FILSMANN: One more question: what will be your position and that of the Filsmann family after all this?

MENCK: The Filsmann family still has its private fortune and also retains a share in the works. To that extent the merger has managed to save the situation. As for the future, all we can do is hope; if the world as we know it stays the way it is, then we did right; if it goes to pot completely, then nothing will matter anymore anyway.

MRS. FILSMANN: And what will be your particular interests in all this?

MENCK: They will be confined to seeing to it that this merger, which unhappily has been forced on us, goes through smoothly and without too much loss or damage.

MRS. FILSMANN: Good, and now I'll invite you for lunch . . . I see the future is dark enough, but I'm glad that I still have food to offer you . . . I was beginning to doubt even that, you see.

HERBERT (enters): I've only just been told that you're here, Mr. Menck. My father is waiting for us upstairs.

MRS. FILSMANN: I think you're worrying too much, my boy. Mr. Menck has just told me all sorts of comforting things about our future.

HERBERT (numbly): Yes, well, I hope you'll all be safeguarded. . . . I think Mr. Menck will do his best.

MENCK: Well, and you—you're still here too, my friend.

MRS. FILSMANN: Mr. Menck is staying for lunch . . . I'm very glad about that. . . . Meanwhile I'll leave you. (She starts to leave.)

HERBERT (as if coming to a sudden decision): Yes, Mother—but please excuse me today . . . I won't be able to stay for lunch.

MENCK: That's really a pity, Filsmann.

MRS. FILSMANN (looking at him searchingly): You really can't stay?

HERBERT (averting his eyes): No . . . no . . . I can't . . . I have

an appointment with the lawyer . . . and after that I have
to go right on to the office.

MRS. FILSMANN (*slowly*): I see . . . but you'll be here in the
evening, my boy?

HERBERT: Yes . . . in the evening . . . I'll be here . . . for sure.

MRS. FILSMANN (*sighing*): All right, then. (*She starts to leave.*)

HERBERT (*his eyes on his mother*): Good-bye, Mother.

MRS. FILSMANN (*comes back and gives her son a kiss*): There . . .
good-bye, my boy . . . and if you decide to stay for lunch
after all, then this didn't count. (*She nods to* MENCK *and
leaves.*)

MENCK: Your mother is a wonderful woman.

HERBERT (*smiling rigidly*): Yes . . . if it weren't for my mother . . .

MENCK: I've got some good news for you, by the way. I've been
talking to Berlin on the telephone. The stock exchange has
got wind of the matter already, and Filsmann stocks are up
twelve.

HERBERT: The Filsmann Works have become a bunch of shares
for me, like any others . . . I have very little interest in the
matter.

MENCK: I still don't understand why you attach so much importance to your family's majority share . . . those times are
long gone, after all.

HERBERT: Not for my father . . . and not for me either . . .

MENCK: You can rest assured we've done the best thing possible
under the circumstances . . . and besides, you're completely
protected by your syndicate agreement.

HERBERT (*shrugging his shoulders absently*): Syndicate agreement
. . . from this day on the Filsmann Works have no right
any longer to bear that name.

MENCK: Your family remains exactly what it has always been . . .
and you'll see, Filsmann, that we'll be able to work together
with Martin Durig quite well. The main thing is to get this
wage question straightened out with him now.

HERBERT: Not me . . . I told you that in the beginning.

MENCK: You're an impossible blockhead.

HERBERT: You may well be right with your opportunistic policies
. . . I admit I'm beaten, but I'm not going to sit down to
talk with any Mr. Lauck—or with any Mr. Durig either.

MENCK: With all due allowance, I'm afraid I can't go along with
you on that.

HERBERT: As far as I'm concerned Right is Right and Left is Left
—and there's nothing I can do about that.

MENCK: You can see for yourself what your own policies have achieved: rioting workers, machines broken by acts of sabotage . . . God only knows what else may happen if we don't put an end to it right now. . . . There's an evil wind blowing in Germany . . . and—don't you forget that it was me to whom you left the task of bolstering the shares from which the bottom was about to drop out.

HERBERT: An honorable death would be better.

MENCK: And what about the responsibility for your family, which I share now?

HERBERT (*staring at him with meaning*): Yes.

MENCK: Well, there, you see!

HERBERT (*rigidly*): Yes.

MENCK: Well then, I think it's time we went to see your father.

HERBERT: One more thing. I just wanted to tell you that I can't bring myself to meet Durig this afternoon . . . I must ask you to take care of that, too . . . I'm no longer the master in the Filsmann Works.

MENCK: But these are pure formalities, my dear Filsmann.

HERBERT: They're meaningful enough as far as I'm concerned to prevent my taking part in the conference . . . since you cannot speak for all my family's interests, I shall instruct my lawyer.

MENCK: Surely you don't propose to stay away from the meetings of the Board of Directors? You can't do that!

HERBERT (*very absently*): Yes.

MENCK: If only for your father's sake!

HERBERT (*getting up stiffly*): Yes . . . my father is waiting.

MENCK: Have you prepared him? (*He rises also.*)

HERBERT: Yes . . . but all he thinks of is Gelshausen.

MENCK: I'll tell him that there are prospects of reopening Gelshausen . . . that'll make him as receptive as possible . . . and, with God's help, maybe we'll actually manage to do it some day.

HERBERT (*absently*): Yes . . . that'll make him as receptive as possible . . . (*Bursting out.*) For Heaven's sake, Menck, spare me this . . . you go to see him alone . . . I can't.

MENCK: What am I to do with you? Listen here, Filsmann, you've got to . . . Come on . . . you have to do this, if it's the last thing you do.

HERBERT (*stubbornly*): I can't . . . I can't.

MENCK (*strongly*): You're risking everything, Dr. Filsmann.

HERBERT (*weakly*): It's the last thing I'll ask you.

MENCK (*taking him under the arm*): Come along, Filsmann . . .

HERBERT (*obediently*): Yes . . . let's go . . . (*Very softly.*) . . . it's the last thing.

MENCK (*looks at him searchingly, stops, and says pleadingly*): Listen, Filsmann . . . stay here for lunch . . . it'll please your mother . . .

HERBERT (*shaking his head, softly*): No.

MENCK: But you will be in your office this afternoon . . . you'll promise me that?

HERBERT (*numbly*): Yes, I promise you that . . . let's go . . .

(*They go arm in arm.*)

CURTAIN

SCENE 4

SOUND EFFECT: *The slow and halting rattle of a typewriter's keys. It gets slower and slower, the intervals longer and longer. Finally it stops.*

There is no film.

Curtain goes up. EVA GRÖNER's *room. Very simple furnishings.* EVA *sits at the typewriter, her arms hanging down.* LAUCK *is in a corner of the room.*

LAUCK: Are you going to be through soon?

EVA (*without moving*): No.

LAUCK: I have to go in a moment; I've got a meeting with Menck this afternoon.

EVA: Go on, then.

LAUCK: What are you typing?

EVA: You know what . . . any typing job I can get.

LAUCK: Things can't go on this way . . . I'm not going to let you live like this any longer.

EVA: You ought to have thought of that sooner.

LAUCK: But it was an impossible situation . . .

EVA (*quiet and suppressed*): Since you claim to be a Socialist you should have been particularly glad that I had work of my own and could lead my own life . . . but I realize now that you just wanted to make me dependent on you . . . to get me completely into your power . . . you're not a Socialist at all —all you care about is power.

LAUCK (*fanatically*): Yes, I care about power—but only to use it in the service of the Ideal.

EVA (*very quickly*): And with me? With me too, of course!

LAUCK (*amazed*): But that's something completely different . . . it was simply intolerable for my fiancée to be mixed up in plots against my own class—even if only as a secretary . . . (*Haltingly.*) . . . the woman that I love.

EVA: A man who thinks only of his party can't love, you're lying.

LAUCK: It's not a matter of the party; it's a matter of the Idea.

EVA: There you see how you're lying—you're not at all aware of the fact that you've got a living human being before you.

LAUCK (*stunned by her words, he makes as if to approach her and says softly*): I love you.

EVA: Don't touch me . . . (*Sullenly.*) . . . no, don't touch me. I'm not going to let myself be swallowed up by you and your Idea—I'm still a human being.

LAUCK: But this is madness, Eva.

EVA: No, your Idea is madness . . . everything you people do is madness . . . Rychner had to be murdered because of the Idea.

LAUCK: Plenty of people have died for the sake of a higher goal . . .

EVA (*more and more agitated*): Those are just propaganda slogans —that's the only way you know how to talk . . . all your ideas are just propaganda slogans . . . I'm only just realizing it . . . you've all got your ideas and all you ever say is nothing—nothing but a bunch of propaganda slogans . . .

LAUCK (*alarmed*): If you believe that, Eva, there's no way we can communicate anymore.

EVA: No, there's no way we can communicate anymore.

LAUCK: You didn't always think this way.

EVA (*breaking down and crying*): Oh, if I could only go back . . . I want to go back to my job.

LAUCK: And I thought you were one of us!

EVA: Yes, that's all that was important to you. . . . Oh, I can see through it all now—do you hear, I can see through it all now . . . I know you kept after me because you figured you could pry some secrets about the management out of me . . . that's what I was important for . . . and that's all! . . .

LAUCK: Eva . . .

EVA: I despise you . . . you and your ideas both. (*She is screaming by now.*)

LAUCK (*hides his face in his hands*): What was the point of it all, then . . . everything that happened!

EVA (*almost hysterical*): What was the point of it? . . . You still want to know?

LAUCK: Didn't you . . . (*Haltingly.*) . . . ever love me, then?

EVA (*hysterically*): Love you? . . . You? . . . (*Screaming.*) . . . I pitied you . . . Oh God, how I pitied you! . . . because you were a weakling . . . because you were so miserably weak and burned out . . . and you wanted to get everything done just through your will power alone . . . and I thought you had to be helped . . . because you were weak and deformed . . . you . . . you're a . . . (*She has jumped up.*) . . . you're a hunchback . . . a hunchback, and you're uglier than anybody else . . . that's why I pitied you . . . and I followed you . . . yes, I followed you . . . yes, followed you with your hump—you've got one, all right, there it is . . .

LAUCK (*bursting out*): I'm going, Eva . . . that's enough . . . I'm going . . .

EVA: Yes, go, go to your ideas . . . go and don't come back . . .

(LAUCK *dashes out;* EVA *screams at the closed door.*)

. . . go on, you and your hump . . . go on, go on . . . I don't want to see you ever again . . . he's got a hump . . . (*She collapses.*) . . . he's a hunchback . . . (*Sobbing.*) . . . he's a hunchback, he's a hunchback . . . (*Her sobbing becomes quieter.*) . . . a hump . . . (*Very weakly.*) . . . a hump . . . Oh, he's deformed . . . all deformed and helpless . . . so helpless, so helpless . . . oh, I love him . . . (*Suddenly bursting out again.*) I love him, I love him.

CURTAIN

SCENE 5

SOUND EFFECT: *The murmur of a crowd, rising and falling.*

FILM: *Deserted factory workrooms, some with wrecked machines.*

Factory wall and lantern (the scene of the murder). Some workers, mostly young men with some women among them, are huddled together, at stage right, some standing, some squatting on the ground. WORITZKI's *mother is alone at left. This scene should be played in a subdued, shadowy, marionette-like manner. All movements should be silent, even when the characters are running across the stage.*

FIRST WORKER (*he is hidden in the group and speaks softly*): Move on when the police come. Assemblies are forbidden.

(*Pause. No one moves.*)

SECOND WORKER (*ditto*): Why don't you move on yourself, then?

FIRST WOMAN (*ditto*): Where are we supposed to move on to?

VOICES (*hoarsely*): Where are we supposed to move on to? . . .
Where to? . . . We're unemployed . . . unemployed . . .
Where to?

OLD MRS. WORITZKI (*shrilly*): It wasn't him.

(*Pause. Nobody moves.* BEREND *enters, right, slinks across,
and exits, left. Pause.*)

FIRST WORKER (*tonelessly*): That was Berend; he's a Christian.

FIRST WOMAN: He's proud; he doesn't care about us.

SECOND WOMAN: They'll hire him again for sure . . . or they'll
take him at Durig's . . .

SECOND WORKER: Where are we supposed to go? . . .

A WORKER (*jumps out of the group and onto the base of the lantern, from which he hangs by his right hand like a sailor from
a mast*): It's lunchtime . . . (*He speaks in a low, hoarse
voice.*) . . . which one of you has had anything to eat?

(*No one moves; the crowd stares at the speaker without
moving. Pause.*)

FIRST WORKER (*whispering*): Get down—get down off there
quickly or they'll arrest you.

OLD MRS. WORITZKI: It wasn't him.

THE SPEAKER (*softly, from the lamppost*): I'm not getting down.
. . . Workers' blood was poured out here. One of us fell here
in the fight against capitalism . . . which one of you has
had any lunch?

OLD MRS. WORITZKI: It wasn't him!

THE SPEAKER: He was hungry too . . .

VOICES (*hoarsely*): We're unemployed . . . we're hungry.

THE SPEAKER: He was hungry too . . . and what if he did do it?
Who led him on? We'll never find out about that . . .

SECOND WORKER (*in a low, hoarse voice from the middle of the
unmoving group*): Down with the exploiters! . . . Down
with them!

VOICES (*hoarsely*): Down with the exploiters! . . . Down with
the murderers!

FIRST WOMAN (*in a low voice*): Quiet, quiet . . . the police!

VOICES (*slightly louder; the group sways forward a bit; some arms
are raised hesitantly*): We're unemployed. Where are we supposed to go?

THE SPEAKER: Which one of you has eaten any lunch?

(*The group freezes again.*)

SECOND WOMAN: The Durig workers have food.

THE SPEAKER (*in a low, hissing voice*): The capitalists like to close down one factory so that they can get all their profits out of another one. We're glad the Durig workers are still earning money . . . but soon enough they'll be in the same boat as we.

SECOND WOMAN: Our children are hungry . . .

(*The group moves slightly forward again and opens up somewhat.*)

THE SPEAKER (*hoarsely, almost as if telling a secret*): The Durig workers have their Mr. Hügli, too, someone who'll promise them that he'll keep wages up but who'll break his word to them, too, and throw them out on the street . . . (*The group breaks up.*)

VOICES: Down with Hügli . . . Down with Filsmann . . . Down with Hügli . . . Smash his windows . . . to Hügli's . . . (*The voices are low, muffled, and hoarse.*)

FIRST WORKER: Careful . . . quiet . . .

(*The* SPEAKER *has jumped down. The group has broken up and runs off left, making threatening gestures. They drag* OLD MRS. WORITZKI *with them. Shouts of "To Hügli's" are heard. Some of those who have remained behind make signs to the wings, off right, from where little groups of three or four workers appear who wave others on after them, always whispering "To Hügli's" to each other. This action should not have the appearance of being the beginning of a revolution. Not more than twenty people should be involved, even with those who are waved on afterward.*)

VOICES (*from offstage*): To Hügli's.

(*Empty stage.*)

CURTAIN

SCENE 6

The murmur of the crowd swells. Shouts of "Down with HÜGLI." *The murmur breaks off.*

Curtain goes up. A room in Hügli's house. Windows along one wall. HÜGLI *and his wife are sitting at the table, having just eaten. She holds her baby in her arms.*

HÜGLI: Mr. Menck asked me to undertake the reorganization of the Durig Works today.

MRS. HÜGLI (*indicating the baby*): Look how sweetly he sleeps.

HÜGLI (*looking at the baby*): I'd be in charge of all three plants then . . . a challenging job.

(MRS. HÜGLI *starts singing a lullaby.*) *

All the same, it's not an easy decision to make.

MRS. HÜGLI: You'll be even less at home with us then.

HÜGLI: It would be a case not only of defending my position against Dr. Filsmann, but probably against Mr. Durig as well.

(*The hum of voices is heard from the street.*)

MRS. HÜGLI: What's that?

HÜGLI: Obviously another demonstration.

MRS. HÜGLI: The workers? . . . Or is there another election?

(*Cries of "Down with Hügli" are heard from outside.*)

HÜGLI (*springs to the window*): Well, that's the limit now!

(*The noise gets louder. A shrill voice is heard crying once, "It wasn't him!"*)

MRS. HÜGLI (*runs to her husband to try and pull him back, her child in her arms*): Get away from the window . . . Get away from the window!

(*Stones fly into the room, breaking the window panes.* HÜGLI, *who has not yet got to the window, suddenly falls back, clutching his arm.*)

MRS. HÜGLI (*screaming*): You're hit!

HÜGLI: It's nothing.

(*The shower of stones stops. Shouts of "Police!" "The police*

* His son will grow into a great big laddie,
A famous engineer just like his daddie
Now he's still small, he's got to sleep,
Dream and sleep and never weep.
For him the sun is shining bright
So his dreams may be happy and light.
He's our love and our joy,
Our sweet beloved, our little boy . . .

are coming." "Police pigs!" can be heard; then a voice yells
out the command, "Break it up, or we'll shoot!")

HÜGLI (going back to the window): Scandalous!

MRS. HÜGLI (wailing): Don't go to the window!

HÜGLI (looking out of the window): It's all quiet now . . . the
street's empty already . . . scandalous! . . . that these people . . .

MRS. HÜGLI (screaming): Aaaaaah . . . (She holds the child in
front of her and sways toward HÜGLI.)

HÜGLI (quickly taking the child from her): What, in Heaven's
name . . . what?

MRS. HÜGLI (breaking down): He's . . . he's . . . he's dead!

HÜGLI (feeling the child's face with a trembling hand): No, no,
that isn't possible . . . no, no . . . he's only got a scratch
. . . he's laughing . . . you, you . . . (Dully, suddenly petri-
fied.) . . . killed.

CURTAIN

SCENE 7

SOUND EFFECT: Chorus of many typewriters.

FILM: Interior of the Berlin Stock Exchange. Milling crowds.

Curtain goes up. MENCK's office.

MENCK: I must ask you to forgive me for being so late, but I had
to go and visit poor Hügli.

DURIG: A terrible affair . . . killed just like that. Poor little thing.

MENCK: A stone hit it on the forehead . . . it doesn't take much
with a little kid like that.

DURIG: And there's no way of finding out who did it . . . he just
goes unpunished.

MENCK: It's a horrible time we live in . . . (After a pause.)
. . . we'll lose Hügli. He wants to get out of town with his
wife as soon as possible.

DURIG: I can well imagine he would . . . does he want to go back
to Switzerland?

MENCK: I think he'll go to Russia after a bit . . . he had an offer
from there once before.

DURIG: To the Bolsheviks . . . now that this has happened to
him?

MENCK: Well, he says he's a technician . . . he's always going to have to be together with workers . . . and what're you going to do—that's the way it goes.

DURIG: And we keep asking ourselves what it all means.

MENCK: You know what's really terrible, Durig? The fact that even this has its good side . . . not only that this poor dead little thing is going to give us a good lever in the negotiations with those people, but it should also be obvious to you that you'll have to take over the technical direction of all of the works now.

DURIG: Wouldn't you prefer to engage a general manager from outside? . . . Filsmann would hardly agree to anything else.

MENCK: We've got to save money, my dear Durig . . . besides, Filsmann has the legal training and you're a technical man . . . so it's only natural to do it this way . . . and you'll find you'll be able to work together quite well after a bit.

DURIG (*smiling*): Yes, well, neither of us is going to find it easy at the start.

MENCK: Which reminds me, I must tell him you're here . . . (*Goes to the telephone and rings several times; very disconcerted.*) . . . that's funny, he doesn't answer . . . and I promised him that I'd . . . oh well, perhaps he's gone to see Hügli . . . things are in a bit of mess with us today. . . . We'll just have to get our business done without him if he doesn't show up.

DURIG (*obviously relieved*): Well now, I'm really sorry to hear that.

MENCK: We've already announced the general meeting at which you're to absorb the Filsmann Board of Directors.

DURIG: We have too . . . have you decided yet who will join our board in addition to yourself—the old Filsmann or the young one?

MENCK: I thought Herbert Filsmann would be better . . . (*The telephone rings.* MENCK *answers.*) . . . very good, ask the gentlemen to wait a moment . . . (*To* DURIG.) . . . Lauck and his boys are here; do them good to wait a bit. There's one other thing I wanted to tell you: Filsmann stocks are up twelve percent today.

DURIG: That's the way! Let's hope it keeps up . . . though not at the expense of the Durig stocks.

MENCK: We'll see to that together . . . you see, the trouble with Herbert Filsmann is that he sees everything from either the viewpoint of the victor or the defeated; he still hasn't learned that there are never any victors.

DURIG: Maybe—but in this wage question we've got to come out on top.

MENCK: Yes, well, one Pyrrhic victory more or less won't matter —the point is that Pyrrhic victories are the only kind there are . . . even your Agricultural Bank, which we managed to polish off so nicely . . .

DURIG (*guffawing*): That *was* pretty good . . . when you've figured everything, it still amounted to a discount of over forty percent . . .

MENCK: Maybe, but even this Agricultural Bank affair is going to end badly for me . . . I predict that I'll still end up saddled with the Institute.

DURIG: You're insatiable, my dear Menck . . . (*He laughs.*) . . . really you are.

MENCK: Yes, I keep eating my way through that Big Rock Candy Mountain, and the Mountain grows and grows . . . and finally it'll end up eating me . . . but I think it's time to end the quarantine . . . (*Telephoning.*) . . . ask the gentlemen to come in . . .

DURIG: If you've got no Big Rock Candy Mountain to work for, life isn't worth living . . . (*Indicating the door.*) . . . and not for those either . . .

MENCK: Of course . . . things aren't really bad until you know it isn't there.

(*Enter* LAUCK, KRAITSZAK, BEREND, *and* KÖNIGER.)

MENCK: Welcome, gentlemen.

LAUCK: My name is Lauck.

KRAITSZAK (*stiffly imitating* LAUCK): My name is Kraitszak.

BEREND: Berend, Christian Trade Union.

KÖNIGER: Königer, National Trade Union.

MENCK: This is our friend, Mr. Durig . . . (*They bow to each other.*) . . . please sit down, gentlemen. Gentlemen, we've asked you to come to this meeting because matters have come to a point that demands rapid action . . . I would gladly have postponed this meeting since our General Manager, Mr. Hügli, is unable to attend as a result of the criminal events that took place this morning, but the seriousness of the position is such . . .

KÖNIGER: The members of the working class deplore such Communist excesses as strongly as possible.

LAUCK: Hunger no longer has anything to do with party affiliations . . .

MENCK: We're not here to judge anything . . . you say that it's

a question of hunger . . . very well, we're ready to reopen
the plants, even though it's our machines that were wrecked
and even though the critical economic situation hardly permits such a reopening . . . the problem, in other words, is
to find out under what conditions we can accomplish this.

BEREND: A truly Christian attitude, but these conditions must
not hinge on additional sacrifices by the workers.

KRAITSZAK: Capitalism has never had a Christian attitude.

DURIG: I don't see any representative of the Durig Works among
you, gentlemen. Are you authorized to deal for them too?

KRAITSZAK: We're not authorized to deal at all . . . all we can
do is inform our comrades . . . the decision is up to all of
them.

LAUCK: The employees of the Durig Works are of the opinion
that there's no need for them to negotiate anything at all
since their factory is operating anyway.

KÖNIGER: Nor can the Filsmann plants resume operations except
at the old wage rates.

DURIG: Our factory is on the point of being closed down . . . we
weren't forced to merge for nothing.

LAUCK: Well, we'll just have to wait for it to be closed down.

MENCK: Do you want to start a fire so that you may call the
firemen?

KRAITSZAK: Whether you gentlemen open up a factory or close it
down, it's always the stockholders' profits that come first.

MENCK: That's the way it ought to be, but one look at our books
will show you what kind of profits we're making . . . they're
open for public inspection, you know.

LAUCK: Yes—except for the secret entries.

KRAITSZAK: Political donations are taken out of the workers'
pockets, too.

MENCK: Political donations come primarily out of union funds.

KÖNIGER: If you're going to make such accusations, I'll have to
leave.

MENCK: There's your answer, you see—politics is a luxury that no
one can afford anymore . . . stockholders used to be independently wealthy people—but these days they're all down
and out.

LAUCK: We can hardly expect to be overcome with pity at the
plight of the independently wealthy.

KÖNIGER: We can't tolerate drones in today's society.

BEREND: The hard-working labor man must be protected from
poverty and need.

KRAITSZAK: The luxury of politics? Who lives in luxurious villas anyway? As far as I know, it isn't the workers—and you still want to cut his wages!

DURIG: Nobody can accuse me of living luxuriously.

KRAITSZAK: I'll change with you any time.

MENCK: Gentlemen, these arguments are not worthy of you. You're degrading the worker to the level of a son complaining about a stingy father without taking any notice of the fact that there isn't any money left in the house anymore.

KRAITSZAK: You look hard enough, you'll find something hidden away in a corner.

LAUCK: Quite the contrary, it is the boss who is still assuming the father role and playing it for all it's worth.

MENCK: That may have been true under old Mr. Filsmann . . . indeed, it's my impression that all of you are still longing for this situation from way back around 1880 and that, in fact, your socialism is striving to revert to these conditions . . . very reactionary basically.

DURIG: It doesn't make any difference nowadays whether somebody sits up in the front office or is just a handyman around the works—the fact is we're all workers standing in the same trench together.

KRAITSZAK: Yeah, but you're in it for your own profit.

KÖNIGER: It's high time that management got it through its head that it's part of the people, too . . . see that you act that way.

DURIG: That's exactly what we're trying to do.

LAUCK: The only way you'll ever be able to act is capitalistically.

MENCK: Granted, granted—but you forget one thing in this whole matter: namely—to put it metaphorically—that the world today is like a gamblers' club in which one of the gamblers has won all the chips or all the gold of the other players, so that things have got to the point where neither the winner nor the losers really could go on playing . . .

LAUCK: And naturally the game itself has no point any longer.

MENCK: Exactly, but no one wants to admit that—you don't, either, gentlemen; and nor, for that matter, do I . . . the whole world wants to go on with the game, so the winner keeps lending his partner bigger or smaller piles of chips . . . naturally, under such circumstances, it's only a phony game. To make it a real game once again all the winners would have to start betting on their own losses—something no gambler likes to do.

LAUCK: In that case the only thing to do is to redistribute the chips all over again . . . not even you, Mr. Menck, can avoid

the force and ineluctable logic of Communist theory . . .
(*Fanatically.*) There's more than enough food in the world
so that no one has to go hungry—there's no need to burn
any wheat . . . Socialism is the political instrument that's
going to force the necessary redistribution.

KRAITSZAK: Just you wait till the proletariat sits down at those
gambling tables of yours!

KÖNIGER: We don't need any international chips, even if they're
made of gold. Germany has had enough of those cheats.

MENCK: Yes, yes, gentlemen, all I can do is agree with you, of
course. Like you, I'm aware that gold is only an expedient
and a chip in the game and that we're in the middle of a
crisis of economic distribution . . . but I'm still hoping that
it will be possible to build things up again within the old
system and avoid any revolutionary bloodshed. All that would
be needed is a little common sense and fairness.

BEREND: That's exactly what we expect from you.

MENCK: And, of course, we do have to face facts. Right now the
old game is still being played, and even if we want to call
it a phony game, the fact is that Germany is one of the losers
and that its economy is sustained by a make-believe game
played with borrowed money. We may win that money from
each other, but it doesn't really belong to any of us . . . and
that's the down-to-earth reality of our capital assets.

DURIG: Only a swindler would permit himself to squander borrowed
money.

KRAITSZAK: In that case we'll just have to get it ourselves.

DURIG: If you mean you're going to strike . . . the Durig Works
are prepared for that. We can hardly lose more money than
we're losing right now.

KÖNIGER: All I get out of this is that you're talking as defenders
of foreign capital. The German worker is not going to let
himself be enslaved anymore; he knows how he has to answer
to that.

KRAITSZAK: You think you can starve the workers till they do what
you want.

LAUCK (*shouting the others down*): You think we're weak . . .
you think we're crippled . . . but the power of our Idea gives
us the strength to sacrifice ourselves . . . we have the strength
to go on starving . . . as revolutionaries we can only rejoice
if you don't give in since this will only help to strengthen the
determination of the masses to achieve victory . . .

DURIG: Well, well, so we've come right back to where we started
from.

KRAITSZAK: And we don't give a damn if your private opinions favor Communism, Mr. Menck—all we care about is that you want to cut down the wages of a few thousand people.

MENCK: That, Mr. Kraitszak, is by far the most intelligent remark any of us has made so far. The circumstances are what we have to deal with, and they don't care one little bit about our private views . . . (*Strongly.*) Gentlemen, innocent blood has been spilled today . . . it is absolutely essential for us to discuss matters calmly and rationally.

(*Silence.* LAUCK, *who had sprung to his feet, begins to pace up and down.*)

BEREND: That's exactly what we want.

MENCK: Have you come here with any specific proposals in mind?

KÖNIGER: We came to hear yours.

KRAITSZAK: Any wage cutting that you have in mind has to start with management's salaries.

MENCK: Very good . . . that opens up an avenue for discussion right away. If you mean that the highest salaries should be cut to a proportionately greater extent than the lower ones, I'm sure we'll be able to come to an agreement on that point.

LAUCK: (*sitting down again*): We're not there yet by a long shot.

MENCK: Well now, let's get down to facts . . . do any of you gentlemen smoke? (*He brings a cigar box over to the table.*)

KRAITSZAK (*stiffly*): No thanks, I don't smoke.

DURIG (*the only one to take a cigar*): I have here before me a statistical table of wages . . .

LAUCK (*nervously, taking out one of his own cigarettes*): If you'll allow me . . .

DURIG: . . . including the wages of both the Filsmann and the Durig Works. The first thing you'll notice is that the wages are graduated in the . . .

(*The door is ripped open, and a servant bursts in.*)

SERVANT: Mr. Menck . . . (*He is unable to go on.*) . . . Mr.—Mr.—Mr. Filsmann . . . (*He makes a gesture indicating hanging.*)

AN OFFICE EMPLOYEE (*one of several who have followed*): Mr. Menck . . . Mr. Filsmann . . . has hanged himself . . . in his office . . . on the bars of the window . . . we've just found him . . . dead.

CURTAIN

SCENE 8

SOUND EFFECT: *Recorded Negro spirituals.*

No film.

Curtain goes up. THEA's *living room. Dusk.* THEA *and* HASSEL *are drinking tea. The Gramophone plays.*

THEA: Tell me, Hassel, do you really care for nothing but knowledge?

HASSEL: Besides yourself.

THEA: I don't believe either the one or the other.

HASSEL: How can I prove it to you? I'm prepared to propose marriage to you any time . . .

THEA: That's nice—and how about knowledge?

HASSEL: Well, I'll get my books written yet . . . it just seems such superfluous work to me . . . it doesn't fit into the times.

(The record comes to an end.)

THEA: Right now I'd like you to take that record off the machine before it gets scratched . . . records are expensive.

HASSEL *(at the Gramophone)*: Do you want me to put on another one?

THEA: No, that's enough of music . . . I keep thinking about the poor Hüglis, anyhow . . . people like us have it much too good.

HASSEL: What's Menck got to say about it?

THEA: I haven't spoken to him . . . it's his big day today.

HASSEL: Oh yes, the Durig affair . . . he really wrapped that one up . . . well, I certainly wouldn't want to be in Filsmann's shoes today . . .

THEA: Menck's quite a fellow, all right . . . which reminds me, I must ask him to do something for Eva . . . her engagement to Lauck seems finally to be really finished and done with.

HASSEL: And you want Menck to patch it up again?

THEA: Don't be silly—I want him to give her her job back . . . now that he's got the Durig Works as well . . .

HASSEL: Her job's probably been taken long ago by some general's daughter . . . that's the way it should be, really—a Socialist's girl is hardly the right person for a company director's secretary.

THEA: Her father was a privy councillor . . .

HASSEL: So much the worse—bourgeois society doesn't tolerate renegades.

THEA: Menck will fix it up for my sake.

HASSEL: Thea . . .

THEA: Yes.

HASSEL (*hesitatingly*): Thea . . . it is said that you're . . . you're going to marry Menck.

THEA (*thoughtfully, shaking her head*): No.

HASSEL: But . . .

THEA: No buts . . . (*Smiling.*) Or can you really imagine me functioning as the wife of a big businessman?

HASSEL: But what if he gives it all up, as he's always wanted to?

THEA: Menck's no good for idyllic holidays in the South anymore . . . nor am I, for that matter. The moment he gives up his business, he'll be a very old man—and he knows it.

HASSEL: Thank God, in that case that leaves only me.

THEA: You've got your search for knowledge.

HASSEL: I'll give it up.

THEA: You'll be good enough to do nothing of the sort . . . people like us—that's all we have; that and our lives . . . and that's the main thing, after all.

HASSEL: What a pity you're such a good pal, Thea; it's really a pity.

THEA: Yes—I'm afraid I wouldn't be much use as a wife.

HASSEL: A terrible shame—but somehow I have a foreboding that sibling marriages are coming back into style.

THEA: We'll just have to wait and see about that, Hassel.

HASSEL: Together? Hand in hand?

THEA: If you like . . . but it's high time we put some lights on now. (*She turns on the lamp.*)

HASSEL: It was nicer the other way.

(*The doorbell rings.*)

THEA: Who could that be now?

HASSEL: Shall I go and see?

THEA: No, my cleaning woman is still here.

(*Short pause.*)

MENCK'S CHAUFFEUR (*coming in quickly*): I have a message from Mr. Menck. He wants Miss Woltau to please take his car and go to Mrs. Filsmann right away . . . He's there himself already. Something terrible has happened.

(THEA *and* HASSEL *jump up.*)

CURTAIN

SCENE 9

No sound effects and no film.

Curtain goes up. The Filsmann living room, dimly lit. The stage is empty.

THEA (*entering with* GLADYS *through the center door after a short pause*): How did your father-in-law take it?

GLADYS: He asked about Gelshausen.

THEA: That's his real child.

GLADYS: I keep wondering about so much now . . . about everything—about being here and not at home with Mother, about having had a husband, about . . . oh, Thea . . .

THEA (*leads her to an armchair, but remains standing herself*): You'll find yourself again, Gladys.

GLADYS: You can't find anything again . . . (*Numbly.*) everything's gone to pieces since I came back here . . . it had to turn out this way . . . because everything was crumbling already . . . oh, Thea . . . I don't see any future for me . . . I want to talk.

THEA: Well then, talk, Gladys.

GLADYS: I can't.

THEA: You're not . . . not . . . going to go back there?

GLADYS (*numbly*): No . . . he's dead, too . . . everyone's dead . . . I know.

THEA: You've still got your own life . . .

GLADYS: I don't know about that . . .

(MRS. FILSMANN *slowly enters at the center door.*)

MRS. FILSMANN: Here you are, children . . . come, sit by me. (*She sits on the sofa with both women crouched at her feet. She puts her arms around them.*)

GLADYS: How is father?

MRS. FILSMANN: He may be quite well, really . . . he doesn't think very much.

THEA: You're so calm . . . I think you're lovely.

MRS. FILSMANN: I think a great deal . . . yes, a great deal . . . and perhaps I know some things, too.

GLADYS: I don't know anything anymore . . . everything is over.

MRS. FILSMANN: You two—you couldn't know anything . . . you don't have any children . . . you can only know if you've had a child and lost it.

THEA: That's terrible.

MRS. FILSMANN: Yes, it is truly terrible . . . because we can't be alone . . . we exist only through our men because they give us our children . . . and after that the men mean nothing to us.

GLADYS: He's dead . . . and nothing was true at all.

MRS. FILSMANN: All men are dead . . . and then the child is dead too, but it did exist . . . and we exist because it did.

THEA: I don't want that.

MRS. FILSMANN: You don't want it . . . it doesn't make any difference what you want . . . you have to surrender yourself to life, and then life becomes your child.

GLADYS: No, no . . . I want to go back to my mother.

MRS. FILSMANN: We all want to go back to our mothers . . . but it doesn't do us any good . . . our mothers are dead, too, and we are no longer their children . . . we too are dead to our children, and still we only live through them.

THEA (softly): Does it have to be that way?

MRS. FILSMANN: It will be that way . . . and it will be that way for you, too . . . when you turn to face life.

GLADYS: I don't see life anymore . . . what has passed, is forgotten, and what is to come—that is forgotten too.

MRS. FILSMANN: We carry the fate of women in us. For us women there is no past and no future; for us there is only a now— and in the now, the past and the future are the same.

THEA: Men live in the past, and they live in the future without any present.

MRS. FILSMANN: And love lives in the present.

CURTAIN

SEBALD's voice is heard singing his folk song.

SCENE 10

SOUND EFFECT: SEBALD's folk song continues and then breaks off. No film.

Curtain up. A small set on the stage apron. An open landscape. A wayside shrine. SEBALD, *with a knapsack on his back and his cap in his hand, is standing in front of the shrine. Bright sunshine.*

SEBALD (*spelling out the words on the wayside shrine's plaque*):
>   We wander and we know not where we go,
>   I am surprised how happy I do grow.

(*He looks up, wipes his forehead, looks at the landscape, and smiles.*)
>   It's strange that I can still feel glad and free
>   Although I have so little time.
>   It's strange that I can still sing happy songs
>   Although the wind sweeps down so sharp.
>   I walk alone through little space,
>   And still enjoy the sight of bush, of tree,
>   Of open field stretched out before my eyes,
>   Of branches swaying in the wind.
>   There's little time and only little space.
>   I walk along the edge of life
>   Along the pit that waits my fall.
>   Oh, world of graves through which we have to pass,
>   You last one heartbeat in eternity,
>   Then fade into the everlasting pit.
>   A wondrous heartbeat although full of grief,
>   A momentary glance at questions without answer,
>   Rushing to death while asking where we go.
>   I am surprised how happy I do grow;
>   I go abroad, a cheerful wanderer
>   And yet and still the death's lament returns.

(*He throws his jacket over his shoulder and marches off.*)

CURTAIN

Darkness; the sound of gongs leads into the Epilogue.

EPILOGUE: THE DEATH LAMENT

SCENE 1

The sound of the gong fades out. Curtain goes up. The same conference room as in Act I. Pale grayish light giving the impres-

sion of a foggy day in winter. Seated around the table are COUNT
SAGDORFF, *who is in the chair,* MENCK, DOLFUSS, GUMBING, WENGER,
DURIG, KÖHLER, ERHARDT, *and the notary,* KETTLER, *as well as*
KRAITSZAK *and* BEREND, *as representatives of the workers. This first
scene is to be played as if by automatons, with stiff movements
and wooden, toneless voices.*

SAGDORFF: I hereby declare the meeting of the Board of Directors
in session and greet those present, particularly Mr. Kettler,
our notary (*They bow to each other.*), and request our Recording Secretary, Mr. Wenger, to submit his report.

WENGER (*rises*): Report submitted to the honorable Board of
Directors of the F. J. Filsmann Company . . . (*He clears
his throat.*) . . . The company held its seventh extraordinary general meeting on November 10th of the present year.
The legally certified minutes of the meeting were printed and
were distributed to the members of the Board of Directors
. . . (*Clears his throat again; short pause.*) . . . The Company particularly laments the passing

(*The members of the board rise as one man.*)

of Dr. Herbert Filsmann, member of the Board of Directors,
who was snatched away by a sudden death. The deceased
through his exemplary efforts and his tireless industry in the
service of our company has earned its everlasting gratitude
and, through his passing, has left a void among us that cannot be filled. A true friend to his fellow workers and to his
subordinates alike, a model of the strictest devotion to duty
as a businessman, the deceased will always be honored by the
faithful regard of the company and all of its employees.

(*The company resumes its seats.*)

Our honored Vice-Chairman of the Board, Mr. Friedrich
Johann Filsmann, has taken the deeply regretted resolve to
resign his office with the Board of Directors on grounds of advanced age. The company accepts his resolve with deep regret
and takes the opportunity to extend its heartfelt thanks to
Vice-Chairman Friedrich Johann Filsmann for his services.
The Board of Directors has decided to extend its thanks to
Mr. F. J. Filsmann as founder of the Filsmann Works and
its wishes for a happy and peaceful retirement and to express
the hope that Mr. Filsmann will nevertheless continue to give
the company the benefit of his rich experience by putting
his advice at its disposal.

SAGDORFF: I call the question; all those in favor, please raise their hands.

(*Everyone raises his hand.*)

Motion passed unanimously.

WENGER (*reading on monotonously*): Mr. Ernst Hügli, General Manager and chief engineer, has felt obliged by circumstances to cancel his contract with the company prematurely. The company has accepted his resignation. Mr. Hügli has simultaneously resigned his position on the Board of Directors. The Board of Directors has taken note of Mr. Hügli's decision with deep regret and has resolved to pass a vote of thanks to him for his services.

SAGDORFF: I call the question; all those in favor, please raise their hands.

(*Everyone raises his hand.*)

Motion passed unanimously.

WENGER (*continuing to read*): The Board of Directors has resolved to fill its three vacant places with the following new members: Mr. Martin Durig, Mr. Justice Köhler, and Mr. Emanuel Erhardt, director of the Agricultural Bank of Berlin.

SAGDORFF: I take pleasure in greeting our new members and welcoming them into our midst.

DURIG (*rises*): I have accepted my appointment with thanks and would like to express my gratitude for your cordial reception. (*He sits.*)

ERHARDT (*rises*): I too have accepted the appointment and would like to express my profound obligation. (*He sits.*)

KÖHLER (*rises*): For my part, I wish to express my thanks for your kind welcome. (*He sits.*)

WENGER (*reading on monotonously*): The Board of Directors has resolved to appoint Dr. Albert Menck to the Vice-Chairmanship left vacant by the resignation of Vice-Chairman F. J. Filsmann.

SAGDORFF: I call the question; all those in favor, please raise their hands.

(*Everybody except MENCK raises his hand.*)

Motion passed.

MENCK (*rises*): Much honored by your choice, I accept the appointment with gratitude. (*He sits.*)

WENGER (*reading on monotonously*): The general meeting has taken cognizance of the establishment of a compact with the

Durig Works to be based on a quota system of manufacture
. . . (*The scene becomes dark; in the darkness* WENGER's
voices drones on, becoming less and less distinct.) . . . to be
divided between the Filsmann and the Durig Works. The
general meeting hopes that this action . . . (WENGER's *voice
fades out.*)

(*The sound of the gong leads into the second scene.*)

SCENE 2

*The curtain rises while the gong continues to sound. An abstract
room in semidarkness. The* FIRST MOTHER *stands in the middle.
Like the other women, she is dressed in impersonal robes, the*
THREE MOTHERS *being in gray and the* SIX YOUNG WOMEN *in blue.
The women enter in the order of their speaking, alternately from
left and right, except for the* OLD MOTHER *at the end, who comes
in through the middle. The sound of the gong ends.*

FIRST MOTHER (WORITZKI's *mother—she stands center without
moving*):
The men took hold of him and led him out
In the gray dawn.
Men on all sides of him,
And his mother not with him.
I sat at home, counting the seconds,
I sat and screamed.
And they tied his hands behind his back
And tore the buttons off his coat,
And he was left alone.
He had fingers and limbs like all other children
And a lovely body,
And they threw him under the axe,
And they cut off his head,
The head that was on his body,
The head that called its mother with its mouth,
The head with all the thoughts that were in it—
They cut it off.
Oh.
FIRST YOUNG WOMAN (MRS. HÜGLI):
They murdered a little child,
My son.
Men threw stones.

They hit my child on the forehead.
Oh, the sweet little head.
What a delicate child it was,
And everything was white in his room.
His father was a big engineer
And that is why the little child had to die.
Oh.

BOTH:

Oh, heaven above, stretched out over the blossoming
    earth,
Oh, comforting breeze, touching the temples lightly
Of playful children and of breathing men
As they are led to death.
Oh death of children when they awake to loneliness.

SECOND YOUNG WOMAN (GLADYS):

I welcomed men into my bed,
One without joy, the other with utmost longing,
And both are shadows now.
I was their naked love in the midst of the nights.
And like shadows they slipped away
To things that are strange and far to me,
And that are death, and buried by oblivion.

THE THREE:

Oblivion, the horrifying oblivion!
The dead rob us of the lives of the past,
The dead rob us of whatever was.

THIRD YOUNG WOMAN (PROSTITUTE):

The dead men came to me,
Rigid, and showing their teeth in the rotting smile,
Forcing themselves into me like corpses,
With corpse tongues and the breath of corpses,
Stiff rigid corpses.

THE FOUR:

Coffins are we for the eternal dead.
Coffins under the blossoming sky,
Dead ourselves,
Killed by the dead.

FOURTH YOUNG WOMAN (WORITZKI'S *wife*):

A man made children in me.
A murderer he was,
And yet the children live.
His breath was in my breath,
His flesh in mine . . .
Murderer!

Murder in every man!

THE FIVE:

Murder is the way of men,
Murder and murder upon murder.
The mist sinks screaming
Over the dying world.

FIFTH YOUNG WOMAN (EVA):

Let us lament the murder,
For they murder out of weakness,
Flight is their furious murdering,
Fright is their senseless thinking,
And they meet their death like animals,
Loveless,
In the dark.

THE SIX:

Loveless in the dark . . . !
The mountains crash down nightly,
And godliness is muffled in the dark.
Woe that the laments no longer penetrate
The bowl of brass.
The earth is ringed with black,
And the silent scream
Is shattered.

SIXTH YOUNG WOMAN (THEA):

Where has life escaped to?
Where has the light gone to
Under the sounding dome?
Lament upon lament fades away,
Whereto does the path lead, my sisters?

THE SEVEN:

We stand on the shore
And wait for the ferry.
We stand in the night
And look for the path.
We weep for the dead
And look for life.
We glean the stones
With bleeding hands.
We weed what is withered
And wait for the sowing.

*(The scene has meanwhile become completely dark. Behind
the scenes men's voices are heard calling, "Mother, Mother."
During the following the scene slowly becomes lighter again.)*

SECOND MOTHER (RYCHNER's *mother—she enters and stands next to the* FIRST MOTHER *while the* SIX YOUNG WOMEN *form a shadowy group*):
>   Helpless am I.
>   My son was killed,
>   Was it yours that killed him?

FIRST MOTHER:
>   I came to you.
>   I asked you,
>   And then it was no longer him.
>   Helpless am I.

BOTH MOTHERS:
>   We know not the answer.
>   Our knowledge means death.
>   Our knowledge is dead.
>   Your son was mine,
>   My son was yours.
>   In the death of the sons
>   We became but one.
>   My womb is empty,
>   Empty we both.
>   Helpless we are:
>   The future is empty . . .
>   Oh, we are no longer two,
>   Oh, we are no longer many,
>   We are but one from now on.
>   We see ourselves no longer,
>   And hear ourselves no more:
>   We are from now but one.
>   We live without knowledge
>   Our eyes are blinded,
>   Our future is blinded,
>   We hesitate and grope
>   Guessing at what is to come,
>   Like children deaf and dumb.
>   We are from now but one:
>   A deaf-mute child.
>   Helpless and blind,
>   How can I lead you now?

(*Voices of women are heard behind the scenes crying, "Mother, Mother." The light changes from gray to blue, without, however, changing the semidarkness of the scene.*)

THE OLD MOTHER (MRS. FILSMANN, *who walks slowly to the center*

to stand between the two other MOTHERS; *the* SIX YOUNG
WOMEN *form a semicircle around them*):
> The eyes that have looked on so much,
> See in the darkest night as well.
> The night sinks slowly,
> And slowly, ever slowly,
> Grows the fear.
> We have arrived here from one end,
> And slowly near the other,
> The one is hidden now,
> And hidden still the other,
> And yet we slowly wend from rest to rest.
> The end in view, the lamentations cease,
> For then all crumbles into dust.
> And who among you weeps, weeps for the child eternal,
> Embodies our lament and, in herself, becomes the entire
>   world.
> Who lives long time traverses many days,
> And many days bloom in the morning light.
> That men must die is the eternal plaint,
> The dead die too, and death turns into light.
> In your laments you have each other found
> And love each other now in dismal sisterhood.
> Bound by pain, now are you freed from pain.
> Oh, dreaded pain from which so many worlds are born:
> Go on lamenting now for evermore,
> For from your pain the world will rise once more.

SIXTH YOUNG WOMAN (THEA):
> Perfection will arise out of the womb of pain,
> For women's pain will build a world anew.

FIFTH YOUNG WOMAN (EVA):
> Blessed be the one who'll rise in that perfection.

ALL SIX:
> The leaves rustle over the graves,
> The graves are covered by love,
> Love, born of the most painful desire.
> Over the graves the stars gleam bright,
> And in the farthest reaches of their light
> Behold the path of godly loving fire.

BOTH MOTHERS:
> We hear the rustling, we hear the sounds,
> We mothers together, deprived of sons,
> Blessedly blind and blessedly deaf,
> Merged with each other, all difference gone,

Extinguished in pain . . .

THE OLD MOTHER:

. . . and led by pain . . .

BOTH MOTHERS:

. . . encompassed by pain . . .

THE OLD MOTHER:

. . . reclaimed for the future.

THE SIX YOUNG VOICES:

We suffer the pain
Of those that have died without need.
We bemoan the pain
Of those who have never been.
We carry the burden of all the times to come,
To which the voices of the mothers lead us on,
We are the voices of the future carrying the stars.
We call the eternally unending space,
We call the unity that we conceived . . .
Behold the godly love-encompassed path . . .

THE END

CHRISTOPHER COLUMBUS

by KURT TUCHOLSKY
and WALTER HASENCLEVER

TRANSLATED BY MAX SPALTER AND GEORGE E. WELLWARTH

Characters

TEACHER

FIRST PUPIL

SECOND PUPIL

LUIS DE SANTANGEL

ANTONIO DE QUINTANILLA

COLUMBUS

PAGE

CARDINAL-ARCHBISHOP OF
TOLEDO

FATHER GONZALA

FATHER BERNARDI

FATHER GASPARE

OFFICER

ISABELLA

OFFICER OF THE GUARD

MARQUISE OF MOYA

PEPI

VENDRINO

OFFICIAL

FIRST OFFICER

SHIP'S DOCTOR

DIEGO

RODRIGO

SHIP'S COOK

CABIN BOY

SLEEPING SAILOR

OFFICERS and SAILORS

CHIEF

DRUMMER

MEDICINE MAN

HUNTER

NATIVE

ANACOANA

KING

LACKEY

AMERIGO VESPUCCI

MARIE

Drop-curtain. A painted schoolroom with many youngsters around twelve years old, wearing short pants. Facing them a bench with three living pupils. A rostrum with a TEACHER. *The* TEACHER *indicates the* FIRST PUPIL.

FIRST PUPIL (*stands up*): 1489!
TEACHER: Wrong.
FIRST PUPIL: 1490.
TEACHER: Wrong.

(SECOND PUPIL *shoots his hand up eagerly.*)

FIRST PUPIL: 1491.
TEACHER: This is like an auction! You've learned nothing!

(SECOND PUPIL *even more eagerly.*)

TEACHER (*to a painted pupil*): Well, Braune, you back there? No answer again, as usual. You're a doomed man. Just you wait and see what'll happen to you when you get out of here. . . . Emil Ludwig is certainly not going to write a biography of *you!* (*To the* SECOND PUPIL.) Well—?
SECOND PUPIL: 1492!
TEACHER: Correct. America was discovered in the year 1492. (*To the* SECOND PUPIL.) By whom?
SECOND PUPIL: By Christopher Columbus.
TEACHER: Correct. (*To the* FIRST PUPIL.) Well, Okonowski, tell us how that came about.
FIRST PUPIL: America was discovered in the year 1492. Christopher Columbus was a Spaniard from Genoa who begged Queen Isabella to help him. This she did and gave him some money, as well as two steamships, and with these he kept steaming around the world because at that time the world was round. America was overjoyed at being discovered and that's how Columbus landed in jail.
TEACHER: Sit down. You are a pack of dullards. God must have created this school when he was in a bad mood. Whoever does not know his stuff within the next hour, will not be taken along to the aquarium.
SECOND PUPIL: May I be excused?
TEACHER: You can be excused after the discovery of America.
SECOND PUPIL: But I have to *go!*
TEACHER: Learn to control your body, you clumsy scamp! Pay attention! In 1492 the eyes of the whole world were directed

109

at mighty Spain; everyone spoke of the bold seafarer—stop picking your nose, Lichtner—who set out for the unknown.

(SECOND PUPIL *puts his hand up very nervously*.)

The Queen said to him—you don't have to go out now—that she would overwhelm him with honors, since he had the trust of the entire court. You mustn't imagine that things were the way they are today when everything is quite ordinary . . . that was a great and powerful time! People forgot their petty, everyday worries because of this fantastic discovery— it was a turning point in the history of mankind. But what did Columbus need most for this sea voyage? What does one need for that? Well? A com . . . a com . . .

FIRST PUPIL: A companion.

TEACHER: A compass! And so Columbus, on the third of August of the year 1492, weighed anchor in Palos and sailed in bright sunlight westward over the blue ocean.

(*During the last sentence the scene has darkened; the voice of the* TEACHER *fades away.*)

Scene 1

A *hall in the castle of Santa Fé. The Chancellor* LUIS DE SANT- ANGEL *and the Treasurer* ANTONIO DE QUINTANILLA, *two elderly diplomats with graying hair.*

QUINTANILLA: I'm not a magician. I'm only a human being, after all.

SANTANGEL: You are not a human being. You are a Minister of Finance.

QUINTANILLA: It's a mystery to me how we're supposed to pay our debts.

SANTANGEL: Draw on the Bank of Spain's reserve stocks!

QUINTANILLA: First of all, that's illegal; secondly, I am on the Board of Directors; and thirdly, the reserve stocks are ex- hausted.

SANTANGEL: Then levy taxes.

QUINTANILLA: We've already taxed everything down to the last pants button, my dear Chancellor.

SANTANGEL: At this historic moment, when one of history's great- est events faces us . . .

QUINTANILLA: Can't you make it cheaper?

SANTANGEL: With the eyes of the whole world directed at us . . .

QUINTANILLA: All of a sudden you need scaling ladders!

SANTANGEL: It is high time that Granada was conquered. We are close to the final victory.

QUINTANILLA: At least wait until autumn.

SANTANGEL: My dear Quintanilla, the Queen has taken an oath not to change her shift until the city is liberated from the unbelievers. It is now January . . . If she would have to wait until August . . .

QUINTANILLA: Just between us, Señor Santangel, is that story about the shift true?

SANTANGEL: Can you keep a secret?

QUINTANILLA: As a man whose business is handling income-tax returns . . .

SANTANGEL: Then I'll tell you a secret. She does not wear the shift.

QUINTANILLA: Who does?

PAGE (*enters*): There's a gentleman outside.

SANTANGEL: I'm busy. I'm in conference.

PAGE: The gentleman says it is very urgent.

SANTANGEL: Who is it then?

PAGE: A sea captain.

SANTANGEL: Let him wait.

(PAGE *exits.*)

QUINTANILLA: I can't wait to hear. Who wears the shift?

SANTANGEL: Her lady-in-waiting, the Marquise of Moya. Her Majesty has the glory of having created a new fashion: the Isabella-color.

QUINTANILLA: The Marquise of Moya . . . tell me, isn't that that small, sharp-tongued girl with the good figure? Reputed to be a great disappointment in all other respects.

SANTANGEL: My dear Quintanilla, if she disappointed you, it must have been your fault.

QUINTANILLA: I must tell you a story about her.

(PAGE *reenters.*)

What's the matter?

PAGE: The gentleman can't wait any longer. He has an appointment.

SANTANGEL: What's his name?

PAGE: Captain Christopher Columbus.

SANTANGEL: Columbus . . . that sounds vaguely familiar . . .

QUINTANILLA: Isn't that that pest from Portugal who wants to sail to India?

SANTANGEL: Yes, that's right . . . I've got a note about it here: Half-past ten—meeting of the Spiritual Council under the chairmanship of the Archbishop of Toledo. Rendering of an expert opinion on the matter of a sea route to India. By command of Her Majesty, the Queen. (*To* PAGE.) Tell the gentleman I shall receive him shortly.

(PAGE *exits.*)

QUINTANILLA: By command of the Queen?

SANTANGEL: Her Majesty has romantic inclinations.

QUINTANILLA: Allow me to warn you, my dear colleague. This fellow is nothing but a cynical adventurer.

SANTANGEL: We'll see about that right away. (*He rings. A guard appears.*) Go upstairs to the chief of the secret police and tell him I want the Columbus file.

(*Guard exits.*)

We've got our hands full with affairs of state, and then we have to go to the trouble of assembling archbishops and abbots simply because some swindler gets a bee in his bonnet.

QUINTANILLA: Why don't you let the King do his own dirty work?

SANTANGEL: That idiot!

(*The guard has come in.*)

Can't you knock?

(*The guard salutes.*)

Give it here!

(*The guard hands over the documents.*)

Ask Señor Columbus to step this way.

(*Guard exits.* SANTANGEL *opens the file.*)

You were going to tell me that story about the little Moya girl.

QUINTANILLA: Well now, it was this way. Do you know Gomez?

SANTANGEL: I know two.

QUINTANILLA: I mean the other. With him she . . . (*He whispers; one can make out only fragments of the story.*) . . . and then he made her . . . and then she made him . . . behind a curtain . . . in bed . . . and then she says: With whom do I have the honor?

(COLUMBUS *enters.*)

SANTANGEL: Impossible!

QUINTANILLA: As I live and breathe! (*They laugh.*)

SANTANGEL (*to* COLUMBUS): One moment! (*To* QUINTANILLA.) What does her husband have to say about that?

QUINTANILLA: Just imagine: he knows nothing about it!

SANTANGEL: He knows nothing?

QUINTANILLA: He hasn't the faintest idea.

SANTANGEL: Husbands never have the faintest idea. (*To* COLUMBUS.) Come a little closer, please.

COLUMBUS: I was asked to present myself to the Commission.

SANTANGEL: Are you from Portugal?

COLUMBUS: I am a seafarer from Genoa and have to beg because kings do not want to accept my empires.

SANTANGEL: I hear there is a warrant out for your arrest—is that right?

COLUMBUS: My father is Count Colombo of Montserrat, a descendant of the Roman general Colonius.

SANTANGEL: What else?

COLUMBUS: In a number of memoranda to Their Spanish Majesties, I have developed my thoughts . . .

SANTANGEL: We know all about them.

COLUMBUS: I have at my disposal geographic calculations which prove that the western sea route to India . . .

SANTANGEL: Make it short, please.

COLUMBUS: I have . . .

SANTANGEL: Do you have any money?

COLUMBUS: I have certainty.

SANTANGEL: You wish to sail to India, then. And what do you expect to gain by that?

COLUMBUS: The opening up of a new world.

SANTANGEL: You think we've got nothing better to worry about?

QUINTANILLA: And who is supposed to finance all this?

COLUMBUS: God has inspired me. He will find a way.

SANTANGEL: You keep talking about God. Are you Jewish?

COLUMBUS: I am a devout Catholic, Señor . . . Luis Santangel.

SANTANGEL: Very well, very well! So am I!

QUINTANILLA: As far as religious matters are concerned, that will be decided by those better qualified than we. What do you live on, anyway?

COLUMBUS: Her Majesty's grace has provided me with a small income.

QUINTANILLA: And where do you pay your taxes?

COLUMBUS: I am poor, to be sure, but not so poor that I have to allow Spain to give me something for nothing.

QUINTANILLA: In other words, you have not paid your taxes.

COLUMBUS: I will soon be richer than all of you.

SANTANGEL: Who tells you that?

COLUMBUS: An inner voice.

SANTANGEL: Just as long as you don't consider yourself an unrecognized genius, Señor Columbus. We're crawling with explorers here, and they all have a different story to tell.

PAGE (*announcing*): The Cardinal-Archbishop of Toledo, and the lords of the Spiritual Council!

(*A folding door opens; the* ARCHBISHOP OF TOLEDO *enters with* FATHERS BERNARDI, GONZALA, *and* GASPARE, *followed by priests and abbots who arrange themselves in the background. Those present kneel. During what follows the serving brothers place a large cross upon the table and a number of thick parchment Bibles are distributed. The whole thing is done with a certain ceremony.*)

ARCHBISHOP: Pax vobiscum! (*He makes the Sign of the Cross. Those kneeling arise.*) My dear Chancellor, I missed you at yesterday's auto-da-fé.

SANTANGEL: Pressing affairs of state, Eminence . . .

ARCHBISHOP: Pity. A great pity. The stake at which the heretics burned offered an unforgettable spectacle. The show was excellently attended. Many prominent personages of the court were present. For a moment it looked as if it was going to rain, but it cleared up again. And so it was a great success . . . just right. (*He seats himself in an armchair halfway along the length of the table.*) Gentlemen, please take your seats.

(*The three fathers and both ministers group themselves around the table. A page gives* COLUMBUS *a chair.*)

I call the meeting to order. At the behest of Her Majesty we are to render an expert opinion upon the proposal of Captain Christopher Columbus. We have the honor to welcome to our midst a beacon of scholarship: Father Bernardi, Professor of Theology at the University of Salamanca. Father Gonzala, a member of the Holy Inquisition, will assist us with his counsel. Father Gaspare, the Apostolic Nuncio at the Spanish court, represents the Holy Father. I give the floor to the Captain.

COLUMBUS (*stands up*): Honorable members of the Council! For centuries mankind has tried to discover new routes across the seas. We get important products from the Far East, but the land route to Asia is threatened by the Turks. Therefore, bold seafarers have sailed along the coast of Africa, in order to get to India. In vain. These are the thoughts that moved me when God inspired me. Among educated Christians there is no longer any doubt as to the global form of the earth. On the basis of this fact I declare that the world stands on the brink of a new discovery. One can reach the east by way of the west.

GONZALA: You assert that God has inspired you. Are your thoughts in harmony with Holy Scripture?

COLUMBUS: May I please have a Bible. (*One is given to him. He opens it up.*) It is written, Psalm 104: "O Lord my God, thou art very great . . . Who layeth the beams of his chambers in the waters . . ."

GONZALA: What do you deduce from that?

COLUMBUS: That the earth is round.

GONZALA: Pardon me. (*He opens up his Bible.*) Psalm 104: ". . . who stretchest out the heavens like a curtain." So the earth cannot be round.

COLUMBUS: Pardon me, please, Isaiah 65:17: "For, behold, I create new heavens and a new earth."

GONZALA: That proves nothing.

COLUMBUS: I have reference to Seneca. (*He recites from memory.*) "In the latter years of the earth, a time will come—since the ocean will loosen the bond between all things—when a great land mass will open up and a new seaman will discover a new world."

GASPARE: Do you consider yourself that seaman?

COLUMBUS: Yes.

GONZALA: Let us stick to facts. John 20:8: "And Satan will go out in order to lead astray the heathens in the four corners of the earth." A globe does not have four corners.

BERNARDI: A segment of the prevailing opinion is of another mind, Father.

GONZALA: In what way?

BERNARDI: The roundness of the earth is at least debatable.

GONZALA: The earth is not a ball.

BERNARDI: But it is a ball.

GONZALA: Anyone who represents this theory is obsessed with the devil.

BERNARDI (*striking the table furiously*): What are we?

GONZALA: A shameless, puffed-up piece of scum!

BERNARDI: Scum yourself! Juggler!

ARCHBISHOP: But, gentlemen! With all due respect for science, I would still appreciate your keeping this discussion within the bounds of Christian tact. What was your point, professor?

BERNARDI: I have a question for the Captain. If the earth is a globe—and only an ignoramus would contend otherwise—then you would be proceeding downward on this globe. Very nice. But how would you get back up on the other side?

COLUMBUS: By following the motion of the globe.

BERNARDI: That sounds utterly muddled to me.

GASPARE: Perhaps you will show us what you mean by that.

COLUMBUS (*approaches the table and uses the Bibles to make a map*): If Spain lies here, then that is Portugal. And there—that empty space—is the ocean. Europe ends here. There, where the cross is, begins the mainland of Asia. India lies here.

BERNARDI (*shoving the cross away*): No, India lies over there.

COLUMBUS (*putting the cross back to its original place*): No, India lies over here. Consequently, if I sail steadily westward, I will reach the east coast of Asia and land in India . . .

GONZALA: So over here there's another continent?

COLUMBUS: Yes, over here there is another continent.

GONZALA: Then it is a heretical continent!

COLUMBUS: I must sail toward the west. Toward the west.

GASPARE: Are you aware that the Holy Father has promised all future discoveries west of Europe to the crown of Portugal?

SANTANGEL (*wakes up*): What's that, Your Grace? First I've heard of it! Since when?

GASPARE: By decree of the three papal bulls *Quia notum est, Ubicumque terrarum*, and *Veniet supra marem*.

SANTANGEL: This is incredible! I protest in the name of all who care for our country. Spain needs colonies.

GASPARE: Get in touch with Lisbon.

SANTANGEL: We are Spaniards, thank God, and not Portuguese. No foreign power is going to dictate to us.

GASPARE: I will not be spoken to in that tone, Excellency!

ARCHBISHOP: Peace, gentlemen. We do not even know yet what countries are in question.

SANTANGEL: It is a question of Spanish interests.

GONZALA: It is a question of the Holy Scriptures. Captain Columbus asserts that his inspiration stems from God. I can nowhere (*To* BERNARDI.), and I mean nowhere, find a sea route to India mentioned in the Scriptures. Consequently, there is none. The whole thing is blasphemy. The matter should be taken up by an entirely different court of justice.

ARCHBISHOP: We don't want to go that far, Father.

GONZALA: Pity, the matter has a smoky odor.

COLUMBUS: Honorable members of the Council! I see nations that long to be received into the bosom of the one true Church. Liberate these poor people from the torment of unbelief. Save their souls.

GASPARE: That's just a yarn. Do you think that God has been waiting for you?

ARCHBISHOP: How do you know that your way is the right one?

COLUMBUS: I know it, Eminence.

GONZALA: But we have proved to you that this way does not exist!

COLUMBUS: I know it nonetheless.

ARCHBISHOP: I believe we can close the discussion. Does anyone else have any questions? Lord Chancellor?

SANTANGEL: Thank you. We are not interested.

COLUMBUS: Even if you were able to wipe out the national debt with the gold I would bring back?

SANTANGEL: Gold?

COLUMBUS: Remember the reports of famous travelers who wrote about the legendary treasures of India.

QUINTANILLA: You can't run the nation's finances on fairy tales.

SANTANGEL (*quietly to* QUINTANILLA): I wouldn't go so far as to say that.

COLUMBUS: I must sail westward. Westward.

(*Fanfares. The folding door opens. A column of bodyguards enters.*)

AN OFFICER: Her Majesty, the Queen!

(*Those assembled rise. The Queen enters and sits down at the table. All others remain standing.*)

ISABELLA: Please, gentlemen, don't let me disturb you.

(*All sit down.*)

Well, how is the matter going?

ARCHBISHOP: I'm afraid we cannot report anything favorable to Your Majesty.

ISABELLA: Has the expert opinion been given?

ARCHBISHOP: We are about to withdraw for consultation.

ISABELLA: We await your judgment.

(*The priests leave the hall.*)

(*To the ministers.*) His Majesty the King has ordered you
to report. I should like you to be back here when the Council
returns.

(SANTANGEL *and* QUINTANILLA *bow deeply and go. The Queen
and* COLUMBUS *remain alone.*)

When did I see you last, Captain? Two years ago in Madrid.

COLUMBUS (*kneels*): I throw myself at Your Majesty's feet.

ISABELLA: Stand up. Step toward the light. Your hair has gone
gray.

COLUMBUS: May I speak openly?

ISABELLA: Speak!

COLUMBUS: When Your Majesty had the grace to receive me in
Madrid, I believed that it was a turn in my destiny. For the
first time I saw eyes that did not mock me. They were the
eyes of my Queen.

ISABELLA: That did not stop you from going to Portugal. You
offered your project to a foreign court.

COLUMBUS: A long road of suffering lay behind me. Does Your
Majesty know how one feels when one cannot eat or sleep?
When one is constantly pursued by a single thought?

ISABELLA: Are you married?

COLUMBUS: I was married. When one has no more peace, when
everything revolves around this one point . . .

ISABELLA: Is your wife still alive?

COLUMBUS: She is dead, Majesty.

ISABELLA: And where do you live now?

COLUMBUS: I just wander about in the world.

ISABELLA: You lead a lonely life.

COLUMBUS: In sleepless nights I traverse the ocean. Westward,
Your Majesty, westward. Across the endless wilderness of the
sea . . . upon the traces of the sinking sun.

ISABELLA: Have you no one who is close to you?

COLUMBUS: I have belief.

ISABELLA: What would you do if I fulfilled your wish?

COLUMBUS: I would carry Spain's flag to the ends of the earth.

ISABELLA: Spain's flag . . . And if I could not do it?

COLUMBUS: Isabella is almighty.

ISABELLA: Isabella is a woman. The King is against your plan.
If the expert opinion turns out to be unfavorable, the responsibility will be mine alone.

COLUMBUS: Don't listen to your councillors, Majesty. Follow your
feelings!

ISABELLA: You are Italian, Captain?

COLUMBUS: I was born in Genoa.

ISABELLA: It is said that Italians are very passionate.

COLUMBUS: I wish I could prove that to Her Majesty.

ISABELLA: Are you courageous?

COLUMBUS: I am prepared to die for my Queen at any time.

ISABELLA: Do you have to die right away?

COLUMBUS: I have decided to stake my life. My last cry will be: Long live Spain!

ISABELLA: Pity. You are a man whom women could take to.

OFFICER OF THE GUARD (*announcing*): The reverend fathers!

(*Reentrance of the councillors and ministers.*)

ISABELLA (*to the* ARCHBISHOP): You have the floor, Eminence.

ARCHBISHOP: After thorough examination, the councillors have come to the conclusion . . .

ISABELLA: Do you even consider the expedition possible?

ARCHBISHOP: The expedition is wholly without prospects. I must add that certain statements of the Captain's sound almost heretical.

ISABELLA: I have just convinced myself that the Captain is a devout Christian. Chancellor, what do you think of this undertaking?

SANTANGEL: Given the condition of the realm, there is no room for experiments in foreign policy. I strongly advise against it, Your Majesty.

ISABELLA: And you, Treasurer?

QUINTANILLA: We could not survive any further demands on the Treasury. I should like to associate myself with the view expressed by my distinguished colleague.

ISABELLA (*very quietly*): Very good, gentlemen. In that case, we'll do it.

(*General astonishment.*)

I am not unaware of the difficulties, but am of the opinion that Spain must take her part in the conquest of the world. I want India to be united to my crown before other countries get ahead of us.

ARCHBISHOP: The Church will raise no objections to an expansionist policy on the part of Spain. I, myself, have always defended such a policy.

SANTANGEL: An exploratory expedition under the auspices of the state could have most advantageous results.

QUINTANILLA: I should like to associate myself with the view expressed by my distinguished colleague.

ISABELLA: Eminence, I thank you and the Council for your efforts. Implore the blessing of Heaven for our undertaking.

(*All sink to their knees.*)

ARCHBISHOP (*makes the Sign of the Cross*): In the name of the Father, the Son, and the Holy Ghost!

(*The Council members exit. All stand up.*)

ISABELLA: Chancellor, be so good as to arrange the business aspects with the Captain.

SANTANGEL: Majesty, I see only one difficulty. The equipping of the expedition will require an immense amount of cash.

ISABELLA: Are we then completely out of money?

(SANTANGEL *shrugs his shoulders.* QUINTANILLA *shrugs his shoulders as well.*)

Pawn my jewels.

QUINTANILLA: They are already pawned, Your Majesty.

ISABELLA: Then pawn them again.

QUINTANILLA: We'll do that business with England. The people are unpleasant but they've got money.

COLUMBUS (*kneeling in front of the Queen*): Exalted Queen! With undying gratitude I kiss the hem of your dress.

(OFFICER OF THE GUARD *enters and salutes.*)

ISABELLA: What's up?

OFFICER: The milliner, Your Majesty

ISABELLA: I'm coming. (*To* COLUMBUS.) I hope you will not disappoint my expectations. (*To* SANTANGEL.) Send me the contract for my signature. (*Fanfares. Queen exits.*)

SANTANGEL: Please take a seat, Señor Columbus.

(COLUMBUS *sits down at the table next to the two ministers.*)

I propose that we give you the rank and income of a captain in the service of Spain. You will command one ship . . .

COLUMBUS: Three ships.

SANTANGEL: How's that, please?

COLUMBUS: I require three ships.

SANTANGEL: One thing at a time. For your personal equipment you will receive a subsidy the size of which will be determined by the Minister of Finance. You will be obligated to give an exact accounting of all proceeds. Have you any other wishes?

COLUMBUS: I require the title of Viceroy and the office of Governor-general of all lands that I shall discover, promotion to admiral, and ten percent of all money taken in.

SANTANGEL: Tell me, my dear fellow, have you taken leave of your senses?

COLUMBUS: I am not finished yet. I want ownership of one eighth of these lands and the income therefrom. All rights, titles, and ranks are to be inherited by my descendants.

QUINTANILLA: This is the most extraordinary piece of insolence I've ever heard!

SANTANGEL: Are you in earnest?

(QUINTANILLA *laughs resoundingly*.)

COLUMBUS: Completely.

QUINTANILLA: I thought you were an idealist, Señor Columbus.

SANTANGEL: Do you imagine that you can bargain with us in that tone?

COLUMBUS: I am not bargaining. I am informing you of my conditions.

QUINTANILLA: You come here as a beggar and then you set conditions?

COLUMBUS: Pity. (*He stands up.*)

SANTANGEL: Sit down. As far as the titles are concerned, there is room for discussion. You can become Admiral for all I care. But you will not get any money.

COLUMBUS: If my conditions do not suit you, gentlemen . . .

SANTANGEL: Let us try to come to an agreement, Señor Columbus. Five percent and the Viceroyalty.

COLUMBUS: Ten percent.

SANTANGEL: Seven and one-half. And that's as far as I'll go.

COLUMBUS: Then I'm sorry. Good-bye. (*He goes to the door.*)

SANTANGEL: Where to?

COLUMBUS (*at the door*): To the King of Portugal.

SANTANGEL: Nine and a half percent . . . and that settles it. But as for the right of possession, that's out of the question. We're making ourselves ridiculous.

COLUMBUS: I insist on all points.

QUINTANILLA: Then go off to . . . the King of Portugal.

PAGE (*announcing*): The Marquise of Moya.

SANTANGEL: Show her in.

(*The Marquise enters.*)

Dear Marquise!

MOYA: Her Majesty would like to know if the terms have been agreed upon.

SANTANGEL: It's a good thing that you've come. You'll see right away how our modern explorers behave.

MOYA (*inspecting* COLUMBUS *through her lorgnette*): Señor Columbus, himself? Very interesting.

COLUMBUS: Have the goodness, Madam, to convey to Her Majesty my most respectful farewell.

MOYA: You wish to leave us?

COLUMBUS: I am going back to Portugal.

MOYA: One moment, gentlemen. (*She speaks quietly to the ministers.*) Listen, that's impossible. The Queen insists on the contract.

SANTANGEL: But one can't talk to this man.

QUINTANILLA: Tell me, is it true that you are wearing the Queen's chemise until Granada falls?

MOYA: That's a state secret.

QUINTANILLA: But you can tell us.

MOYA: Officially, the Queen is wearing the chemise. Semi-officially, I am.

QUINTANILLA: And who actually does wear it?

MOYA: My chambermaid.

SANTANGEL: Well, what about the contract?

QUINTANILLA: That fellow's trying to cheat us.

MOYA: Then you cheat him. I'm always for everyone earning something.

SANTANGEL: Not bad . . . at all . . . (*To* COLUMBUS.) Señor Columbus, we accept your conditions. We would even like to participate in the affair. But we can undertake the risk only if a Civilian Commissioner goes along.

COLUMBUS: I cannot share my command with anyone.

SANTANGEL: There is no thought of that. We need a trustworthy man to examine revenues and expenses.

QUINTANILLA: But whom do we take for that?

SANTANGEL: Yes, whom do we take?

MOYA: You have a very qualified man in the Ministry of Finance, Señor Vendrino.

QUINTANILLA (*with a glance at* MOYA): Vendrino? Oh, yes.

SANTANGEL (*quietly to* MOYA): Still?

MOYA: I think we're in the midst of a business deal.

SANTANGEL (*rings. A guard appears*): Tell Finance Inspector Vendrino to come up.

(*Guard exits.*)

QUINTANILLA: I propose that we establish a private trading company. There's just one obstacle . . . Have you any money?

COLUMBUS: No.

QUINTANILLA: Can you give us any security?

COLUMBUS: I am staking my life on this venture.

QUINTANILLA: That's hardly the sort of capital we can rely on.

PAGE (*announcing*): Finance Inspector Vendrino.

(VENDRINO *enters. He is a corpulent and active man in his forties.*)

SANTANGEL: Inspector, we've a matter here of . . .

VENDRINO: I know.

SANTANGEL: How do you know?

MOYA: Señor Vendrino has been informed of the facts.

SANTANGEL: So much the better. Would you be willing to accompany the expedition as the government's Civilian Commissioner?

VENDRINO: What does the position pay?

QUINTANILLA (*aside*): You'll be a partner.

VENDRINO: Done!

SANTANGEL (*to* COLUMBUS): Be so good as to put your conditions in writing. In the meantime, we'll consult with each other.

(COLUMBUS *sits down at the table and writes, his back to the public. What follows takes place behind his back.*)

QUINTANILLA: How do you feel about a private trading company with its headquarters in Madrid?

VENDRINO: Naturally enough, things will have to be done a little differently now. We'll establish—let me finish, please—we'll establish a limited liability company with stock distribution. Each of us accepts his share of the liabilities, and we all share in the profits.

QUINTANILLA: Then we'll have to pay in cash.

VENDRINO: In Spain, yes. But we're going to do the whole thing in the Republic of Andorra—there we don't have to pay in cash. Well?

MOYA: Isn't he clever?

VENDRINO: My way has the additional advantage of not obliging the partners to identify themselves. How about that?

SANTANGEL: Put me down for fifty thousand.

QUINTANILLA: And the same for me.

VENDRINO: Put me down for thirty thousand. (*He makes a note of the figures.*) And another thirty thousand for Señora Moya.

MOYA: Where do you suppose I'm going to get that much?

VENDRINO: We don't pay here; we just enter figures in our little book.

SANTANGEL: And if the thing turns out badly?

VENDRINO: Then he'll have made a very bad mistake.

SANTANGEL (*aloud*): Captain . . . excuse me . . . Admiral . . .
we've come to an agreement. The Civilian Commissioner
will take care of all further arrangements.

(COLUMBUS *hands* SANTANGEL *what he has written.* SANTANGEL
keeps the sheet in his hand.)

VENDRINO: One more question! Who's going to take care of the
deliveries? I mean the fitting out of the ships and the purchase of provisions? Let me finish, please. I'll take care of
it. I know my way around when it comes to that. I used to
be purchasing agent for the city of Madrid. (*To* COLUMBUS.)
May I request your company in my office? You don't have
anything to worry about, Señor Columbus—I'll do everything
myself! (*He takes* COLUMBUS' *arm and goes off with him.*)

MOYA: Now what if he really discovers something? Then he'll
be getting far too much.

QUINTANILLA: How come?

MOYA: You have accepted his conditions!

(SANTANGEL *slowly tears up the sheet with* COLUMBUS' *conditions.*)

CURTAIN

SCENE 2

*Room in an inn in the port of Palos. Curtains at the windows,
pictures on the wall, a ship's model, a map, a peasant with a live
bird.* PEPI *leans out of the window—from the street guitar music.
In the middle of the room a large, open trunk. All the cupboards
are open, pieces of clothing on the chairs. Everything indicates
that someone is moving out.*

PEPI (*comes back into the room and sings to the accompaniment
of the mandolin; actually, he half whistles and half sings
while packing*):

> She wears a rose behind her ear
> > a rose behind her ear
> Pepita!
> And I, poor fool

> My heart did lose
> No other did I choose
> Than Pepita—than Pepita—
> With the rose behind her ear.

You'd think he could have bought himself new stockings—just take a look at these excuses for socks! (*He holds a pair of socks in his hand and continues to pack.*) There's just no woman in the house, and when there is no woman in the house, then we miss the woman's touch, if I may be permitted to say so. Just take a look! (*He rummages in the cabinet and finds a bottle.*) I just knew he had some left. Fourteen-hundred and forty-four! This would never survive the crossing anyway. (*During what follows he finishes the bottle while packing.*) The new trousers and the old trousers . . . since we became admiral, we've had a full-dress uniform made up. All for the Indians! The tailor says, how many stripes, says he. So I say, put another fourteen stripes on it—the savages will just love that. I say we represent Spain. A walking stick! Very important at sea . . . (*He packs the stick; now he slowly gets drunk. He squeaks the wet cork along the bottle.*) Shut up! He wants to establish a new state. (*He spreads out a pair of underpants with holes.*) With these underpants we can't establish a state. But it's good for the ventilation.

(*The guitars play a solemn tune outside. He sings while packing.*)

> I am already mother of eight children,
> But you have scorned my heart
> Love cannot prevent that
> Even if time does pass . . .
>
> You sued for my hand so hotly.
> My little mother turned you down.
> But if you did die happily,
> I'd sob each Sunday on your grave!

(*He wipes his nose with his sleeve and drinks. Now he is wholly drunk, and he unpacks all that he packed.*) What's he going to need boots in India for? Are we going to be walking around there? No, we are not going to be walking around there. They'll be carrying us around on their shoulders there, and we'll ride on ele . . . ele . . . elephants with the rose behind the ear! All those books! (*He throws every-*

thing out of the trunk upon the floor.) Either we sink, in
which case we won't need any books, or we get there, and
then we certainly won't need any. Away with the books! I
say to him, Lord Admiral, I say, how about a few girls on
board? He says, says he, you've got no idea of how a real
sailor acts. I say, that's no wonder—I'm from the land. He
says, so long as I am Admiral, no female foot will step on
the "Santa Maria." (*He notices the picture on the wall, a trashy
portrait of a woman.*) The pictures . . . the pictures have to
go along, too! (*He takes the pictures from the walls and
packs them, along with a wooden ship's model. He throws
everything into the trunk.*) The ship too! What does the old
fellow want to go to India for? Insanity, to travel to India in
the summer! I rather like him, the old fellow—but he's off
his head. He's so off his head that he sometimes talks to
himself. (*He places a ladder at the window and climbs up.*)
The curtains! Of course, we can't travel without curtains!
What would the savages think of us!

(*Meanwhile,* COLUMBUS, *in dressing gown, has entered.*)

PEPI (*looks through the empty bottle as if through a telescope*):
I see land!
COLUMBUS: Tell me, what do you think you're doing up there?
PEPI: I'm packing.
COLUMBUS: Come down from there immediately!
PEPI (*slides down the ladder*): Of course, Lord Admiral. (*He
stands laboriously at attention.*)
COLUMBUS: What's all this mess here? Like a pigsty! My uni-
form, boy . . . what are you stuffing into the chest? (*He
takes the ship and the pictures out.*) Are you out of your
mind? That doesn't even belong to us! What will the innkeeper think! Put that ship back!
PEPI (*obeys totteringly*): Lord Admiral, we must bring something
with us for the savages. (*He presents* COLUMBUS *with an
oil painting.*) For the sake of culture.
COLUMBUS: Come over here. Breathe upon me. Completely drunk.
One hour before departure . . . to get as drunk as that!
At this solemn moment . . . (PEPI *burps.*) Well, just wait,
lad, we'll discuss this when we get aboard. Thank God
there's no whiskey over there—you won't know what do
with yourself.
PEPI: Lord Admiral, such a land should not be discovered.
COLUMBUS: Shut your mouth and pack! (*He goes across the room
in long strides.*)

PEPI: Lord Admiral . . . do we want to take the woolen socks or not?

COLUMBUS: Damn it all! I've got other worries.

PEPI: I'm just asking. In case of rain.

COLUMBUS: Has the innkeeper brought you the bill?

PEPI: The bill . . . where did I put the bill? . . . Damn it, I packed it. (*He rummages in the trunk.*) Here.

COLUMBUS: Four bottles of wine per day? How did that happen?

PEPI: To dull the pain of departure.

COLUMBUS: Go down and pay up.

PEPI: Lord Admiral, couldn't we send the money from over there? We are . . . that is to say . . . that is to say, we are out of funds.

COLUMBUS: But I just gave you the rest of the money yesterday.

PEPI: That went to the tailor. We have so many debts—it's a good thing we're leaving.

VENDRINO (*tears the door open and remains standing with the door in his hand. He speaks alternately to* COLUMBUS *and to someone outside who is not visible.*): Everything ready? (*To the outside.*) What else do you want? I have . . . I have told you—we need ten barrels of butter—let me finish—and I don't pay regular prices—I've never done so in my life, and I'm not starting with you! (*To the inside.*) I'll be with you in a moment. (*To the outside.*) Anyone can deliver goods cheap. You've got to deliver them cheaper! (*To the inside.*) Are you finished packing? The trunk will be picked up in twenty minutes. (*To the outside.*) But of course. No. Ship's biscuit. Naturally, the eatable kind and the other—give us both kinds. Your brother-in-law . . . your brother-in-law . . . the fact that it's your brother-in-law—it's all the same to me —I have enough problems with my own relatives! (*To the inside.*) I still have something important to tell you . . . (*To the outside.*) Soft soap? I don't need your soft soap. Anything that has to be soft-soaped around here we'll do ourselves. (*To the inside.*) One moment . . . Excuse the disturbance! (*To the outside.*) Well, that's a different matter altogether, of course. Send the bill to Madrid. Naturally, I promised you payment in cash—that is, if I pay at all, but I'm not paying! Lllllll-eave me alone! (*He throws the door shut.*) You have it made. You are a seafarer. We merchants . . . tomorrow. (*He collapses on the trunk, which* PEPI *has meanwhile closed.*)

(COLUMBUS *is absorbed in a wall map.*)

PEPI (*quietly and carefully to* VENDRINO): Señor Commissioner!

VENDRINO: Everything at the last moment! They've had time to make their deliveries for months now! (*He dries his brow.*) I've been sweating like a pig today!

PEPI (*louder*): Señor Commissioner!

VENDRINO: Supply three ships—I'd like to see anyone else do that! And this trouble with the sailors . . .

PEPI (*bellowing*): Señor Commissioner!

VENDRINO (*almost falling from the trunk*): Why are you bellowing like that, you lout?

PEPI: Couldn't you give us a small advance? We have to pay the bill here.

VENDRINO: How much?

(PEPI, *totteringly, holds up the bill in front of* VENDRINO's *nose.*)

Well . . . you didn't stint yourselves.

PEPI: Señor Commissioner, as admiral, we want to live, too.

VENDRINO: That exceeds your charge account. (*He writes his name on the bill.*) In my office.

PEPI (*off singing*): I am already a mother of eight children, but you, you scorned my heart . . .

VENDRINO (*to* COLUMBUS, *who is striding up and down the room*): How do you feel, Admiral?

COLUMBUS: Do you think the crew is reliable?

VENDRINO: Tip-top. Nothing but first-class lads. We'll bring those Indians to their senses.

COLUMBUS: Were there many volunteers?

VENDRINO: We helped things along a bit. (*He starts to patter across the room next to* COLUMBUS, *who walks in great strides.*) There wasn't too much enthusiasm for it at first. Why are you walking so fast?

COLUMBUS: That's how one goes on board.

VENDRINO (*beginning to walk like* COLUMBUS): In short . . . when nobody volunteered anymore, we went to the jails. And then everything went smoothly all of a sudden.

COLUMBUS (*stops walking suddenly*): You recruited criminals?

VENDRINO: But very good men in all other respects.

COLUMBUS: I'm supposed to conquer a land with criminals?

VENDRINO: It won't be the first time.

PEPI (*sticks his head through the doorway*): Señor Commissioner, there's a woman to see you.

VENDRINO: I'm too busy to see any women now.

PEPI: This isn't a woman; it's a lady.

VENDRINO: How would you know?

PEPI: She arrived in a sedan chair. But the sedan chair has left.

VENDRINO: Wait a moment. (*To* COLUMBUS, *who stands in front of a wall map.*) It's almost time, Admiral. You have to get dressed.

COLUMBUS: I'll take a course toward Africa and sail in the direction of the Canary Islands.

VENDRINO: But you can't sail in your dressing gown.

COLUMBUS: Then I'll go as far as latitude twenty-eight and from there to the west . . .

(VENDRINO *maneuvers him quietly and carefully into the next room. To* PEPI.)

VENDRINO: Bring the lady in! (PEPI *exits.* VENDRINO *goes to the mirror and spruces up.*)

(*A heavily veiled lady enters the room.*)

With whom do I have the honor?

THE LADY (*disguising her voice*): Do you still remember Seville?

VENDRINO: One moment . . . there, to be sure, I knew a lady . . . Are you perhaps Juanita?

THE LADY: Right the first time!

VENDRINO (*kisses her hand*): There was the charming evening when we met on the sly. Your husband was away . . . that is, he was not really away at all and, besides, it wasn't your husband. Why did you stop writing me?

THE LADY (*tears off the veil; it is the* MARQUISE OF MOYA): You blackguard!

VENDRINO (*very startled*): My dear child . . . that was before your time!

MOYA: Before my time? How long do we know each other? Two years. And when were you in Seville? Three months ago.

VENDRINO: Darling . . .

MOYA: I am not your darling. I'm through with you. I'm fed up with your eternal unfaithfulness. I never want to see you again.

VENDRINO: First of all, give me a kiss. (*Embrace.*)

(PEPI *sticks his head through the doorway but disappears immediately.*)

MOYA: Was someone there?

VENDRINO: No one.

MOYA: Who lives here?

VENDRINO: The chief.

MOYA: Very nice here. But come closer, let's see how you look! One needs only to leave you men alone . . . (*She opens his jacket and closes it, pulls at his vest, straightens out his cuffs; all this while they continue to talk.*)

VENDRINO: Such a surprise! When did you arrive?

MOYA: This morning. I came here with the Archbishop. He's got things to do here in Palos.

VENDRINO: You must have gotten up very early. That's a change for you.

MOYA: I wanted to see you again.

VENDRINO: With whom are you faithful to me these days?

MOYA (*pulls at his ruff*): Men—they are a silly sex!

VENDRINO: Do you love me?

MOYA: Yes. Otherwise I would be much kinder to you. But I can't be alone all the time. Seize the day!

VENDRINO: Stop playing with my collar. Come here. Sit down. (*They sit down on the trunk.*) Beatrice, you can't imagine how busy I am. I'm handling everything around here. Just yesterday somebody tried to palm expensive white flour off on me. What did your clever Vendrino do? He purchased good stuff for the officers and cheap stuff for the crew.

MOYA: They're wearing very small hats in Madrid now. It's a crazy fad.

VENDRINO: Do stop looking at yourself in the mirror!

MOYA: You should see the way Quintanilla's wife acts—she keeps painting her face all day. I have a commission from the Queen . . .

VENDRINO: For me?

MOYA: That would suit you fine, eh? For Columbus. She sends him a letter.

VENDRINO: A letter? What's it say?

MOYA: No, my dear. Don't trouble yourself. We women stick together when we don't happen to love the same person. When I think of how you'll be carrying on in India! Just don't come back to me with Indian women!

VENDRINO: Oh, do be quiet! A lot you've got to complain of! Think of Gomez.

MOYA: That was before your time, if you please!

VENDRINO: Which Gomez was it anyway? Don Fernando or . . .

MOYA: The other one. His name was Don Juan on top of everything else. Ah, my dear God!

VENDRINO: Why didn't you hold on to him?

MOYA: Whom does one really want to hold on to? What has your

Admiral got here? (*At the birdcage.*) Tittittittitt! Let's hear you sing!

VENDRINO: He doesn't sing because he's smart.

MOYA: Does your Admiral sleep here? I could never sleep in the same room with a bird. Do you get along with him?

VENDRINO: With the bird?

MOYA: Idiot. With the Admiral.

VENDRINO: He's a strange man, Beatrice. When you ask him something, he looks at you so curiously, as if his mind were on something else completely. Aside from that, he does everything wrong. Nonetheless . . . there's something about him. He's got something. He may well make something of himself yet!

MOYA: He's not my type at all. I like small, fat men.

VENDRINO: He can thank his lucky stars that he has me. I made him, after all. I think we made a good deal. You'll earn plenty of money, Beatrice.

MOYA: And who gave you the idea?

VENDRINO: I did. (*He taps her cheerfully on the back.*)

MOYA: No, I. Stop being so mean. I always told you you didn't have good manners and you didn't have bad manners: you don't have any manners at all. You're much too loud. Even at court. That's no way to build a career.

VENDRINO: How does one build a career?

MOYA: Like this. (*She kisses him.*)

(PEPI *sticks his head into the doorway and again disappears immediately.*)

VENDRINO: Was someone there?

MOYA: No one. Are we going to eat together later? I like eating with you.

VENDRINO (*pulls a little notebook out of his pocket and turns the pages*): Leave Palos the third of August, four P.M. . . . I don't know if we have enough time left. When will you be going back? I mean . . . one must . . . one should really . . .

MOYA: What are you thinking of! (*Grandly.*) I am traveling in the entourage of the Archbishop.

VENDRINO: Pity.

MOYA: Yes, José . . . it really is a pity.

VENDRINO: It is too much of a pity.

MOYA: Do you promise to write to me?

VENDRINO: I'll write you every day, my child.

MOYA: Write me everything. Write me what the Indian women wear. I'm crazy to know about that. And if they wear nothing, then write me about that as well. (*She licks her lips.*) And how well developed the men are. You must write me everything, José. And be careful not to catch cold during the crossing. You're the kind that catches cold when a closet door is open. Dress warmly, do you hear? And don't do anything silly with those Indian women. Just be careful! Come back to me in good health!

VENDRINO: My little worrier, good-bye! (*Long embrace.*)

(PEPI *comes into the room to fetch the trunk. He is not noticed and carefully pulls the trunk away from under them.*)

VENDRINO: Damn it all!

MOYA: Why, what's the matter?

VENDRINO (*to* PEPI): You must have been bitten by a wild Portuguese!

PEPI (*stiffly*): I'm here to get the trunk, Señor Commissioner!

VENDRINO: And you couldn't let us know you were in the room?

PEPI: I've already been here twice . . . but Señor Commissioner was so busy . . .

VENDRINO: It was a matter of confidential communications.

PEPI: I could see that. (*He drags the trunk out.*)

(COLUMBUS *enters wearing his Admiral's uniform.*)

MOYA: Lord Admiral, I am here on a commission for the Queen. She sends you this letter. (*She takes out a sealed letter and gives it to him.*)

COLUMBUS (*breaks the seal and draws out a gold crucifix on a chain. He touches the cross with his lips and hangs it around his neck*): Tell Her Majesty that I shall wear the cross as a sign of her grace. I shall show myself to be worthy of that grace.

PEPI (*bursting into the room*): Admiral—the Archbishop!

COLUMBUS: Why don't you accompany the Marquise, Señor Commissioner?

(MOYA *and* VENDRINO *exit with* PEPI. ARCHBISHOP *enters.* COLUMBUS *kneels.*)

ARCHBISHOP: Stand up, my son. I wanted to see you one more time before your departure. The port is full of people. So you're really going?

COLUMBUS: I am ready, Eminence.

ARCHBISHOP: Have you done justice to your Christian duties?

COLUMBUS: I have gone to confession and received the blessing of the Church.

ARCHBISHOP: And how do things stand when it comes to earthly matters? Hopefully, your intentions are pure?

COLUMBUS: I have no intentions. I have an idea.

ARCHBISHOP: You are reputed to have quite a head for business, Admiral. How do you reconcile that with your idea?

COLUMBUS: Eminence, do you think that I like bargaining? I know nothing about business. I am not a merchant.

ARCHBISHOP: Why do you bargain then?

COLUMBUS: Because I have been swindled too often. These people respect only those who act the way they do. Anyone who is not out for money, they consider stupid. My only weapon is to be hard. Whenever I can't get any further with them, I repeat with the stubbornness of the weak: ten percent, one-eighth of the proceeds, ten percent. That's not avarice. That's self-defense.

ARCHBISHOP: I don't know what I should admire more: your courage or your adroitness.

COLUMBUS: I beat them this time despite the odds against me. I can board my ship in peace. This time I won't be cheated.

ARCHBISHOP: Who are you really, Señor Columbus? Are you of noble blood?

COLUMBUS: I am the son of a poor weaver from Genoa.

ARCHBISHOP: In other words, you lied.

COLUMBUS: Eminence, do you believe that if I hadn't anyone would have taken me seriously?

ARCHBISHOP: And you are always talking about God?

COLUMBUS: There is one basic principle that I act on in my affairs. The end sanctifies the means.

ARCHBISHOP: That is relevant only to success.

COLUMBUS: I shall conquer the sea for Spain. I am sailing beyond the borders of our world, out of the realms of the Church . . .

ARCHBISHOP: No one can sail out of our realms—the entire earth is Catholic

COLUMBUS: And what about the heathens?

ARCHBISHOP: You are not only carrying a flag; you are carrying the cross to the west, Admiral. Keep your mind on the words of Holy Writ: Go everywhere in the world and teach all of the nations.

COLUMBUS: And if the nations are not interested?

ARCHBISHOP: Out of the question. They are Christians. Only they don't know it.

COLUMBUS: May one convert them by force?

ARCHBISHOP: The Church knows only God's commandment—its execution she leaves to the politicians. We can do no more than bless the weapons that bring redemption to other peoples. The rest is not our task. I wish you a successful voyage!

COLUMBUS: Well, Eminence, where exactly does the Church stand?

ARCHBISHOP: On the side of power, my son. (*Exits.*)

(PEPI *enters with the dagger and plumed cap of an admiral.* COLUMBUS *girds himself with the dagger and puts the cap on.*)

COLUMBUS: Well, Pepi, now we can start. (*He looks around.*) Do we have everything?

PEPI: Yes, indeed. What about the bird?

COLUMBUS: We're taking him with us.

PEPI: The Lord Admiral has specifically ordered that no animals be taken aboard.

COLUMBUS: That's not an animal. That's a bird.

PEPI (*takes the birdcage under his arm*): If only he doesn't get seasick!

VENDRINO (*bursts in, ready to go*): The rifle club of Palos wishes to escort Your Excellency to the port. (*He calls out through the window.*) Ready, gentlemen!

(*A brass band plays a popular march.* COLUMBUS, VENDRINO, *and* PEPI *go to the door. As they get to it, an* OFFICIAL *enters the room.*)

OFFICIAL: One moment! Your passports, please!

VENDRINO: Make it snappy! (*He hurriedly pulls out the passports.*) We're in a hurry.

OFFICIAL: But you don't have any exit permits!

VENDRINO: What d'you mean—no exit permits? (*Through the window.*) Stop it! Stop the music! (*The music ceases.*) Where are you from?

OFFICIAL: From the Ministry of Finance. The Admiral has neglected to pay his taxes.

VENDRINO (*to* COLUMBUS): Is that right?

COLUMBUS (*to* PEPI): Is that right?

PEPI: That's right.

COLUMBUS: But officers from lieutenant colonel on up are not subject to taxation. I have the rank of general.

OFFICIAL (*pulls out a roll of paper*): This concerns the time when you were still only a captain.

VENDRINO (*takes the roll of paper away from the* OFFICIAL): Give
that here! Ah, I see! Pay attention now. (*Very rapidly.*) According to the decree of the 24th of April, 1488, the income
quota which is not derived from public utilities is reckoned
up with the capital proceeds in such a manner that the purchase tax in addition to the house-rent tax and with the deduc-
tion of the ground-rent tax is reckoned up with the remaining ten percent of the household tax. Agreed that the sum
total was due the first of July, the decree of the 18th of November, 1474, takes effect, whereby the tax-free share of the
income tax does not remain subject to the jurisdiction of
the finance divisions. Today is the 3rd of August, 1492. So
the sum total is not due till the 1st of January, 1943. Do you
understand?

OFFICIAL: Yes . . . but . . .

VENDRINO: Obviously you do not know your own regulations.
Get out of here immediately!

(OFFICIAL *exits.*)

VENDRINO (*brandishing the passports triumphantly*): How did I
handle that?

PEPI: First-rate.

VENDRINO: You see, Admiral: anyone can sail to India. But to
get out of Spain—that is a real feat! (*He winks out the
window. The music plays again.*)

CURTAIN

SCENE 3

On board the "Santa Maria." The stage is divided into three
parts: bridge, top deck, and lower deck, which are connected by
stairs. Top left the bridge, behind which lies the Admiral's cabin,
wheelhouse, and flagstaff. From the bridge, one staircase leads to
the top deck on the right, where the officers' cabins are situated.
Here rises the mast with the mainsail; the crow's nest is barely
visible. In addition, there is on the top deck a small lavatory with
a carved-out heart on the door and the inscription: "Here." From
the top deck, a second staircase leads to the lower deck, where the
crew's quarters are located. There one finds hammocks, kitchen,
and storeroom. Top deck and lower deck are conceived of as two
tiers, one over the other.

COLUMBUS, VENDRINO, PEPI, FIRST OFFICER, SHIP'S DOCTOR, *the sailors* DIEGO, RODRIGO (*a somewhat dissipated fellow*), *the* SHIP'S COOK, *the* CABIN BOY, *and a* SLEEPING SAILOR. OFFICERS *and* SAILORS.

The bridge is empty. The top deck remains empty at first; later, the SHIP'S DOCTOR *goes up and down there. On the lower deck a* SAILOR *is asleep in his hammock. The* COOK *stands at his hearth. The* CABIN BOY *sits up in the crow's nest.* DIEGO *is playing his guitar.* RODRIGO *is scraping carrots. The* COOK, DIEGO, *and* RODRIGO *are already singing, before the curtain rises, to the melody: "It's a long way to Tipperary!"*

> It's a long way to Barcelona—
> It's a long way to Madrid.
> Should I be off for Tarragona,
> Then you would go with me.
> It's a long way to Granada
> And to the Alcazar!
> It's a long way into your arms, dear,
> Where I once lay happily!

RODRIGO (*always speaks very slowly, sleepily, and awkwardly*): Well, what did the Ship's Doctor tell you?

DIEGO: That prescriber! He said that he had heartburn himself, and that I should get some exercise. (*He scrapes carrots.*)

RODRIGO: Perhaps you can climb the mast ten times each day— good for the digestion.

DIEGO: Since we're on the subject of digestion . . . when do we eat lunch?

COOK: When you're finished with the carrots.

DIEGO: Exactly the way I always pictured the sea voyage to India. Scraping carrots!

RODRIGO: Say, did I ever tell you the story of how I almost escaped from the Toledo jail?

DIEGO: Only about a hundred times! I know all your stories as well as I know your face. How long have I had to look at your stupid mug? Seventy days! Every day . . . take a look at yourself in the mirror. (*Holds a mirror to him.*) That's what I've had to look at every day.

RODRIGO: You want me to tell it? All right, I'll tell it. There we were standing at the wall, Gonzalez, red Philippo, and me. Philippo, he was small and fat, and . . .

DIEGO: And so he hopped on your shoulders, and up over the wall, and you they left in there, and so you were the sucker. I know! I know! God's blood, if I could only get off this damned floating box!

COOK: Just step off!

SLEEPING SAILOR (*turns over in the hammock*): Can't a sleeping man get any peace and quiet in this hotel?

DIEGO (*to* RODRIGO): If only you had stayed in your jail! That's where you really belong!

COOK (*to* DIEGO): Yeah, and you?

DIEGO: I'm a sailor.

COOK: You haven't always been one.

DIEGO: Thank God, I haven't always been one. I've been a porter, tinker, donkey driver, and banker.

COOK: You a banker! (*He laughs.*)

DIEGO: To be sure, I was a banker. In an exchange office. And if someone gave us money, it was as safe as in the Bank of Spain. He never got it back.

RODRIGO: There were plenty of bankers in the jail I was in. But they never stayed long. They had work to do on the outside.

CABIN BOY (*has slid down from the mast and come into the crew's room*): Ahoy!

COOK: Did you see anything?

CABIN BOY: Nothing but water. The sea is smooth as an oil cake. No sign of land

RODRIGO: You won't earn the reward either.

CABIN BOY: Ten thousand . . . is a pretty penny. But I'm not going to be caught . . .

COOK: Fetch us a sack of peas. What won't you be caught at?

CABIN BOY (*grubbing around in the storeroom*): I'm not going to be caught yelling "Land!" too soon. If it turns out to be a mistake . . .

COOK: Then you don't get the reward. Quite right, m'boy.

DIEGO: Man, if the officers told us to paint our asses green, the cook would still say, quite right, quite right. Some are born assholes—there's just no help for that!

CABIN BOY (*drags a sack out of the storeroom*): Boy, this one's heavy!

COOK (*empties the sack*): Hey, what's this?

(*All step closer.*)

DIEGO: There are stones in there! How about *that!*

RODRIGO (*very slowly*): Who does get the reward?

DIEGO: You're always about two steps behind, aren't you? Better take a look at that heap of stones. Everything here is ready to break. Touch a rope, it falls apart. Turn the wheel, a spoke remains in your hand. I'd just like to know what dog did the purchasing for this ship. He sure didn't do badly for himself.

COOK: It's been quite a while since I made a complaint.

DIEGO: Well, make one! Go ahead! Complain! I've had a bellyful of you, you old bumbler—you and the rest of this crap.

PEPI (*who has meanwhile come down from the bridge*): Good morning. The old man would like to know who had the watch last night.

DIEGO: Ah, the Staff Officer! Good morning, Excellency! Had a good night's sleep?

PEPI: Who had the night watch?

DIEGO: What a silly question!

SLEEPING SAILOR: What? How? Night watch? I had the night watch.

PEPI: The old man wants to know if around half-past one you saw something light up in the sky.

SLEEPING SAILOR: I didn't see a thing. And besides that, I'm sleeping now. (*He turns over, making a vulgar gesture.*)

PEPI: I look at that in my quiet, calm way . . .

COOK: How do things look above?

DIEGO: Man, when do we arrive?

PEPI: We play around a lot with the compass. The Chief writes all night.

DIEGO: That won't get us there any earlier. But what's he saying?

COOK: Tell us something!

PEPI: Our hopes are up.

RODRIGO: What was lighting up the sky?

DIEGO: He'll be late for his own funeral. But, Excellency, if we don't sight land soon, you and your Admiral up there will damned well wish we had. That refugee from Genoa!

PEPI: I think I'm in the way here. You gentlemen are so excitable.

DIEGO: I've had it up to here. I don't want to discover any sea route to India. Count me out. I gave up a quiet life . . .

PEPI: In jail, by your leave.

DIEGO: I suppose it's my fault I didn't have a castle to live in?

(PEPI *exits.* DIEGO *follows him.*)

Arse-licker! Shirker! Jerk! This is no place for a proper seaman to be. Everything's unnatural here. Rockets are falling out of the skies, and grass grows out of the sea. It stinks here. You all remember how we saw fishes fly?

(*All cross themselves.*)

Why, there's no such thing. If a fish can fly, then he can't swim. I want to see something I can tell about when I get home. Nobody's going to believe I saw fishes fly.

CABIN BOY (*plays quietly on his guitar and hums along*): It's a long way to Barcelona . . .

(*All hum along and scrape carrots.*)

Top Deck

OFFICER *and* DOCTOR *meet on the top deck.*

OFFICER: Good morning, Doctor.

DOCTOR: Good morning, Lieutenant.

OFFICER: Tell me, you've studied zoology. How do fish manage to have wings? The crew was so scared they damn near crapped in their pants.

DOCTOR: Those fellows are so crude. It's really all very simple. The fish have feathers on their fins, and that's how they fly. Do you understand?

OFFICER: No.

DOCTOR: It's the so-called *Piscis aviaticus Oceani*.

OFFICER: Oh! Now I get it.

DOCTOR: Speaking of fish—do you know the joke about the salmon? Two unbelievers sit in a theatre, and one says to the other . . .

OFFICER: That's enough of your unbelievable jokes. You've already told me all of them.

DOCTOR: The voyage is taking too long.

OFFICER: The voyage is taking much too long. (*They walk silently.*) You're out of step.

DOCTOR: Sorry. (*He changes his step.*) Now you're out of step.

OFFICER: No, I'm not.

DOCTOR: Yes, you are.

OFFICER (*nervously*): No, I'm not.

DOCTOR (*even more nervously*): Yes. You are.

OFFICER (*stops walking*): Do you know what you can do to me?

DOCTOR (*threateningly*): Please, no intimacies!

OFFICER: Sorry, it wasn't meant that way.

DOCTOR: It's nerves. You go completely crazy on this ship. (*They resume walking next to one another.*) Speaking of the ship: where are we, anyway?

OFFICER: Take a look at the sail. No wind. We're completely lost. The angle of the sun . . . no, as a layman, you wouldn't understand. And that's the way the "Santa Maria" has been going for days.

DOCTOR: I was up above yesterday.

OFFICER: With him?

DOCTOR: He doesn't sleep anymore. He's feverish. No wonder, he's calculating day and night.

OFFICER: The man's fighting for his life. At night he stands there without moving, looking at the stars. It's positively uncanny.

DOCTOR: Just between us: do you really believe in this nonsense?

OFFICER: What nonsense?

DOCTOR: That we're going to hit land.

OFFICER: Shhh! . . . As long as the crew doesn't notice anything. One has to stop people thinking: otherwise they come up with nothing but idiocies. (*They resume walking next to each other in silence.*)

Lower Deck

DIEGO: They stop everything we do. Lately we've been playing the game with the spider: if the spider climbs left, then we'll see land by evening, and if not, not. Along comes the First Officer and stops it. Everything gets stopped! They've stopped us singing the bird song . . .

(CABIN BOY *plays the melody of the satirical song "A Bird Is Flying Across the Blue Sea" on the guitar, and whistles in accompaniment.*)

COOK: You're not supposed to sing that song!

DIEGO: Says you! We'll see once and for all. (*To* RODRIGO.) Come on, stand at the door and keep watch. Alfonso, play!

(*The* CABIN BOY *plays the satirical song;* DIEGO *begins to sing in a whisper; single lines are sung by all the men, but always in a whisper. The whole text should not be sung in chorus.*)

CABIN BOY: A bird is flying across the blue sea.

ALL: Seville and Valladolid.

CABIN BOY: And where does that little bird come from?

ALL: From Seville and Valladolid.

CABIN BOY:

A ship out of Madrid
Is bringing Columbus.

For India he's looking—
Yes, cooking . . . Yes, cooking . . .

ALL:

> Christopher, stick your head out of the cabin—
> Christopher . . .

(OFFICER *has heard the melody upstairs, eavesdrops, and descends carefully.*)

RODRIGO (*bursting into the crew's room*): Watch it! The First!

(DIEGO *gives the youth a sign. The latter immediately changes the melody, and all sing harmlessly.*)

ALL:

> When the sun goes down—goes down—goes down,
> You don't see it anymore—anymore—anymore.
> When your sweetheart goes from here—from here—from
>   here,
> Then he's never coming back—coming back.
> (*In a drawl.*)
> Weeping willows
> And a bunch of rosemary!
> He who loves must suffer much—
> And thus I think of you—think of you—think of you.

OFFICER (*has meanwhile come in and listens amiably to the singing*): Good morning, men!

ALL (*laconic and annoyed*): Good morning, Lieutenant.

OFFICER: Singing, eh? That's fine. Always nice and lively. Is the food good?

COOK: The food is first-rate. Would the Lieutenant like to taste some?

OFFICER (*tastes something from a dish presented by the* COOK): Why, it's great. Tastes first-rate. As far as that goes, you've got no grounds for complaints. Any other problems? (*Dull silence.*) Well?

RODRIGO: It's about the peas.

OFFICER: What peas?

(*The sailors make gestures at* RODRIGO *to keep him from talking.*)

RODRIGO: Diego has said there are too many peas among the stones . . .

DIEGO: He's a bit stupid, Lieutenant. I've already told him a hundred times, you're so stupid, you ought to be an officer . . . I mean . . .

OFFICER: Well, well, so everything is in order. Good morning, men. (*Exits. No one returns the greeting.*)

COOK (*to* DIEGO): You can't ever keep your trap shut even when no one's around.

RODRIGO (*has gone behind the* COOK's *back to the pots, where he is now tasting. The* COOK *hits his fingers with a ladle.*): The tomatoes are no good. Tomatoes have to have something sweet in them.

DIEGO: I wouldn't mind something sweet myself—seventy days without a woman. For God's sake.

CABIN BOY: I miss the women a lot myself.

DIEGO: Oh, come on now . . . you're lucky if you can hit the pot right.

RODRIGO: Are there eats or are there no eats?

COOK: Just pick out the peas over there!

(*All do so. The* SLEEPING SAILOR *remains on his back the entire time.*)

Top Deck

OFFICER *comes up from the lower deck.*

DOCTOR: Well?

OFFICER: There's something not quite right down there. I don't like the way those people are acting.

DOCTOR: As long as the Chief doesn't notice.

OFFICER: At first he took care of every little bit of nonsense himself. Every complaint had to be taken to him. (*He opens the door to the lavatory.*) He even had a window installed here. (*He slams the door shut again.*) Well, I soon cured him of that. As a captain he can do that sort of thing, but not as an admiral. Let him watch the compass. The crew is my department.

DOCTOR: Are you writing all that in the log?

OFFICER: Naturally, you can't write that sort of thing down. I'm a realist. Besides, I have a family.

DOCTOR: Tell me, why did you sign on in the first place? Did you have to?

OFFICER: I've got my eye on a governorship in the colonies; there's nothing doing back home.

DOCTOR: I'm supposed to get general's rank in the Medical Corps out there.

OFFICER: Best of luck.

(*Noise on lower deck.*)

I don't know what's wrong with the crew.

DOCTOR: They need women. Speaking of women: last year I was physician-in-residence at the baths in San Sebastián. The place teemed with women! You only had to wink.

OFFICER: Did you wink?

DOCTOR: Every night. There was one charming woman who came to me one day . . .

PEPI (*opens a cabin door*): The Commissioner requests the staff doctor's presence. The Commissioner has a stomach ache.

DOCTOR: Right away.

(PEPI *exits.*)

Anyway, she came to me and said she had spiritual difficulties. Have you ever heard of anything like that? Of course, as a layman you can't understand that. I examined the lady . . . everything there . . . flawless. I said: "How long have you been married, dear madam?"—She said: "Twelve years." Then it dawned on me.

PEPI (*in the doorway*): The Commissioner requests the staff doctor to come immediately because of the stomach ache.

DOCTOR: I'm coming!

(PEPI *exits.*)

One night I went to her secretly, for a consultation, and naturally I charged her double. Imagine if her husband had caught me!

OFFICER: Did he?

DOCTOR: Not a trace. Do you know what he did?

OFFICER: What?

DOCTOR: He didn't pay the bill.

PEPI (*at the door*): The Commissioner says that he doesn't need the staff doctor anymore: his stomach ache has gone.

DOCTOR: Well, there you are!

OFFICER: Come on! I have some inspecting to do on the other side. (*They go off to the right.*)

Lower Deck

DIEGO: Now in the White Vest in Seville—do you know the White Vest?

COOK: Of course, I do. Some women they got there! I was once thrown out of that place because I was so drunk. That's a very fine house.

DIEGO: Do you know the big blonde, Alice?

COOK: Do I know Alice!

DIEGO: Brother, if we get back all right, I'm off to Seville—that's the first thing I do. No other place!

CABIN BOY: I'm going along.

DIEGO: They won't even let you in without a set of instructions!

COOK (*to* DIEGO): Both of us will go there.

DIEGO: Both of us. Downstairs they've got that big palm tree in a pot, and then inside, to the left, is the drawing room . . .

COOK: With the two pictures . . . "Mother-love" and "Sorrow" . . .

DIEGO: First of all, we order a real old Tarragona, and then I go upstairs with Alice. For Christ's sake!

COOK: What are you going to do?

DIEGO: Go upstairs with Alice.

COOK: No. I'm going with Alice.

DIEGO: You're going with Alice?

COOK: First me. Afterward you can go.

DIEGO: We'll see about that. First I go, and then, as far as I'm concerned, you can go.

COOK: I know Alice longer than you do. And I go first.

DIEGO: I go first.

COOK and DIEGO (*together*): Me first—Alice—you blockhead! First me—damned galley slave—first me—(*They fight.*)

SLEEPING SAILOR: Say, what's the fighting for?

COOK and DIEGO (*letting each other go*): Yes, why? Well, yes . . . that's true . . . Alice . . . there's no Alice here . . .

RODRIGO (*slowly*): Who is Alice?

COOK and DIEGO (*turning on* RODRIGO): What are you sticking your nose into things for, you ox!

RODRIGO: I . . .

DIEGO: I've had a bellyful. And let me tell you guys something once and for all: When I start thinking about women, I start feeling funny all over. How long is this here going to go on? No one tells anyone anything. The old man is in hiding. When do we arrive? It's high time someone told us that.

COOK: He's right.

DIEGO: We've got to send a delegation and force the old man to tell us what's what.

COOK: Just to get things straight. Who's going?

DIEGO: I'd be glad to sacrifice myself for my comrades. I'll go. That is . . . maybe someone else would like to go?

COOK: Just to get things straight. We'll draw for it.

DIEGO: Get four small pieces of wood.

(COOK *and* DIEGO *look for the wood on the floor and whisper to one another.*)

COOK (*quietly*): Are you really going?

DIEGO (*likewise*): I've been playing games like this for years— leave it to me.

COOK: Well, now we draw for it. The one who draws the short piece, goes.

DIEGO: Give it here. There! (*He offers the pieces of wood to* COOK, *looking very conspiratorial. The* COOK *winks at* DIEGO *and draws.*)

CABIN BOY: Me too.

DIEGO: You wait till you get a bit bigger. (*To the* SLEEPING SAILOR.) Well, now you. Come on! What are you doing?

SLEEPING SAILOR: I'm the opposition.

DIEGO (*to* RODRIGO): Well, then you. (*He manipulates the pieces of wood like a juggler.* RODRIGO *draws. They compare the pieces.*) Rodrigo's got it.

(COOK *grins.*)

RODRIGO: I'm supposed to go?

DIEGO: Naturally—you. I give you the official command.

RODRIGO: All right then—I'll go. (*He goes to the door.*)

DIEGO: You dumb ox—you don't even know what you're supposed to say. Sit down.

COOK: He's supposed to ask when we'll get to India.

DIEGO: Nonsense. You go upstairs and say you want to speak to the old man. When the old man comes out, you say that you're the delegation and would like to inquire about the date of arrival.

COOK: The exact date of arrival.

DIEGO: Pay attention. You say, the crew . . . no. The crew has been seized by a state of exhaustion, you say. And remember exactly what he says. Understand? Now get up there.

RODRIGO (*off; on the staircase he turns around and comes back in the cabin*): What has seized the crew?

DIEGO: You hopeless oyster—the crew has been seized by a state of exhaustion. Now get up there!

(RODRIGO *goes slowly up the staircase and grumbles: "State of exhaustion—state of exhaustion!"*)

Top Deck

VENDRINO (*steps out of his cabin with a sun helmet on his head*):
How do I really feel? Do I still feel ill? I can't look at all
that water anymore. (*He casts a glance at the sea.*) Horrible.
Come over here, Pepi!

(PEPI *appears with a brush and a pair of top boots.*)

How is the sea today?

PEPI: The sea is satisfactory, Señor Commissioner.

VENDRINO: Big waves?

PEPI: Not a ripple as far as the eye can see. (*He spits on his boots
and brushes.*)

VENDRINO: Stop spitting. It makes me nervous.

RODRIGO (*stands at the top of the stairs and mutters*): State of
exhaustion.

VENDRINO (*to* PEPI, *who is brushing right in front of him*): Stop
rocking back and forth like that, fellow. How often do I have
to tell you that!

RODRIGO: —has been seized. (*He goes to the Admiral's staircase.*)

VENDRINO: What does that man want?

PEPI: Hey! Where you going?

RODRIGO: To the Admiral.

PEPI: You're not allowed to go up there.

VENDRINO: What do you want?

RODRIGO: The situation is namely that . . . I am a delegation.

VENDRINO: What are you?

RODRIGO: My comrades have delegated me concerning the state
of exhaustion which has seized them.

VENDRINO: I don't understand a word.

RODRIGO: Then I'll have to ask again. (*Turns to exit.*)

VENDRINO: Halt! You stay here! Now I'll do the talking. I'm an
old seaman. I'm not going to put up with any sloppiness
around here. If you have something to say, then say it to me.
Otherwise I'll lock you up for three days.

RODRIGO: The situation is namely that . . . I am to go to the
Admiral . . .

VENDRINO: The Admiral is not available just now.

RODRIGO (*unperturbed*): And when he comes out, I am to say:
We would like to ask about the time of arrival.

VENDRINO: Why?

RODRIGO: Because I drew the shortest piece of wood.

VENDRINO: Did you ever see anything like that! (*In a rage, to*
PEPI.) Stop rocking back and forth! (*To* RODRIGO.) It sounds

like you're all crazy down there! Comes up here and wants to disturb the Admiral! Whose messenger boy are you, anyway?

RODRIGO: They can't take it anymore. The crew's taking over. We want to know, once and for all, when we'll get there.

VENDRINO: Ah, that's different, of course. Now I'm going to tell you something. As long as there remains a drop of blood in our veins, we keep going. Spain expects every man to do his duty. Even if we never get there. Understand?

(PEPI *spits on the boots.*)

RODRIGO: Yes, indeed, Señor Commissioner.

VENDRINO: About face.

(*Stiffly,* RODRIGO *turns and goes down the stairs. To* PEPI, *who is again spitting on his boots.*)

I would just like to know why you keep spitting!

PEPI: So that they shine, Señor Commissioner.

VENDRINO: Set up a deck chair over here! And bring me something to read—the *Spanish Observer!*

(PEPI *brings the chair and a roll of parchment—*VENDRINO *stretches out and reads.*)

Lower Deck

RODRIGO *comes down.*

ALL: Well? What happened? What did he say?

RODRIGO: He said that as far as he's concerned, things are rolling. And he's waiting for Spain. And he said that we'll never get there.

DIEGO: What?

COOK: Is that what the old man said?

RODRIGO: The old man's got his door shut. You can't get up there.

DIEGO: Then who did you speak to?

RODRIGO: To the fat one. The Commissioner.

DIEGO: And he said we'll never get there?

RODRIGO: As sure as I'm standing here.

DIEGO (*takes a few plates and flings them crashingly to the floor*): God's blood! I've had it!

RODRIGO (*likewise throws whatever he can reach to the floor*): Me too!

CABIN BOY (*trampling on the peas*): Me too!

ALL: We want to go home—home—home!—

(DIEGO *begins to sing the satirical song—first not too loud,
then louder and louder. The others join in the refrain, blowing on cans and beating time on plates.*)

A bird is flying across the blue sea
—Seville and Valladolid.
And from where does that bird come here?
From Seville and Valladolid.
A ship out of Madrid
Is bringing Columbus.
For India he's looking—
Yes, cooking . . . Yes, cooking . . .

ALL:

Christopher, stick your head out of the cabin—
Christopher, the Indians are not at home—
Christopher, you great admiral—
Go search for it! Go search for it!
We aren't under cover.
And us it is
That you may well discover!

(*Refrain is sung twice. They are overcome by the song. In
rhythm, they march up the stairs. From all sides of the ship,
sailors step forth and sing along. An* OFFICER *and the* SHIP'S
DOCTOR *rush on the scene and try in vain to stop those singing. They shout: "Halt! Back!"* VENDRINO, *frightened, rushes
back and forth. The officers are forced back to the Admiral's
staircase. The top deck is now filled with mutinous, singing
sailors. At this moment,* COLUMBUS *appears on the bridge.
The singing stops suddenly.*)

COLUMBUS: What do you want?
ALL: Go back home! Go back home! Search for that—search
for that! Go back home!
COLUMBUS: Quiet! (*He descends the stairs, shoves aside a few
sailors who stand in his way, and now stands among the
crew.*) What have you to say to me?
VOICES: Back to Spain! We've had it! Stick your head out of the
cabin! Christopher!
COLUMBUS: Let one speak.
DIEGO: Lord Admiral . . .
COLUMBUS: What is your name?
DIEGO: Diego.
COLUMBUS: Speak.

DIEGO: We've been deceived. We were promised land. For seventy days we've been wandering around on the sea. There is no land. (*To* COOK.) Now you speak!

COOK: Lord Admiral, the provisions are running out. The biscuit is getting moldy. The water is putrid. Therefore we request that the Lord Admiral turn back before it is too late.

COLUMBUS: Sailors! For seventy days you were brave . . . Do you want to be cowards on the last day?

DIEGO: Better once a coward than to starve for a lifetime.

COLUMBUS: You complain about the length of the journey. Do you think that will make the return trip shorter? The worst is over.

A SAILOR: Throw him overboard, the foreigner!

COLUMBUS: I'm not afraid for my life! I entreat you, believe me! Up there I went on my knees and prayed to God. My calculations are correct. We are close to the goal . . .

(*He is interrupted by an outbreak of noise: "Lies! Fraud!"*)

DIEGO: In short, Admiral, do you want to turn back or not?

COLUMBUS (*to an* OFFICER): Arrest that man!

OFFICER: We are in the minority, Admiral. The wishes of the crew strike me as not entirely unjustified.

DOCTOR: The men are not in the best of health, Admiral. There are a number of cases of scurvy.

COLUMBUS: I see . . . And you, Commissioner?

VENDRINO: If I believe, on the one hand, that going on with the journey is to be recommended, I believe also, on the other hand, that specific political considerations operate against the continuance of that journey.

COLUMBUS: What do you really mean?

VENDRINO: As an official, I am for going on. As democrat, against.

COLUMBUS (*touches the Queen's crucifix*): I gave the Queen my pledge. I keep my word. I am going on.

VENDRINO: From a strictly legal viewpoint there is nothing against your seeking a hero's death. The only question is whether we join you. I propose that we put the matter to a vote.

COLUMBUS: Sailors! The flocks of birds we have seen show that we're close to land. Yesterday a green branch floated in the sea. Do you want to give up everything you've worked for now that you've seen these signs? Think of the riches that await you! Who follows me? Volunteers up front! (*No one moves.*) I'm taking the wheel. (COLUMBUS *is immediately surrounded by a crowd of sailors.*)

VOICES: Turn the sails! (*Silence.*)

COLUMBUS: Go back. One against all. Not the sea but my men have conquered me. I refuse to give up. With the first ship I'll sail back west! (*Slowly, he goes up the stairs to the bridge and into his cabin.*)

COOK: The old man has guts. He just turns his back to us.

DIEGO: Courage he's got. But he's completely crazy. Now we're in command. Everyone aloft to man the sails!

(*The sailors slowly climb up the rope ladders.*)

DOCTOR (*to* OFFICER): Is all this going into the ship's log too?

OFFICER: Not by a long shot—you can't put *everything* down! (OFFICER *and* DOCTOR *disappear quickly into their cabins.*)

COOK: What are we going to say when we get home? I mean . . . when the women ask. We've discovered no land . . . brought back no souvenirs . . .

DIEGO: Man, you don't know what you want either. First you want to go home, and then you don't.

CABIN BOY: And when we get back, they'll throw us all in jail!

DIEGO: You, shut your trap, or I'll kick your ass from here all the way back to Spain!

PEPI: Well, it's all over with India now. (*He throws his boots in a high arc into the sea.*)

RODRIGO: They've got cannibals there and men with three heads and women as big as trees.

COOK: That's all stuff you could have told your old lady when you got back. Now we just look like a bunch of fools.

(RODRIGO *scratches his head.*)

DIEGO: What do you think, Pepi?

PEPI: I'll have to think about it in peace and quiet. (*He takes the large key that hangs on the lavatory and disappears in there. Meanwhile the sail has been turned and a large section of the sky has become visible.*)

COOK: Just think—another seventy days back . . . seventy days and seventy nights . . .

RODRIGO: I wonder if they'll be able to digest us properly . . .

COOK: Who?

RODRIGO: The cannibals!

(*Tremendous racket from the lavatory.*)

PEPI (*bursts forth and cries*): Land! Land!

ALL: Where?

PEPI: There!

(*The cry "Land" grows like wildfire.* OFFICERS *and crew throng around the lavatory. The* CABIN BOY *climbs the mast like a monkey.*)

Land, Señor Commissioner, land!

(VENDRINO, OFFICER, *and* DOCTOR *appear.*)

VENDRINO: Well, what did I tell you?
ALL: Admiral! Admiral!
CABIN BOY (*on the mast*): Land, ahoy!

(COLUMBUS *appears on the bridge. Everyone becomes dead silent.*)

VENDRINO: Lord Admiral, deeply moved, may we extend our most hearty best wishes . . .
COLUMBUS (*interrupts him with a gesture of his hand*): Well, well, now everyone's eager. All hands on deck! Raise the flags! Let us sing the national anthem. Sailors, the new world lies before us. Long live Spain! (*He exposes his head. The stage is full of flags.*)
ALL (*singing*):
      Bravery, unity, and honesty
      Can only be found in Spain
      Spain, my fatherland.
      Thrift, integrity, diligence, and chastity
      Can only be found in Spain.
      That's not a little thing
      Long live our gracious King!—

CURTAIN

SCENE 4

A palm-fringed inlet by the ocean. Left, an open hut with animal skins. Right, a fireplace, at which four brown men in bathing suits are sitting on low stones. They are playing bridge and smoking thick cigars. The CHIEF *sits on the right with the* MEDICINE MAN *opposite him and the* DRUMMER *between them. The fourth man, a* HUNTER, *sits with his back to the audience. All are wearing gold jewelry on their ears.*

CHIEF: One spade.
DRUMMER: Three diamonds.

MEDICINE MAN: Three spades.
HUNTER: Pass.
CHIEF: Pass.
DRUMMER: Double.

> (*All the others pass. They play. A* NATIVE *comes running in from the direction of the sea. During the following, the four continue playing calmly.*)

NATIVE: Chief! Chief! A battleship!
CHIEF: Battleships don't exist anymore.
NATIVE: With cannons. I saw it with my own eyes.
DRUMMER: Fairy tales. We've abolished cannons.
NATIVE: They're strangers. A bunch of white men with funny-looking hats. They've got guns and look very nervous.
CHIEF: What kind of savages could be coming here with guns?
MEDICINE MAN: Could they be cannibals?
DRUMMER: My great-grandfather always used to talk about a great continent to the east where the people kept killing one another.
NATIVE (*running back and forth*): Chief! The strangers have lowered a boat and are landing!
CHIEF: Contract fulfilled.
MEDICINE MAN: You even made an extra trick.
NATIVE: Chief! The strangers are coming!
CHIEF: Let them come. We're busy playing.
DRUMMER (*to* HUNTER): You had no business throwing out your king, there.
HUNTER: I only did it because you were bluffing.
CHIEF: Gentlemen, are we chatting or are we playing! Your deal.

> (DRUMMER *deals the cards. In the meantime,* COLUMBUS, VENDRINO, OFFICER, *and* SHIP'S DOCTOR *approach.*)

DRUMMER: One no trump.
MEDICINE MAN: Two hearts.
HUNTER: Watch it! Risky bid!

> (COLUMBUS *and his men have arrived. He is wearing his dress uniform and a feathered hat. The others are dressed splendidly, especially* VENDRINO. *The savages stand up slowly. There is an embarrassed pause; no one knows what to say.*)

VENDRINO: Well!
CHIEF: Nice day.
COLUMBUS: Very nice.
CHIEF: Did you have a good crossing?

COLUMBUS: Yes, thank you.

CHIEF: With whom do I have the honor?

COLUMBUS: We come in the name of Their Spanish Majesties. I am Christopher Columbus, Admiral-in-Chief of the Ocean and Viceroy of this country.

CHIEF: I am the chief. That is the medicine man, that the drummer, and this gentleman is one of my brothers-in-law.

COLUMBUS: We come with peaceful intentions. We merely wish to take possession of this country.

DRUMMER (to VENDRINO): Pardon me—are you a cannibal?

VENDRINO: I am the Civilian Commissioner. We're going to establish order here. (He looks around.) Well now, all this is going to have to go. We've got to have regular houses here. You don't even have a proper harbor. What's the meaning of these miserable-looking huts? They're made of straw! Don't the building inspectors have anything to say about that? We'll have to get a bit of order into things here. But the first thing we've got to do is take over the country.

CHIEF: Won't you sit down?

(All seat themselves.)

COLUMBUS: Their Spanish Majesties send you their greetings. We have discovered you. I hope you will show yourselves worthy of this honor.

CHIEF: Do you like it here?

VENDRINO: You should come to Madrid some time. That'll open your eyes!

CHIEF: What is your country called?

COLUMBUS: Spain.

CHIEF: Is it a big country?

COLUMBUS: The biggest country in the world.

CHIEF: Then why did you come here?

COLUMBUS: We need colonies.

CHIEF: What is that?

COLUMBUS: Colonies are countries that we civilize. We bring you the blessings of culture. We show you that your morals and manners are barbaric, and that you must live the way we do.

CHIEF: And then?

COLUMBUS: Then you belong to us.

CHIEF (smoking): Very interesting.

MEDICINE MAN: Really very interesting. (He smokes.)

DRUMMER: Extraordinarily interesting.

(All three blow thick clouds of smoke in front of them.)

CHIEF: I am afraid you are going to be disappointed. There's not much to conquer here.

COLUMBUS: Why not?

CHIEF: Because there's nothing here.

VENDRINO: May I see what you have there in your ear.

MEDICINE MAN (*takes ring out of his ear*): Of course.

VENDRINO: Gold! Hallmarked? No. (*He hands the ring to* COLUMBUS. *The ring goes from hand to hand.*) Do you have any more of these?

MEDICINE MAN: Of this worthless metal?

VENDRINO: Worthless . . . ! Allow me . . . ! You people wear rings like this in your ears?

MEDICINE MAN: We take a new one every morning.

VENDRINO: Perhaps we can trade a little. You give us gold, and in return we'll give you merchandise.

DRUMMER: What shall we do with that?

VENDRINO: Go into business!

DRUMMER: But we don't need anything.

VENDRINO: Since when is merchandise here to be used? The important thing is production. A modern state must sell its products to other nations.

CHIEF: And they sell to you?

VENDRINO: They would like to, but we do not allow it. Only we are allowed to sell.

CHIEF: What happens if the others don't want to buy?

VENDRINO: Then we declare war on them.

CHIEF (*smoking*): Very interesting.

MEDICINE MAN (*smoking*): Really very interesting.

DRUMMER (*smoking*): Extraordinarily interesting. But if all are at war and no one can buy anything, why don't you open your borders and trade freely?

COLUMBUS: Because we are a nation.

CHIEF: But what if another nation says the same thing?

OFFICER: Then it's not a real nation.

(*The natives smoke quietly and blow thick clouds of smoke.*)

COLUMBUS: You are a small nation, and we are a large nation. Submit to us and give up your weapons.

CHIEF: We have no weapons.

VENDRINO (*strikes his fist on a rock*): Are you trying to make fun of us? We are the conquerors here.

CHIEF: We misunderstand each other. We really have no weapons. We have a few spears and arrows for hunting—that is all.

COLUMBUS: Have you then no army?

CHIEF: We had an army. We also had battleships and weapons. We even had money. That is all a long time ago. Our ancestors, who were very wise, recognized that these things bring men to no good. And so they did away with all of that. Since then we've had peace.

VENDRINO: How can one live on such a low cultural level! But things can't go on like this. Things have to be organized around here! We'll establish a commercial colony. Under Spanish control, of course. We shall protect your legal rights . . .

NATIVE (*bursts in in great agitation*): Chief! Chief! The strangers are taking away our earrings!

CHIEF: Is that the protection of legal rights?

VENDRINO: No, it's confiscation.

COLUMBUS: I forbid all looting. Lieutenant, see to it that discipline is maintained.

OFFICER: At your service, Admiral! (*Goes off stiffly.*)

MEDICINE MAN: Why is that man making such strange movements? Is he ill?

SHIP'S DOCTOR: No, he's obeying orders.

MEDICINE MAN: Do you people always have to obey orders?

SHIP'S DOCTOR: Whenever a superior commands.

CHIEF: Which one of you is the superior?

SHIP'S DOCTOR: Whoever gets more money.

CHIEF: Very interesting. (*He smokes.*)

MEDICINE MAN: Really very interesting. (*He smokes.*)

DRUMMER: Extraordinarily interesting.

(*They blow great clouds of smoke.*)

COLUMBUS: What are those fiery things you have in your mouth?

MEDICINE MAN: These are cigars.

CHIEF: Please, help yourself. (*He offers cigars.*)

VENDRINO: Do these grow here? (*He bites into one.*)

MEDICINE MAN: They're not for eating. They're for smoking. (*He lights up* VENDRINO's *cigar with his own.*)

COLUMBUS: Peculiar customs.

VENDRINO (*blowing through his cigar*): Doesn't taste bad. (*To* COLUMBUS.) Can you imagine the Queen putting something like that in her mouth? (*Swallows the wrong way and coughs. The* MEDICINE MAN *hits him on the back.*)

MEDICINE MAN: You must draw, not blow.

DOCTOR: You sit around like this all day, smoke fat cigars and do nothing?

CHIEF: What should we do?

DOCTOR: Work. In Spain one works from morning to night.

CHIEF: Have you got that much work?

VENDRINO: If we have none, we create it.

(*The sound of muffled drumming from afar. The* DRUMMER *fetches a drum from the bushes and listens.*)

COLUMBUS: What is that?

DRUMMER: Quiet. A news report.

COLUMBUS: From this village here?

DRUMMER: No. It is very far away. (*He listens and then strikes the drum rhythmically.*)

COLUMBUS: What are you doing there?

DRUMMER: I am passing the news on. (*He resumes beating the drum.*)

VENDRINO: Well, that has to stop! Where would we be if everybody drummed! There would be no more bank secrets.

DRUMMER (*while beating the drum*): 90—92—95—

VENDRINO: Are those prices?

DRUMMER: No, scores. We go around and hit a small ball into holes with a club, and he who makes the least strokes, wins.

VENDRINO: That strikes me as rather idiotic.

COLUMBUS: And that is what you're drumming across the whole country?

DRUMMER: It's the only thing that really interests us.

VENDRINO: Peculiar people.

CHIEF (*rising*): We have a request. I don't dare put it into words.

COLUMBUS: Speak!

CHIEF: I am afraid you may feel insulted.

COLUMBUS: Is there anything I can do for you?

CHIEF: We would like to finish our rubber. Perhaps we can continue with our conversation tomorrow. Naturally, you will be my guests for the night. (*To* COLUMBUS.) May I offer you my humble hut. (*He points to the hut.*)

COLUMBUS: I can't accept that. (*Bows.*)

CHIEF: But I implore you. (*Bows.*)

COLUMBUS: Would the gentlemen be my guests on board ship tomorrow at noon? A small snack. (*Bows.*)

CHIEF: Very kind of you, but we don't want you to go to any trouble. (*Bows.*)

COLUMBUS: Quite the contrary. We look forward to it. It would be an honor for us. (*Bows.*)

CHIEF: In that case permit us to invite you to dinner tomorrow evening. (*Bows.*) I hope you will take to our cooking. We eat everything raw.

SHIP'S DOCTOR: Does that agree with you?

MEDICINE MAN: We drink cold water with our food.

VENDRINO: Ice cold water?

MEDICINE MAN: Ice cold water.

VENDRINO: Horrible.

CHIEF (*to* COLUMBUS): We realize what we owe to such a great chief. The most beautiful dancer of our tribe will share your quarters tonight.

COLUMBUS: Please don't go to any trouble. (*Bows.*)

CHIEF: Or did you bring your own women with you?

COLUMBUS: No, we didn't, but . . . I am rather tired from the journey.

CHIEF: Our dancers are very talented. It will remain a lasting memory for us.

COLUMBUS: Very good of you. But perhaps one of my officers . . .

CHIEF: That would be a gross insult.

COLUMBUS: For goodness sake!

CHIEF: Make yourselves entirely at home here. Gentlemen! It has been a pleasure. (*Bows. The natives pick up the cards and leave.*)

COLUMBUS: A fine mess, that business with the dancing girl!

VENDRINO: You will have to sacrifice yourself.

COLUMBUS: What would the Queen say to it!

VENDRINO: Far greater sacrifices have been made for the fatherland before now, Admiral.

COLUMBUS: Then you do it!

VENDRINO: After you, Admiral.

COLUMBUS: That's not what I came to India to do. I am an explorer, not a lover.

VENDRINO: Sometimes the two are one and the same. The girl could turn out to be very pretty.

COLUMBUS: A colored girl? Impossible! I have Spanish blood!

VENDRINO: From Genoa.

COLUMBUS: What did you say?

VENDRINO: Nothing. The only thing I have to say is, we mustn't insult these people.

COLUMBUS: Tell me, Doctor . . . is there a health hazard in dealing with such a girl?

DOCTOR: For whom?

COLUMBUS: I'm no coward. But this is going too far.

DOCTOR: We are pioneers, Admiral.

COLUMBUS (*to* DOCTOR): Doctor, do me a favor. Go to the beach and get Pepi. Tell him to come right away. I want to have myself shaved.

(DOCTOR *exits.* COLUMBUS *strides back and forth.* VENDRINO *tries to keep up with him.*)

VENDRINO: I'd like to give you a few suggestions about the occupation. Because of technical and administrative factors, we
have to set up a military base. I'll set up a central authority
for gold. Then colonial merchandise: lavender, myrrh, cam-
phor, and all the cinnamon. Yes, that's right—cinnamon as
well. This is purely financial-political . . . why are you walking so fast?

COLUMBUS: I walk as I please.

VENDRINO: Sorry. Negotiations won't get us anywhere here. This
is a different state of affairs altogether. We'll have to take
direct action here.

COLUMBUS: These are quiet, harmless people who bother no one.
I want no killing.

VENDRINO: In that case I must decline all responsibility.

COLUMBUS (*stops*): I release you from it with pleasure. I have
the confidence of the court.

VENDRINO: You forget, Admiral, that a good part of your success
is due to me. Without me, you would still be sitting in
Spain. I obtained the money. I equipped the ships. I recruited
the crews. And you? What did you do?

COLUMBUS: I had the idea.

VENDRINO: Yes, Admiral, you had the idea. One man has the
idea, and another carries it out. What would you be without
me?

COLUMBUS: And what would you be without me?

VENDRINO: Your part is over. Now it's our turn.

COLUMBUS: My part begins the moment I set foot on this land.

VENDRINO: You have something much more important to do. Be
a figurehead!

COLUMBUS: And who carries the responsibility?

VENDRINO: There is no responsibility. There is only a risk.

COLUMBUS: I know what violence is. I want peace.

VENDRINO: I know what peace is. I want to do business. (*He
bows.*) Admiral . . .

COLUMBUS: Commissioner!

(VENDRINO *off.* COLUMBUS *goes into the hut, takes off his
topcoat and sits down on a cot.* PEPI *appears with razor, soap,
brush, towel—a thick cigar in his mouth.*)

What are you puffing on there?

PEPI: This is my second one, already. The Chief, himself, gave me this one. (*He ties the towel around* COLUMBUS *and works up a lather.*) I like it here very much, Admiral. Lots of brown girls with such eyes! And they're all so friendly. . . . In my own quiet way, I observe things. The savages are quite happy. A little naked. And they do spit. But otherwise, splendid fellows. The cook received two earrings from a savage, and the savage got one pound of ham in return.

COLUMBUS: From the ship's stores?

PEPI: No. This was a private ham. Damnation . . . !

COLUMBUS: What's wrong?

PEPI: I feel peculiar.

COLUMBUS: That's from too much smoking.

PEPI: One moment, Lord Admiral. One moment!

(*He goes into the bushes.* COLUMBUS *sits, his face covered with soap. Sound of music. The forest is suddenly illuminated by torches. Behind the palms appear brown girls in bathing suits with* ANACOANA, *in their midst. They bow before* COLUMBUS *and dance a fantastic native dance. Meanwhile,* PEPI *returns and finishes shaving* COLUMBUS. *When the dance ends, the girls disappear and* PEPI *sneaks after them. The torches go out, the music stops.*)

ANACOANA: Did you like it?

COLUMBUS: I liked it very much.

ANACOANA: Do you people dance like that, too?

COLUMBUS: Not yet. But we will soon.

ANACOANA: May I come a little closer?

COLUMBUS: Please do.

ANACOANA: So you are the foreign chief. How old are you actually?

COLUMBUS: I'd rather not talk about that.

ANACOANA: Our chief isn't all that young anymore either. You're wearing a pretty dress.

COLUMBUS: This isn't a dress. It's a uniform.

(ANACOANA *laughs loudly.*)

What's there to laugh about?

ANACOANA: What kind of strange tubes are those?

COLUMBUS: Those are trousers.

ANACOANA: Do you always wear them?

COLUMBUS: What questions you ask! I don't inquire about your secrets. Trousers are trousers.

ANACOANA: Take them off.

(COLUMBUS *is shocked.*)

Have I said something improper? Is one not allowed to say that?

COLUMBUS: No, you can't say that.

ANACOANA: Why not?

COLUMBUS: Because . . . one doesn't say such things.

ANACOANA: Oh! Now I understand. It's taboo!

COLUMBUS: What is taboo?

ANACOANA: Taboo is something you are not allowed to touch. Otherwise, you die of it.

COLUMBUS: It's not all that serious. Let's not exaggerate. There are, however, things one does not say because they are indecent.

ANACOANA: If they are indecent, why do you wear them?

COLUMBUS: Tell me, are you always so inquisitive?

ANACOANA: I am not inquisitive. I would just like to know everything exactly.

COLUMBUS: By the way, what is your name?

ANACOANA: Anacoana. That means: flower of the wild waters.

COLUMBUS: Anacoana—I like the name.

ANACOANA: And what is your name?

COLUMBUS: Christopher.

ANACOANA: Christopher . . . do you have many wives?

COLUMBUS: Among us each man has only one wife.

ANACOANA: Oh God! Are your women beautiful?

COLUMBUS: Very beautiful.

ANACOANA: More beautiful than me?

COLUMBUS: They're not all so well developed.

ANACOANA: Do they also wear trousers?

COLUMBUS: Yes. But differently.

ANACOANA: Oh! They wear them on top!

COLUMBUS: No!

ANACOANA: Where then?

COLUMBUS: You should not be so curious.

ANACOANA: But I want to learn something. What do your women do when they love a man?

COLUMBUS: They marry him.

ANACOANA: What do they do?

COLUMBUS: They go to church and make a pact for life.

ANACOANA: They do something quite different here. Are you married?

COLUMBUS: No.

ANACOANA: Do you want to make a pact with me for life?

COLUMBUS: First of all, you can't rush something like that.

Second of all, among us, it's not the women who ask that question, but the men.

ANACOANA: Ask me, Christopher!

COLUMBUS: Come here, my child. I must have a serious talk with you. Sit down here. There.

(*She sits at his feet.*)

Now pay attention. A barbaric custom of your tribe requires that I . . . that you . . . that I and you . . .

ANACOANA: Then you don't want to make a pact with me for life?

COLUMBUS (*smilingly strokes her hand*): No.

ANACOANA (*looking at his hand pensively*): Are you so white all over?

COLUMBUS: All over.

ANACOANA: Show me. May I see? (*She opens his jacket at the neck and finds the Queen's golden cross.*) What have you got there?

COLUMBUS: A cross.

ANACOANA: Did a medicine man give you that?

COLUMBUS: No. A queen.

ANACOANA: Do you love her?

COLUMBUS: One may not love a queen.

ANACOANA: Does she love you?

COLUMBUS: When I think of her now . . . maybe she did really love me.

ANACOANA (*has with lightning speed torn off the cross*): I don't want other women to love you.

COLUMBUS: Give me that cross immediately! (*He seizes her by the arm and tries to tear the cross away from her.*)

ANACOANA: Let go! (*She bites him.*)

COLUMBUS (*realizing that force will not do the job*): If you don't behave yourself, I'll send you away.

ANACOANA: But I won't go.

COLUMBUS: Then I'll call my men and have you carted off.

ANACOANA: Then I'll scream. In this country, if a woman wants something, a man must obey. Here the woman is always in the right.

COLUMBUS: Don't the men have any rights here?

ANACOANA: Oh no. They're allowed to take care of us, nourish our children, and say yes to everything. Say yes!

COLUMBUS: What is it you really want?

ANACOANA: I want to experience an adventure.

COLUMBUS: Now, in the middle of the night?

ANACOANA: You must embrace me just once. (*She draws out the cross.*) Then you get the cross. Do you promise to do that?

COLUMBUS: Yes, but . . .

ANACOANA: I'll throw it in the woods! One-two-

COLUMBUS: I promise.

ANACOANA (*gives him the cross*): Now you are in for it.

COLUMBUS (*very embarrassed*): I can't just simply embrace you.

ANACOANA: If you don't embrace me, I'll call for help!

(*He kisses her.*)

At last!

COLUMBUS: What a way you have with you! I feel like a schoolboy.

ANACOANA (*sits on his knee*): But Christopher, you are so famous. And we women love famous men.

COLUMBUS: Am I really famous?

ANACOANA: Frightfully famous. The whole village is talking about you.

COLUMBUS (*pulling her to him*): Then come.

ANACOANA: Wait. Not yet. Tell me how you got here. But exactly. I want to know everything. I am tremendously excited.

COLUMBUS: On the third of August of the year 1492 I weighed anchor in Palos and, in bright sunlight, sailed westward across the blue ocean . . .

(*The curtain falls slowly.*)

SCENE 5

A table in the castle at Madrid. A cosy breakfast for seven has been laid out. The table is in the form of an open rectangle: five places along the length, one place at each end. A small orchestra is on the balcony; it has not yet begun to play when the curtain rises. The MARQUISE OF MOYA *studies the menu.* SANTANGEL *enters.*

MOYA: So punctual, my dear Chancellor?

SANTANGEL (*kisses her hand*): I am never too busy to give some time to a beautiful woman. Anyway, there's nothing to do.

MOYA: I thought governing was frightfully exhausting.

SANTANGEL: Only when nothing is happening. That's when one's inferiors get particularly critical. When things get serious, however, one issues decrees. Who else has been commanded to breakfast by the King?

MOYA: What is the seating arrangement actually? No, that's impossible. (*She switches the place cards at the ends.*)

SANTANGEL: What are you doing there?

MOYA: I'm avenging myself. I am displacing your Finance Minister.

SANTANGEL: What did poor Quintanilla do to you?

MOYA: He has reduced officials' salaries again. My husband will have me running around naked soon.

SANTANGEL: Then the economic crisis will have had at least one good result. And who is the lucky man who will sit next to you?

MOYA: Vendrino.

SANTANGEL: Correct. He's expected back today. Is he still in favor?

MOYA: I can't wait to hear what happened in India.

SANTANGEL: I can.

MOYA: But you've gotten shiploads of gold!

SANTANGEL: Who says so?

MOYA: Official proclamation.

SANTANGEL: Dear child, if we just had the gold that this whole swindle has cost us, we wouldn't need to reduce salaries.

MOYA: Why are you lying, then?

SANTANGEL: So that other countries will burst with envy. The least we can expect for all our money is some Portuguese irritation. Otherwise the discovery of America would just be a bore.

MOYA: Do you really think that Columbus is competent?

SANTANGEL: You know I was always against the fellow.

MOYA: Why don't you send someone else out there?

SANTANGEL: He's sitting pretty. The Queen is deaf to every complaint. Her darling is to have his triumph, even if everything goes topsy-turvy.

MOYA: Señor Santangel . . . what if something happened . . .

SANTANGEL: You mean . . . a change in personnel . . . ?

MOYA: India is far. Do you have anyone in mind?

SANTANGEL (*after a pause*): Vendrino?

MOYA: Vendrino is the only reliable man around.

SANTANGEL: Vendrino as Columbus' successor. Not bad. And . . . who will be Vendrino's successor . . . the Marquis?

MOYA: That remains to be seen.

SANTANGEL (*kisses her hand*): You have a remarkable understanding of politics. Pity you are not a man.

MOYA: Luckily for you I am a woman. By the way, I have the honor of sitting next to you at the table.

SANTANGEL: I thought Vendrino was sitting next to you.

MOYA: I am sitting between you.

SANTANGEL: Excellent.

QUINTANILLA (*enters hurriedly and gives* SANTANGEL *a letter*): Just arrived by courier. What do you say?

SANTANGEL (*reads*): This is crazy!

MOYA: What is it?

QUINTANILLA: Top secret, my dear Marquise.

SANTANGEL (*to* MOYA): I believe the moment you were speaking of has arrived.

MOYA: Has something happened?

SANTANGEL: More than you imagine. This letter will finish him off. (*He sticks the letter in his pocket.*) This is going to be an interesting breakfast.

MOYA: But do say something!

SANTANGEL: Eat hearty!

(*A flourish of trumpets from the orchestra. Entrance of* KING, *Queen, and the* CARDINAL-ARCHBISHOP. *Lackeys move the chairs back. First Their Majesties, then the others sit down. To the side, on the left,* QUINTANILLA; *from the left, at the longer side:* ARCHBISHOP, KING, *Queen,* SANTANGEL, MOYA. *The seat at the shorter side remains empty at first.*)

KING (*speaks and looks like a postal official suffering from stomach troubles*): Who sits in the empty seat?

SANTANGEL: Civilian Commissioner Vendrino, who has just returned from India.

KING: But he's not sitting there. If I ask who is sitting there, and no one is sitting there, then one cannot tell me that some-one is sitting there. Sssississs . . .

ISABELLA: Ferdinand, please!

SANTANGEL: He is expected any moment now.

ISABELLA: Let us begin.

LACKEY: Clear bouillon in cups. A soft-boiled egg for His Majesty.

(*The food is served. The orchestra plays.*)

KING (*still in a bad mood*): Why are we using the good dishes?

ISABELLA: We always use the good dishes on Sundays.

KING: Isabella, do you know what the doctor said yesterday?

ISABELLA: Well, what did he say?

KING: He said that he's never seen such a stomach. And he's not happy with the bowel movements either.

ISABELLA: Ferdinand, please!

ARCHBISHOP (*to* KING): How did Your Majesty like yesterday's organ concert in the old cathedral? The *Te deum* poured through the halls like a stream. The new organist made a good first impression.

KING: He played so loud that one couldn't hear what one was saying.

ISABELLA: Do take some more bouillon, Señor Treasurer. (*To* ARCHBISHOP.) Who is this organist?

ARCHBISHOP: The son of a pastry cook. His father is a most respectable man.

SANTANGEL (*quietly to* MOYA): The respectable pastry cook has eight illegitimate children.

MOYA (*quietly to* SANTANGEL): When does the man find time to do his baking?

LACKEY: White port, vintage 1487.

KING: Where is my milk? Quintanilla, don't drink so much wine. It's bad for your bile. You keep that up and one day you'll get a stroke, and then you'll be crippled.

QUINTANILLA: Heaven forbid, Majesty!

KING: Or dead. Whichever you prefer. If you want to grow as old as the hills, drink milk.

LACKEY: Broiled perch with whipped butter. Carrot purée for His Majesty.

KING (*looks carefully at the other plates. To* ARCHBISHOP): Eminence, what have you got over there! (*He takes the serving of fish from his plate and gives him another.*) Here—take this—it's the best! The other was much too indigestible. That fish is overcooked.

ARCHBISHOP: Tastes excellent, Majesty.

QUINTANILLA: It couldn't be better.

KING: Pity.—I propose a toast to the health and happiness of the royal family, of Spain, and of my . . . one, two, three, four . . . dear guests! Your health!

(*Flourish of trumpets. All drink to one another. The* KING *drinks the toast in milk. For a while, one hears only: "To health and happiness! To health and happiness! To great health and happiness!" The music resumes.*)

What kind of racket is that? Stop the music!

(*The music stops.*)

ISABELLA: Help yourself, Chancellor!

KING: Why do you always need him?

ISABELLA: Ferdinand, please—don't eat so fast! First of all, it does not agree with you, and then you know: when you finish, the plates are changed—perhaps the others still want to eat.

KING: Leave me alone. I know my stomach. And the others should not eat so much.

ISABELLA (*to* MOYA): My dear, where do you have your work done these days?

MOYA: Majesty, at today's prices . . . what I'd really like is to find a little seamstress.

KING: What's the difference—the milk is too warm, I've said it a hundred times, I want cold milk!—What's the difference between a big seamstress or a little one?

MOYA: The little one copies the big one, works just as well, and charges half as much.

KING: Why don't you go to a little one then?

MOYA: The little one wants cash, Majesty.

LACKEY: Mixed vegetables with cold greens. Thick gruel for His Majesty. Sherry, vintage 1441.

KING: Why isn't the music playing?

(*The music starts.*)

MOYA (*to* SANTANGEL): Where is Vendrino?

SANTANGEL: Longings?

MOYA: Curiosity.

QUINTANILLA (*to Queen*): Majesty, have you consented to be patron to the big charity festival?

KING: I don't know anything about that.

ISABELLA: I was just going to tell you.

KING: No one tells me anything!

ISABELLA: I shall patronize the event—the poor people!

QUINTANILLA (*his mouth full*): Yes, this poverty . . . it's horrible! The state's revenues have gone down again too, but don't let it worry you—we're living in a time of transition.

KING: Isabella, take a look at the violinist up there! The man looks so yellow. I wonder if he's got a bad liver. My court is nothing but a sanatorium. I'm the only healthy specimen around here.

MOYA: Santangel, why are you constantly stepping on my foot?

SANTANGEL: You are enchanting today, Marquise.

MOYA: First India—then love.

LACKEY (*announcing*): Civilian Commissioner Vendrino!

VENDRINO (*hurries in*): Majesty, I beg your pardon a thousand times . . . the coach broke down.

ISABELLA: Have a seat, my dear Vendrino. You must be hungry. Eat something.

VENDRINO: Very kind, Majesty. (*He sits down right, at the end of the table.*) Lord Chancellor! Marquise!

LACKEY: Baked spring chickens with mushrooms in Madeira sauce. Oatmeal gruel for His Majesty.

KING (*grimacing*): Oatmeal gruel! (*He takes the Queen's plate and sniffs it.*) Let me see. Maybe I can have some of the sauce?

ISABELLA: Ferdinand, please! You know what the doctor has told you.

KING: I'm fed up. All doctors are to be put in prison and fed oatmeal gruel for three days. Do you hear, Chancellor?

SANTANGEL: Yes, indeed, Majesty.

VENDRINO (*quietly to* SANTANGEL): Are you going to do that?

SANTANGEL: If I were to do everything I'm ordered to, we'd be in a fine pickle!

ISABELLA (*to* VENDRINO): What's new from India, Commissioner?

VENDRINO: A great surprise, Majesty! (*He gives a sign to a lackey.*)

ISABELLA: A pleasant one?

VENDRINO: Your Majesty will be amazed.

ISABELLA: You're making me curious.

(*A large sack is brought in and placed at the front of the stage.* VENDRINO *stands up and opens it cautiously.*)

KING: That is a sack, as far as I can see.

VENDRINO: Quite right, Majesty, a sack. (*He reaches into the sack and brings out potatoes, which he places on the table.*)

ISABELLA: What is that? Gold?

VENDRINO: No. Gold it's not. The moment we introduced a gold economy, the gold suddenly disappeared. What I have here is far more valuable than gold.

KING: What is it then?

VENDRINO: This is a new fruit, Majesty. A colonial product. The so-called potato.

(*The potatoes are passed from hand to hand.*)

ISABELLA: Can they be eaten?

KING (*bites into a potato and spits it out*): Ugh—it tastes awful!

VENDRINO: In a raw state, the fruit is inedible. I've asked the kitchen to prepare a dish of it. If Your Majesty permits, it can be served up right away. (*He sits again.*)

ISABELLA: What is the dish called?

VENDRINO: The savages have an odd name for it. They call it potato pancake.

ISABELLA: Potato pancake?

VENDRINO: Majesty, this dish will conquer the world!

KING: Away with oatmeal gruel!

(*All the guests' plates are removed.*)

VENDRINO (*to* LACKEY): What's gotten into you! Give it here— I'm not finished yet! (*He grabs the plate back.*)

MOYA: José! The King has finished eating!

VENDRINO: Just one more bite. I am so hungry.

MOYA: Behave yourself. You are at court and not among your Indians.

VENDRINO (*eating*): Do you love me?

MOYA: I am proud of you. You've gotten fatter again.

VENDRINO: To be fat is a philosophy of life.

ARCHBISHOP (*to* QUINTANILLA): What do you think of the fruit?

QUINTANILLA: If this is all we're going to import, we might as well have stayed at home.

(*Everyone looks at the fruit suspiciously.*)

MOYA: Tell me, José—what was it really like?

VENDRINO (*stuffing himself with bread*): Am I hungry! What do you want to know?

MOYA: How did you discover the country? Who saw it first?

VENDRINO: Good old Pepi.

MOYA: From where did he see it first?

VENDRINO: From where? I can't say that out loud. (*He whispers in her ear.*) And that's what it was like, exactly.

LACKEY: Potato pancake. Also for His Majesty.

(*A large silver tray is passed around.*)

KING: Isabella, do you think I can eat it?

ISABELLA: Be careful, Ferdinand. It appears to be very greasy.

KING: After all, I am King.

ARCHBISHOP: Try it, Your Majesty!

ISABELLA: If it does not agree with my husband, I won't be able to sleep the entire night.

KING: Nonsense. I'll simply eat it.

(*All try it. Everyone looks distinctly uncomfortable.*)

SANTANGEL (*quietly to* MOYA): Tastes like the bark of a tree with grease.

QUINTANILLA (*quietly to* ARCHBISHOP): Eminence, this would make good nourishment for heretics!

MOYA (*quietly to* VENDRINO): José, for God's sake, what did you bring with you?

ISABELLA: Well . . . I must say: I've tasted better.

KING (*has tried it cautiously, eats and eats more and more quickly*): Tastes great to me.

ARCHBISHOP: A very interesting dish.

QUINTANILLA: Has its own unique character. A certain charm.

SANTANGEL: The more one eats, the better it gets.

VENDRINO: Well, what did I tell you?

ISABELLA: It lacks something. (*To* LACKEY.) Go to the kitchen and fetch cranberries.

KING: Well, from now on this will be served at court every Sunday. Eat, Eminence! (*He eats avidly.*) Quintanilla, don't pretend to be exhausted! It's good for your bile. Eat, my little Isabella!

SANTANGEL: Is Your Majesty going to command that this food be introduced into the kingdom??

KING: Potato pancakes for the people? Are you out of your mind?

(*The cranberries are brought in.*)

To health and happiness, Commissioner! You've finally brought something sensible with you. India is coming along nicely. I am very pleased with you!

VENDRINO (*jumps up, upsetting his glass in his excitement, and toasts with a potato pancake*): To health and happiness, Majesty!

SANTANGEL (*quietly to* VENDRINO): How does it really look out there?

VENDRINO (*gloomily*): Well, that's a horse of another color.

SANTANGEL: For God's sake, don't look so desperate! The King wants happy faces to look at. Majesty requires sun.

MOYA: José, smile!

VENDRINO (*smiling constrainedly*): We're not doing any business. Trade is at a standstill. The whole business is costing us a fortune and bringing nothing in. It's a colossal bankruptcy!

ISABELLA: What other news have you from India, Commissioner? Let us have quiet, please.

(*The music stops and does not resume.*)

How is the Admiral?

VENDRINO: Thanks, he's all right. Perhaps . . .

ISABELLA: Speak.

VENDRINO: Perhaps I might say that when it comes to trade policies, he doesn't always have the right touch.

SANTANGEL (*very carefully*): Have you noticed anything about the
Admiral since his last journey from Europe?

VENDRINO: You mean . . .

SANTANGEL: I mean . . . some sign of—how shall I put it—
mental derangement?

VENDRINO: The Admiral, for whom I feel only the sincerest
friendship, has been acting rather strange lately, to be sure.

ISABELLA: Doesn't he feel well?

VENDRINO: He was never completely healthy. He was always a
dreamer.

ISABELLA: A dreamer is not mentally ill. The Admiral is overworked.

VENDRINO: That is the right word, Majesty. Overworked.

ISABELLA: And how are my subjects doing?

VENDRINO: Things are going first-rate with them, Majesty. The
colony is blossoming and flourishing. Spaniards are a healthy
race.

ISABELLA: And the Indians?

VENDRINO: As far as we can tell from the few that are still left . . .

ISABELLA: Have they emigrated?

VENDRINO: No, they are dead.

ISABELLA: Dead?

VENDRINO: Unfortunately, we had to resort to drastic measures.
Nothing could be done to help those people.

ISABELLA: But, for God's sake, why were they done away with?

VENDRINO: There weren't many anyway. Then there was continual
unpleasantness with the occupation authorities. They didn't
want to deliver any gold and pay any taxes. And they didn't
want to become Christians, either.

ARCHBISHOP: But that's no reason for killing people.

ISABELLA: How could the Admiral permit it?

VENDRINO: Too weak, Majesty, too weak.

KING (*strikes the table*): This is disgraceful!

ISABELLA: Ferdinand, please.

KING: You always know better. I've been opposed to this from
the start. But you never listen! You've got to have colonies.
Well, now you have your colonies.

ISABELLA: Who paid for the expedition? You or I?

KING: And who was taken in by it? I or you?

ARCHBISHOP: Majesty, I must raise my voice in warning. When
the Holy Father learns of these abominations, the conse-

quences will be more than anyone can foresee. The Church wants believers, not corpses.

KING (*to* ISABELLA): Now we are in for religious difficulties as well! You didn't bring gold back with you—just aggravation. Why do you kill people? Wouldn't it be preferable to sell them something?

ISABELLA: You mustn't get excited, Ferdinand.

KING: I always get excited when I'm not supposed to. But we're through with explorations now!

ISABELLA (*to* VENDRINO): Commissioner, I am shocked. When they led the first natives to me as slaves, I ordered that they be returned to their homeland as free people. Who is responsible for this butchery?

VENDRINO: Majesty, I am just a small official . . .

KING: It's all your darling Columbus' fault.

MOYA (*quietly to* VENDRINO): Whoever is not present is in the wrong.

VENDRINO (*quietly to* MOYA): I think I'm getting the upper hand.

ARCHBISHOP: Majesty, a man who conducts himself in so unchristian a manner, can no longer enjoy the confidence of the Church.

KING: Dismiss him! Dismiss him!

ISABELLA: The Admiral may have made mistakes. But he did have the idea. After all, he did discover the sea route to India.

SANTANGEL: What did he discover, Majesty? (*He pulls the letter out of his pocket.*) I've just received news from Portugal. Vasco da Gama discovered the sea route to India.

ISABELLA: Who?

SANTANGEL: Vasco da Gama.

ISABELLA: Discovered the sea route to India?

SANTANGEL: By sailing along the west coast of Africa. Here! (*He hands the letter to the Queen.*)

ISABELLA (*helplessly*): Well, was it all lies?

KING: Naturally, the Portuguese! That nation of shopkeepers!

ISABELLA: Yes—for Heaven's sake, what *did* Columbus discover?

SANTANGEL: Very likely, not a thing. A few small islands.

ISABELLA: And I trusted him! A swindler! (*She stands up. All stand up.*) Lord Chancellor, we are issuing a cabinet order. Admiral Christopher Columbus is to be relieved of all his offices and titles. He is to be arrested, brought back to Spain, and tried before a court of law. As his successor, we designate (*She hesitates a moment;* SANTANGEL *points out* VENDRINO.) the present Civilian Commissioner José Vendrino. Present this order to me for my signature. This dinner is concluded.

(*She turns quickly and goes. All follow her save* MOYA, SANTANGEL, *and* VENDRINO.)

SANTANGEL: I congratulate you, Governor-General. This is the end of an adventurer.

VENDRINO: Pity about the man.

SANTANGEL (*with a glance at* MOYA): I hope that now we will finally be able to collaborate fruitfully. Good-bye, Marquise! (*Exit.*)

MOYA (*throws herself into* VENDRINO'*s arms*): José, I am so happy!

VENDRINO: Well, my little jewel, how did I handle that? Now you will be sailing with me as Lady Governor-General.

MOYA: Next time. (*With a glance at the door.*) There is still a little matter I must take care of here.

CURTAIN

SCENE 6

At the Golden Anchor in Seville, February 5, 1505. A small, smoke-filled tavern for sailors. In the background, a bar with bottles, behind which a hidden staircase leads to the cellar and kitchen. Left, a large cask, from which wine is tapped. Right, the entrance. From the ceiling hang ships' models, on the wall, pictures of sea life. When the curtain rises, the pretty waitress, MARIE, *is wiping a table up front; then she fetches from the bar a sign with the word "Reserved" on it and puts it on the table. Meanwhile,* AMERIGO VESPUCCI *enters. He is an elegant young man wearing a lorgnette.*

AMERIGO: Pardon, Miss. Is this the Golden Anchor of Seville?

MARIE: Yes. What does the gentleman wish?

AMERIGO: I am looking for someone.

MARIE: And who is that?

AMERIGO: A famous man.

MARIE: We don't get famous men here. Only sailors spend their time here. (*She continues wiping.*)

AMERIGO: What is your name, my child?

MARIE: Marie.

AMERIGO: Bring me a glass of port, Marie. (*He sits down front at the big table.*)

MARIE: Excuse me, sir, that table is reserved.

AMERIGO: Why, who's sitting here?

MARIE: That table is reserved for the old India sailors. They come twice a week. Perhaps the gentleman would care to take a seat over there.

AMERIGO (*sits down at a smaller table nearby*): Tell me, my child, surely you know the greatest man of the century?

MARIE: No, I don't know him.

AMERIGO: Admiral Christopher Columbus?

MARIE: Oh! The retired admiral! Yes, I know him. He comes here sometimes too. Is he really famous?

AMERIGO: You mean you people don't know? Why, he discovered America.

MARIE: He's always telling about his travels. But he never said he got that far. Is today Thursday?

AMERIGO: Today is Thursday.

MARIE: Then he's definitely coming. So you're in luck. You'll be able to speak to him yourself.

(*Enter* COOK, DIEGO, RODRIGO, *and* CABIN BOY, *who is now a grown man. They seat themselves at the big table. A chair with armrests in the center remains empty.*)

COOK: Good evening to all of you! Little Marie, my angel—give your sweetie a kiss!

(MARIE *kisses him.*)

DIEGO: You're not being faithful to me. Who is your sweetie here, little Marie?

(MARIE *kisses him.*)

CABIN BOY: Me too!

(MARIE *kisses him.*)

COOK: Now he's learned how. Innkeeper! Innkeeper!

DIEGO: Innkeeper!

RODRIGO (*very slowly*): If I could perhaps receive a kiss also . . . ?

(MARIE *kisses him.*)

ALL: Innkeeper! Service! Innkeeper! Innkeeper!

(PEPI *emerges from the cellar stairs behind the bar.*)

COOK: Well, you old bunghole, there you are!

MARIE: Four pea soups for the regulars!

PEPI (*calling down into the cellar*): Four pea soups for the regulars!

DIEGO: Well, Pepi—today we're in the mood to drink something decent.

PEPI: How about a Santa-Maria-Flip?

CABIN BOY: I want Tarragona.

COOK: Do you still have the old Malaga, from 1492? (*He kisses* MARIE.)

PEPI: And I just stand here looking at all this in my quiet way . . . Leave that girl alone, for Christ's sake. I'm still here!

COOK: Well, do you think we come here to look at your beautiful nose?

ALL: Wine! Wine!

PEPI: We're out of Malaga. You can have port. (*He starts filling glasses.*)

DIEGO: Stop! First, grace. Who starts?

RODRIGO: Me.

COOK: Man! You sing like a drunk frog! (*To* CABIN BOY, *who has fetched a guitar from the wall and is strumming on it.*) Let's go!

(*Only the lines indicated should be sung in chorus in the following.*)

CABIN BOY:
       Blue are the waves in the ocean, Santa Maria . . .
       What was our proud boat called?
       Santa Maria.
       From morn to sundown
       We sailed straight on our course
       And India we never did find.

ALL:
       Santa Maria—Santa Maria—
       Happy Santa Maria!

DIEGO:
       Proudly our flag flutters in the wind—

ALL:
       Santa Maria!

DIEGO:
       Our cook, he eats our bacon all alone!

ALL:
       Santa Maria!

DIEGO:
       Our cook, he drinks our rum all alone.
       We sailed around in world history,
       Till we got deep into geography—

ALL:

> Santa Maria—Santa Maria—
> Happy Santa Maria!

(COLUMBUS *has entered and seats himself in the chair with the armrests.*)

COOK:

> And when the sailor's life comes to a close—

ALL:

> Santa Maria!

COOK:

> Then we're happy once more to sit at home—

ALL:

> Santa Maria!

COOK:

> And if our fair Marie gets a kid,
> Then we don't ask who the fathers are,
> Since we do our loving in company

ALL:

> Santa Maria—Santa Maria—
> The lovely Santa Maria!

MARIE (*has in the meantime served the pea soup. She grimaces at the singers. All eat. Then* MARIE *goes over to* AMERIGO *and indicates* COLUMBUS): That's him!

AMERIGO (*goes to* COLUMBUS): Permit me to introduce myself. My name is Vespucci. (*Pause.*) Amerigo Vespucci. (*Pause.*) Surely, you have heard of me.

COLUMBUS: Sorry. What was the name?

AMERIGO: Amerigo Vespucci. The new continent is named after me. I've published a book about my expedition.

COLUMBUS: Congratulations.

AMERIGO (*solemnly*): Admiral, I must shake your hand. You were the first. You are truly a great man. You discovered America.

COLUMBUS: I discovered what?

AMERIGO: America exists. I verified the fact myself.

COLUMBUS: America? I discovered the sea route to Asia.

AMERIGO: You discovered something much greater. A new continent.

COLUMBUS: There is no new continent.

AMERIGO: The calculations of the last century are incorrect. Asia is in another direction entirely.

COLUMBUS: Are you trying to give lessons to an old man? Here, ask my shipmates. Do you still recall what you swore to on our last journey?

COOK: We swore solemnly that we had reached the continent of Asia.

DIEGO: Yes, indeed, that we did.

RODRIGO: And we all signed our names to it. On a big piece of parchment!

COLUMBUS (to AMERIGO): And now you are trying to tell us that we weren't even in Asia! Don't be absurd.

AMERIGO: Admiral, what kind of people are these! Just a bunch of jailbirds!

COLUMBUS: And I?

AMERIGO: That was a regrettable misunderstanding.

COLUMBUS: I wasn't aware of that while I was in prison. I was treated like the worst criminal. They brought me back to Spain in chains. I was robbed and swindled. I've nothing left. And now I'm supposed to believe it was all a mistake? No, young man, I know what's what.

MARIE: Would you like some pea soup too, Admiral?

COLUMBUS: Bring me two eggs with bread and butter.

MARIE (calls to PEPI): Two eggs for the Admiral!

PEPI (calls into the kitchen): Two eggs for the Admiral!

AMERIGO: Why don't you write your memoirs?

COLUMBUS: Memoirs? What for? I have nothing to hide.

AMERIGO: So that posterity will know how it really was.

COLUMBUS: But it wasn't like that at all! The ridiculous things I've had to live through! No one would believe me.

AMERIGO: Excuse me, Admiral, world history is not ridiculous; it is significant.

COLUMBUS: What do you know about it?

AMERIGO: I have written a book about it.

COLUMBUS: And I was there.

AMERIGO: That is not the point. We require heroes as a means of justifying ourselves.

(MARIE has put down two eggs, bread and butter.)

Besides, there are historical events that have really happened. For example, that business with you and the egg.

COLUMBUS: What business?

AMERIGO (takes an egg and crushes it upon the table so that it remains standing): The egg of Columbus!

COLUMBUS: What is that?

AMERIGO: But, Admiral, don't you remember? When the ship's mutiny broke out, someone said: We have as much chance of sighting land as we have of making an egg stand on its end. At that, you took the egg and put it on the table like that.

COLUMBUS: I'm supposed to have done that? Not a word of truth in it.

DIEGO: Such a swindle! Did we ever mutiny? There one can see how you are lying.

CABIN BOY: We were fire and flame.

PEPI: And I climbed up the mast and called out "Land."

DIEGO: Children, those were our best days!

COLUMBUS (*takes the egg, removes the shell, and eats*): Señor Amerigo, if you ever write another book, be a bit more careful. The egg of Columbus is a charming story, but, unfortunately, a fiction from A to Z. I fear it will be the same with your America.

AMERIGO: My thanks for teaching me a lesson, Admiral. One should admire great men, but one should never make their acquaintance. Farewell!

(*He departs with a deep bow. Laughter behind him. The* CABIN BOY *takes the guitar.*)

PEPI (*sings*):
Earth is dry and water is wet—

ALL:
Santa Maria!

PEPI:
Then the people come and try to say—

ALL:
Santa Maria!

PEPI:
That back there stands a continent,
But we were there and none did see.
Perhaps it just lies across the way . . .

ALL:
Santa Maria—Santa Maria—
The happy Santa Maria!

MARIE (*comes out from behind the bar with a book and goes over to* COLUMBUS): It must have been frightfully interesting among those savages, Admiral. Were they all naked?

COLUMBUS: Not completely.

MARIE: What did they wear?

COLUMBUS: Bathing trunks.

MARIE (*disillusioned*): Oh . . . ! Since you're such a famous man, Admiral . . . please, give me your autograph.

COLUMBUS: But what am I to write?

MARIE: It doesn't matter—I can't read anyway.

COLUMBUS (*writes and hands the book back to her*): Here, my child.

MARIE: Thank you very much. (*To the sailors.*) Well, children, what's going to become of the land you discovered?

DIEGO: What should become of it? There's only monkeys and parrots there.

PEPI: It'll never amount to anything. In a hundred years nobody'll be there at all.

MARIE: And what do you think, Admiral?

(COLUMBUS *rises. While he speaks, jazz music begins to make itself heard, first quietly, then stronger and stronger. The walls of the room disappear, the horizon is illuminated. As if conjured up, a vision of New York suddenly appears: Times Square with skyscrapers and fiery neon advertisements. It is as if those present were sitting not in the tavern but on Broadway.*)

COLUMBUS: One day this land will be quiet and peaceful. I see a plain and frugal people. God's Chosen will live in this new land. Even the poorest will be respected and none will go hungry and none will be oppressed. This people will open the doors of its treasure houses and distribute its gold to all other countries. A statue will stand at the ocean's edge and from out its mouth will issue the words: "Give me your tired, your poor,/Your huddled masses yearning to breathe free." This is the earthly paradise!

CURTAIN

THE CAPTAIN OF KÖPENICK

A German Fairy Tale in Three Acts

by CARL ZUCKMAYER

TRANSLATED BY CARL RICHARD MUELLER

"No," said the dwarf, "let us talk of men! Whatever has life in it is dearer to me than all the treasures of the world."

THE BROTHERS GRIMM, *Rumpelstiltskin*

CHARACTERS

WILHELM VOIGT
FRIEDRICH HOPRECHT
FRAU HOPRECHT
MAYOR OBERMÜLLER
FRAU OBERMÜLLER
ADOLF WORMSER, a uniform tailor
WILLY WORMSER, his son
WABSCHKE, a tailor's cutter
CAPTAIN VON SCHLETTOW
TWO POLICE SERGEANTS
POLICEMEN
DR. JELLINEK
SOLDIERS
GRENADIER
PAUL KALLENBERG, known as KALLE
WAITERS
POLLY
CIVILIAN
KNELL
HIRSCHBERG
OFFICE WORKERS
APPLICANTS
DELTZEIT, Schlettow's orderly
FLOPHOUSE KEEPER
ZECK
HÖLLHUBER
BUTTJE
JUPP
GEBWEILER
SERGEANT
CORPORAL
CHAPLAIN
PRISONERS
PRISON DIRECTOR
WARDEN
BULCKE
PUDRITZKI
HELMUT OBERMÜLLER
IRENE OBERMÜLLER
FANNY, the Obermüller's servant
WOMAN

MAN
YOUNG A.D.C.
READER OF Vorwärts
YOUNG LIEUTENANT
FAT MAN
SICK GIRL
AUGUSTA VICTORIA WORMSER, Wormser's daughter
CAPTAIN VON SCHLEINITZ
MAJOR KESSLER
FRAU KESSLER
DR. TRUMP, a young lawyer
KRAKAUER
FIRST YOUNG PERSON
SECOND YOUNG PERSON
COLONEL
COUNCILLOR
FIRST NURSEMAID
SECOND NURSEMAID
FIRST OFFICER
SECOND OFFICER
THIRD OFFICER
FIRST SENIOR OFFICER
SECOND SENIOR OFFICER
VETERAN
FIRST OLD LADY
SECOND OLD LADY
FIRST RAILROAD OFFICIAL
PORTER
SECOND RAILROAD OFFICIAL
COMENIUS, a Municipal Councillor
RAU, a Municipal Councillor
KILIAN, Municipal Policeman
WASHERWOMAN
KUTZMANN, Municipal Secretary
WENDROWITZ, farmer, landowner
ROSENCRANTZ, Municipal Treasurer
TWO POLICE INSPECTORS
CHARWOMAN
MILKMAN
TWO MILKMAIDS

TAXI DRIVER
NEWSBOY
POLICE COMMISSIONER

STUTZ, a prisoner
PASSPORT COMMISSIONER
CHIEF OF POLICE

SCENE

Berlin and its environs.

TIME

Before World War I.

The first act takes place around the turn of the century.

The second and third acts take place ten years later.

The actual facts involved serve merely as the occasion for the present play. Materials and individuals have been handled with complete freedom.

ACT I

SCENE 1

Army March Number Nine is heard played before the curtain rises. It comes from a military marching band. After a powerful crescendo, both the music and the measured steps of the troops coming off guard fade gradually away. Distant military music accompanies the entire scene. The curtain has meanwhile risen. The stage shows the interior of A. WORMSER's uniform shop in Potsdam. There is a counter in the foreground along with an area for tending the customers. Toward the rear are glass shop windows; through them we see the street and the queue of the squadron of guards as they march to the music. The windows are decorated with individual parts of uniforms, including helmets, caps, sabers, and patent-leather riding boots. Complete officers' uniforms are worn by wooden dummies without heads. Upstage center is a double glass door with a bell over it. The panes of glass bear in reverse order, as we see it, the name of the establishment in gold letters: "A. Wormser, by Special Appointment to His Royal Imperial Prussian Highness." On the counter are bolts of cloth, buttons for uniforms, epaulets, gloves, battlefield slings, and the like. On the wall is a portrait of the Royal Family along with autographed photos of high-ranking officers. There is also a framed honorary diploma and the acceptance of HERR WORMSER into a uniformed students' fraternity. A side door leads to WORMSER's private office. WABSCHKE, the tailor's cutter—diminutive, humpbacked—stands on a stool and helps CAPTAIN VON SCHLETTOW into the jacket of his new uniform.

SCHLETTOW: No, no, Wabschke, there's something just not right about the uniform. There's something wrong. That's the feeling I have.

WABSCHKE: Feeling, Captain, feeling! But that's the way it is. Always. Whenever I step into a new pair of pants—even tailored ones—perfect to the last button—I have that strange feeling too. Finally I realize it has nothing at all to do with feeling—it's the newness of the article.

SCHLETTOW: No, no, Wabschke, you mustn't try to deceive me. After all, I'm only a captain; I can't be ordering a new uniform every day. And being a member of a regiment, you know, costs a pretty penny too. But—when I order a new uniform, everything must be in absolutely impeccable shape. I suppose that makes me strange, does it? (*He laughs.*)

WABSCHKE (*straightening the coattails*): Ah, perfect. Fits like a glove.

SCHLETTOW: So you say!— (*Looks at himself from all angles in the mirror.*)—Well, yes, I suppose you could say it fits well in front, all right. Oh, but back here! Back here! Just look at these buttons back here! Those have certainly not been put on as I ordered.

WABSCHKE: But, Captain, sir, I assure you, it fits like a glove. If you'd been born with them there they couldn't look more perfect.

SCHLETTOW: Six and a half centimeters between the buttons! That's right, Wabschke—six and a half centimeters is regulation. These are at least eight centimeters apart—and don't contradict me—that's the feeling I have.

WABSCHKE: But, Captain, sir, no one's going to measure that close.

SCHLETTOW: That's the feeling I have. There is nothing to argue about. These buttons will be changed, Wabschke.

WABSCHKE: I'll have to rip open the whole gathering back here, and then the waistline will be all wrong.

SCHLETTOW: Wabschke, your every movement demonstrates to me you were never in the Kaiser's service. Talk back like that in the army and you'd spend your life in the stockade.

WABSCHKE: That's why I never complained about this back of mine. Being light-fingered and keeping my mouth shut— believe me, that was no sport for my father's youngest born.

SCHLETTOW: That's what you lack, Wabschke, that is what you lack! You may be a first-class tailor, but as a human being you lack polish, you lack manners, you lack deportment—in fact you lack everything that has to do with proper bearing!

WABSCHKE: Well, Captain, sir, I can stand at attention the same as anyone else, and press down my chin till it folds over my collar. (*He simulates a rigid attitude.*)

SCHLETTOW (*half-laughing, half-indignant*): Stop it, Wabschke, stop it, it's too much!

(WORMSER *enters quickly.—He is chubby, rosy, and grayish-blond, with only slightly Jewish characteristics.*)

WORMSER: What's all the racket in here?—Wabschke, stop tormenting the Captain! Good-day, Herr von Schlettow! Don't let this clown get on your nerves; he isn't normal! But a better tailor's cutter you won't find in all the rest of Germany. Wabschke, hold your tongue! I have told you time and again, the next insolent action you perform here, out you go!—Ah, you're looking splendid, Captain, sir, splendid!

(*Shaking his hands.*) That's what the army does for a man—
fresh air, Kaiser's regiment, eh? Well now, let's see here, let's
see how splendid you look!—Hm, now whatever could be
wrong, I wonder, eh? Let's see where the trouble is.—We'll
get to the bottom of this yet.—Eh?

SCHLETTOW: I just don't know, Herr Wormser, but there's something about the uniform that is just not right. It has a strange
feeling here at the back of my neck, and the buttons at the
rear are simply not sewn on according to regulations.

WORMSER (*calls*): Willy, bring me the measurement book! I shall
investigate this matter, Captain, sir, you shall be personally
convinced. The coat looks splendid on you. Willy, will you
hurry! Magnificent material, eh? What a piece of material!
The only ones to get this material from me are the gentlemen
of the Kaiser's Regiment and the Princes of the Imperial
Family. Take a look at this— (*He runs his knuckles over the
fabric.*)—glossy as a freshly waxed horse's popo—eh?

SCHLETTOW (*laughing*): Splendid, Wormser! Tremendous! Horse's
popo—! The things you think of!

(WILLY *appears with the measurement book. He is sixteen
years old, thin, pale, pimpled, and awkward. His Jewish
characteristics are more strongly marked than in his father.*)

WORMSER: Let's see, Willy, put the book down, open it up,
stop daydreaming, get a move on! Here you are, Herr von
Schlettow—here you have it before your very eyes: black on
white! Buttons for rear of coat to be set six and a half centimeters apart. Am I right, Captain, am I right, eh? What
more can you ask for?

SCHLETTOW: That's what it says, yes—but that is *not* how they
have been sewn on. Measure for yourself.

(*During the last few sentences, from about the time of*
WILLY'*s entrance, a man appears on the street in the background. He stops for a moment, then goes on. He comes back
now, slowly, goes as far as the door into the shop, and stares
through the shop window.*)

WORMSER: Wabschke, give me the measure. Willy, stand straight!
How can you stand hunched over like that! Keep that up
and you'll never get into the army. What's that man doing
there at the door? Willy, go see. Ah, so he's running off now,
eh? (*Measuring.*) Well, if I must be quite exact about it,
Captain, sir, I suppose you're right. You must be a good

shot: shoot the wings off a gnat, I'll wager, eh? The buttons are approximately half a centimeter too far apart.

SCHLETTOW: Precisely the feeling I had. I said that the moment I laid eyes on the garment. You needn't laugh, Wabschke. Obviously you think this is a trivial matter. And it *is* a trivial matter. But trivial matters are what distinguish the soldier. Absolutely everything is based upon it. Do you understand? It's exactly the same with the goose step. People are always complaining that it's annoying. But it's *not* annoying—it has a deeper significance—that's what people must come to understand. You see?

WORMSER: My words exactly, Captain, sir, my words exactly. What am I always saying? Three things they will never copy from us: good old Freddy the Great, the Categorical Imperative, and our Drill Regulations. These and other classics are our contribution to the world. Willy, take your hands out of your pockets and stand straight. Look at the Captain. There's a figure of a man for you. And how did he get that way? He stood straight.

(*The shop bell rings.*)

Well, here he is back again.

(WILHELM VOIGT *enters. He is a man of fragile build, thin and somewhat stooped, with a slight suggestion of bowed legs, a hollow face with heavy cheekbones, gray moustache, and sallow complexion. He wears an old, dark, but by no means tattered suit, a shirt without a collar, a stiff hat, thick boots, and carries a package bound with twine. He holds tightly to the doorknob and looks as though astounded into the shop.*)

WORMSER: What do you want here? Are you delivering something?

VOIGT: No. (*He closes the door and continues on.*)

SCHLETTOW: What does he want? Looks like a corpse on leave of absence.

WORMSER: I can't imagine—unless he wants to order a regimental uniform for himself.

SCHLETTOW: Excellent, Wormser! Very amusing!

WABSCHKE (*to* WORMSER): What we have to do is rip open the whole gathering back here, and then the waistline will be all wrong.

WORMSER: Now Captain, sir, just for a tiny couple of millimeters we're not going to have to cut up this beautiful piece of material, now, are we? Regulations are regulations—but for such a trivial matter I really don't think anything will happen to you.

SCHLETTOW: Oh? You think not? (*Jovially.*) Well now, and what if I should meet his Imperial Majesty walking down Under the Lindens, and His Majesty pulls out a little rule from his pocket and measures the buttons on the back of my coat— what would you have me do then, eh? (*He laughs.*)

WORMSER: What would I have you do then? I'll tell you what you'd do. He will naturally ask you where you had the coat made, and you will tell him: At Adolf Wormser's in Potsdam. "What," he'll cry, "at my dear Wormser's? I have my own work done there! Ah, well, in that case, the buttons are all right, of course, and my rule is certainly wrong! Here's a decoration for you. These plaited shoulder-pieces! And see you keep it up, Major!" (*Bubbling over.*) You see? You're bound to be promoted when you have your work done at Wormser's!!

SCHLETTOW (*with a belly laugh*): Excellent, Wormser! Tremendous! Absolutely splendid! "My dear Wormser!" Splendid!

(*Laughter. The bell at the door rings again.*)

WORMSER: There's that man again.

(*VOIGT stands in the doorway of the shop and looks interestedly at the patent-leather boots displayed in the window.*)

WORMSER (*going toward him*): What do you want here?

(*VOIGT looks at him.*)

Is there something you want? What are you looking for?

VOIGT: I only wanted to ask, sir—

WORMSER: Out! There'll be no begging in here!

(*VOIGT quickly closes the door and strolls off.*)

Can you imagine! In my shop! In broad daylight! The shamelessness of people nowadays! Impudent as—as blowflies.

SCHLETTOW: Don't excite yourself, Wormser! Why not simply reset the buttons?

WORMSER: Good as done, Herr von Schlettow, good as done. If that's what you want—that is what will be done. Willy, help the Captain on with his coat. On Monday morning you will have your new uniform—with buttons strictly according to regulations. Satisfied?

SCHLETTOW: Thank you, Herr Wormser!—Many thanks, Herr Wormser! When I have a new uniform made, absolutely everything must be in impeccable shape. I take great satisfaction in such matters, you understand.

BLACKOUT

Scene 2

A police station in Potsdam. The windows are closed, the air musty; a great deal of paper lies about; there is a cabinet for public documents and a fireproof safe. A picture of the Kaiser hangs on the wall, along with boards to which ordinances and decrees are affixed. Sabers worn by rural policemen hang on clothes hooks. Also hanging there are spiked helmets. The POLICE SERGEANT and the POLICEMAN sit opposite one another at office tables. WILHELM VOIGT, with hat in hand and carrying a package, stands near the POLICE SERGEANT seated behind a low wooden partition. The POLICE SERGEANT writes with a pen that scratches; the POLICEMAN sticks labels on watermarked paper. In the distance we hear the chimes on the Potsdam Garrison Church.

SERGEANT (*pulls out his pocket watch and says in a supervisory tone*): Twelve o'clock. (*He relieves himself of his official capacity, closing the folder of documents with a clap.*)
VOIGT: Begging your pardon, sir, I only wanted to ask, sir—
SERGEANT: In the first place we are closed between the hours of twelve and two P.M. You could have read as much on the door outside. In the second place I am not "sir," but a Police Sergeant and the District Supervisor. You might have told that by my buttons and my sword knot.
VOIGT: Begging your pardon, Herr Commissioner, sir, I've been waiting ever since eleven-thirty—
SERGEANT: And in the third place you will execute one-half step to the rear. Trespassers in public offices are required by law to maintain that amount of distance from those administrative authorities on duty so as to be unable to discern with the naked and unaided eye such inscriptions as may be affixed to folders containing public documents. Why, anyone at all could come and gawk over our shoulders. Do you mean to say you have never heard of: Official Secrets?!
VOIGT: Begging your pardon, Herr Police Commissioner, sir, but

I'm nearsighted. I always need my spectacles to read with. And when it comes to official secrets, I wouldn't want to incriminate myself, so I always look away. But all I wanted was to ask you politely when I could get the residence permit that I applied for. I've been waiting now for—

SERGEANT: Name?

VOIGT: Voigt, Wilhelm.

SERGEANT: Schlickmann, hurry, get me Personal File U–Z. Age?

VOIGT: Forty-six.

SERGEANT: Profession?

VOIGT: Shoemaker.

SERGEANT: Born in . . . ?

VOIGT: Klein-Pinchow.

SERGEANT: Where's that?

VOIGT: Oh, around back there, near Wuhlheide.

SERGEANT: Where are you living now?

VOIGT: No place.

SERGEANT: How's that? You must be able to declare some address.

VOIGT: No, I'm afraid not.

SERGEANT: Well then, where are you registered?

VOIGT: Like I said, no place. The truth is I'm on parole, you see. That's why I'm here—I *want* to register. But before I can do that I need a residence permit.

SERGEANT: Where were you last registered?

VOIGT: Well, like I said, no place. I just got out of the penitentiary at Plötzensee.

SERGEANT (*has found his place in the documents*): Aha! Previous conviction. For the same crime no less. So, you're a heavy con man, eh?

VOIGT: I don't know, Herr Commissioner, sir. You see, I get lighter all the time. Especially since I got out of Plötzensee. All I've got left in my bones is air.

SERGEANT: Stop your blabbering. A bit light-headed too, eh? What do you want here in Potsdam?

VOIGT: Find work.

SERGEANT: That's easy enough to say. Why didn't you work before they sent you to prison? Fifteen years in the penitentiary for falsification of postal documents!

VOIGT: That was a long time ago, Herr Commissioner, sir.

SERGEANT: All the worse, all the worse. And at eighteen, too! Why did you ever get mixed up in such things?

VOIGT: I was just a young puppy then, Herr Commissioner, sir. And altogether it was only three hundred marks.

SERGEANT: That is no excuse.

VOIGT: I'm not trying to excuse myself, Herr Commissioner, sir, but that's the way it was. I was going with a young girl then; she worked in a hotel kitchen. And because of her I just didn't know what I was doing. But I could never spend any money on her, you see, because those who *could,* well, just took her away from me.

SERGEANT: And so you just went in, and you just fraudulently plundered the Imperial Postal Department.

VOIGT: I never thought a big organization like that would ever suffer any from it. But then they arrested me and gave me fifteen years right off. I think that's an awful lot for just a young one like I was.

SERGEANT: That is not for you to decide. The degree of penalty is always in exact accordance with the gravity of the offense.

VOIGT: It doesn't matter, I guess. It's all past now.

SERGEANT: Such things are never past. I'd remember that if I were you. Whatever is recorded here in your personal file is as much a part of you as the nose on your face. Once you have trod that downward path—

VOIGT: That's right.

SERGEANT: What do you mean, "that's right"? *What's* right?

VOIGT: That business about the downward path. You're absolutely right. It's the same as when you put a louse on a pane of glass. It'll crawl and crawl, but always slip back down again.

SERGEANT: Don't try to make excuses. (*Reads in the file.*) After you served your term you left the country.

VOIGT: Yes. I went to Bohemia and then to Bucharest.

SERGEANT: What did you do there?

VOIGT: Worked.

SERGEANT: I see. Who for?

VOIGT: The Wonkrowitz shoe factory. They were Jews.

SERGEANT: Aha! (*Notes something down.*) And why did you come back?

VOIGT: That's hard to say, Herr Commissioner, sir. I made a real good place there for myself.

SERGEANT: Then why didn't you stay there with your Jews?

VOIGT: Because I—I wanted so much just to come home again. It was stupid. The Jews took real good care of me.

SERGEANT: You still have a family in Germany?

VOIGT: No—well, yes, I guess maybe I still do have *some;* a sister, I mean—she's married. But with my record, you see, I wouldn't trust myself to go see them.

SERGEANT: Then why did you ever come back to Germany?

VOIGT: I said it was stupid. But I was homesick. They're different down there, and they all talk different too. But then, finally, everybody has his own language, and even when he has nothing, he's still got that left. You'd never believe what a beautiful place Germany is when you're far away and only think about it. But like I said, it was stupid.

SERGEANT (*reading the file without listening to him*): And then there was another sentence—fifteen months imprisonment for lapse of registration, for lapse of passport, for deceiving the administrative authorities, and for attempted falsification of documents.

VOIGT: All I wanted was to tear the nose off my face.

SERGEANT: What's that?! What's that?!

VOIGT: I mean, what you said before, about a man's record: that you carry it around with you like the nose on your face. As Wilhelm Voigt I couldn't have gotten anywhere. So I said to myself: Enough of this Wilhelm Voigt character; you start all over again from the beginning as Friedrich Müller. Now that wasn't so terrible, was it?

SERGEANT: Nonsense. You see what came of it, don't you?

VOIGT: I just didn't know what to do.

SERGEANT: Let's hope you know what to do *this* time: what the law is, what an offense is, *and* what prison is. You've certainly studied it long enough.

VOIGT: That's for sure. But that's why I need my residence permit now. I'm no good without it. I'd like to work here in the shoe factory, with military boots—you see, knee boots are my specialty—and in prison they taught me how to use machines, too.

SERGEANT: Have you looked for work?

VOIGT: Every day since I got out. I've run holes in my shoes already. The director at the prison gave me a recommendation —(*He rummages through his pockets.*)—but I can't find it to show people. Every place I go they want to see my registration papers, and when I go into the better shops, they think I've come to beg, and run me off.

SERGEANT (*has scarcely listened to him; puts the documents in order*): Come back when you've found work and we'll see what can be done.

VOIGT: But I can't get work until I register. I have to have a registration permit first—

SERGEANT: Then I suggest you forget it. We don't hand out residence permits to jobless criminals. I suggest you forget about working and get on as best you can.

VOIGT: But I *have* to work. How can I live?

SERGEANT: That's your concern. See you become a decent human being. If a person wants work, he'll find work.

VOIGT (*shakes his head*): No, no, that's like a merry-go-round, like —If I'm not registered, I get no work, and if I get no work I can't register. No, no, I'd rather go back again. No, give me a passport with a border visa so I can go back.

SERGEANT: We are not authorized for such things.

VOIGT: You've got the history of my life there in your hands, and if you don't want me here, send me somewhere else to get a passport.

SERGEANT: I told you we are not authorized for such things. If you want a passport, you'll have to go to the authorities where you were born.

VOIGT: I was just there. But they didn't even listen to me. "You've been scratched from our records," they said. "We no longer recognize you here; you were crossed off our records twenty years ago. Go someplace else," they said, "we're ashamed of you here." All right, I said, I'm not asking you to put up a monument to me, all I want is what I've got coming. They ran me out. No, no, I won't go back there anymore.

SERGEANT: Now look here, you, just don't lose your temper!

VOIGT: I'm not losing my temper! All I want is my papers! A piece of paper's worth more now than a man himself! I need that paper worse than food!

SERGEANT (*buckles on his sword; puts on his helmet*): That will do.

VOIGT: No, no, look, I haven't lost my temper at all. But there must be *some* place a man belongs. If I can't register, and I can't stay here, then at least I want a passport so I can get out. I can't just dangle my feet in the air. Only a hanged man can do that.

SERGEANT: Your application for a residence permit will be passed on.

VOIGT: I'd rather you give me a passport. I want out. I just want to get out again, and I promise you I won't be back soon either, you can bet your life on that! I know now—I burned my fingers bad enough to remember for the rest of my life!

SERGEANT: Can't you understand there's nothing we can do for you here? Your passport is out of the question in this office, remember that, it is absolutely impossible. I shall see that your application for a residence permit is passed on, but I cannot recommend it in any way, because your life's history is entirely too questionable. We have quite enough undesirable elements in this city as is. Now that's the end of that.

VOIGT: I want to suggest something to you—I want to suggest you let them ship me back at once, *and in a hurry,* to the prison at Plötzensee!

SERGEANT: Out! He's getting impudent too now! Get the hell out of here!!

VOIGT: Don't worry, I'm going.—Enjoy your lunch. (*He goes off.*)

SERGEANT: Stupid fool. Stole fifteen minutes of my lunch time. And then insults me on top of it. I wouldn't trust him farther than I can see.

POLICEMAN: Me either, Herr Commissioner, sir.

SERGEANT: I'm off to lunch now. I'll relieve you at half-past one. Good day, Schlickmann.

BLACKOUT

SCENE 3

The Café National on Friedrichstrasse. Sunday morning. Only a few guests. No music. At the rear a sign is hung over a curtained doorway: "To the Bonne Queue Billiard Club. Private." From behind the curtain we hear the clicking of billiard balls, and the occasional muffled cries of the players. Several ample ladies, despite the early hour, sit at marble tables with bored and wooden faces, like soldiers determined to maintain a ready battle position come what will. The WAITERS *lounge around the buffet. Downstage right sit* WILHELM VOIGT *and* PAUL KALLENBERG, *known as* KALLE. *His face is small and wizened, though he is considerably younger than* VOIGT. *His eyes are inflamed, and his face seems to have nurtured a pallor inside a prison. He wears a collar and a gaudy tie.*

KALLE: Where did you sleep last night?

VOIGT: At Wannsee Station—and later on a bench in the park. But when it got cold I rode to the Zoo Station and sat in the waiting room.

KALLE: Well, I slept in a bed. Was that ever good!

VOIGT: Where? How did you manage that?

KALLE: I visited my old friend Schmidt—you know, the preacher at Moabit Prison; the one with the popeyes we always called Scrambled Eggs. He gave us his address once so we could send him a picture postcard how we're getting on in our new life and bettering ourselves. So round about eight o'clock I rang his door bell—the maid answered—I stuck my foot in the door and there I was: inside! And there *they* were, sitting around the table, lapping up bowls of red soup. So what do *I* do? I lean on the wall, cover my face with my hands, and cry till the tears run down through the stubble of my unshaved face. I really do that up good with my runny old goggle-eyes. "What a beautiful picture of family life," I blubbered. "Blessed are they who can live such a life!" And so right off he gives me a bowl of soup and then the end of a sausage and a couple mealy potatoes; and finally I get put in his son's bed, and the son has to spend the night on the sofa. "Joachim," he says to his son, "this is an exercise in Christian charity for you." What a draggle-tail!

VOIGT: What happened then?

KALLE: Well, I got some coffee this morning, except all it tasted like was chicory, and a stale roll that must have been from last Wednesday. And then he sent me off to the Cathedral with his family, because it's Sunday. Talk about embarrassed! There I was, walking down Under the Lindens with some crazy preacher's wife and a snot-nosed little brat on each side of her! So when we got to the arcade I made a quick turn and hightailed it into the bushes.

VOIGT: You sure are a card, Kalle.

KALLE: Damn right! But that's what you have to be these days, or you'll die on your feet, drop dead of starvation in front of a delicatessen shop.

WAITER (*comes over, distrustfully sizing up the two of them*): If you're going to sit at a table you'll have to order something.

VOIGT: Smart man. Why else would we be sitting here?

KALLE: To judge the beauty contest maybe. Ah, but no. A man can't live on the enjoyment of art alone. Two cognacs.

VOIGT: Not for me. I'll just have a hot coffee.

KALLE: Two cognacs. Wilhelm, you're my guest. But you can buy your hot coffee yourself if you want to.

(*The* WAITER *goes.*)

VOIGT: Do you have money?

KALLE (*takes a few small coins from his pocket*): The last of the Mohicans.

VOIGT: And when they're gone?

KALLE: I can always sell my suit. It's still in style.

VOIGT: No, listen, don't do a thing like that. The least a man can

do is keep his shell. Believe me, your shell is all you've got.
Once you start running around looking like me—well, there's
not much farther you can sink.

KALLE: Go on, what are you talking about—you're still a fine
young fellow.

VOIGT: You know, in Potsdam I came on one of those funny junk
shops—and, you know, I think you could almost buy yourself
a coat in that place worn by the Kaiser himself; blue patches
in front and all.

KALLE: What are you talking about?

VOIGT: A uniform shop. I saw some high patent-leather boots in
the window, so I went in to ask for work. Oh, and listen, they
had everything there, everything you could imagine, just hanging around empty like skins in a tanner's shop. Just imagine
how surprised I was.

KALLE: You never saw a uniform shop before?

VOIGT: No—well, I mean I did when I was living with the Polacks,
but never here. And I always thought, well, you get your
Kaiser's coat from the quartermaster store when you're a
recruit, and an officer gets his from the Kaiser himself.

KALLE: I always thought you came from Berlin.

VOIGT: I do. Now, of course, most Berliners come from Posen.
And I happen to come from Wuhlheide.

KALLE: You sure don't seem to know your way around Berlin.

VOIGT: Every time I came here they'd lock me up, just like that
—so I don't feel at home here too much.

KALLE: Let's go to the Café Dalles tonight. We'll find us a boss
who needs two youngsters, even if it's only standing lookout.

VOIGT: Not me. I had my fill of that. That's the fastest way I
know to get thrown back in. I'll get a job in some industry.

KALLE: What are you talking about?

VOIGT: Work.

KALLE: Brrrr!

VOIGT: There's a lot of money to be made that way.—I'm a trained
worker.

KALLE: That's right—and they're waiting for you with open arms.

VOIGT: When it comes to independent master craftsmen, of
course, well, they're sure not to take our kind, and quite right,
too. As long as they can get young apprentices, what do they
want with a bag of old bones like us? But in industry—they're
always needing human fodder for their machines.

KALLE: I don't understand such things. I'm going to pull off a job
so big I can afford to rest up for a couple years.

VOIGT: It won't work, Kalle. If you want to pull off a job, a really big job, like you say—then you've got to have a head on your shoulders; and that you haven't got. You have to know exactly what you're doing, don't you see? Now I had an idea once . . . (*He fades off, smiling.*)

KALLE: What was your idea?

(VOIGT *does not answer; he rocks his head, smiling.*)

I bet you never even had one.

(*The* WAITER *comes, puts the tray with the two cognacs and the coffee on the table, and goes off.*)

VOIGT (*shaking his head*): No, no,—I'll try to get another job in a shoe factory.

KALLE: Well—prosit! (*He pushes a cognac toward him.*)

VOIGT (*taking his coffee*): I can't take that on an empty stomach. Besides, I'm not used to alcohol.

KALLE: Me either, but I'm sure *getting* used to it. (*He downs one of the cognacs with a tilting motion, then fishes a half-smoked cigarette from his pocket, straightens it out, and lights it.*)

(VOIGT *slowly slurps his coffee. Both of them are silent.* CAPTAIN VON SCHLETTOW, *in civilian dress, appears at the rear, entering through the curtained doorway that leads into the billiard room. He still holds the billiard cue in his hand and finally gives it to the boy waiter who hurries after him. It is obvious he is not accustomed to wearing civilian clothes. The collar is too high and appears to be choking him.* DR. JELLINEK, *a young medical assistant and also one of the billiard players, appears at the same time.*)

SCHLETTOW: Come, Jellinek, let's have a schnapps. An opponent like you doesn't come along every day.

JELLINEK: No disgrace being beaten by a man of your sort. No, my dear Captain, I'm afraid I'm not much of a match for you. Not by a long shot.

SCHLETTOW (*radiant*): Not bad, eh? How'd you like that double carambole, and then the rearward action to the left? Never thought I'd be able to bring it off.

JELLINEK: No man alive could beat that. Good morning, Dolly. Good morning, Olympia. (*Nodding, he greets some of the ladies.*) There's a table by itself, Captain.

SCHLETTOW: I think I'll have a bite to eat. I'm hungry again. The fact is, I can eat all day long.

JELLINEK: Don't worry, you're the picture of health. More people like you, and we doctors would have to close up shop. Your cheeks are red as apples, your eyes sparkle like sunflowers, and your walk is crisp as a well-baked roll. If I were a woman, you know, I'd do anything to have a child by you.

SCHLETTOW: Delightful, my dear Doctor! You are really delightful! (*They seat themselves downstage left. A* WAITER *has followed them over.*) What'll we have?

JELLINEK: I'll have a double kümmel.

SCHLETTOW: And give me cognac with soda and two eggs in a glass.

(*The* WAITER *goes.*)

(*Calls after him.*) And a few salt sticks with butter, and a small plate of ham!

WAITER (*over his shoulder*): Raw or cooked?

SCHLETTOW: Cooked, but not too fat.

JELLINEK: Not as fat as the Jews eat it, eh?

SCHLETTOW: Delightful! You're a real card! (*Looks around.*) This is certainly a wretched place, I must say. More like a train station. But tell me, are you acquainted with all these ladies personally?

JELLINEK: Let's say I know most of them professionally. I'm an assistant in the women's ward at the hospital. Yes, indeed, we do learn our share of facts there.

SCHLETTOW (*thoughtfully*): As a doctor, of course, you have a much easier way of getting to know—the opposite sex.

JELLINEK: Listen to him! An officer like you can outdo us any day of the week. You're a nobleman, in the Guards—what more do you want?

SCHLETTOW: Well, yes, in uniform we have no trouble at all. It helps us cut a figure, as it were, gives one a solid footing, you might say. Makes a different man of you. Ah, but in these civilian clothes I feel like a fish out of water.

(JELLINEK *laughs.*)

But in a place like this, one has no choice. If the best billiard players in Berlin didn't gather here—well, I assure you I'd never set foot in the place.

JELLINEK: It's really quite harmless. After all, it is not a den of thieves.

SCHLETTOW: Ah, but for the military it's off limits. You must bear in mind that our kind—well, after all, we've been a family of officers since the Seven Years' War; except for grandfather, of course, who was only a common soldier without a "von" in front of his name—and the moment you have a title in front of your name you have to be careful. Being an officer is to be a continual public responsibility; that's what my old father used to preach to me—and *he* made Commanding General. A soldier's jacket must have not so much as a speck of dust to sully it—that is the task I have set myself in this life.

JELLINEK: Yes, of course, I can understand that. I'd like to be on the active list, too, instead of opening up people's stomachs.

(*The* WAITER *comes with the drinks.*)

SCHLETTOW (*absorbed in his own thoughts*): By the way, I've just had a new uniform made at Wormser's. It has a shine on it like the neck of a well-groomed black charger.

JELLINEK (*raising his glass*): To your health!

SCHLETTOW: To your health! The best of luck! And three cheers to top it off!

(*The* WAITER *has meanwhile poured the soda water, and now goes off.*)

Where are the eggs?

WAITER: Right away, sir. They're being cooked.

SCHLETTOW: I hope they've at least been laid.

(*Another lady enters and walks slowly through the café. She is blonde, amply proportioned, still quite young. Her dress is of poplin, and no longer new. Swinging her handbag, she goes toward an empty table and sits down. Smiles of recognition are exchanged between her and* JELLINEK.)

(*Slightly disgusted.*) You mean to say you know that one too?

JELLINEK: Her? That's Polly. She's the hottest piece around. Quite an original, that girl. Did I ever tell you how she first—come closer, I shouldn't say this out loud—

(SCHLETTOW *leans forward toward* JELLINEK *who whispers.*)

KALLE: Well, Willy, what are you thinking about now?

VOIGT: Me? Oh, I'm not thinking. I was just dozing. You know, whenever I stir my spoon around in my coffee cup I always think of an old aunt of mine. "My goodness, Wilhelm," she'd always say when I brought my coffee cup to her with the grounds still in the bottom—"you're going to be something so big one of these days you won't recognize yourself anymore."

KALLE: Looks like you're just about there.

VOIGT (*enigmatically*): There's something to that. Yes. Yes. And
then all that about the stars—there's something in that, too.
Do you think because they're so far away they have nothing
to do with us? Well, then, you don't know, you just don't
know.

KALLE: Willy, I was just wondering about something else.

VOIGT: What?

KALLE: People like us, who've been in jail for so long, have to
build themselves up first. Otherwise they'll never amount to
anything, ever again.

VOIGT: How do you mean?

KALLE: Just what I said. A man who's been in prison all that time
has to lift himself up. The main thing is, a man should be
able to rise up again. Take a good look around. (*He points at
the ladies seated about.*) Look at them! Just look at them
all. What's the matter, somebody turn your blood off?

VOIGT: Well, yes, that's true enough. And a man *would* like to be
a man again, now and then. But—but you don't get things
like that for nothing.

KALLE: It'd be cheaper if we went together. How much have you
got left?

VOIGT: Two marks fifty and a couple of pennies.

KALLE: Let's see. We'll count it up.

(*They bend over the table and count their coins. In the
meanwhile,* POLLY *has sauntered over to the table where*
SCHLETTOW *and* JELLINEK *are seated. At the same time the*
WAITER *brings* SCHLETTOW's *food: two eggs in a glass, ham,
butter, and rolls.*)

POLLY (*swaying a bit*): Hi!

JELLINEK: Well, if it isn't Polly! How's everything?

POLLY: How do you think? Nights are pretty damn dark without
oil in the lamps.

SCHLETTOW (*playing with the saltcellar, obviously displeased*): It
can't be as bad as all that.

POLLY: You don't mind my sitting down here, I'm sure.

SCHLETTOW: You will kindly do us the favor of not. We're having
a conversation. If you'd like a whiskey, I'll have one sent over
to you.

POLLY (*with quiet composure*): Thanks, mister, but why not just
keep it. Eat your eggs before they get cold. I'll bet you spend
Sunday evenings with your old grandmother. (*She goes on.*)

SCHLETTOW (*to* JELLINEK): Disgusting woman! I find such things
absolutely embarrassing. You know, Doctor—I simply cannot

endure vulgarity under any guise. (*Eating.*) And there's no sense in marriage either. Whatever nice girls there may be, have no money.

JELLINEK (*laughing*): Well, I rather think there's an intermediate stage, somewhere between Polly and a countess with an inheritance—eh?

SCHLETTOW: Of course, of course—when you think about it, Berlin is quite large. But it's in a city this size that one is so often alone.

JELLINEK: Surely there's no place closed to a man like you. Don't you often go out in society?

SCHLETTOW: Generally only to official functions. Regimental balls and such. You know—I'm not at all a frivolous person. I take all this frightfully seriously.

JELLINEK (*smoking, disinterested*): Yes. We Germans tend to weight everything down so.

SCHLETTOW: Exactly. I am thoroughly convinced this is a result of our education. Even in the Cadet Corps I used to think deeply about matters. But the rock-bottom fact is, a man still has his job to tend to. Correct? That is far and away the most important thing.—Am I right?—It brings a man back to reality. (*Quite refreshed now.*) Oh, I can assure you, when in the morning a man mounts his old nag and rides out to the rifle range, and then gallops across the country, gives a few commands, and sees a company developing with absolute precision, like clockwork—and then when you come to know every single man in your entire company, why—

JELLINEK: Yes, of course, one's profession is the main thing. Whenever we doctors get a really good case of abdominal pregnancy, or a twenty-pound tumor, or a nice clean Cesarean —well, it makes another man of you, you go around beaming like the sun had got under your skin.

SCHLETTOW: Not for me, Doctor, not for me. I'll take ten hours of rifle drill any day.

(JELLINEK *laughs.*)

I can assure you of one thing—if it weren't for the army, I simply could not . . .

JELLINEK (*bored*): Smoke?

SCHLETTOW: Yes, thank you. (*He helps himself.*)

(*They both puff away in silence, with nothing further to say to one another.* POLLY *has meanwhile gone on and finally ends up in the vicinity of the table occupied by* VOIGT *and*

KALLENBERG. *They follow her with their eyes, look at each other, hesitate a moment, then call.*)

KALLE: Uh, you there, Miss, come over here a minute.

(POLLY *looks at him over her shoulder, smiles.*)

(*With great delight.*) She's the real thing, all right. I knew right off she was the real thing. No, no, don't run off, sit down. Where were you going?

POLLY: Where? The toilet.

KALLE: Can't it wait?

POLLY: Sure, no rush. (*She approaches the table.*)

KALLE: You see? You see? What did I tell you?

(VOIGT *puts on his steel-rimmed spectacles.*)

POLLY: Hey, old boy, looking for something? Don't you like me?

(VOIGT *grins—and with a graciously inviting gesture of his hand pushes toward her his glass of cognac from which he has merely sipped.*)

Thanks, old boy. (*She sits down and drinks.*) Here's to you!

KALLE: Quite a conquest you've made there, Willy!—Hold onto it while it's warm! I said to myself, the first thing I saw you: Now, there's a piece won't turn down a good solid dollar.

POLLY: Well, let's not spread rumors like that, my little man. Nobody paws me for less than five marks a head.

KALLE: Isn't that a little greedy?

POLLY: What do you want to do, bargain? And on a Sunday morning, too, when every honorable person's either in church or listening to the military band in the park! Aren't you ashamed! You think you can mount me like some two-bit old nag?

VOIGT: See there, Kalle?

KALLE: Shut up. Keep out of what you don't understand!—You see, Miss, we're two down-and-out innocent lilies of the field who just got out of the jug after all those years with nothing but bread and water for company; and now we don't have a soul to take care of us or a pillow to lay our heads on—and so you see, Miss, well, I can see you're a kindhearted person, so why not take pity on two unhappy outcasts of human society.

POLLY: Cut the sob story.

KALLE: Where would you find a gentleman with money on a Sunday morning?

POLLY: If I go along with anybody it'll be old grandpa here. He's not at all like you; he's a gentleman, and with fine spectacles like that the two of us could talk real educated—right, Gramps?

(VOIGT *smiles in a friendly manner, but shakes his head thoughtfully.* KALLE *makes a sign for him to say something.*)

What's the matter, Gramps? Swallow the birdy?

VOIGT: Excuse me, Miss—but all I've got is two marks fifty, and I need a couple groschen of that for a flophouse and the streetcar.

KALLE: Streetcar! Once you leave her, you won't need a streetcar! But I'll tell you what we'll do. We'll take his two fifty, and I'll add another five groschen just to show I'm no skinflint— and then the three of us'll go off with a nice Prussian dollar.

POLLY: Go to hell! I'll go with old Gramps here if I go at all. (*She strokes* VOIGT's *hand.*)

(*He grins. At the same time a considerable commotion is heard from the front of the café. We hear the voice of a drunken* SOLDIER *singing the "Song of the Reservists."*)

KALLE: No, Wilhelm, no, you can't do that, it's against our agreement. You can't do that, Wilhelm, not if you've still got a spark of honor left in you.

VOIGT: (*thoughtfully*): No, no, Kalle, I'm not going with her. (*To* POLLY.) I just couldn't do it.

POLLY: My, my, aren't we an honorable little sweetie!

(*A quite drunken* GRENADIER *appears making his way through the revolving door. Directly behind him is a somewhat soiled* CIVILIAN.)

GRENADIER (*singing roughly*):
    "—and it will not last much longer,
    And we will have our rest!"

CIVILIAN: Augustus, Augustus, no! Come to your senses! Don't forget you're still a soldier!

GRENADIER: So what the hell do I care! Tomorrow my two years are up! But today's today! Waiter! Two beers and two double whiskies!

SCHLETTOW: This is unheard of! What does he think he's doing? Besides, this café is off limits. A man from the Third Guard Regiment—an old soldier with a marksman's medal!

JELLINEK: Be reasonable, Schlettow, don't get mixed up in this. You're here as a civilian, remember.

SCHLETTOW: Stand by and endure such a thing?! Never! Never!

JELLINEK: Waiter, the check!

(*But the* WAITER *does not come.*)

POLLY: Sorry, honey, you're worn out.—And besides, I need more than a dollar. I'll take my chances with the grenadiers. (*She rises and goes over to the* GRENADIER's *table.*)

GRENADIER: Hey there, you little bitch, come here!—(*Strikes himself on the chest.*)—This is where the money is! Over here! No, not on the chair, you stupid bitch! Here!—(*Strikes his lap.*)—On the prettiest pair of pointed knees you ever felt! (*He pulls her on to his lap.*)

CIVILIAN: Augustus! You're still in the army!

GRENADIER: Go to hell! I don't give a damn!

POLLY: Man, are you bombed!

GRENADIER: Damn right, baby! So what? Here today, gone tomorrow, like they always say! (*He takes hold of her, and she lets out a scream.*)

(SCHLETTOW *roots around nervously on his seat.*)

JELLINEK (*putting a hand on* SCHLETTOW's *arm*): Waiter, the check!

WAITER (*without coming*): Right away.

VOIGT: You see, Kalle, that's the way it always goes. Let somebody with a bright coat and shiny buttons come along, and we wouldn't stand a chance with ten whole marks.

KALLE: That's right. And we'd be laughed at. And wouldn't that be a nice kettle of fish. Well, we'll just see about that.

VOIGT: There's nothing to see, Kalle. A man gets treated like the way he looks.

KALLE: You, maybe, but not me. I won't stand for it! I won't! (*Hysterically.*) We'll see about that! We'll just see about that!

GRENADIER (*rocks* POLLY *up and down on his knees; sings roughly*):
"Can you really think, my dear,
My little Berlin whore,
That just because I dance with you
That I must love you more?"

KALLE (*goes to the* GRENADIER's *table*): Sir, you will take your hands off that woman—she is my intended!

POLLY: What's the matter, buddy, you got a screw loose, uh? Soft in the head?

KALLE (*shouting at the* GRENADIER): Listen, you goddamn beer-guzzler, you saw this lady sitting at our table!

GRENADIER: What the hell does *he* want? How about a taste of my fist, uh?

POLLY: Ah, let him alone, he had beans for breakfast.

KALLE (*making a fist*): You—I'll smack a five mark piece into your face; it'll take you a month to cash it!

GRENADIER: Same to you! (*He reaches past* POLLY *and gives* KALLE *a sturdy slap on the ears.*)

KALLE: You'll pay for that, you, you'll pay for that! (*He grabs hold of a full mug of beer and throws its contents over the* GRENADIER.)

GRENADIER (*drenched, jumps up in a mad rage and draws his side-arm*): I'll kill you for that! I'll kill you!

KALLE (*retreating*): What's that? Your cheese knife? Put it back, you fool, it's not even sharp!

SCHLETTOW (*jumps up*): This is going too far! I won't endure any more of this! (*Stomping up to the* GRENADIER.) Have you lost your mind? I'll have you arrested! Pull yourself together, man! You're a soldier! Put up your weapon!

GRENADIER (*sheathes his sidearm*): Damn right! I *am* a soldier! So who do you think *you're* spitting orders at?!

SCHLETTOW (*sharply, without shouting*): You will do as I say! I am a Captain in the First Guard Regiment!

GRENADIER: That's easy enough to say. You're just a stinking civilian to me!

SCHLETTOW: You will leave this establishmen at once! You will follow me to the nearest police station! Now stand at attention!

GRENADIER: —A stinking civilian! Change your clothes before you give *me* orders, but not like this, sonny, not like this.

CIVILIAN: For God's sake, don't get into trouble! Don't get into trouble!

SCHLETTOW: You will do as I say! Or I shall call the police! Forward! March! (*He grasps hold of the* GRENADIER.)

GRENADIER: Get your dirty paws off me! Nobody touches *me!* (*He lands* SCHLETTOW *a blow directly on the face.*)

SCHLETTOW (*roaring*): What the hell? You goddamned—(*He grabs hold of the* GRENADIER, *they fight, the table is over-turned, women scream—tumult.*)

POLLY (*at the entrance*): Police! Police!

PASSERSBY (*enter from outside*): What's going on here? Look, they're fighting! Go on! Punch him one! Punch him one!

POLICEMAN (*wearing a spiked helmet, pushes the people apart*): Oh, is that so! Come on! Here! Come on! Let the soldier go!

(*He goes after* SCHLETTOW *and the* GRENADIER *and separates them.*)

SCHLETTOW (*bleeding, his collar torn away*): Arrest this man at once! Take him to the police station!

POLICEMAN (*takes hold of* SCHLETTOW *with the police-hold*): That's enough! Both of you, come with me!

SCHLETTOW: What are you talking about!? That man laid hands on me! I merely took him to account! I'm a Captain in the First Guard Regiment!

GRENADIER: That's easy enough to say! Out of uniform you're a stinking civilian!

POLICEMAN: Out you go! Both of you!

GRENADIER: Hell, anybody can try a thing like that. He's a stinking civilian.

PASSERSBY: That's right. Don't let him put anything over on you. That's why you're a soldier.

POLLY: He says he's a captain, but he's no captain. I know.

VOICES: The nerve of the man! Molesting a grenadier! Hit him on the head!

POLICEMAN: Go on! Make room there!—You're both coming with me!

JELLINEK (*who has remained at his table all the while, frightened, to the* POLICEMAN): Leave him alone, he *is* a captain, I can vouch for him.

POLICEMAN (*stubbornly*): So what! They were both fighting, so they'll both come along.

(SCHLETTOW, *utterly broken, is led off with the* GRENADIER.)

JELLINEK: Well, he brought it on himself. (*He goes off into the billiard room.*)

KALLE (*at the table again, with* VOIGT, *holding his cheek*): Oh, oh! It hurts! It hurts! Oh!

VOIGT: You see, Kalle? It's like I always said: a man gets treated like the way he looks.

KALLE: Oh, oh! (*He cries.*)

BLACKOUT

SCENE 4

The personnel office of the "Axolotl" wholesale shoe factory. Placard advertisements of the firm's reptile symbol appear on the wall in a great number of variations: "Wear Axolotls"—"Axolotl's Oxfords Are the Very Best! Only M. 12.50 a Pair!"—"Axolotl Top Boots, the Choicest Top Boot for City Wear!"—"First in the Field, Axolotl Won't Yield!"—"Testimonials from Leading Scientists Are Proof Positive that Axolotl Has Restored the Natural Shape of the Foot!"—"Comfortable, Inexpensive, Durable!"—etc. At the rear are glass doors; rows of typists seated at long office tables. The sound of typewriters is heard. Downstage are KNELL, *the factory manager, and* HIRSCHBERG, *opposite each other at a desk behind a wooden partition very much like that in a police station.* KNELL *is signing work contracts. Behind him stands a young lady who hands him papers, which she extracts from folders and which she retrieves after he has signed them.* HIRSCHBERG *is seated and is figuring wage lists.* KNELL, *while writing and blotting away, sings in a monotone, all the while maintaining an unchanging expression.*

KNELL:
    "When my wife undresses,
    Her legs are two fat messes,
    You should see the sight,
    They really are a fright."

(*An* OFFICE WORKER *enters, stops, and brings his hand to his cap.*)

    "When my wife undresses,
    Her legs are two fat messes,
    You should see the sight,
    They really are a fright."

(*He continues to sign his name without looking up. The* OFFICE WORKER *stands there at attention.*)

    "When my wife undresses . . ."

(*He finishes the last signature, slaps the folder shut.*) There. That's that.—Hirschberg, make a note for the wage list: twenty-five skilled laborers, twelve girls for the button division, ten young boy machine apprentices, and fifteen newly-hired packers. They'll begin work tomorrow morning.

(*The* GIRL *with the folder goes out.*)

(*To the* OFFICE WORKER.) Well, Krause, what is it?
OFFICE WORKER: There are twenty-five applicants outside about the ad for the new factory in Tempelhof.

KNELL: Skilled laborers?

OFFICE WORKER: Most of them, sir.

KNELL: I can still use another dozen. Let them in one at a time—but hurry.

(*The* OFFICE WORKER *goes out.*)

"When my wife undresses . . ."

(*He stops short. The first* APPLICANT *enters.*) Where'd you serve?

APPLICANT: In the Guards, sir.

KNELL: Ah, yes, and you're from Bavaria, too. Very good. When were you in?

APPLICANT: 1899 to 1901, sir.

KNELL: And how were you discharged?

APPLICANT: As a corporal in the reserves, sir.

KNELL: Good. What's your name? We'll hire him. Show me your papers.

(*The* APPLICANT *does so.*)

All in order. You'll start work tomorrow at the Axolotl shoe factory in Tempelhof.

APPLICANT: Very good, sir. (*He goes off.*)

KNELL: You see, Hirschberg, you must talk to these people in a straightforward military manner; that way you get the quickest and clearest answers.

(VOIGT *has in the meanwhile entered.*)

Where'd you serve?

VOIGT: With several master craftsmen, and then I was trained in the city shoe factory.

KNELL: What was your standing, I mean?

VOIGT: Standing?—About all I did was sit.

KNELL: Your rank, your rank!—Weren't you in the army?

VOIGT: No, I never made it. I had a previous conviction.—I'd rather tell you that now than have it come out later. I thought they wouldn't be so particular in a factory. I'm a specialist at working machines.

KNELL: Well, show me your papers.

(VOIGT *removes a paper from an envelope and shows it to him.*)

(*Looking at it.*) What do you call this? You call this papers?

VOIGT: The director at the prison told me, "If you're willing to work, this recommendation will get you more than you can take care of."

KNELL: Show me your police registration first, or your passport.

VOIGT: They won't give me one till I have work

KNELL: I can't give you a job until your papers are in order. Why did you bother coming? This is an orderly establishment here Every man's personal papers must be in order before he works for us. If you'd been in the army, you know, these ways would have been ingrained in you by now.

VOIGT (*quite calmly and drily*): I thought this was a factory, not a barracks. (*He goes out.*)

KNELL: Out you go! Damned insolence! Whoever heard of such a thing. Well, there you have it, Hirschberg, there you have it. Don't tell me I don't know what I'm doing when I hire only former military personnel. With these Social Democrat agitators around nowadays a man has to be careful who he takes into his house. How else can a person put any trust in his employees? (*To the third* APPLICANT *who in the meanwhile has entered.*) Where'd you serve?

BLACKOUT

SCENE 5

An elegantly furnished room in Potsdam. Plush easy chairs, knick-knacks; photographs of military celebrations, and pictures of famous battles are hung on the walls. SCHLETTOW *has his coat off.* DELTZEIT, *his orderly, stands in front of him with a helpless expression on his face.*

SCHLETTOW: And now, my dear Deltzeit, let me thank you again for all you have done. You were above reproach. Always absolutely punctual. You are to return to your company now, where you will continue in your duty and gain the satisfaction and approval of your new master—in fact I expect that of you.

DELTZEIT: But, Captain, sir, I—I just don't understand.

SCHLETTOW (*in a gruff but friendly manner*): Nor is it any of your concern. As an officer's orderly you must understand such things. When such an occurrence happens in public to an officer, there can be only one solution; hand in his papers.

Understand? The men in the company will, of course, realize
that I was not guilty of . . . of forging a check, for example,
or—(*He gazes numbly into space.*)

DELTZEIT: But the Captain couldn't do anything about it—the
Captain only—

SCHLETTOW: Don't talk nonsense, Deltzeit. The main thing is, no
soldier should ever have so much trouble. Bad luck is also a
disqualification. But that's enough of that.

DELTZEIT (*with a gulp*): The Captain was always so kind—

SCHLETTOW: That's enough! Pull yourself together, Deltzeit. After
all, you're a man. (*Gives him his hand.*) Goodbye—and out
you go now.

DELTZEIT: Goodbye, Captain, sir. (*He does an about-face and goes
out.*)

(SCHLETTOW *stands there gazing numbly in front of him.
The doorbell rings.* DELTZEIT *reappears immediately at the
door.*)

DELTZEIT: Excuse me, Captain, sir, for intruding—the tailor's here
with your new uniform—shall I tell him—

SCHLETTOW (*bites his lips*): Let him come in. Go on! Tell him to
come in.

DELTZEIT: Right away, Captain, sir. (*He goes off.*)

(SCHLETTOW *gives a shrug and passes his hand over his hair.*
WABSCHKE *enters with a new uniform wrapped in tissue
paper.*)

WABSCHKE: Here it is, Captain! And I assure you, when you get
this on you won't have that "feeling" anymore.

SCHLETTOW: Let's see it.

(WABSCHKE *takes the uniform from the tissue paper, holds it
high, the rear buttons toward the front.* SCHLETTOW *examines
it, keenly measures it with his eyes, and nods his approval.*)

Perfect, yes, everything in order. I can see that at first glance.
(*He takes the jacket and slips into it.*)

WABSCHKE (*tugging at the bottom of the jacket to set it in order*):
A work of art, Captain, sir. This is no longer a jacket, it's a
part of a living human being. It's your better skin, so to
speak.

SCHLETTOW (*in front of the mirror*): Not a thread out of place.
Absolutely perfect.

WABSCHKE: Would you look at that, sir—even the mirror's come
to attention. You can almost hear its heels snap.

SCHLETTOW (*turns around, unbuttons his jacket*): Very well, you will now take it back to the shop, and you will ask Herr Wormser to try to sell the uniform on commission. I am afraid I can't use it. If he is unable to dispose of it, then, of course, I shall pay for it. And if he is forced to sell it at a loss, it is understood I will make up the difference.

WABSCHKE: But, Captain, sir, what is it? Why should you send back your nice, new—

SCHLETTOW (*with forced gaiety*): Change of plans, Wabschke, change of plans. Figured I'd try my hand at a little farming. I've always had something of the sort in mind. A small inheritance, you know, raise crops, breed horses; much better than soldiering and having to wear these colored jackets. (*He has taken off the jacket and gives him a five mark piece.*) There. Now pack it up.

WABSCHKE (*wraps up the uniform*): Thank you, Captain, sir. (*After a slight pause, during which* SCHLETTOW *whistles.*) The Captain shouldn't take this so much to heart.

SCHLETTOW: Whatever do you mean?

WABSCHKE: I don't know anything about it, sir—it's none of my business. I only meant—(*Almost tenderly, with caution.*)— well, the military is a fine thing, but then again it's not the only occupation in the world. The world's a big place, and every morning the sun comes up no matter what. But when a person's young, and healthy and—and straight-limbed— well, what I mean is—when a man's a good honest human being—that's all that matters, isn't it?

SCHLETTOW: Off you go now. And my best regards to Herr Wormser.

WABSCHKE: Thank you, sir. (*In the doorway.*) I mean, after all, that *is* all that matters, Captain, sir. (*He goes off with the uniform.*)

SCHLETTOW (*alone*): Maybe—maybe he has something there.— Oh, hell!

BLACKOUT

SCENE 6

A flophouse in the northern sector of Berlin; clean wooden walls patched with tar paper and newspaper; double-deck bunks of wood and meshed wire, straw mattresses, and carbide lamps. Most

*of the bunks are already occupied. Men are seen waiting their turn
at the door in the rear.*

FLOPHOUSE KEEPER (*at the door in the rear*): Room for seven
more. Don't shove. That won't get you nowhere. Come on.
Can't take more than I got beds for. First come, first served.
You others I can't help. Try the Salvation Army. There's
always room there.

A VOICE (*from outside the door*): Hell, they'll make us sing
hymns. I'd rather sleep in the park.

FLOPHOUSE KEEPER: Don't shove. Quiet there, quiet. You have to
be in line to get in. Six pfennigs a bed ticket and a groschen
a ticket for food if you want soup and bread in the morning.
(*To* ZECK, *who enters first.*) Zeck! Back again, uh?

ZECK: Don't cry, old man, but you won't be seeing me around
here anymore.

FLOPHOUSE KEEPER: Seems I heard that one before—sounds
familiar.

ZECK: No, it's a fact. I got a job with a traveling show. World
champion prizefighter. I start tomorrow. I already hit them
for fifty pfennigs.

FLOPHOUSE KEEPER: Just watch it you don't crack no ribs, or you'll
be out on the street again. (*To the next* MAN.) Well, what
are you supposed to be?

HÖLLHUBER (*in Bavarian mountain dress, with short pants, and a
peculiar beard*): A yodeler soloist.

FLOPHOUSE KEEPER: What's that?

HÖLLHUBER: I'm a yodeler soloist with the Alpine Rose and Edel-
weiss Glee Club. But the director kicked me out because I
got in a fight.

FLOPHOUSE KEEPER: And what do you do now?

HÖLLHUBER: Now? Now I'm going home.

FLOPHOUSE KEEPER: Where's that?

HÖLLHUBER: Hiaglgwimpffen near Sanktmariageschwändt.

FLOPHOUSE KEEPER: You're in for quite a trip—better get a good
rest.

ZECK: Watch you don't catch cold with them legs sticking out.
(*Slaps him on the knee.*)

HÖLLHUBER: Keep your paws to yourself, you bloody swine!

ZECK: Can't you take a joke? Where'd you grow up? With savages?

FLOPHOUSE KEEPER: Let him be, Zeck. He's worried 'cause he's so
far from home. (*Meanwhile he has let in* GEBWEILER *and*
JUPP.)

HÖLLHUBER: Bloody swine, that's what you are, a bloody swine! (*Sits down at the side, grumbling.*)

FLOPHOUSE KEEPER (*lets* VOIGT *in*): Find work yet?

VOIGT: No.

FLOPHOUSE KEEPER: Don't you want a food ticket?

VOIGT: Thank you anyway—I don't have a groschen.

FLOPHOUSE KEEPER: So have one on credit. You'll need a spoonful of something in your belly tomorrow.

VOIGT: I'll pay it back soon as I get some money. Thank you kindly.

KALLE (*behind* VOIGT): I'll have a ticket on credit too, please.

FLOPHOUSE KEEPER: Where's the groschen you just had in your hand?

KALLE: I kind of thought I'd be needing that in a day or two.

FLOPHOUSE KEEPER: All right, but don't try it too often. I have to buy meat for the soup or you'd pour it down the sink.

BUTTJE (*enters*): Hello, Pop!

FLOPHOUSE KEEPER: Look at that! A Hamburg carpenter in the house!

BUTTJE: Yep, back again. (*Sings.*) "I just got back from Hamburg—"

ZECK: Ah, shut up! I know you. He's a sailor from the slums. Never saw Hamburg *or* salt water.

BUTTJE: How about *you*? What do *you* do?

FLOPHOUSE KEEPER: I'm warning you, Zeck. You start a fight and I'll call the cops.

ZECK: You can't scare me with that. I'd as soon sleep in jail as in your flophouse.

FLOPHOUSE KEEPER: Good night. Time to hit the sack. Soup's at six tomorrow.

ZECK: 'Night, Pop! If I find any fleas in my mattress I'll save them for you. You can start a flea circus.

FLOPHOUSE KEEPER: No fleas in my place. And if there are, you brought them. (*He goes out, closing the door behind him.*)

ZECK: Hey, how about a drink! (*Pulls a whiskey bottle from his pocket and takes a mighty draw.*)

(*Meanwhile the others go to the unoccupied bunks.*)

(*Puts the bottle aside, and starts in again on* BUTTJE.) What do you mean taking two blankets! Who do you think you are!

BUTTJE: I need one under my head; I'm used to it.

ZECK: Oh, a blanket for under your fat head, uh? And this kid over here goes with nothing? (*Pointing to* GEBWEILER, *sitting on one of the bottom bunks.*) Look at him shivering over there.

BUTTJE: So what? Uh? So what?

ZECK (*tears the second blanket from him*): Here's a blanket for you, boy. Your face looks like chalk it's so pale. Have a drink of brew, it'll warm your belly. (*Gives him the bottle.*)

(GEBWEILER, *a puny young boy, takes a swallow without looking at* ZECK.)

He ain't even got a jacket. And those pants. Why, those are army pants. Where'd you get them?

(GEBWEILER *turns toward the wall.*)

You don't have to tell me. It's none of my business anyway.

BUTTJE: Damn right it's none of your business, you dirty gutter rat!

ZECK: Shut up! (*Takes another drink.*)

KALLE: Zeck! How about six pfennigs of schnapps?

ZECK: I don't sell schnapps. Go to a tavern.

KALLE: Then give me a drink. I'm awful weak.

ZECK: Wouldn't think of it. I don't like your kind.

KALLE: That's real charity for you, uh?

ZECK (*drinking; to the others*): I know a Prussian saying goes like this: "To each his own, but the most to me." Anybody here know how to play skat?

JUPP: Me. But I only play for gold.

ZECK: There's my man! Now where's a third?

(*Two others join them.*)

Right. Gambling ruins a man's character. What are we waiting for?

(*They sit somewhere upstage.* ZECK *shuffles the cards. Throughout the succeeding dialogue we hear improvised exclamations from the card players in half-loud voices, along with the slamming down of cards, shuffling, and low whistling.* VOIGT *and* KALLE *are seated on a bed downstage.* KALLE *unwraps a piece of cheese and some bread from a kerchief he had in his bag.*)

KALLE: How about a feast? Here, here's some cheese. Dig in.

VOIGT: No, no, Kalle, you eat it yourself. I'm not hungry.

KALLE (*eating*): You're hiding something, Willy, I can tell. Brooding about it won't do no good. Something on your

chest, tell me about it. I won't go blabbing it out, you know
that.

VOIGT: If you want to join in, Kalle, that'd be fine with me. I
could never do the job alone.

KALLE (*moves close to him*): What? What is it? Any money in
it?

VOIGT: In Potsdam—the police station—there's no bars on the
windows and they look out onto a courtyard. There's no
guard either. We have to get over the wall first—the two of
us could do that—and then all you do is push in a window-
pane. The filing cabinets have ordinary locks, you could pick
them with a bent pin.

KALLE (*disappointed*): A police station in Potsdam? What do you
want in there? They've got nothing to steal.

VOIGT: Kalle, they've got my whole life down there in a file. I
can find it right away under V. I tried to register there and
they brought it all out: the conviction and the prison dis-
charge and all the police records—and all I have to do is
throw it in the fire and it's gone forever.

KALLE: Willy, you're out of your mind.

VOIGT: No, Kalle, no. I looked around real careful, and there's a
whole cabinet of passes, all kinds of beautiful passports and
permits just waiting to be filled out or renewed. And then
there's rubber stamps for working, and duty stamps, and
rubber-stamped papers, and everything you need for your
whole life is there.

KALLE: Is there a cashbox?

VOIGT: *Sure* there's a cashbox, there'd *have* to be a cashbox, of
course—they collect court fees and taxes there, too.

KALLE: Without a cashbox I'm not interested.

VOIGT: The cashbox is all yours. All I want is enough for a ticket
to the Bohemian border, and that won't cost much.

KALLE: I'll have to think about it. Without a cashbox—

VOIGT: Well of course there's a cashbox. And a cabinet full of
blank forms. And all the personal files. I'll put an end to it
all. I'll be dead. And I'll get across the border where there are
all those shoe factories, you know, in Prague and Budweis—

KALLE: If you're sure there's a cashbox, we might talk about it.

VOIGT: They *have* to have a cashbox. It's Potsdam! There's money
all over the place. And there's always a cashbox in a police
station.

KALLE: I guess we could peek in and see. We sure couldn't get in
trouble just for *that*.

VOIGT: I'd have a passport then—I could start all over again—

Carl Zuckmayer

("*Taps*" *is heard in the distance.*)

BUTTJE: Time to hit the hay. (*He sings to the tune of the bugle.*)

"A musketeer stood by his broad
And wanted to do it again, O Lawd
Too late, too late, too late!"

ZECK: Tell them to shut up that noise! I can't think! Keep it quiet!

(*There is excitement among the* PLAYERS.)

BUTTJE: If I want to sing, I'll sing! People who don't like music ain't worth the salt they eat! They should have their ears cut off. (*Sings.*) "So on we sail, and on we sail, over the blue, blue waves . . ."

ZECK: Look, you stop singing, or marry some blasted merchant's daughter in Grünewald with a music room! But in here you keep your trap shut!

BUTTJE: How'd you like to chew your own teeth, uh? (*But for safety's sake he keeps quiet, takes out a harmonica, taps it a few times, and plays.*)

JUPP: He ought to join the Salvation Army.

ZECK: Damn! Lost again! What do you want to do, Jupp? Steal the last button off my trousers? That why you came to Berlin?

JUPP: You're playing like you lost your mind, old boy. (*He shuffles the cards.*)

ZECK: What are you doing in this hole in the wall anyway? Aren't you a miner? Go to the coal country!

JUPP: Got a bad reputation in the mines. Killed an overseer once.

ZECK: How'd *that* happen? Tell us.

JUPP: Nothing to tell. He was some dirty skunk; always did what they told him, and spitting down on the likes of us—that's the no-good kind *he* was.

ZECK: We know his kind. Go on.

JUPP: He was always giving me trouble—more than anybody else. "Jupp, your lantern's not cleaned!" "Jupp, your leather's all dirty!" "Jupp, your hammer's rusty!" So I listened to it for a couple years, till I had enough. One Monday he comes along with a hangover from the weekend, and growls, "You better say good morning to me, Jupp!" "No," I said back, "I don't bother with dirty swine like you." "Take your cap off," he screams at me, "or I'll report you!" So I raised my pickax and brought it down on his skull.

ZECK: Serves him right, the dirty dog!

JUPP: Real fine gentleman, too—stiff collar every Sunday.

ZECK: What did they give you?

JUPP: Since it wasn't planned, they couldn't do much. And all my friends stood up for me, too. Two years. But my name's not worth much in the mines anymore.

ZECK: Prosit, Jupp! You're a good man! Have a drink! (*Gives him the bottle.*)

JUPP: Spades are trumps. Lay it on the table. (*He plays.*)

KALLE: If you want to, Wilhelm, we can pull the job tomorrow night. I've even got a Browning.

VOIGT: Leave it at home. Where'd you get a thing like that anyway?

KALLE: I stuck my hand in a rich man's pocket once; I thought it was a purse. But it wasn't a bad pinch. (*Shows him the revolver.*) See?—It's loaded, too.

VOIGT: We won't need a revolver. There's no guard on duty. Forget about it. If anything goes wrong and you've got a gun, you're done for.

KALLE: Why would anything go wrong?

VOIGT: Nothing will go wrong. I just mean you shouldn't tempt the good Lord too far.

KALLE: Let's sleep on it.

VOIGT: No, I can't sleep anymore, Kalle. It's always going around in my head, and I hear . .

KALLE: Hear what?

VOIGT: Drums. And bells. You know? Real clear sometimes, like glass tinkling. And then louder and louder, like listening in a seashell.

KALLE: That's your dirty ears, Willy, it's the wax. Spit on your little finger and clean it out.

VOIGT: When I was all alone in jail, I always laid with my ear to the stone wall. For a long time there was nothing—and then finally a soft rustling came from the stone, right from inside it. I always used to say the stone's growing again.

KALLE: Growing, uh? What? The bee in your bonnet?

VOIGT: No, Kalle, no, the stone. You don't understand such things. Your mind is still too small. You think what's built is built, and what's solid stays solid. But that's not so. Everything grows, a stone the same as an apple seed. It just happens slower and nobody sees it.

KALLE: Willy, you're mad! About all you *can* notice growing is the whiskers on your chin.

VOIGT: Under a big city like this with all its fine buildings and walls, there's still earth, isn't there?—Sand and clay and water? And inside a man's head there are thoughts, and words, and even dreams—and they keep growing, and get bigger, and—and nobody ever knows what's going to come of them all.

KALLE: I'll sleep on it and let you know in the morning—maybe. (*He lies back and pulls off his boots.*)

VOIGT (*laughs softly*): Once I have a passport—and get across the border—I could go the rest of the way on foot. I'll have to cross those enormous Bohemian mountains—they're really big.

KALLE (*yawning*): I can't wander around like that anymore, Wilhelm. I've got bad feet. And autumn's coming on, too.

VOIGT: It's always so nice in September. And in the valleys they'll be threshing the summer corn, they still do it by hand, you know, and so there's always a way to earn a little soup and bread.

KALLE: That's not fit for a dog.

VOIGT: You mustn't say that. But you're free out there, even if you do freeze sometimes—but there's always the road ahead of you. And if it rains, then you think the next day will be nicer . . . oh, let me tell you—if I ever get out there—

FLOPHOUSE KEEPER (*suddenly opens the door and whistles*): Come on, let's get those lights out! The bugle blew a long time ago. The Night Patrol always comes in if they see a light. If it's dark, they go on—and that might be the best thing for some of you. (*He goes off.*)

ZECK: So let the blasted patrol come! Spades are trumps! Out with the ace!

GEBWEILER (*has all the while lain with his face to the wall, but now suddenly turns around, very pale, and almost screams out*): Put out that light!

ZECK: Why should I? I just lit it! How can we play cards without a light? (*He throws down a card.*)

GEBWEILER (*even more alarmed*): Put out that light! Put out that light!

ZECK: Pull the blanket over your head if you can't sleep.

(GEBWEILER *crawls up under his blanket.*)

BUTTJE: What a crybaby! (*He gets up and goes over to* HÖLL-HUBER, *who has sat alone and dejectedly on a chest.*) Say, you're from the Tyrol, aren't you? They like to sing there. (*Sings.*)
   "The Tyrol is happy, the Tyrol is gay . . ."

HÖLLHUBER: Let me alone. I'm not from the Tyrol either. I'm from Bavaria.

BUTTJE: Oh, a Bavarian! Well, that's about the same. Hey, I know a Bavarian tune. Listen to this. (*He sings a Bavarian melody.*)

> "My father keeps a tavern,
> And I serve drinks in glasses;
> My father corks up bottles,
> And I cork up the lasses."

How's that for a Bavarian song!

HÖLLHUBER (*rises and gives him a box on the ears*): Dirty pig! Dirty no-good pig! What do you mean "Bavarian"!

BUTTJE (*running away*): Hey, not so rough there!

ZECK: Bravo! Good one, boy! You hold onto that! You'll need it! (*He roars with laughter.*)

GEBWEILER (*from under the blanket, as though suffocating*): Put out that light! They're coming! They're coming!!

(*A knock at the door. The door is suddenly opened from out side. The* FLOPHOUSE KEEPER *lets in the Night Patrol. The room is deathly silent.*)

SERGEANT: Everybody up! Stand away from your beds! (*To the* FLOPHOUSE KEEPER.) Papers in order?

FLOPHOUSE KEEPER: They're all right. They're old customers.

SERGEANT: We'll just test a few just to make sure.

BUTTJE (*pulls* GEBWEILER *from bed with thorough officiousness*): Everybody up! Can't you hear! Get up! Get up!

SERGEANT (to ZECK): Show me your permit.

ZECK: Jeez, I must've left it in the toilet.

SERGEANT: Look, you got a permit or not?

ZECK: I said I did, over there in the toilet, at the Dirty Dog's. See for yourself—unless maybe it fell in.

SERGEANT: What's that in your hand?

ZECK: The best hand of cards I ever had. Take a look. (*Holds the cards out to him.*) But don't tell.

SERGEANT: I could arrest you. Got any other papers?

ZECK (*reaches into his pocket*): I'll see. Oops, here's my permit after all! (*Hands over the permit with a grin on his face.*) Excuse me, I must have made a mistake.

SERGEANT (*confused*): Good thing you found it. If it's not in order, you're coming along to the station.

ZECK: Always wanted to see the place. I heard the schnapps is good there.

SERGEANT: Shut up! Or you'll get more than a schnapps! (*Looking at the permit.*)

BUTTJE (*has meanwhile left* GEBWEILER *who stands chattering in the shadow beside his bed; he goes to the* SERGEANT): Here's my traveler's permit, stamped by the police authorities.

SERGEANT (*pushes him aside and rapidly inspects the permits held out to him by the others; he looks at* VOIGT): What's this supposed to be!

VOIGT (*giving him the paper*): My dismissal from Plötzensee Prison. They didn't give me a regular permit.

SERGEANT (*looking at the paper*): All right. But be sure you get one.

VOIGT: Thank you, I'll do my best.

SERGEANT: That'll do for today. Now let's have some quiet in here.

FLOPHOUSE KEEPER: I'll take the lamps out, Sergeant.

ZECK (*as the* SERGEANT *hands him back his permit*): Anything wrong with them, Sergeant? I'd sure be sad if there was.

SERGEANT: You shut up, or you'll come along with me!—Forward march!

CORPORAL (*has stared at* GEBWEILER *all the while, who has become more and more uneasy*): Excuse me, Sergeant, I just noticed something.

SERGEANT: Noticed what? What is it?

CORPORAL: That man there in the corner—that man in the corner looks like Louis Gebweiler—the deserter—the one they've got the arrest warrant out for.

(*The* SERGEANT *goes toward* GEBWEILER.)

He was in the Sixth Regiment, but I saw him often enough in the barracks yard.

SERGEANT (*looks sharply at* GEBWEILER): Are you Gebweiler?— The deserter?

(GEBWEILER *doesn't answer.*)

Show me your papers!

(GEBWEILER *doesn't move.*)

Come with me!

GEBWEILER (*deathly afraid*): No, no, that's not me—

CORPORAL: It *is* him, it's *him!* Didn't you hear him! He's an Alsatian! (*Imitates him.*) "That's not me! That's not me!"— It's him, all right!

SERGEANT: Good catch, Corporal! Take that man with you. (*To the* CORPORAL.) Tomorrow at Parade I'll bring you to the Company Commander's attention.

(*The* CORPORAL, *delighted, salutes smartly.*)

GEBWEILER: No, no, that's not me, that's not me—

SERGEANT: Grab hold of him!

(*The* SOLDIERS *grab hold of him.*)

GEBWEILER (*with a sob*): Mother! (*He grows silent.*)

BUTTJE (*laughs*): He called for his mother!

(*The others are silent.*)

SERGEANT: Crazy fool. What's he running away for? We don't bite people. The two years would do him good—it's healthy. You learn a trade, so you can make something of yourself when you get out. But now they'll send you up for five years at least, and bust you to soldier second class. You could have saved yourself all this. Well, what can you expect from a dumb Alsatian! And he's still got his army pants on. Stealing government property makes it even worse. In wartime he'd have been shot.

(*Everyone has listened to him silently. No one moves.*)

All right!—Forward—march! (*Not without geniality.*) Help the man there, you expect him to go by himself? He's too dumb for that. Good night. (*He goes off.*)

(GEBWEILER *is led off between the two* SOLDIERS, *led on by the* CORPORAL.)

FLOPHOUSE KEEPER: Terrible thing . . . Terrible thing . . . (*He takes the lamps away.*) Go on now, get to bed.—The poor devil, they should have let him go. He was only a boy.

ZECK: The dirty louses! If it was up to me, I'd blow up all their barracks and their prisons and their Parliaments—and everything else.

FLOPHOUSE KEEPER: Stop your swearing, Zeck, there's got to be order. Now get to bed. (*Goes off with the lamps.*)

(*Everything grows dark.*)

ZECK (*to himself*): Dirty louses!

VOIGT (*on his bed, downstage; softly*): Kalle—Kalle—

KALLE: What?

VOIGT: Tomorrow night, Kalle. You won't let me down, will you, Kalle? I have to have a passport, Kalle, I have to get out of here.

KALLE (*already half asleep*): Without a cashbox—(*He breathes deeply.*)

VOIGT: Kalle—are you asleep, Kalle?—My God—if I could only
    get out of this—

BLACKOUT

SCENE 7

WORMSER's *Uniform Shop in Potsdam.* WILLY *leans on the counter*
and reads a newspaper. Military music is heard in the distance,
drums and fifes. WORMSER *comes out of his office.* WILLY *quickly*
hides the newspaper.

WORMSER: I knew it, I knew it—he's reading the paper again!
    Must you always read? What's in it? Show me. Aha, just as I
    thought, reading the entertainment section! The entertain-
    ment section! Read other things, if you want to read the
    paper! Read the market reports, trade reports, politics! Take
    an interest in practical things! Now what's this you've marked
    here? "Gerhart Hauptmann Premiere at the Deutsches The-
    ater, by Alfred Kerr." What do you read stuff like that for?
    You don't even understand it. All you have to do is see if it's
    a success, and how many curtain calls it got, and so on, to
    know if you should go or not. And don't grin at me like that!
    You know as little about such things as your father. What's
    this, what's this? (*Reads.*) "Potsdam—Sensational Arrest at
    Police Station . . ."—tsk-tsk-tsk-tsk-tsk—that's a fine kettle of
    fish! Broke into our police station last night—into the police
    station, mind you!—And tried to steal the cashbox! Why, these
    good-for-nothing tramps nowadays are becoming as bold as
    blowflies. They even used a gun. But they got caught all
    right. Two former convicts, naturally. Why do they let them
    out in the first place, when all they ever do is start in burgling
    again!—Now here's some interesting news—"His Majesty The
    Kaiser's Hunting Party at Rominten."—How marvelous! Six
    reigning Princes were among the guests!—Oh, what I'd give
    to have been there! Even if only as a waiter! Our Kaiser is
    an imposing fellow, all right. There's a touch of greatness
    about him. Here, read the speech he made at the banquet—
    you might learn something from it. There's style for you,
    there's genius, there's inspiration! What is it, Wabschke?
WABSCHKE (*has entered from the side with* SCHLETTOW's *uniform*
    over his arm): Why not hang it in the window till somebody

comes along who wants it? Think of all the work we went to
with those buttons!

WORMSER: And it's not even paid for yet. Well, at least I don't
have to remind him of it. Too bad about Schlettow. He was a
fine fellow. Hang it up and take away the tunic—it's out of
fashion now; it's only worn now in silver gray.

(OBERMÜLLER *enters. He is about thirty years old, well built,
with a visible propensity toward corpulence. A pince-nez and
a small blond moustache give his face a somewhat concerned
expression, which is in keeping with his voice and manner of
speech. Despite this, however, everything he says has about it
the stamp of a man both well read and idealistic. He wears
the uniform of a one-year conscript with the rank of sergeant.*)

OBERMÜLLER: Good morning, Herr Wormser.

WORMSER: Good morning, good morning, my dear Sergeant—now
what was your name again—?

OBERMÜLLER: Obermüller. Doctor Obermüller from Köpenick.

WORMSER: Of course, of course, excuse me, haven't seen you in a
long time—what can I do for you, Doctor?

OBERMÜLLER: Well, you see, it's about—

WORMSER (*interrupting*): Ah, but I'll bet I can guess! I suspect
congratulations are in order, eh? How's that? How's that for
a guess?

OBERMÜLLER: Very well done, indeed, sir. The Adjutant of the
Battalion has just informed me I've been promoted to
Lieutenant in the reserves. It came as quite a surprise, I
assure you. But now I have to see about putting my uniform
and equipment in order. I do hope you can help me, Mr.
Wormser, sir—

WORMSER: It's as good as done, sir, as good as done! But I must
remind you, good work takes time. And of course you'll want
to be an example in all your splendor. I'm delighted for you,
sir, absolutely delighted. And it was only your second year,
too, eh?

OBERMÜLLER: The third, Herr Wormser, the third. I encountered
a bit of difficulty with my shooting tests—my nearsightedness,
you know. But—all that's behind me now, thank God.

WORMSER: And quite right, too. Ah, it must be a wonderful feeling to be addressed as Lieutenant for the first time—it must
make your ears absolutely tingle. But you know what I always
say: Darwinism begins with the rank of Corporal, but Mankind begins with Lieutenant. Right? Right? Eh?

OBERMÜLLER: Well, I wouldn't exactly say that—but—well, it's certainly useful for my career. I really need the uniform very urgently, Herr Wormser, I—

WORMSER: Wabschke, the measurement book! You're a Civil Servant, aren't you, Lieutenant, sir?

OBERMÜLLER: Well, you see, my mother-in-law's coming for a visit, and she places great importance on such matters—coming from a family of officers. But I'm only a Civil Servant in the administration. Of course, I did want to go into politics —I thought I might do something as a political economist in the Progressive Party—all for the common good, you know—but mainly through my writing—ah, but one needs means for such plans.

WORMSER: A Civil Servant is no mean position.

OBERMÜLLER: Of course. And the promotions are good, too. Presently, for example, I'm a Civic Magistrate in Köpenick; and with good luck I'll one day be Mayor of Köpenick— (*With a quiet smile.*)—and a position like that, of course, is *also* directed toward the common good of the community.

WORMSER: But the main thing is, you're a Lieutenant now, and that's what you have to be nowadays—for social reasons, professional reasons, and everything else. A Doctor's degree is only a visiting card, but to be an officer in the reserves opens the door to everything. It's the foundation—that's what it is!

WABSCHKE: That's what it is.

WORMSER: Quiet, Wabschke, nobody asked you. I'll tell you what I can do, Lieutenant, sir. It occurs to me I have just what you need.—I mean, if you're in a hurry. Now just slip into this jacket. It should be about the right fit for you. (*He takes* SCHLETTOW's *uniform from the stand.*)

OBERMÜLLER: But this is a Captain's jacket, Herr Wormser, I haven't got *that* far yet! (*He laughs.*)

WORMSER: The day will come, sir, the day will come! All we need are a few alterations, and different epaulets, and we're all set. Button the jacket, Wabschke.

WABSCHKE: Looks like it was made specially for you. A little tight around the hips, maybe.

OBERMÜLLER: I suppose I do have a rather large posterior—an occupational disease, you might say—comes from too much sitting.

WORMSER: I'll tell you what. You take this uniform. I'd need at least a week to make a new one. And besides, this one will cost you less, and it hasn't even been worn yet—brand new— I took it to sell on commission. The gentleman it was made for was forced to leave the service. (*Lowers his voice.*) You must have heard about *that* scandal—*cherchez la femme*, as they say.

OBERMÜLLER: No, I'm afraid I don't take much interest in scandals. Such matters are always distorted in the mouth of the public.

WORMSER: My very words, Lieutenant, sir, my very words! Just what I've always said! No idle gossip for me! Half of it's always lies, and the other half's none of my business. So many stories are brought into this shop, I don't even listen to them anymore. Well now, let's have a look in the mirror. How do you like yourself as an officer?

OBERMÜLLER: Not bad! Not bad! (*Takes a step to the rear, removes the pince-nez, and regards himself from top to bottom.*) Clothes do make the man, I must say. There's something very forceful in a uniform like this. It radiates a kind of magic—

WORMSER (*meanwhile makes some marks in chalk on the back of the jacket*): You see, Wabschke, right here—and here—and here—nothing to it at all. Of course, Lieutenant, sir, of course, it brings out a man's real value, eh? But the best of all is, you've become something that not everyone can become. That's where the real fun lies, eh? Hand me those pins, Wabschke!

OBERMÜLLER: On the contrary, my dear Herr Wormser, quite on the contrary! The important thing in our country is the idea of a People's Army; an army in which every man assumes the proper place assigned him by the social structure of our communal society. A man of merit knows no limitations. That's the motto of our glorious German nation! The concept of individual freedom and the concept of the constitution unite, and the whole of society is rendered capable of development. Our system may be monarchical, I admit; but the actual fact is, we are a—democracy. I'm absolutely convinced of it.

WORMSER: True, true! Just what I always say! Why, we have more freedom here than any republic you could mention. They might take a lesson from us! Well now, everything seems in order. Quite a stroke of luck you had with this uniform, Lieutenant, sir.

OBERMÜLLER: I suppose; as long as it takes less time. Naturally I'd have preferred a new one—but—considering the rush—

WORMSER: It'll be ready for you tomorrow. And of course you'll want an officer's sword belt and sword, a sash, cap, helmet— what's your head size, Lieutenant, sir?

OBERMÜLLER: Nine and a half—I have a rather highly developed skull.

WORMSER: With plenty inside it, too! Willy, help the Lieutenant into his jacket! Make yourself useful.

(*A military brass band is heard approaching.*)

What splendid Prussian marches we have, eh? Makes a man want to stand up and salute! Goes right to the marrow of your bones!

WABSCHKE: Enough to make a frog learn the polka.

WORMSER: Quiet, Wabschke—you have no soul for music. Congratulations again, Lieutenant! I'm delighted!

OBERMÜLLER: Thank you, thank you, Herr Wormser.

WORMSER: Let's say, you can pick it up tomorrow at the same time, eh?

OBERMÜLLER: Very well, Herr Wormser. My mother-in-law's coming tomorrow for a visit—I've already telegraphed her, but, of course, I'd like to . . .

WORMSER: In your uniform—of course—I understand! Your mother-in-law will be very proud of her splendid Lieutenant!

OBERMÜLLER: Yes, that's right, you see, my mother-in-law places great importance on such—well, *au revoir,* Herr Wormser, *au revoir!*

WORMSER: *Au revoir,* Lieutenant, *au revoir!* (*He bows him to the door and out.*) Well, so *he's* done it too! What they don't turn into officers these days! Let this be an example to you, Willy!

BLACKOUT

The sound of the military brass band is very near and very loud.

ACT II

SCENE 1

The prison chapel in the Prussian prison at Sonnenburg. It resembles a dismal lecture hall with a raised platform. The individual seats for each of the prisoners are separated from one another by high, back and side partitions, so that each appears to be seated in a wooden box open only at the front. The windows are barred. Guards are seated right and left of the exit. The WARDENS *sit elsewhere on separate chairs. The* CHAPLAIN *is on the platform, directing the singing. The* PRISONERS *are standing with hymnbooks in hand, singing the chorale.*

PRISONERS:
" 'Tis here our Heavenly Father's brought us,
   In token of His love . . ."

CHAPLAIN (*after the verse has been sung*): That will be all for today. Collect the hymnbooks.

(*The* WARDENS *gather up the hymnbooks.*)

In place of a sermon we will celebrate the fortieth anniversary of our great victory at Sedan by hearing a patriotic address delivered by the Director of our own prison.

A PRISONER (*unseen*): Ohhhh!

CHAPLAIN: Who was that? I will assume it was an expression of genuine appreciation. You are all familiar with the innumerable privileges and amenities which the goodness of our prison Director has bestowed upon you. You will therefore behave accordingly. Be seated! (*He goes out.*)

(*The* PRISONERS *sit down. The* DIRECTOR *enters. The* PRISONERS *jump to their feet. The* DIRECTOR *is a distinguished old gentleman with a long gray beard parted in the middle. Above the beard we see a round, rosy, friendly face with a bald shiny forehead. He wears a gray frock coat.*)

DIRECTOR: Good morning, gentlemen!

PRISONERS (*bellowing*): Good morning, sir!

DIRECTOR (*on the platform*): Count off!

(*The* PRISONERS *count off in military fashion from one to thirty.*)

Very good! Very well done! Numbers one through seven will be cavalry, eight through twelve artillery, thirteen through twenty-four infantry, and the rest: engineers, supply, and ambulance corps. Be seated!

(*The* PRISONERS *are seated.*)

As you are well aware, today is the second of September. It

occurs to me at the moment that tomorrow, the third of September, one of you will be completing his sentence. Now who would that be?

(VOIGT *rises.*)

Ah, so it's you, Voigt.

VOIGT: Yes, sir.

DIRECTOR: How long have you been with us?

VOIGT: Ten years, sir.

DIRECTOR: And why were you brought here in the first place?

VOIGT: For breaking into a Potsdam police station. All I wanted was . . .

DIRECTOR: Yes, of course. Well now, my good man, may I say that your exemplary conduct and industry has earned you the respect of your superiors. Let's hope that—ah, but we'll talk about that tomorrow, won't we?

VOIGT: With pleasure, sir.

WARDEN (*jumps up at this point and runs toward one of the back rows of seats*): Hands up! Hands up! Finally caught you, uh?

DIRECTOR: What is it! What's the meaning of this!

WARDEN: They've been smuggling again at the back. I've had my eye on them since they came in.

DIRECTOR (*scoldingly*): I should not have expected this of you today. What have they got there?

WARDEN: This one here traded a quarter pound of canteen sausage for ten cigarettes, and he's got a piece of paper stuck under his arm.

DIRECTOR: A piece of paper? What does it say?

WARDEN: Nothing. It's a drawing.

DIRECTOR: Show it to me.

WARDEN: Excuse me, sir, but it's dirty.

DIRECTOR: You should be ashamed. I won't even look at it. (*He crumples the paper and sticks it into his pocket.*) The cigarettes will be confiscated. You have no idea the harm you're inflicting upon your health with such poisonous materials. I personally do not smoke. He may keep the sausage, but for eating purposes only, not for barter.

WARDEN (*gives the* PRISONER *the sausage*): Here, shove it in your pocket.

DIRECTOR: *Place* it in your pocket. You know well enough how I insist upon courtesy toward our inmates.

WARDEN: I'm sorry, sir, it just slipped out that way.

DIRECTOR: Very well.—And so we find ourselves assembled here on the second of September to commemorate the anniversary of Sedan. Sixty million German hearts beat with great excitement at the thought that forty years ago today our glorious army won a decisive victory on the field of battle which has made us what we are today. Many of our fellow citizens think back with great pride upon those members of their families who helped in winning this victory. As all of you know, I, too, had the unforgettable good fortune as a young volunteer to stand face to face with the enemy on that great day. The supreme good fortune of being able to fight for one's country can, of course, not be the share of every generation. And yet those who serve their country between times, in peaceable employment, are also fulfilling a high mission. Above all, however, the blessed institution of Universal Compulsory Military Conscription Duty has provided our country's standing army with great living force, a force which even in peacetime protects not only our moral stability, but our spiritual and physical welfare as well. Many of you, of course, were prevented by the stroke of fate from belonging to this army and marching shoulder to shoulder with your joyful comrades in the Brotherhood of Arms. What you have lost in regard to those things which alone make life worth living, I have endeavored to my greatest capacity to make up to you in this institution, in the attempt to educate you anew and place you upon a new and righteous path. Many a man, who, before beginning his sentence here, could not distinguish between a noncommissioned officer and a general, has left this institution, if not as a trained soldier, then at least as one trained in the ways and the disciplines of our German army. And this will enable him to hold his own even in civilian life, however difficult that beginning may be.—But let us now return to the historical occasion of today's celebration. As you all know, I was personally blessed with the good fortune of taking part in the storming of that extremely important Hill Number 101—an action which, though it may not have been the ultimately decisive one, nevertheless was instrumental in bringing *about* that decisive result. General von der Tann's three battle-ready infantry divisions were faced with the enemy's superior power of numbers in the form of four army corps under the leadership of the French General Boulanger. We were supported by the artillery of the Third Corps and the First Bavarian Cavalry Division under Lieutenant General Prince Donnersmarck.—I hope you are well versed in the strengths and dispositions of the various troop formations. Who can tell me the composition of an army corps?—Bulcke?

BULCKE (*a tall man with gigantic hands, rattles off*): An army
corps consists of two infantry divisions, a division of two infantry brigades, a cavalry brigade, and an artillery brigade. A
brigade consists of . .

DIRECTOR: Thank you! It's obvious you were a soldier.—Now, how
many companies constitute a battle-ready infantry regiment?
—Pudritzki?

PUDRITZKI (*a small man with a stubble beard and a Polish ac-
cent*): It—it—varies, sir.

DIRECTOR: Nonsense! Can't you ever learn! Sit down!

(VOIGT *raises his hand along with various others.*)

Very well, Voigt! You needn't answer that one. I'll give you
a harder question. What do we understand by the term
cavalry division?

VOIGT (*clearly and without hesitation*): A cavalry division is an
independent unit subject to the army and under orders to the
Army Commander to dispose of as needed. It consists of
three, and at times four, cavalry regiments with the added
support of a section of mounted field artillery.

DIRECTOR: Bravo, Voigt! Excellent! Excellent, Voigt! You have
not merely paid careful attention here but you have learned
something as well. On some future day you shall see just how
useful that information will be. Step forward now, Voigt.
You are to take command of the attack regiments. After all,
today is the last time you will take part in our exercises.
Warden Lorenz will detail six men, two from each main
division. The pioneers and reserves won't be needed till we
advance.

WARDEN (*rather roughly*): Fall out! One-two—one-two—one-two!

DIRECTOR: Come up here onto the platform so everyone can see
you. Bulcke, you will represent the Bavarian Cavalry Division.
Voigt more to the fore! These others will stand behind you to
represent the Second and Third West Prussian Grenadier
Regiments. No, no, more over there—there's a ground depression here, and to the right of it a swamp. The artillery will
take cover under the platform—that's right, duck down, duck
down! You will come into view only after the First Cavalry
attack has been repulsed. You will assume the spot on which
I am standing to be the enemy's main force; and this stool to
represent Hill Number 101. The time is eleven in the morning. Directly ahead of you is a windmill, and behind it you
see a small white cloud rising into the sky. What does that
signify, Bulcke?

BULCKE: Bad weather, sir.

DIRECTOR: Come now, Bulcke. That's not the answer I was expecting from you! What *can* it mean but the firing of the enemy's artillery?

BULCKE: Begging your pardon, sir, but last time you said it started to drizzle at eleven o'clock, and so I thought—

DIRECTOR: Quite right, Bulcke, that's very good; that shows me you were paying attention. A light passing shower has somewhat impaired visibility. But the weather improves toward noon. Now, while the cavalry proceeds at a slow trot in the direction of the windmill—go on, go on—no, more over this way, you're dipping your right wing into the swamp!—Voigt, what are you doing?

VOIGT: Keeping myself prepared; and in any case I have to have one regiment to form a line of skirmishers. My trumpeter will give the signal. (*He imitates the appropriate signal.*)

DIRECTOR: Bravo, Voigt! Your grasp of the military situation would almost suggest to me you were present there yourself. How do you come by this?

VOIGT: It's in a Prussian's blood, sir. (*Turns to the man behind him.*) Group, right wheel—march! Forward—march! Slow step—march!

DIRECTOR: What's this, what's this! Voigt! Where are you marching that man!

VOIGT: That's the Second Regiment, sir. It's in reserve now, and meanwhile I'm letting them march off to the field kitchen. With warm soup in their bellies, they'll be all fresh again.

DIRECTOR: Splendid, Voigt, splendid! You're a true example to the troops! (*To the others.*) This is precisely what I mean by thoughtful self-reliance in a noncommissioned officer, so necessary in a time of crisis. Pity it's too late, Voigt! You're a born soldier despite your bowlegs. But the cavalry's at a gallop now and proceeds to the attack! Forward—march!

BULCKE AND THE OTHERS (*storming forward*): Hurrah! Hurrah!

BLACKOUT

SCENE 2

The living room of the Hoprecht house in Rixdorf. Middle-class furnishings consisting of a sofa, a mirror, cheap prints, a calendar, and gas lighting. There are two doors, one leading outside, the other into the bedroom. FRAU HOPRECHT, *standing, has just hung a noncommissioned officer's uniform on a hanger over the wardrobe door and is busy polishing the brass buttons with a cloth soaked with a cleaning solution.* WILHELM VOIGT *is seated at the table, with his hat and a tied package on his knees, and a cup of coffee in front of him. He is dressed as he was earlier.*

FRAU HOPRECHT: Now, Wilhelm, put your hat and package away, and make yourself at home. We can't offer you much, so you'll just have to be happy with what there is.

VOIGT: Thank you, Marie. The coffee tastes good.

FRAU HOPRECHT: Did you put sugar in it? Go on, take a good spoonful of sugar. There's not much coffee, everything's so expensive nowadays. Friedrich's whole pay goes just for the household, and my soap business almost doesn't pay for itself. They don't use much soap here in Rixdorf, and we have to fight for the little business we do get with all the druggists and hairdressers. Besides, there's no license for selling soap.

VOIGT: Marie, listen—you mustn't think I'll be a burden to you. I only came to say hello. And now I'll be on my way.

FRAU HOPRECHT: No, Wilhelm, no, you can't do that. Imagine my husband, if I let my only brother run off before he even gets to know you.

VOIGT: He won't take much pleasure in that, will he?

FRAU HOPRECHT: Wilhelm you shouldn't say such things; you don't even know him. Why, my husband is goodness itself, that's what he is. He can't bear to see a fly caught in a spider's web. Of course, in the magistrate's office where he works, it's quite different. He knows how to be firm there; even severe, if he has to. And besides, he can't stand anything that's irregular. But no, Wilhelm, you mustn't get the wrong idea. Outside his office he's goodness itself, like I said. And his heart's in the right place, too.

VOIGT: I thought about it a long time—whether I should come up or not—I even went past the house a couple times first.

FRAU HOPRECHT: But, Wilhelm, you should have come to your sister's long before this! Who knows, maybe everything would have been different.

VOIGT: Before—well, I wouldn't have belonged here at all, Marie. I wouldn't have dared.—But now . . .

FRAU HOPRECHT: No, Wilhelm, no, it was wrong of you to stay away all these years. And if you'd written, just once, if we'd only known what prison you were in, I'd have sent you a Christmas package.

VOIGT: That's very nice of you.

FRAU HOPRECHT: Well, of course I would have; we're brother and sister. I might not have recognized you, because it's been such a—my goodness, just think, I was only a child! Oh, and when I remember the time mother died . . .

VOIGT: Not about mother, please . . .

FRAU HOPRECHT: Not if you don't want me to, Wilhelm. I just thought you'd like to hear about it.

(VOIGT *shakes his head.*)

He ought to be here soon. They get off today at half-past five. —I mean the volunteers and reservists. They have to be at the barracks tomorrow to practice for the Kaiser's maneuvers. That means being there at four in the morning.

VOIGT: Is it voluntary?

FRAU HOPRECHT: Sure! He'd much rather have been in the army, but we'd just inherited the shop from Auntie and thought we could do better with it. I think sometimes if he didn't go out to drill once in a while he'd just pine away. It means everything to him. Otherwise there's nothing much else—a game of skittles now and then, smoke a pipe, and at most a glass of beer, even if he is a sober man.

VOIGT: You picked a good man, Marie.

FRAU HOPRECHT: You're right, Wilhelm. I can't complain. I only wish things would work out a little better, you know—not that they don't, but it is a little difficult.

VOIGT (*looks around*): It's very nice here . . .

FRAU HOPRECHT: The ceiling has to be painted and the floor needs polishing, and the rugs are eaten up by moths—there just isn't enough money for everything.

VOIGT: It looks new enough to me.

FRAU HOPRECHT: You're not used to it anymore, Wilhelm. But at least it's clean.

VOIGT: You could shave here in the moonlight—wouldn't even need a mirror.

FRAU HOPRECHT: Right now he's specially anxious about his volunteer duty. They're supposed to make him acting-sergeant— he's up for it at least. But don't mention it; he's keeping it a secret. He's just like a child—he talked about it in his sleep. Oh, and look here— (*She opens the wardrobe and shows him an object wrapped in paper and hidden away.*) —he's already bought himself a sword with a sword knot on it—he's allowed to buy it himself, you know, when he's made acting-sergeant. But you mustn't tell him I know—he wants to surprise me.—

Oh, listen to that, she's calling again! I'm coming, I'm coming!

(*A thin, distant voice, like that of a child, is heard calling.*)

We're having a little trouble right now. That's our tenant. We've got a room looking out onto the yard—we always thought of it as a nursery.—Friedrich wanted so much to have one, but I was sick then, and now it's too late, so we rented it out. She's a very nice girl, not even sixteen yet. She worked in a shop where they sewed linens, but there's something wrong with her chest now; been in bed for almost two months. She can't pay, of course, because she's an orphan, and Friedrich wanted to send her to the hospital; but she'd cry, and he let her stay here.—He's such a good man. (*While talking, she has put away the polishing materials, and then hears the voice again.*) Yes, yes, I'm coming! She hates to be left alone because she's afraid. I'll be right back, Wilhelm . . . (*She goes off.*)

VOIGT (*remains seated at first, then rises, places his hat and package on the chair, goes to the wardrobe and gives the uniform hanging there a good looking-over. He studies the shoulder straps, and says half to himself*): The Twenty-first Grenadier Guards. Hm. Imagine that! (*He looks at the helmet hanging on a clothes hook.*) Infantry helmet. Hm. (*He touches it as though wanting to take it down. At the same moment, the wall clock begins to strike six in a thin clear sound, interrupted by a strange, soft, rattling noise. VOIGT turns around and takes a few hesitant steps toward the clock.*) Look at that—the old clock!—Imagine that! (*He stands there staring at the clock.*)

(*Meanwhile we hear the sound of a key in the outside door, along with the opening and closing of the door, and then footsteps. HOPRECHT enters the room. He is younger than VOIGT, a broad and powerful man, with a clear, strong face. He is simply dressed.*)

VOIGT (*still looking at the clock; then turns around slowly*): Good day, Herr Hoprecht.
HOPRECHT: Hello. Who are you?
VOIGT: Your brother-in-law. Wilhelm Voigt.
HOPRECHT: I see. (*He ponders for a moment, then goes to VOIGT and extends his hand.*) I'm glad. Nice of you to visit us. Sit down, sit down. Where's Marie.

VOIGT: The sick girl just called; she went back.

HOPRECHT: I see. Have you been here long?

VOIGT: No—a half hour. I thought I'd . . .

HOPRECHT: Your things are still here. I'll put them away.

VOIGT: I was just going to leave.

HOPRECHT: Certainly not. We must get to know each other first. Or don't you have time?

VOIGT: Oh, I've got time, all right.

HOPRECHT: Well then. Sit down and rest. You'll stay the night. I insist.

VOIGT: I don't know if I should. I don't want to disturb you.

HOPRECHT: Nonsense! Excuse the expression, but it's true. Eh? (*He hangs* VOIGT's *things in front of the door; comes back and looks at* VOIGT.) I want to tell you something. I won't beat around the bush, because I can't. But you're my wife's brother, and so I have some claim to you too. You're welcome here anytime.

VOIGT: That's good of you. Thank you.

HOPRECHT: Nothing to thank. (*They sit down.*) How are things going now, Wilhelm?

VOIGT: Oh, all right. I have to start all over again first. I've been away from the world for ten years now, you know.

HOPRECHT: I know. When did you get out?

VOIGT: Just this morning. I didn't know where to go. You forget your way around after all that time.

HOPRECHT: Haven't you any more friends?

VOIGT: No. Before that I was in for fifteen years, and then in between I was in Moabit Prison for a year and a half, and the rest of the time out of the country. I only know the people in jail, you see, and, well, I'd rather just not know them anymore, you see.

HOPRECHT: I understand. That's all right, Wilhelm. And if you don't mind my saying so, I think you'll start all over, right from the beginning. Eh? A person can always start over again; no one's ever too old for that.

VOIGT: That would be nice, all right.

HOPRECHT: That's right, Wilhelm. And we'll help put you on your feet. And soon too.

VOIGT: I hope so. If only they let me.

HOPRECHT: You'll find work. They're not so particular nowadays.

VOIGT: Maybe so. But I mean the police—because of my permit.

HOPRECHT: It's not as bad as all that. They're not cannibals! I'm a civil official myself.—Take a good look and you'll see they're human beings too, eh? (*He laughs.*)

VOIGT (*laughing with him*): You know, I was so afraid of you, I can't say.

HOPRECHT: Do you have a place to stay yet?

VOIGT: No. But I've got a little money—I did some special work there. I won't have to sleep in the flophouse yet.

HOPRECHT: Save your money, you'll be glad you did. You'll stay with us until you get a job.

VOIGT: No, Friedrich, I can't. I can't let you do that.

HOPRECHT: Why not? You have to. That's a regimental order, understand? No back talk now. If you mean you don't want it for nothing, you can help my wife in the shop till you find something else.

VOIGT: That's not why I came up here, it really isn't. I just wanted to talk to a human being again

HOPRECHT: I believe you, Wilhelm. But it would be nice to have a man in the house while I'm away at maneuvers. Marie's so careless about the cashbox, she just lets it sit around open, and so you can keep an eye on it for me, eh?

VOIGT (*is silent for a moment, then extends him his hand*): You know, Friedrich, with more people like you in the world we wouldn't need prisons.

HOPRECHT: You're exaggerating, Wilhelm. (*Slaps him on the shoulder.*) What I mean is, what's done is done. So now you have to stand on your own two legs and keep your chin up.

VOIGT: I will, Friedrich. I promise you. You see, it's just that I couldn't do it by myself anymore. Ten years ago, why all I wanted was to get away, over the hills, and—but now—you just get so dead tired, you see—

HOPRECHT: Everything will be fine now.

VOIGT: If it ever happens again—if I ever go down again—it'll be the end of me. It'll be all over.

HOPRECHT: You forget that and go straight on ahead. Your legs will get you there all by themselves.

VOIGT: I'll manage, Friedrich.

FRAU HOPRECHT (*enters*): Good evening, Friedrich, you're home already. She was all soaked through with sweat; I had to change her bed. Well, I see you've gotten acquainted. I was right, you see? Not letting him go off. He was going to leave and I said, you must get acquainted first, he doesn't bite.

HOPRECHT: You know what, Marie? Your brother and I just arranged for him to stay here for the time being. Until he gets a job. He can even help you a little in the shop.

FRAU HOPRECHT (*not too eagerly*): Well, all right, Friedrich, if you think so—is he going to sleep here too, you mean?

HOPRECHT: Of course! We have this nice sofa over here that nobody ever sits on. It's all right with you, isn't it, Wilhelm?

VOIGT: I should say! And there's the old clock hanging over it—
the one from the hall at home, eh, Marie?—I mean, if it's all
right with Marie . . .

FRAU HOPRECHT: I'll have to get out some bedclothes.

HOPRECHT: Then get them out. You've got a whole chestful.

FRAU HOPRECHT: Of course—I just mean I have to get them out.
(*She starts off.—In the doorway.*) I'll get supper ready.
(*Off.*)

HOPRECHT (*laughs*): That's the way she is. A good soul but a little
fussy. Look here, Wilhelm, I want to show you something.
(*Leads him to the wardrobe.*) If everything goes right, I'll be
promoted to acting-sergeant this time. This'll be my second
year as a volunteer reservist. She doesn't know about it yet,
because I want to surprise her. She's just like a child in such
matters. Look, I've even bought my sword already—you're
allowed to buy it yourself—look. (*He opens the paper covering a bit so that the hilt of the sword is visible, and then
looks anxiously at the door.*) I'll come home with it and with
my buttons and cockades. (*With a smirk.*) You'll keep it
under your hat, won't you, Wilhelm? She shouldn't know
anything about it.

VOIGT: Of course, of course!—And then when there's a war you
might become a warrant officer, and who knows, maybe even
a field lieutenant.

HOPRECHT: I must say, you know a lot about ranks.

VOIGT: It always interested me, though I've never been in myself.

HOPRECHT: That's too bad. That's the best thing in life. (*He puts
away the sword.*) Well now, how about a quick drink to welcome you back? Just us two men, eh? I've got a bottle here
they gave me at the office for a New Year's present. It's real
brandy. (*While saying this, he takes the bottle, which is
three-fourths full, from the sideboard and fills two small
glasses.*)

VOIGT: Friedrich, listen, I want to ask you something. Like you
said, you work in the magistrate's office, where everything
comes through—so I was wondering about a permit to stay
here, so they don't make me leave—or refuse me a passport
like they always did before—and I can't get work without a
registration form, too—I mean—do you think you could do
something about it—when the papers come through?

HOPRECHT: Things must take their course, Wilhelm. There's nothing you can do. So let's not even discuss it, eh? You must go

about such things in the right way, and it'll all turn out in the end. Doing such things under cover would be against the law. You'll get exactly what you deserve; that's the nice thing about living in Prussia. Well, Wilhelm, here's to a new life. And don't worry. Things must take their course!

VOIGT: Well—prosit!

(*They clink glasses.*)

BLACKOUT

SCENE 3

The bedroom of MAYOR OBERMÜLLER *in Köpenick. A wide double bed of fine wood, but very pretentious; night tables, curtains, lamps, wardrobes. Over the husband's side of the bed hangs the "Madonna della Sedia" of Raphael, and over the wife's side the "Adam" of Michelangelo. A clock ticks on the wall, and an alarm clock sits on the night table; both show 3:15. A telephone is on the wife's night table.* FRAU OBERMÜLLER, *a Junoesque apparition, sits on the bed in her nightdress and embroidered night jacket, beneath which she wears a corset confining her bosom. Her hair, robbed of its pads and other paraphernalia, is piled high on her head, and held there by hairpins and clasps. The telephone receiver is at her ear and she drums excitedly on the telephone carriage, at the same time shouting into it.*

FRAU OBERMÜLLER: Potsdam! Pots—dam! Potsdam 324! Wormser!

OBERMÜLLER (*half of his face shaved, the other half still covered with soap; he is dressed in an open bathrobe with a full set of woolen underwear beneath it, in addition to stocking suspenders, and military boots with spurs; he storms out of the bathroom*): Got it, Mathilde? Where in heaven's name is Fanny?

FRAU OBERMÜLLER: Good Lord, I'm not a magician! (*She presses a bell which sounds shrilly.*)—Potsdam, Potsdam 324.—Go back and finish shaving, or you'll never be ready!

OBERMÜLLER: Finish finish finish! How can I finish when everything's against me! Where in heaven's name is Fanny?!

FRAU OBERMÜLLER (*ringing furiously*): The silly goose is still in bed! No one answers—

OBERMÜLLER: If that Wormser fails me with this uniform, I'll

have to go in the old one!—I can't very well go to the
Kaiser's maneuvers dressed in my underclothes! And I must
be there exactly at four—

FANNY (*the servant, half asleep, enters in night clothes*): Yes?

OBERMÜLLER and FRAU OBERMÜLLER: Where's the uniform?!

FANNY: Not here yet . . .

OBERMÜLLER: Then bring me the old one, goddamn it! Bring me
the old one!!

FANNY (*drowsily*): The old one?

FRAU OBERMÜLLER: Of course! Hurry! Down the hallway!

FANNY: But it's to be sold.

OBERMÜLLER (*screaming*): Bring it here!!

FANNY: All right, all right. (*She goes off.*)

FRAU OBERMÜLLER: Potsdam!! Potsdam 324! Stop standing around
like that and wipe the soap off your face. Yes, Potsdam—well,
finally! Mayor Obermüller calling from Köpenick—Mayor
Obermüller, from Köpenick—no, no,—not Spandau—where
do you get Spandau?—Köpenick!

OBERMÜLLER (*tears the receiver from her hand*): Wormser,
Wormser, is that you?—the uniform tailor in Potsdam?—you
promised me my new uniform by midnight at the latest,
midnight at the latest is what you said—you know perfectly
well I must be with my regiment at four A.M., and I'm not
about to go stark naked!—How can you do this to me, I—
What?! This isn't Adolf Wormser? Well, who is it then?—
What? What's that? He doesn't answer? Well, why *doesn't*
he answer? The middle of the night? But it's already light
outside!! This is unheard of—(*He lets the receiver sink down.*)
—he doesn't answer. Wormser—doesn't answer.

FRAU OBERMÜLLER: I could have told you that right away. It's
midnight.

OBERMÜLLER: But it's already light outside. At four o'clock I have
to be—

FANNY (*enters with the old uniform*): Here it is. I thought it was
to be sold.

FRAU OBERMÜLLER: Then *stop* thinking for a while and help my
husband! Hurry, hurry!

OBERMÜLLER: In any case the trousers will still fit me. I'll have to
keep them up with safety pins. (*He has stepped into his
trousers.*) Oh, but the coat!! (*He tries putting it on.*)

FRAU OBERMÜLLER (*helping* FANNY *pull the coat on*): You've
grown much too fat—I've told you that for a long time now.

OBERMÜLLER: Nonsense! The material's shrunk! I'm the same now

as five years ago! Good God! I can't cut myself down *now*!
It won't fit— (*He pulls on the coat, groaning, but it won't
button.*)

FRAU OBERMÜLLER: You should have thought about that sooner.
Look, the children! What are you doing up at this time of
night?

(HELMUT *and* IRENE, *in their teens, look in, dressed in their
night clothes.*)

IRENE: How can we sleep with all the noise?

HELMUT: I thought I could hurry over to the uniform shop on my
bicycle.

OBERMÜLLER (*going after them*): Rubbish! Now get back to bed!

HELMUT (*offended*): All right, forget it! (*He goes off with* IRENE.)

OBERMÜLLER (*in dull despair*): I'll have to call the Adjutant at
once—say I had a sudden heart attack—or, no, a fever—
bronchial pneumonia—or no, no, the heart, the heart's better—

FRAU OBERMÜLLER: Go on out, Fanny!

(FANNY *goes off murmuring.*)

You are not going to make that call. You will pull yourself
together. All we need now is for you to give up—with everything at stake! (*She tries to use force in buttoning the coat.*)

OBERMÜLLER: Ouch! Ouch!

FRAU OBERMÜLLER: What do you mean "ouch"! I'm not hurting
you! Hold still! There—(*She has torn off a piece of the uniform in the attempt.*)

OBERMÜLLER (*sinking onto the bed*): And that's the end of that—

FRAU OBERMÜLLER (*screaming into the receiver as though demented*): Potsdam!! Potsdam 324!!!

OBERMÜLLER (*tragically*): Never mind. That won't do any good.—
Why did I sign up for training this year in the first place?

FRAU OBERMÜLLER: Potsdam 324!!!

OBERMÜLLER: I didn't have to. You're the one who wanted it.

FRAU OBERMÜLLER: But I must get through!! 324!!

OBERMÜLLER: You wanted to brag. Sheer female vanity. All because of your women friends.

FRAU OBERMÜLLER: Oh, so now it's my fault, is it?

OBERMÜLLER: The important things I've left undone in my office—

(*The doorbell rings.* FRAU OBERMÜLLER *is startled.*)

FRAU OBERMÜLLER: The bell! It rang!

OBERMÜLLER (*utterly distraught*): Rang? What do you mean "rang"?! You mean it rang?!

FRAU OBERMÜLLER (*jumps up, tidies herself*): Wormser!

OBERMÜLLER: It rang?!

(*The children storm in,* WABSCHKE *behind them with a new uniform over his arm.*)

IRENE: Father! It's here! We've got it!

HELMUT: Hurry, Father! You can still make it with a taxi!

WABSCHKE: There's a taxi waiting outside—the meter read seventeen marks fifty when I arrived—Potsdam's a long way. Good morning, sir—good morning, madam! I trust you had a good night's sleep!

OBERMÜLLER (*jumps up, a new man*): Why all the excitement? I knew it would all turn out. Wormser would never let me down at a time like this, eh? Give it here.

FRAU OBERMÜLLER (*getting after* WABSCHKE): Now you listen to me! Not let us down, eh? This is unheard of—you promised the uniform by midnight at the latest, and now you bring it at the last minute!

WABSCHKE: But, madam, the last minute is always the best. What would your husband have done with the uniform at midnight? He was better off in bed at that hour.

FRAU OBERMÜLLER: Do you suppose we even closed our eyes last night?

WABSCHKE: That's terrible. Ah, but the Mayor probably won't get his customary sleep on maneuvers either. How does it go?— (*He sings.*)

"When midnight lies upon the land,
All alone my guard I stand—"

(*The children join in the song.*)

OBERMÜLLER: Quiet!! My sword! Bring it here! (*He has put on the uniform, and* WABSCHKE *pulls it into perfect place for him.*)

WABSCHKE: Now what do you say to that! Is that a good fit or isn't it?

OBERMÜLLER (*buckles on his belt and puts on his cap*): Fanny! My suitcase! My coat! No, put them in the taxi! Hurry!

FANNY (*appears in the doorway*): The Mayor look very correct now. Just like an officer.

OBERMÜLLER (*in the best of humor*): What do you *expect* me to look like? A mailman? Well, Tilly, how does it look?

FRAU OBERMÜLLER: Perfect! At least you can be seen now!

IRENE: It looks so sweet, Papa!

HELMUT: Is the sword sharp? Don't you have a revolver?

OBERMÜLLER: Come, children, you may walk with me down to the taxi. Adieu, Tilly! Good-bye!

FRAU OBERMÜLLER (*kisses him*): And you'll telephone the first free evening you have—we'll come out to see you; I'll even bring little Hans along. All right?

OBERMÜLLER: Of course, Tilly. Be good, children. Do I have my watch? Yes—good Lord, I need some money!

WABSCHKE: Not a bad idea!

OBERMÜLLER: Good-bye!—Are you riding with me, Wabschke?

WABSCHKE: No, I'll take the streetcar. Enjoy yourself, Mayor, sir! Onward to victory! Hip hip, hooray!

(OBERMÜLLER *goes off with the children.*)

Believe me, madam, that was quite a job. We started work at six and worked all night long without even eating. Ah, but there's nothing too good for the fatherland! Eh?

FRAU OBERMÜLLER: Here, you may as well take the old uniform along with you. Give Herr Wormser my regards and tell him to take it as part payment on the new one.

WABSCHKE (*looks at the uniform*): Not much use left in that. It was secondhand when the Mayor first bought it.

FRAU OBERMÜLLER: What are you talking about?! My husband wearing secondhand clothes! It's just that he's grown too heavy, otherwise it would be in perfect condition.

WABSCHKE: For a masquerade, perhaps.

BLACKOUT

SCENE 4

A hallway in the Rixdorf police station. Bare walls, a bench, a door. A sign on the door reads: "Room 9." It is the permit office of Rixdorf. About ten people of both sexes are seen waiting on the bench. Some drum with their fingers, or else cough nervously. A short, elderly man is reading the Socialist paper Vorwärts. *Most of the people stare dumbly in front of them.—The door opens. Everyone looks up, and the one whose turn is next rises. A* POLICEMAN *comes from inside the room and lets out a* WOMAN.

WOMAN (*talking tearfully over her shoulder*): Oh, but I just didn't know—I didn't know I had to report to the police station when just relatives visited me! How could I know that? It's not my fault! (*She goes off, her handkerchief to her nose.*)

(*The* MAN *next in line tries to enter.*)

POLICEMAN (*barring the way*): Sit down, you!

MAN: But why? It's my turn.

POLICEMAN (*without answering*): Herr Scheitrum!

(*An official enters with a bundle of documents.*)

POLICEMAN: The Chief wants to see you, Herr Scheitrum. (*He opens the door and the official enters; he closes the door behind him and once again stands in front of the door.*)

MAN: But it's my turn to—

POLICEMAN: I said, sit down.

MAN (*sits down*): I wonder if I'll ever get in.

POLICEMAN: You'll get in when it's your turn.

ANOTHER MAN (*reading the Socialist paper* Vorwärts; *in a thin little voice*): Excuse me, but this is a bit too much. Does a public office like this exist for the people—or the people for the office?!

FIRST MAN: Well, you know the saying: "A soldier's life is spent vainly waiting!"

(*Some of them laugh.*)

READER OF Vorwärts: I beg your pardon, but we are not *soldiers,* we're *free citizens!* And we have other things to do than stand around here decorating your walls! Hear?!

POLICEMAN: If you've got time to read that Socialist crap, you've got time to stand here.

READER: Look here, you, that's none of your business! I happen to subscribe to the Vorwärts—that's right, I do—and I read it every day, if you'd like to know. But that will *not* stop me from demanding my civic duties—what I meant to say was rights.

POLICEMAN: Keep your shirt on. You've got a long wait ahead.

READER: This is more than I can take! There's someone from another office in there, and they're telling each other dirty stories!

POLICEMAN (*going up to him*): They're doing *what* in there?

READER: Well, how should I know what they're doing in there? All I want is my turn. (*He peers into his paper.*)

POLICEMAN: You get in around here when your turn comes. (*Returns to the door.*)

VOIGT (*enters from the side, quickly, excitedly*): Excuse me, is this room number nine?

POLICEMAN: Can't you read? Sit down.

VOIGT: Excuse me, Sergeant, I just wondered first if I was in the right place. He told me to try room number nine, but if that's not right—if that's not the right place—

POLICEMAN: Sit down. You'll find out soon enough.

VOIGT: But, you see, by the time I get there it'll be too late, and it'll be no use. I'm on parole, you see, and I'm staying with my brother-in-law, and when I went to the headquarters they said there was no parole office in Rixdorf, and I'd have to move on, because that's the procedure—but he didn't know exactly, so he said to try room number nine—

POLICEMAN: All right then, sit down.

VOIGT: But what if I don't get there in time—or if room number nine is the wrong room again—then it'll be too late!

POLICEMAN: Shut up and sit down.

VOIGT: I'm staying in a respectable house, you know, so they really don't have to send me on. I only wanted to tell that to somebody—somebody with authority—

POLICEMAN: Sit down.

(VOIGT *sits down. Herr Scheitrum comes out of the office and goes off, biting his nails.*)

All right, next. (*He opens the door and goes in with the next in line.*)

(*There is a stir among those waiting.*)

READER (*with an asthmatic wheeze*): He's a bully, that's what he is, a bully! Steps all over anybody below him, and cringes to his superiors.

WOMAN: They've got all the time they want.

READER: But it's *our* time they're wasting, and *our money* they stuff their bellies with! Their rudeness and their tricks make me sick! My name's Klawonn, I'm a merchant, I worked my way up honorably, and now they're barking down my back, all because of a license. And why? Oh, I know why, all right! I say I can think whatever I want, but I'll still demand my civic duties—what I meant to say was rights— (*He chokes and coughs.*)

POLICEMAN (*comes from the office*): Quiet in here! They can hear you inside! (*He suddenly snaps to attention and looks straight down the hallway.*)

YOUNG LIEUTENANT (*with an adjutant's scarf, enters quickly*): Room nine?

POLICEMAN (*at attention*): Yes, Lieutenant, sir!

LIEUTENANT: You can close up shop, Sergeant. We'll be quartering troops in here. (*He enters the room, followed obsequiously by the* POLICEMAN, *who closes the door after them.*)

READER: So now we just pack up and go. It's all over. They've got all the time in the world for the military, but none for the ordinary citizen. Just let a smart young lieutenant come along, and—eh—eh—

FAT MAN (*who has sat motionless till now, staring directly in front of him, jumps up*): How dare you talk like that about our Prussian soldiers! You couldn't pass an army physical if your life depended on it! You're barking up the wrong tree, you little pip-squeak!

READER: Oh, I am, am I?! All I am asking for are my civic—

(*The* POLICEMAN *opens the door. All talk stops and they look at him. He silently hangs a sign on the door that reads: "Closed for the day." He nods significantly to those waiting, and indicates the door with a movement of his head.*)

VOIGT (*with a cry of alarm*): But I have to get in there! I have to—or it'll be too late!!

(*The* POLICEMAN *goes back into the room, closing the door loudly behind him.* VOIGT *sinks down onto the bench.*)

READER (*as the others go off*): You might as well forget it. You'll never get in there today. You'd be sitting here all night. (*He goes off.*)

(VOIGT *stays behind, alone. He sits with his back bent forward, as if he had been dealt a deathblow. After a moment raised voices are heard from inside the room.*)

VOICE OF THE LIEUTENANT:—There will be no exceptions! An order's an order, and I suggest you act accordingly!

(*The voice dies down again.* VOIGT *raises his head, listens—then he rises, goes tiptoe to the door, and—looks through the keyhole.*)

BLACKOUT

SCENE 5

A small room with a bed, a window looking out onto a courtyard, and a door into a hallway. VOIGT *is seated on a chair beside the bed. The bed is so situated that the person in it is scarcely visible —except for a hand, which* VOIGT *holds in his own. Colored illustrations cut from newspapers are pinned to the wall over the bed. From down in the courtyard a man and a woman are heard singing a melancholy song. They are accompanied by a mandolin.*

GIRL: Uncle Wilhelm, I hear something—what is it?

VOIGT: It's the street singers. They're sometimes known as scavengers. They go to sing in the royal courtyard so the Kaiser has to throw down a groschen to get rid of them.

GIRL: Oh, I've got a groschen, too—over there, on the washstand, under the box of tooth powder. Throw it down to them, will you?

VOIGT: If it'll make you happy.

GIRL: Yes, throw it down.

(VOIGT *takes the groschen, goes to the window and opens it. The song of the singers is heard more clearly.*)

> "And so I say once more
> The days of youth are fine
> The days of our happy youth
> But they never will come more."

VOIGT: I'll wrap it in a piece of paper. There— (*He throws it down.*)

GIRL (*sitting up*): Did they get it? Did they catch it?

VOIGT: Oh! It fell right on top of the old buzzard! But I don't think it made a hole.

(*The* GIRL *laughs.*)

(*Turns around.*) You better lay down and cover up, you little rascal, or you'll never get well. (*He has hurried over to her and covered her up. The voice of the male singer is heard addressing the crowd.* VOIGT *hurries to the window and closes it.*)

GIRL: Why did you close the window so I can't hear?

VOIGT: He's stopped singing now—he's making a speech. I can do that for you myself. (*He strikes a pose.*) "Honorable ladies and gentlemen! We who wander through the countryside on the wings of song—we are like unto the birds of heaven, of whom it is written in the Bible: 'They sow not, neither do they reap, but a dry crust feeds them.' And therefore, my dear people, throw us down a little something, even if it's only half a groschen. It will lay up interest for you in heaven, so that one day you will be a millionaire there—if you live a long life down here, and, like a good man, keep building up your reserves."

GIRL: You do that very well. It's almost like you were one of them.

VOIGT: Who knows? One day I might be like that.

GIRL: Tell me, Uncle Wilhelm—did you get around much in the world?

VOIGT: Did I! I never did like the quiet life. I've been to all the five continents—did you know that? And once I even crossed the mountains of Bohemia. That was really something.

GIRL: Herr Hoprecht went to sea once as a young boy. And they even had a storm, and—and a real nigger. But he doesn't tell it very well. You do it much better.

VOIGT: Well, you see, I pictured it all in my head. Oh, but you must go to the mountains. Once you're well you must go there for a rest. Maybe the insurance will help pay for some of it. And then you'll be in the mountains!

GIRL: I was in the Müggel Hills once. But I was still just a child then. It was an orphanage picnic. I almost don't remember it anymore.

VOIGT: Oh, but those are nothing but little molehills! Pinch a flea and he could leap over the whole lot of them. No, no, my child, you could never in the world imagine what really big mountains are like. They're so high they're right up in the clouds—no, higher than the clouds, and sometimes even way up above the clouds—just imagine! And there's beautiful sunshine up there—while down below it's raining!

GIRL: Is there always sunshine above the clouds?

VOIGT: Certainly! The sun's there all day long, eh? And all the clouds do is float around the globe of the earth. Once you've been there you know such things. They have nothing at all to do with heaven. They're only mist and dampness from the water down here below.

GIRL: Isn't it cold up there?

VOIGT: Cold? That close to the sun? Why, when the sun's high in the sky, even in the middle of winter, in the snow, you can run around in nothing but your shirtsleeves and not even notice the frost! And you'd never believe all the things that

grow up there. What is there down here! A couple scraggly
fir trees, a patch of heather and a juniper bush or two. But
up there the air tastes as sweet as a bowl of fruit. And there
are flowers, too, but not in gardens—no, but in every meadow
the eye can see, just like in a picture book. You never saw
such a sight.

GIRL: But, Uncle Wilhelm, why is it so beautiful up there, and
down here there's nothing special?

VOIGT: I'll tell you. I've thought it all out. It's like this—the
earth is alive, and you can see that, because it always changes.
And what's alive wants to rise up, get to the top, way up
high, like a blade of grass, or a seed potato, or a child, eh?—
And it's the same with the crust of the earth. Water's heavy,
so it runs downward, into the ocean. But the real earth, the
true earth, grows higher and higher, raises itself up, don't you
see? But down below here we're closer to the ocean, and
that's why there's more sand and mud, you see? Oh, but up
there, up there there's all kinds of rose-colored quartz and
rock crystal. And so it's bound to be nicer up there.

GIRL: Uncle Wilhelm—we'll go there together!

VOIGT: Of course we will, child, of course.

GIRL: And you'll take me with you, won't you? The next time
you go up!

VOIGT: Of course—there's nothing I'd like better.

GIRL: Listen! They're singing again. The song about "Püppchen."
I like that so much!

(*Through the closed windows, and from a great distance, we
hear the street singers singing.*)

VOIGT: Yes, that's "Püppchen" all right.

GIRL: You know—I don't think we'll ever get there.

VOIGT: Where? What do you mean?

GIRL: To the mountains. We'll never get there—the two of us.

VOIGT: Don't be in such a hurry, child. We can't know such
things. (*He caresses her.*)

GIRL: Don't go away—please—

VOIGT: Of course not—where would I go? I have to look after the
house. Papa Hoprecht is at maneuvers and Marie's at work,
so I couldn't leave you if I had to.

GIRL: Would you read me something, please?

VOIGT: Do you have a book, or a magazine?

GIRL (*fishes out a book from under her mattress*): I'm really too
old for this. But I like it so much, I can never hear it too
often. Frau Hoprecht would make fun of me if she found it.

"You're not a child anymore," she always says to me. I made a scratch with my fingernail where I stopped. It's the story of "The Bremen Town Musicians."

VOIGT: Let's see—Aha! *Grimm's Fairy Tales. (Puts on his glasses.)*

GIRL: I'm really too old for this.

VOIGT: That doesn't matter. I like to read them too, and I'm a little old myself, you might say, eh?

(The doorbell rings.)

GIRL *(sits up)*: Don't go away! *Please!*

VOIGT: But, child, I have to answer the door. Who knows, it might even be important.

GIRL: Maybe someone only got lost on the wrong floor. We're not expecting anyone.

VOIGT: I'll be right back, child.

GIRL *(clinging to him)*: But it's nothing! They're already gone!

(The bell rings again.)

VOIGT: You see? I'll just go answer it and come right back.

GIRL: But you won't close the door, will you? And you'll turn on the light—please? It's growing so dark outside—and the window gets so light and bright—like an eye—

VOIGT *(quickly lights the gas lamp and pulls shut the curtains at the window; the bell rings again, loudly)*: There. Better? Now I'll go have a look.

GIRL: But please leave the door open!

VOIGT: Of course. You'll hear me all the way to the hall door. *(He goes out, leaving the door open behind him.)*

VOIGT'S VOICE: What is it?

STRANGE VOICE *(from outside)*: Does Wilhelm Voigt the cobbler live here? The one who's on parole at the police station?

VOIGT'S VOICE: Yes. One minute. I'll open up.—I'm the one you're looking for.

STRANGE VOICE: Sign here. A letter for you from the police station.

(Silence for a moment. The music outside stops. VOIGT *returns. In his hand is a large envelope with an unbroken official seal on it.)*

GIRL *(very softly)*: Did you get a letter, Uncle Wilhelm?

VOIGT: It's nothing—nothing. *(He sticks it into his pocket.)*

GIRL: Don't you want to read it?

VOIGT: No hurry. It's all so tiresome anyway. I'd rather read to you. *(He sits down and picks up the book.)* Now we'll go on from where you left off.—" 'How can one be happy when his life's at stake?' answered the Cat. 'Just because I'm getting old, and my teeth are worn down, and I'd rather sit beside the stove than chase mice all day long, they want to drown me! I may have escaped them this time, but now I'm at my wit's end. Where shall I go?'—'Come,' said the Cock, 'we'll find something better than death.'" (*He stops and looks at the* GIRL.) What is it, child? Hm?—Are you asleep? (*He bends over her—she breathes deeply. He lays the book down on his knees and quickly takes the envelope from his pocket, hesitates a moment, then breaks the seal and reads in a muted monotone.*) "Notice from Police Headquarters of Rixdorf, Reinickendorf, Neukölln, Gross-Lichterfelde.—You are required—within forty-eight hours—" (*Reads silently, then again in half-voice.*)—"In the event of failure to comply—compulsory eviction—in the event of return—imprisonment up to—" (*He grows silent.*)

GIRL (*after a pause, suddenly*): Uncle Wilhelm—you're not reading!

VOIGT (*picks up the book once more*): " 'Come,' said the Cock, 'we'll find something better than death.' "

BLACKOUT

SCENE 6

A raised box in the great banquet hall of Dressel's Restaurant. Bright lights, elegant decorations completely in white and silver, artificial flowers, mirrors. The hall is so situated as to appear larger than it really is. In the box is a table laden with champagne glasses, bottles in ice coolers, dessert plates, fruit and compote dishes, ashtrays and liqueur glasses, crackers, cotillion favors, and flowers. At the table are HERR WORMSER, WILLY WORMSER, MAJOR *and* FRAU KESSLER, DR. TRUMP. WORMSER *is in evening dress, and his shirt front is already quite rumpled as a result of all kinds of exertions, eating, laughing, talking, sweating.* WILLY *is dressed in a Hussar's uniform of the most elegant officer's cut, though he is only a trooper; he presents a quite lamentable figure.* MAJOR *and* FRAU KESSLER *are an elderly but well-to-do couple. He is pensioned, dressed in civilian clothes, and very much at ease.* TRUMP *is somewhat a rake, humorous, and a bit intoxicated. At the start of the scene,* FRÄULEIN AUGUSTA WORMSER *is seen standing on the steps at the side of the box, as if on a podium turned toward the hall. She is dressed in a uniform of a captain of the Potsdam Grenadier Guards. The uniform spans her amply proportioned figure, and her rather too blonde hair spills in coquettish curls from under the officer's cap on her head. She is singing the final verse of an original composition in honor of the occasion. All listen attentively, and* WORMSER *appears to take in every word.*

AUGUSTA (*sings to the faint accompaniment of an unseen piano*):
"And so, proud Hussars, we welcome you
As honored guests, so brave and true!
You have given us great delight
To watch your grand maneuver's fight!

(*Coquettishly.*)

But you are not the only one—
For I'm here, too, and want some fun!
But I, alas, am infantry,
And so, I'll never ride, you see!"

(*The band strikes up the refrain. General applause and shouts of "Bravo!"* AUGUSTA *thanks them partly with military salutes, partly with hand kisses sent off to all sides. She then disappears into the hall, surrounded by the enthusiastic admirers who drag her off.*)

KESSLER (*at the table, applauding loudly*): Bravo! Excellent! Who composed the words?

WORMSER (*beaming*): The words? She composed them herself, and I knew nothing about it! (*He sings with the music.*)

"But I, alas, am infantry
And so will never ride, you see—"

How's that, eh? How's that!

FRAU KESSLER: Oh, she's so sweet! So absolutely precious! And how charming she looks in her uniform!

TRUMP: Marvelous! Congratulations, Herr Wormser! Your daughter is a perfect prima donna! She could go on the stage this minute!

WORMSER: She gets that from her old papa! In my student days I used to get up and sing like that at all the parties. We had someone there who knew all about acting, and he always said to me: "Wormser, you should go on the stage! You're made for it!" You know, I studied law for a year or two, just like you. That rather makes us colleagues, eh, Trump?

TRUMP: Prosit! (*He drinks.*)

(AUGUSTA *sweeps in, breathless.*)

WORMSER: Ah, so there she is! Come here, my sweet. You did that really splendidly. (*Kisses her.*)
AUGUSTA: Hurry! A glass of champagne! God, I'm so hot!

(*The others applaud.*)

FRAU KESSLER: Oh, so sweet! So absolutely precious! I could fall in love with a captain like her, just like that!
KESSLER: Millie, my dear! Shall we be a bit less eccentric?
AUGUSTA (*has downed one glass of champagne and reaches for another*): Oh, I was so excited!—If I hadn't drunk half a bottle of champagne beforehand, I'd have stuck out like a sore thumb! (*She laughs shrilly and without motivation.*)
WORMSER: Gussie, Gussie, don't drink so fast; you're already on fire! Ah, the temperament of that girl!
AUGUSTA (*sits on his lap*): Oh, Papa, you're such an angel! And you're all such dears!
TRUMP: Thank you, thank you! I must naturally apply that remark to myself above all. And so, to your health, my dear!
AUGUSTA: Prosit! And you're an old rascal, you are! (*Drinks again.*)

(CAPTAIN VON SCHLEINITZ *enters the box. He is a typical cavalry officer, smart and dapper.*)

WORMSER: Ah, the Captain! Good! Excellent! Willy, will you stand in the presence of your superior officer!
SCHLEINITZ: For heaven's sake, don't get up! That's quite unnecessary. (*To* AUGUSTA.) My dear young lady—or rather, my dear comrade-in-arms—may I, in the name of us all, express my thanks and admiration. You were really very smart.
AUGUSTA: And what do you think of me as a soldier? Am I ready for inspection? (*She stands at attention.*)
SCHLEINITZ: May I say, I have never yet kissed the hand of a comrade from the Grenadier Guards. (*He does so, and the others laugh.*) Herr Wormser, I should like to say a few words on behalf of the officers present. So if you will kindly rap your glass, if you please.
WORMSER: With pleasure, Captain, with pleasure! Splendid, ah, how really splendid! (*He raps his glass and calls into the hall.*) *Silentium! Silentium strictissimus* for Captain von Schleinitz!
SCHLEINITZ (*stands on the stairs, and despite the incoherence of*

his sentences, speaks with complete assurance and nobility of bearing): Ladies and gentlemen! It is my duty, since the Potsdam Guards have in so charming a fashion, on the occasion of today's ball, given by the Sixth Hussars, this year, with the cooperation of the good citizens of Potsdam, has been arranged for us, by our dear friend, the Councillor of Commerce, Herr Adolf Wormser, in the most delightful manner. For this reason, ladies and gentlemen, on behalf of the assembled officers of the Sixth Hussars present, to extend our heartfelt thanks and compliments above all else to our charming representative of the Potsdam Grenadier Guards; but it is also my pleasant duty to say to those who arranged this entertainment—ah, but since I'm no orator, let's simply give them three cheers! Hip hip hooray!

(*The band strikes up, glasses are clinked, and cries of "Hip hip hooray!" are shouted out.*)

WORMSER: Captain, it was splendid! Simply staggering! And the calmness, the assurance in the way you did it all! I envy you. I do. I envy you. I'd have sweated up a storm myself.

SCHLEINITZ: Well, I'm not exactly running for Parliament, Herr Wormser. I'm a cavalry officer, not an orator, eh?

WORMSER: Prosit! Prosit!

(*They all clink glasses with* SCHLEINITZ. *Dance music is heard from the hall.*)

AUGUSTA (*to* SCHLEINITZ): And prosit to my brother-officer-in-arms! Why I could almost attend a regimental dinner with you in this uniform! Oh, dear, I'm really feeling tipsy!

SCHLEINITZ: Ah, but it makes you quite charming.

WORMSER: Augusta, I think it's time for you to change. It's very nice, but after all this isn't a masked ball.

FRAU KESSLER: That's out of the question! No, no, no! She must first dance with me! Come, Gussie, my dear, do you know how to lead?

KESSLER: Millie! You will kindly be a bit less eccentric!

AUGUSTA: Well, of course I'll dance. I simply love dancing as a man.

WORMSER: But only *one waltz*, and then you'll change!

AUGUSTA (*humming along with the music; to* KESSLER): With your permission, Major! (*She takes* FRAU KESSLER's *arm, and as she goes off says to* SCHLEINITZ.) May I have the next dance, Captain? (*She disappears into the hall.*)

WORMSER (*calling after her*): But as a lady, if you please! You will change your clothes first! The child's gone mad this evening!

SCHLEINITZ: But charming all the same. Look how she keeps that monocle in her eye—it almost seems to be part of her.

WORMSER: She's certainly not short on ideas, I assure you.

SCHLEINITZ: What a terribly successful evening you've arranged, Herr Wormser. The General is in a remarkable mood. He's even asked about you.

WORMSER: Asked about me? In that case, I'll go right over. Come, Willy, I'll introduce you to the General. Hurry! Excuse me for a moment, gentlemen.

SCHLEINITZ: Of course, of course.

(WORMSER *goes off with* WILLY. SCHLEINITZ, TRUMP, *and* KESSLER *are left alone; they draw up their chairs.*)

TRUMP: Well, Schleinitz, there's your chance. You could certainly use it.

KESSLER: Not bad—not bad at all.

TRUMP: Everything's in your favor—including money.

KESSLER: All the same, Schleinitz, let me give you a bit of a warning. Marrying a rich wife makes a man lazy, and he's apt never to rise above the rank of major. It's a proven fact.

SCHLEINITZ (*with a gentle smile*): But debts make a man even lazier, Major.

WORMSER (*returns with* WILLY): He just left. It's really amazing, Captain, I trust you will deliver my respects to His Excellency.

SCHLEINITZ: Of course—and I shall say some very nice things about you.

WORMSER (*to* KESSLER): I must say, those two women are dancing like they were possessed. Augusta's doing it only as a joke, but I'm afraid your wife is going a bit too far. You won't mind my saying so, Major, but I felt it my duty to tell you.

KESSLER: I'll go out immediately and ask her for a dance.

TRUMP (*to* WORMSER): And with your permission, I'll see to your daughter.

(*All three go off into the hall.*)

WORMSER (*to* WILLY): Why don't you get interested in something for a change! I'd be ashamed, the way you sit around all the time! You don't smoke, all you drink is soda water, and you don't dance! What are people to think of you? A young man like you, with every opportunity in the world! You've been in the army for six years now, and look at you! Still a lance corporal! But it's no wonder, the way you sit there like a block of wood! You should pay a little attention to the Captain. That's what you ought to do! Fill his glass when it's empty, offer him fruit, give him a light when he takes out a cigarette.

AUGUSTA (*rushes into the box, flushed and overheated, fans herself with her cap, and collapses into a chair*): I want a compote! (*To* WILLY, *who, in his confusion, has jumped to his feet as though in the presence of a real officer.*) No, not the peach, the pineapple! I can't endure peaches. They're always so soft and wobbly. (*She attacks the compote with a spoon.*)

WORMSER (*hurriedly to* AUGUSTA, *just as* TRUMP *appears on the stairs*): You will kindly watch your manners! It's disgraceful! What would Captain von Schleinitz think! Oh, if only I'd never have permitted this nonsense! Be careful, don't drop any on your lovely uniform!

AUGUSTA: "Lovely uniform!" That's a good one! (*To* TRUMP.) It was secondhand when he bought it back!

WORMSER: You will kindly not talk business in public!

AUGUSTA: From the Mayor of Köpenick! (*Laughs.*)

WORMSER: The way you're acting, I'm glad I didn't make a new one for you!

AUGUSTA: Oh, I feel so wonderful, I'd like to found a ladies' regiment and start a war!

TRUMP (*behind her*): Nonsense, Augusta, you must get married!

AUGUSTA (*eating*): But to who? You perhaps? Or Schleinitz?

WORMSER: You will kindly not make fun of Captain von Schleinitz! He's a remarkable man. The second-best rider in the army. He rode his horse in front of the Kaiser and got a decoration for it.

AUGUSTA: Oh, I think he's just the sweetest thing!

(SCHLEINITZ *enters with* FRAU KESSLER, MAJOR KESSLER *bringing up the rear.*)

FRAU KESSLER: Captain, I must confess you dance as well as you ride.

AUGUSTA: I didn't lead too badly myself, though, did I?

FRAU KESSLER: We were an absolute sensation!

AUGUSTA: Would you like some pineapple? (*She piles heaps of compote on two glass dishes, for herself and* FRAU KESSLER.)

SCHLEINITZ (*sits down beside* TRUMP; *softly*): Let me tell you, that was quite an undertaking. (*He takes a cigarette from his case and taps it nervously on the back of his hand.*)

(WILLY *quickly strikes a match and holds it ready.*)

(*Not noticing, lowers his cigarette.*) Do you ladies mind if I smoke?

AUGUSTA: Well, certainly not, if you don't mind us eating compote.

(*They all laugh.*)

SCHLEINITZ: Well then—since we have arrived at a mutual agreement— (*He lifts his cigarette again.*)

(WILLY, *whose match has by this time gone out, strikes another, jumps up in desperate haste to offer* SCHLEINITZ *a light across the table. In the process, he overturns the champagne cooler, the glasses, the compote dishes, and the vases of flowers. Everything manages to be spilled on the two ladies. Cries of alarm. Waiters rush in. General confusion.*)

WORMSER: Willy, have you lost your mind! For God's sake! Waiter! Waiter!

FRAU KESSLER: My dress! My lace!

KESSLER: Hurry! Bring some hot water!

(*They all jumped up; the gentlement dab madly at the dresses of the soaked ladies with napkins.* WILLY *stands there horrified.*)

TRUMP: It's nothing, it's nothing, it'll come off!

(AUGUSTA *laughs hysterically.*)

WORMSER: Must you laugh so loud! Oh! That beautiful uniform! All I can do now is give it to the old-clothes dealer!

AUGUSTA: That's where it belonged in the first place!

BLACKOUT

SCENE 7

The HOPRECHTS' *living room in Rixdorf. Afternoon. The clock strikes four.* FRAU HOPRECHT *is alone by the table set for afternoon coffee. She places a cozy over the coffeepot. From outside we hear the sound of a key in the lock of the hall door, and then the door closing.*

FRAU HOPRECHT: There he is— (*She removes the cozy and starts toward the door.*)

(HOPRECHT *enters. He is dressed in his uniform—but there are no sergeant's stripes on it. In one hand he carries a small handbag, in the other the sword, still wrapped in brown paper.*)

HOPRECHT: Hello, Marie.

FRAU HOPRECHT (*hiding her disappointment*): Hello, Friedrich. (*Kisses him quickly.*) I'm so glad you're back. I was waiting for you.

HOPRECHT: Yes, I know—I'm late.

FRAU HOPRECHT: The coffee's still hot, though.

HOPRECHT (*lost in thought*): That's fine. (*He goes to his wardrobe, sets the small handbag beside it, places the wrapped sword in the corner of the wardrobe, and closes it.*)

FRAU HOPRECHT (*looks at him in embarrassment, then pours the coffee*): Here, Friedrich, drink your coffee. There's cake, too.

HOPRECHT (*sits down*): Oh, yes, thank you. It's getting colder out. (*Pause.*) What is it, Marie? Why are you so quiet?

FRAU HOPRECHT: Friedrich, I—I have something to tell you.— Lieschen is dead. Now don't get excited.

HOPRECHT (*staring at her*): What?—

FRAU HOPRECHT: Just—just don't let yourself get excited, Friedrich. There's nothing we can do.

HOPRECHT: What did you say?

FRAU HOPRECHT: Lieschen is—well, she died very quietly, Friedrich.

HOPRECHT: Oh? When?

FRAU HOPRECHT: The day before yesterday—in the middle of the night. We thought she was getting on so well, and then it happened. That evening her breathing was rather heavy, and then she just fell asleep. Wilhelm was with her the whole time. He didn't leave her side once. He said at first she had fantasies in her sleep. She was completely happy.

HOPRECHT: The poor thing.

FRAU HOPRECHT: He's off at the funeral now. I'd have gone, too, but I was expecting you. I locked up the shop for an hour.— Eat something, Friedrich.

HOPRECHT: No, thank you.—That ration bread they serve, always fills me up so.—Everything else in order?

FRAU HOPRECHT: Yes, everything's fine. Business in the shop has been slow.

HOPRECHT: Yes—well—Marie, I—I want to tell you something.

I—well, I thought I—that I was next in line for—for—well, the Captain himself said he couldn't understand it.

FRAU HOPRECHT: Friedrich, what is it?

HOPRECHT: Well—I thought for certain I was to be promoted to sergeant this time—supernumerary, of course, but that was understood all along. I wanted to surprise you; that's why I didn't say anything.

FRAU HOPRECHT: And so, what happened?

HOPRECHT (*somewhat vexed*): What happened? What happened?! Nothing happened! Some new regulation or other cut the budget—for all ranks!—Oh, I don't know; nobody can make head or tail of it. The first in line, of course, are the active military reservists, so naturally only a certain number are chosen from the other reservists, which is figured from the date of enlistment—well, to cut a long story short, I wasn't on the list.

FRAU HOPRECHT: But, Friedrich, it's not your fault.

HOPRECHT: Well, of course, it's not my fault! But that's not the point! What I mean is, everything goes according to the rules, and not according to a man's merits! That's what the Captain said, too. Well, there's nothing I can do.

FRAU HOPRECHT: It's certainly a pity, I must say. A terrible blow.

HOPRECHT: Ah, well! The main thing is a man stays healthy. I can go on just like I am—but not that poor little thing—so young —so young—

FRAU HOPRECHT: Maybe she's better off.

HOPRECHT (*shrugs his shoulders*): You never know. All we know for certain is that all things cling to life.

FRAU HOPRECHT (*after a pause*): I have to run down to the shop for a minute. There are bound to be customers. (*She goes to him, suddenly takes his head in her hands.*) It's nice having you home again, Friedrich. Isn't it?

HOPRECHT (*presses her to him for a moment*): Yes, Marie.—If there was a war, I'd have to go away completely.

FRAU HOPRECHT: Friedrich! Don't talk like that!

HOPRECHT (*laughing a bit*): All right, go to your shop. I'll change my clothes.

FRAU HOPRECHT: Make yourself comfortable, Friedrich. (*She goes out.*)

(HOPRECHT *sits quietly for a moment, then rises and goes into the bedroom, leaving the door ajar.—From outside we hear the sound of a key in the lock of the hall door, then steps.* VOIGT *enters the room. He is pale; his eyes blink from lack of sleep. He is dressed in one of* HOPRECHT's *black suits, which hangs rather too loosely on him. He stands at the door for a moment and stares into the room.—*HOPRECHT *enters from the bedroom. His uniform is unbuttoned. Over his arm is his civilian suit, in his hand his slippers. He, too, like* VOIGT, *remains standing in the doorway for a moment. Then he goes to* VOIGT.)

HOPRECHT: Come in, Wilhelm. How are you? Is the funeral over?

VOIGT: Yes, it's over. Good-day, Friedrich. (*Shakes his hand.*)

HOPRECHT: Who would ever have thought that—that it could happen so quickly. We had the doctor in—did everything we could—

VOIGT (*almost severely*): It's past now.

HOPRECHT: You're right. No sense crying over it. That won't bring her back.

VOIGT: I borrowed your black suit. Mine was too threadbare. I hope you don't mind. I'll take it off right away.

HOPRECHT: No rush—have a cup of coffee—it's over there.

VOIGT: No, thank you. (*He goes to the corner behind the sofa, where his package is lying and his suit is hanging over a chair. He then turns around—smiles.*) So what happened, Friedrich? Where are your big eagle buttons and the silver cockades?

HOPRECHT (*almost casually*): Nothing came of it. It was—it was my mistake. The new regulation says there can't be as many.

VOIGT: But you were the next in line. You had it coming.

HOPRECHT: Yes, I know, I know. But it's all because of a new regulation. Let's forget it now, it's not important.

VOIGT: Important? No, nothing's important; the world's too big for that. But the fact you had it coming is something else. What's right is right, isn't it?

HOPRECHT: What's right is what's legal, Wilhelm. The law knows no favorites; it's the same for everyone. That's the way it is, Wilhelm.

VOIGT: And when a man comes to grief, then he's finished. What good is justice or the law to him then?

HOPRECHT: If a soldier's killed, Wilhelm, he's killed. There's no remedy for death.—But here on earth we always get what we deserve.

(*They have both begun to change clothes.*)

VOIGT: Amen.

HOPRECHT: What do you mean?

VOIGT (*in a friendly way, without scorn*): You've forgotten. Such sentences always end with "Amen." The minister at the cemetery said something almost like that.

HOPRECHT: I don't understand.

VOIGT: You don't have to. Just don't let anyone upset you.—I'll change my clothes—and then I'll go.

HOPRECHT: But where?

(VOIGT *shrugs his shoulders.*)

But why—why do you want to leave, Wilhelm?

VOIGT: That's not the point. I *have* to leave.

(HOPRECHT *takes a step toward him.* VOIGT *takes the paper from his pocket with a deprecating gesture and throws it on the table.*)

Read that.

HOPRECHT (*reads*): Notice—Good God, Wilhelm, didn't you fill out an application?

VOIGT: Twice. They were both turned down. They took no interest in the first one, and they had no time for the second.

HOPRECHT (*helplessly*): But—but where yill you go, Wilhelm?

VOIGT (*with a strange laugh*): Nowhere.

HOPRECHT: Now look—you won't do anything foolish, will you?

VOIGT: No chance of that. Foolish! No chance at all. I'm learning, very slowly.

HOPRECHT: Be sure you see about a permit to stay on in another district—or apply for a passport from the officials in your home town.

VOIGT: Thank you, I know all about that.

HOPRECHT: Then what will you do? How will you get on?

VOIGT: You mustn't worry. It's not that important. (*He laughs quietly again.*)

HOPRECHT: Don't laugh like that! This is serious!

VOIGT: I think it's funny. They won't move *you up*, but they're sure moving *me on!* Like you said: Everyone gets what he deserves, eh?

HOPRECHT: Don't talk like that! You're on the wrong track, Wilhelm! There must be reasons for such things happening, Wilhelm, or else it's all just bad luck.

VOIGT: Bad luck? No. It's not good, but it's not bad luck either. It's nothing but pure and simple injustice. But don't excite yourself, Friedrich. There's plenty of injustice in the world, a good healthy crop of injustice. Believe me, I know.

HOPRECHT: You don't know a thing! You had a stroke of bad luck, that's all. If it was like you say, there wouldn't be any more trust and faith left in the world. So, don't believe it, Wilhelm. You'll never get on this way. You must bear it—like a man.

VOIGT: Bear it? I'm used to that, too, all right, Friedrich. That's nothing. My shoulders are broad enough for any load. But where am I to carry it, Friedrich? That's the question! Where shall I go with it? I've got no place to stay—there's not a single place for me on this earth. I guess my only choice is to walk up into the air.

HOPRECHT: No, Wilhelm, not in the air! Get your feet back on the ground! We live in a civilized country—we live in law and order—and you can't set yourself against that, you have no right! No matter how hard it is—you must work yourself into it again.

VOIGT: Into what? The country? Into law and order? Without a place to stay? Without a passport?

HOPRECHT: You'll work your way in one of these days. One of these days everything will be all right.

VOIGT: Yes—and what will I do once I get back in? What good will it do me then? I'll long have stopped being a human being then.

HOPRECHT: You're a human being only when you place yourself within human law and order. A bedbug is a living thing, too.

VOIGT: That's right, Friedrich! A bedbug's alive, too! And do you know *why* it's alive? Because first comes the bedbug, and *then* the bedbug's laws!

HOPRECHT: The trouble is, Wilhelm, you refuse to submit to authority. But if you want to be a human being, then you *must* submit. Do you understand?

VOIGT: Submit to authority? Yes! But to *what* authority? That's what I want to know! Because law and order must first be right, Friedrich, and that's just what it isn't.

HOPRECHT: But it is! Here in Germany the law is nothing *but* right! Take a look at a troop of cavalry drawn up in rank and file, and then you'll see what I mean. Every man there *feels* it! You must learn the meaning of comradeship, Wilhelm; that's when you'll finally be a human being—and understand human law and order!

VOIGT: It's fine for people who don't have holes in their pants; for those who don't have to sit so straight that they burst their seams. It's all right for those who are safe from bad luck.

HOPRECHT: No! Not here! Not in Germany! We have solid ground under our feet here, not pitfalls. Nothing can possibly happen. Maybe in other countries, yes, where the beams are rotten. In Russia, for example, they have corrupt officials, that's what! And then there's the moujiks who can't read or write, and don't even know their own names. And the immorality of the higher classes, and the women students, and all the terrible things that go on. That's where people get into trouble, Wilhelm; the ground's cracking beneath their feet! Do you understand? But here in Germany everything is sound and solid from top to bottom—and when a thing is sound then it's right, Wilhelm. It's built on a rock foundation!

VOIGT: I see. Then where does injustice come from? From itself?

HOPRECHT: But in Germany there *is* no injustice! At least none that comes from the higher circles. Law and order govern everything here. Any true German can tell you that.

VOIGT: I see. Then what happened to your promotion? Was *that* just?

HOPRECHT: You're twisting everything, Wilhelm. You're the one who first hit out against justice, and then it hit you back. And as for my promotion, that's the way it had to be. I have no complaint. They got raked over the coals in Parliament for the size of our military expenditures, and the size of the army, and so they had to cut the budget, and I was the one who got hit. That's just the way it is. It could have happened to anyone. What's one man compared with the community? Maybe the money being saved on our pay will go to buy another cannon. Who knows?

VOIGT: And then it goes off—and hits you again. Boom-boom and you're dead.

HOPRECHT: All right, so if it goes off, I'm dead. And I'll know why, too. For the Fatherland and for our homes.

VOIGT: I love my home as much as you! As much as anyone else! Then why don't they let me live there! I'd be willing to die for it, too, then, if it had to be! Tell me—where is a man's home, his country? In a police station? Or here, in this piece of paper? I don't even *know* my country anymore! I only know its police districts!

HOPRECHT: I've heard enough, Wilhelm! I mustn't listen to any more! I am a soldier! *And* a state official! Body and soul! And that's what I stand for! I am convinced that here in Germany justice prevails over all things!

VOIGT: And over *people, too,* Friedrich! Over *people* with *bodies* and *souls!* It prevails over a man so that he will never rise again!

HOPRECHT: You were never in the army, Wilhelm. You don't know. If you only knew what our officers are like—of course there's always a young puppy who slips in under the fence now and then—ah, but the others! The real ones! We'd go through fire for them, and they'd do the same for us. We're all there to help one another.

VOIGT: And the people, Friedrich, the community? Who's there to help *them?* What's behind all this, Friedrich? God or the devil? No, they've pushed me around too long by this time! They've brought me to my senses! There are no more flophouses for me! I want to see things as they are!

HOPRECHT: For the last time, Wilhelm, you must take your place in the world! Stop grumbling against it. And if you're crushed by it—well, then you still must keep your mouth shut, because you're still a part of the world, you're a living sacrifice to it! And the world is worth a sacrifice! What more can I say? Where is your conscience, Wilhelm? Where's your sense of duty?

VOIGT: Out there—in the cemetery—I heard it when the clods of earth fell down onto the coffin—I heard it loud then and—

HOPRECHT: Heard? Heard what?

VOIGT: The voice of conscience. Oh, yes, yes, I heard it speak; and everything in the world was dead still; and I heard it say: Old man, it said, everyone has to kick the bucket sometime, including you, it said. And then, then you'll stand before God the Father, you'll stand before the Maker of all things, and He'll ask you straight to your face: Wilhelm Voigt, what have you made of your life? And I'll have to answer—I'll have to tell him: A doormat. I made it in jail, and then everyone trampled all over it. That's what I'll have to tell Him. And then it said: In the end you fought and struggled for a bit of air, and then it was over. That's all you'll have to say to God. But He'll say to you: Go away. He'll say: Get out, He'll say. I didn't give you life for that, He'll say. You are in my debt! Where is it? What have you done with it? And then, Friedrich—and then I still won't have any residence permit.

HOPRECHT: Wilhelm, you're rebelling against all the laws of the universe! It's sinful, Wilhelm, it's sinful! And you can never change it, never!

VOIGT: And I don't want to, I don't want to, Friedrich. How could I, a man all alone and—But I don't want to seem a

miserly being before my God. I don't want to be in His debt
for anything, you understand? I'm going to do something
about it.

HOPRECHT: Wilhelm, you're rebelling against all the laws of the
universe!

VOIGT: That's impossible. That would be stupid. I'd never do a
thing like that. You mustn't worry about it, Friedrich. All I'll
do is have a go at it, that's all. What other people can do,
I've been able to do for a long time. (*Laughs.*)

HOPRECHT: Wilhelm, what have you got in that head of yours?
What are you up to? Tell me, Wilhelm! Tell me, Wilhelm!—Well, don't say I didn't warn you!

VOIGT (*has meanwhile tied up his package and put on his hat*):
Yes, yes, Friedrich, you're a good man. There, your suit's
hung over the chair. Marie can brush it out. (*He goes to*
HOPRECHT *and extends his hand, which* HOPRECHT *takes rather
hesitantly.*) Goodbye, Friedrich. And thank you. (*He goes
off.*)

HOPRECHT (*clinging to the back of a chair*): Why—why, the man
is dangerous!

BLACKOUT

ACT III

SCENE 1

KRAKAUER'S *old-clothes shop in Grenadierstrasse. A gloomy,
windowless establishment, stuffed full of all sorts of articles of
clothing. Steps lead to the street. Placards are seen with such
inscriptions as: "Clothes Make the Man"—"Elegant Outfits
for Gentlemen"—"Inexpensive Winter Coats"—"Costumes and
Masks for Sale or Hire"—"Old Clothes Bought for First-Rate
Prices." Behind the counter,* KRAKAUER, *a legendary ghetto figure,
is serving* WILHELM VOIGT.

KRAKAUER: Do I have something for you! Do I have something
for you!! Let me tell you! A new, beautiful, extra-fine uniform, out there, hanging in the street by the door, and all
the people staring at it like they was struck blind from all the
shine!

VOIGT: I saw it. That's why I came down.

KRAKAUER: Solly! Sol-ly! Bring in the lovely nice uniform from the street! Oh, my good man, it's so beautiful! And wear well! Believe it! And it's genuine!

VOIGT: I need it for a costume ball.

KRAKAUER: That's your business, my good man, that's your business. Here on Grenadierstrasse you buy anything you want, with no questions.

(*Solly enters with the uniform.*)

Look at it, look at it! How it shines! So beautiful! And the material, such expensive cloth, and the lining of silk, the red collar, the shiny buttons—a miracle, I tell you, an absolute miracle! If this uniform could walk around with nobody inside it—I tell you, every soldier would make it such a salute, it's so genuine!

VOIGT (*has taken a step back, and stares fascinatedly at the uniform; then he turns away and shakes his head*): I don't know —if I should.

KRAKAUER: You don't know? You listen to me: I know! I know what you can do: you can take something else. Why do you have to go like a captain? You go to a costume ball, you should enjoy yourself. You go like a captain, you don't enjoy yourself, because when they see you they say: No captain looks like that! You listen to me:—you take maybe something historic. I got all kinds of beautiful things.

VOIGT: No, nothing historical.

KRAKAUER: My dear man, when you want to make a good impression, something historical is always the best. A Roman general, a Nürnberg executioner, an ancient Louis of France—I got it all here. What do you say? Why has it to be an officer exactly? Ah, of course you're right, an officer is always right. Maybe you go like one of Old Fritz's cavalry generals —now there's something for a figure like yours! Potsdam is the fashion.—Potsdam everybody likes. I went there, on Sunday, to Potsdam, with my Solly and his bride Leah. We was going into the castle, and some goy says at the door: "You can't go in; there are officers in there; you will disturb them. The gentlemen don't want to be disturbed." So, "Nebbish," I says to him, "what's a Jew want in a castle anyhow!" So I went and saw the historical windmill, which I recommend, it's very beautiful.

VOIGT (*interested*): There are always a lot of officers in Potsdam, aren't there?

KRAKAUER: More than you can stand on an empty stomach. So

what about a beautiful Pierrot? Here: a white one with blue pompons. Or a Maharajah, or a nice cowboy, or a Boer with a slouch hat?

VOIGT: No, no. I'll take the uniform. (*Takes the uniform from the hanger.*)

KRAKAUER: Good! It's the style! You are absolutely right, Captain! An officer is always best, am I right?

VOIGT: But look at all the spots on the coat.

KRAKAUER: Spots! You should call those spots! Champagne spots! Real ones! Smell! Champagne spots isn't just spots!—Solly, a package of spot removers from Kemnitzer's next door! The captain gets them without charge.

VOIGT (*examines the uniform knowingly*): A star's missing from the shoulder. A captain has two stars, or he's only a lieutenant. And the braid at the edges is all frayed.

KRAKAUER: A star you get extra, and the braid your wife can clean a little at home, or maybe the captain's little daughter.

VOIGT: How much does it cost?

KRAKAUER: Cost? You don't call such a thing cost, Captain! It's a bargain, a surprise, not a cost! For me it's an expense, for you a capital investment: twenty marks.

VOIGT (*puts down the uniform*): No.

KRAKAUER: Eighteen! Seventeen, then, Captain; it's worth seventeen!

VOIGT: Fifteen. And I want a sash with it, and a cap, and a pair of spurs. And a sword to buckle on.

KRAKAUER: Captain, Captain, you're bringing woe and destruction to my house! No, don't say it. It's yours for fifteen marks, but just as a favor. For the sword and the spurs you pay an extra three marks, and you get the spot remover free, and a nice cardboard box, and the string on the box your great-grandchildren will still be using to dry their wash on. Would you like a helmet instead? Two marks, the helmet's yours—it's becoming, and looks like something.

VOIGT: No, thank you. The cap will do. A helmet always slips. Do you have a gray officer's overcoat?

KRAKAUER: Not this minute, but I'll get it for you in a day.

VOIGT: I need it right away. I can't wait.

KRAKAUER: Then go to Kemnitzer; he's a business friend. What he ain't got, I got; and what I ain't got, he's got. We work together for ten percent, so nobody hates the other. Should I pack you in a sword too?

VOIGT: Let me see it; does it have a star on the belt?

KRAKAUER: The Captain thinks of everything! There you see it, Captain: first-class condition and a star!

VOIGT: Good. Now pack it up quickly for me. The spot removers too.

KRAKAUER (with Solly, packs everything up with practiced haste): Whatever you say, Captain. I pack it you don't have to iron it. Can I ask you for the money now, Captain?

VOIGT: Here you are. Eighteen marks. Your prices are shameful.

KRAKAUER: Thank you, Captain, come again. And believe me: this is no purchase, it's an inheritance!

VOIGT: Give it to me. (He is about to leave.)

KRAKAUER (blocking VOIGT's way): Captain, sir! A moment, Captain, sir! Maybe you want something for your wife for the ball? A mask, maybe a black domino?

VOIGT: You're holding me up!—I must report for duty! (He goes out.)

KRAKAUER: Goodbye, Captain! Enjoy yourself, Captain!—Imagine! Him a captain!

BLACKOUT

SCENE 2

An avenue with a bench in the park at Sans Souci. A view of the castle. October sun bathes the scene. The occasional sounds of a barrel organ are heard in the distance. WILHELM VOIGT sits on the bench in the sun. Beside him are his hat and the tied-up cardboard box. He sits erect, with folded arms, and watches the strollers with close attention. Two YOUNG PEOPLE enter from one side.

FIRST YOUNG PERSON: You know, these long, straight avenues make me so proud.

SECOND YOUNG PERSON: Of what?

FIRST YOUNG PERSON: Oh, I don't know. Of human intelligence, I guess. But maybe I really mean something else.

(They go on.—An old man comes along with a stiff, stilted walk. He halts after every two steps, clears his throat in a military manner and spits.)

ANOTHER OLD MAN (with a white beard, meets him): Good-day, Colonel! Out for a walk, I see.

COLONEL: Good-day, Councillor! What else can I do? A man needs a bit of movement now and then.

COUNCILLOR: Ah, yes, and a lovely autumn it is, too! A little walk on a day like this is a ticket to a healthy constitution.

COLONEL (*spits*): Terrible! This blasted bronchitis!

COUNCILLOR: You smoke too much, Colonel. Here, have a licorice.

COLONEL: No, thank you. Sweets make me sick to my stomach. I take Ems pastilles.

COUNCILLOR: Excellent, excellent! I hope you feel better soon, Colonel.

COLONEL: Thank you, thank you. What's the sense of it though? I won't be around much longer. (*Goes on.*)

COUNCILLOR: There, there, there! (*Goes on.*)

(*Two young* NURSEMAIDS *enter; one pushes a baby carriage, the other trudges along beside her. Two very young boys, dressed in colorful officers' uniforms, run ahead of them. The one is dressed as a hussar, the other as a guardsman. The hussar is busy striking at twigs on bushes with his toy sword. The guardsman gallops on a hobbyhorse. A little girl with pigtails walks sadly behind.*)

FIRST NURSEMAID: I'll simply say my mother is sick and I must have the afternoon off. But I'll have to be back by nine at the latest.

SECOND NURSEMAID: That's ridiculous! Things won't even have started then!

FIRST NURSEMAID: Perhaps I can say I missed the train.—Walthari, will you please stop picking up that dirt—it's dog dirt! Imagine calling him Walthari! But whenever I call him Walter, she has a fit.

SECOND NURSEMAID: That's the way they are.

FIRST NURSEMAID (*points into the baby carriage*): This one is called Fredegundes!

(*They both laugh. Walthari bombards* VOIGT *with chestnuts.*)

You leave that man alone! What a rude child you are! I'll give you a slap on the ears in a minute!

(*Walthari sticks his tongue out at her. The boy dressed as a guardsman gallops around in a circle uttering cries of glee.*)

You just wait! I'll tell your father, and then you'll know what his riding crop feels like!

SECOND NURSEMAID: Next year I'll be going into one of the big shops. I'm studying for it now.

(*Three* YOUNG OFFICERS *enter from the other side in animated conversation.*)

FIRST OFFICER: War college! What a lot of nonsense!

SECOND OFFICER: I beg to differ, my good man, but if you'll look at the cartographical division—

FIRST OFFICER: Nonsense! A lot of paper! See it once in actual practice and you'll know how different it all is!

THIRD OFFICER: I've always maintained that our examiners—(*Interrupting himself.*)—damnation! (*Looks at the* NURSEMAIDS.)

(*All three* OFFICERS *laugh softly, cough, turn around several times as they go off.—The* NURSEMAIDS *are also silent, and blush. One of them turns around furtively for another look; then they both look at one another and burst out into excited, giggling laughter.*)

FIRST NURSEMAID: Did you see that blond one? Oh, he was so stylish!

SECOND NURSEMAID: Oh, but the pale one with the scar was much more interesting.

FIRST NURSEMAID: You and your interesting people!

(*Walthari has meanwhile tripped up his galloping companion, who falls into the dog dirt and lies there howling.*)

NURSEMAIDS (*rush to them, each taking one and scolding and beating him*): Stop that! Stop that at once! You naughty, shameless little beast! It serves him right! You filthy, disgusting little snotnose! Come here! You wait till I tell your father! Give that thing here!

FIRST NURSEMAID (*tears the hobbyhorse away from him and puts it on the baby carriage*): You don't deserve to be taken for a walk! That's how bad you are!

(*They go off, with the howling cavalry officers behind them, the little girl crying, and a cooing sound from the carriage.— Two* SENIOR OFFICERS *emerge from the same direction as the* YOUNG OFFICERS *just before them.*)

FIRST SENIOR OFFICER: No, no, no, this Morocco crisis and the Balkans are perpetual powder kegs.—If it ever explodes, here we'll be with our untrained supplementary reserves.

SECOND SENIOR OFFICER: Do you realize you've been going on like this ever since I've known you? Why, it's out of the question. Who in Europe today could think seriously of war!

FIRST SENIOR OFFICER: Exactly! That's just the trouble! No one *is* thinking seriously of war! The only way *to* avoid it is to *think* about it!

SECOND SENIOR OFFICER: Nonsense! War is madness! Think of all our long-range plans. They'd be wiped out in two weeks' time. Certainly not. Wilhelm will continue as the Kaiser of Peace.

FIRST SENIOR OFFICER: I don't trust peace myself. I often hear sounds of thunder. Don't you hear them? There's something in the air.

SECOND SENIOR OFFICER: That's nothing but—what do you call them?—halluminations?

FIRST SENIOR OFFICER (*smiling*): Something like that. Something like that, yes.

(*They continue on. A* VETERAN *with a decoration on his coat enters hobbling. He sees* VOIGT *and goes to him.*)

VETERAN: Ah, you're a veteran, too, I see.

VOIGT: Something like that. Something like that, yes.

VETERAN (*chuckling and tapping the cardboard box*): You're new, eh? Moving into a Veterans' Home? Let me tell you, the food's terrible. Badly managed. Or maybe you're a civil service pensioner. It's better there.

VOIGT (*seriously*): No, no. I'm in the army.

VETERAN: In the army? (*Laughs.*) The army's a good place. Wouldn't mind it myself. (*Going on.*) The food's terrible where we live. Miserable food.—Be careful you don't catch cold. (*Goes off.*)

(*The two* YOUNG PEOPLE *return.*)

FIRST YOUNG PERSON: The leaves! The moss in the trees!

SECOND YOUNG PERSON (*declaims*): "Pure clouds of unhoped-for blue!"

FIRST YOUNG PERSON: Come! Let's run down to the lake! (*Takes him around the shoulder and goes off.*)

(*Two* OLD LADIES *appear in Potsdam costume, with black shawls and bonnets.*)

FIRST OLD LADY: We could sit here for a while before evening falls.

SECOND OLD LADY: But the bench is occupied.

(VOIGT *rises, salutes in military fashion, and picks up his things.*)

FIRST OLD LADY: Oh, that's very kind of you.

(VOIGT *bows and goes off.*—*The* OLD LADIES *sit down.*)

SECOND OLD LADY: You no longer find such manners in the children of today.

FIRST OLD LADY: Yes, well, he's one of the old school, you know.

BLACKOUT

SCENE 3

Berlin. The Silesian Railroad Station. A portion of the main hall is visible with its signs of arrival and departure. On the right is a passageway with a lavatory, above which is painted "Men." One of the two doors is marked "PP," the other "WC." The second door is equipped with an automatic lock arrangement. It is early morning. The station is empty. WILHELM VOIGT *comes through the main hall, the cardboard box in his hand. He goes directly to the lavatory, puts a groschen into the "WC" slot, and disappears. A* RAILROAD PORTER *saunters by, yawning. Two* RAILROAD OFFICIALS *enter from one side.*

FIRST RAILROAD OFFICIAL (*to the* PORTER): Not much doing, eh, Henke?

PORTER: Too early. Nobody's out yet. (*He disappears.*)

SECOND RAILROAD OFFICIAL (*continuing his conversation*): You always think it's only a whim of mine, but it's not, I've figured it all out. The Berlin railway system is divided into eight main routes. But in addition we have eighteen subsidiary routes for branch lines. Now just think of it! Fifteen main depots for twenty-six lines—which is far too few! And the Board of Directors won't admit it until there's an accident. And yet, all they have to do is—

FIRST RAILROAD OFFICIAL: Excuse me. When I get up early I try, but it's no use. Then all of a sudden I have to go. (*He goes into the* WC.)

SECOND RAILROAD OFFICIAL: Of course, of course. But as I was saying: all they have to do is think it over and they'll see for themselves. By all means, let's have the electrical system— except that there could be a short circuit at any time, and what then? Fundamentally we are always dependent on human power.

FIRST RAILROAD OFFICIAL: It's occupied. (*He turns and walks hurriedly.*)

(Both of them cross the stage again.)

SECOND RAILROAD OFFICIAL: And that's why I believe we have to have five new depots, the number of switch signalers must be increased, and working hours must be reduced. Otherwise there'll be an accident. When I told this to the inspector, he laughed. And if you think I took it lying down, you don't know me very well! "Inspector," I said to him, "Inspector, if the president of the railway himself was standing where you're standing now, I'd say exactly the same thing—"

(They disappear for a moment on the other side, their voices still audible; then they return.)

FIRST RAILROAD OFFICIAL: Well, yes, I suppose that's all quite right, but you'll never be able to get it put through. *(He walks faster.)*

SECOND RAILROAD OFFICIAL *(almost running at his side)*: I'll never get it put through? Never get it put through? Why, I've planned every last detail! Five depots is simple enough. Let's consider the stretch between Berlin-Spandau, Berlin-Stahnsdorf, Berlin-Köpenick—

FIRST RAILROAD OFFICIAL: For God's sake! He's still in there!

SECOND RAILROAD OFFICIAL: Berlin-Köpenick, and then the southern stretch and the eastern stretch, which is already taken care of, so to speak. And now what I'd like to know is, what could it cost? Compared with the total building budget, it would be next to nothing, it couldn't cost more than—

FIRST RAILROAD OFFICIAL: Yes, you're right, you're right; no doubt about it. *(He turns.)*

SECOND RAILROAD OFFICIAL: You see, you see? But just listen to this! The main thing, the question of personnel— *(Takes him by the arm.)* no, just a minute, listen—

FIRST RAILROAD OFFICIAL: This is going too far. *(Goes to the WC and bangs on the door.)* Goddamn it, how long do you need for a shit!

(The door opens. VOIGT, dressed in a complete captain's uniform, steps out. The FIRST RAILROAD OFFICIAL starts with shock and does his best to stand at attention. VOIGT looks at him calmly and with self-possession.)

VOIGT: Were you in the army?
FIRST RAILROAD OFFICIAL: Yes, Captain, sir.
VOIGT: Then I presume you also learned how to control yourself. What regiment were you with?

FIRST RAILROAD OFFICIAL: The Sixth Silesian Infantry Regiment of Prince Joachim Albrecht, First Battalion, Third Company.

VOIGT: Wait here a minute. (*He takes a few steps into the main hall and calls.*) You! Porter! Come here!

(*The* PORTER *comes running.*)

Get my package from in there and take it to the Luggage Office. And be quick about it! I'll be right there. (*He pulls on his gloves.*)

(*The* PORTER *dashes off with the package.*)

(*To the* RAILROAD OFFICIALS.) Very well. You're dismissed. But next time learn to behave a bit more properly.

FIRST RAILROAD OFFICIAL: Whatever you say, Captain, sir!

(VOIGT *salutes with a finger at his cap and goes off.*)

BLACKOUT

SCENE 4

Entrance hall of the Köpenick Town Hall. At the rear, a wide-open folding door onto the street. It is raining outside. The interior rests in deep peace and calm. KILIAN, *the municipal policeman, fat and ungainly, squats in his little open guardroom at the right of the main entrance, reading a paper. Municipal Councillor* RAU *and Councillor* COMENIUS *enter from one side. Both are busy unwrapping their sandwiches for lunch.*

COMENIUS: Let's take a quick break for lunch. They'll be in there for hours. By the time they get around to naming the new streets, we'll have been back long ago.

RAU: Quite right. We'll go down to the Rathskeller and have a small bottle of red wine.

COMENIUS: A large one couldn't do us any harm either. There's no rush. The Mayor hasn't even arrived yet.

RAU: But that's not his department. Rosencrantz sees to that. When the time comes to vote on the new taxes—

COMENIUS (*eating*): Nothing will come of it, nothing at all. Kilian!

KILIAN: Yes, sir?

COMENIUS: If they need us to vote, come down to the Rathskeller and get us.

KILIAN: Very well, sir.

(COMENIUS *and* RAU *go out through the door with a sign over it, which reads: "To the Rathskeller." Kähndorf, the* WASHER-WOMAN, *a girl in a thin dress, with rain-soaked hair, enters from outside.*)

KILIAN (*rather gruffly*): What are you doing back here again?

WASHERWOMAN: I had to—because of my passport—I have to have it.

KILIAN: I've told you three times already, the passport office isn't here!

WASHERWOMAN: But I've *got* to have it!

KILIAN: How dumb can you be! Passports are issued only at the County Councillor's Office. Don't you understand? This is a municipal office, and no papers are issued here!

WASHERWOMAN: But I'd have to go there by train, and I haven't got that much free time, and so I thought—

KILIAN: You thought! You've got no business thinking, and I suggest you realize that!

WASHERWOMAN: I don't even have a certificate to show where I was born. But I know I come from Spreewald—

KILIAN: Then go back to Spreewald, for God's sake! Get out of here!

WASHERWOMAN (*going*): I just don't know what I'll do now. (*Goes off.*)

KILIAN: Stupid idiot! (*He sits down and takes up his newspaper again.*)

(*At the same time* MAYOR OBERMÜLLER *and Municipal Secretary* KUTZMANN *appear in the entrance. They close their umbrellas and shake them out.*)

OBERMÜLLER (*in the midst of speaking*): I'm sorry, my dear Kutzmann, but I maintain my original position: there will be no special treatment for any of them. How can we pass a regulation for steam laundry owners when it doesn't apply to the smaller concerns as well? These people are earning money hand over fist as it is.

KUTZMANN: Quite right, Mayor, sir, but one must also consider that they are our community's principal taxpayers. One might say that they're the very ones who pay our salaries. (*He laughs.*)

KILIAN (*at their appearance has jumped up, and eagerly relieves them of their umbrellas*): I'll keep the umbrellas down here, Mayor, sir—otherwise they'll drip in the anteroom and leave quite a little puddle, sir.

OBERMÜLLER: Thank you, Kilian. But don't fail to remind me of it on my way home.

KILIAN: You won't forget it, Mayor, sir; Kilian will see to that, all right. And the galoshes, too, if I may. They leave footprints on the stairs.

OBERMÜLLER: Yes, of course, thank you.

(KILIAN *pulls off* OBERMÜLLER's *galoshes.*)

Is the meeting in session?

KILIAN: Yes, sir, Mayor, sir.

OBERMÜLLER: Herr Kutzmann—would you have a look in, if you please? That's Rosencrantz's department. And then you might hurry the minutes over to me.

KUTZMANN: Of course, sir, gladly.

OBERMÜLLER (*walking on with him*): No, I regret to say that your view of the laundry question and mine simply do not agree. (*On the steps.*) Extra concessions for bigger taxpayers would constitute an outright breach of our entire system. It's a matter of principle, my good man. It's quite out of the question.

(*Both go off.*—WENDROWITZ, *a simple farmer, a powerful man in a wet mackintosh, enters.*)

WENDROWITZ: Brrr! (*He shakes himself off.*) Blasted weather! (*Kicks the mud off his shoes.*)

KILIAN: You there, what are you doing! There's a boot-scraper outside for that.

WENDROWITZ: Boot-scraper?

KILIAN: If everyone came in with dirty boots it'd soon look like a pigsty!

WENDROWITZ: A *real* farmer's pigsty, my dear friend, will be a good deal cleaner than your own front hall. There's no such thing as a dirty pigsty.

KILIAN: What's that got to do with me? What do you want here?

WENDROWITZ: To visit you, of course; to bring a little amusement into your life. Why else would I drive twelve miles cross-country in the rain?

KILIAN: Are you a farmer?

WENDROWITZ: Aha, you've noticed that, have you!

KILIAN: Then you must belong to the district of Teltov.

WENDROWITZ: I do, but I deliver my potatoes to Köpenick; and I've come to complain about the rural duties put on them. Here's the notice I got.

KILIAN: Very good. Go upstairs.

WENDROWITZ: But where? I don't know my way around here.

KILIAN: There's a plan on the wall over there. Room thirty-six.

WENDROWITZ (*goes to the plan, framed on the wall, with its numerous directions*): No. I don't even know what it means. Looks more like neighbor Schmudike's vegetable garden.

KILIAN: Try a little harder and you might figure it out. It's simple. Second floor, left, straight down the corridor, right, and straight through.

WENDROWITZ: I wouldn't find that in three weeks. Couldn't you take me there?

KILIAN: That's not my job. I have other things to do.

WENDROWITZ: I believe it. You must be a big man around here, eh?

KILIAN (*listening to noises in the street, out of which we soon hear the shouts of children and the regular tread of marching soldiers*): What's the matter? There's something the matter out there!

WENDROWITZ: What do you expect? It's the guard coming off duty.

KILIAN: There's no guard here—it's—

VOIGT'S VOICE (*from outside*): Platoon—halt! Front! 'Ten—shun! Eyes right! Fix bayonets!

(*Each command is accompanied by the sharp execution of it by the group.*)

KILIAN: What's this—why, it's, it's, it's real!

(*VOIGT enters as the captain, and with a rapid military stride goes to KILIAN, who jumps from his guardroom and springs to attention.*)

VOIGT: Are you the only guard here?

KILIAN: Yes, sir, Captain!

VOIGT: And where is the Police Inspector?

KILIAN: In his office, sir, room number twelve.

VOIGT: You will obey my orders.

KILIAN: Whatever you say, Captain, sir. Shall I call the Inspector?

VOIGT: Not just now. Does this Town Hall have any other exits, except for the front and rear?

KILIAN: None, sir, except for the Rathskeller.

VOIGT: Good. (*Goes back to the entrance and gives commands to the men outside.*) The first man will remain at the main entrance, the second will take his post at the rear door, and the third will guard the entrance to the Rathskeller. No one will be allowed to enter or leave the Town Hall without my personal permission. This is a state of siege—understand? All entrances will be locked. The rest of you will follow me. Corporal, bring them along. (*To* KILIAN.) Take me to the Mayor's office.

KILIAN: Very good, Captain, sir!

CORPORAL'S VOICE (*from outside*): By fours—right turn—march!

(*The soldiers appear at the entrance.* KILIAN *has begun marching up the stairs as quickly as his corpulence will permit.*)

VOIGT: Forward—march! (*He marches up the stairs with the* CORPORAL *and the six grenadiers following him.*)

(WENDROWITZ *stares dumbly at them. The door at the rear is slammed shut.*)

BLACKOUT

SCENE 5

Private office of the Mayor. A portrait of Bismarck and a photograph of Schopenhauer hang on the wall. OBERMÜLLER *sits in a comfortable armchair behind a diplomatic-looking writing table. A municipal clerk stands behind him taking dictation.*

OBERMÜLLER (*dictating*): And therefore it is impossible for us to meet with you in regard to this matter. Got that? In regard to this matter. The heads of a municipality, whose main contingent consists of an industrial population—industrial population—can only be actuated by the principles of modern liberal social political measures. Here in Köpenick we have no garrison, nor do we have need of one like other communities, which must necessarily pay special regard to the military authorities—Yes? What is it?

KILIAN (*sticks his head in, eyes bulging*): Mayor! Mayor Obermüller, sir!—

OBERMÜLLER: What is the meaning of this! How dare you burst in here without so much as knocking!

VOIGT'S VOICE (*from outside*): Two men will accompany me as guards with the corporal as orderly. The others will remain at the door for the present to await orders. Make way there.

(*He shoves* KILIAN *to the side from the rear and enters. The soldiers are seen in the doorway with their fixed bayonets.* OBERMÜLLER, *speechless, slowly lifts himself from his armchair.*)

VOIGT: Are you the Mayor of Köpenick?

OBERMÜLLER: I certainly am.

VOIGT (*to the clerk*): Leave us alone.

OBERMÜLLER: Now look here, what's the meaning of this—

VOIGT (*raises his left hand, indicating that* OBERMÜLLER *is to be quiet, clicks his heels together, and lifts his hand to the brim of his cap*): By order of His Imperial Majesty, the Kaiser, I declare you under arrest. I have orders to take you directly to the Headquarters of the Imperial Guards in Berlin. You will prepare yourself to leave.

OBERMÜLLER (*pale but with some composure*): I don't understand! This must be a mistake!—What is the meaning of this?

VOIGT: What does it mean? (*Indicates the soldiers behind him.*) Doesn't that speak for itself?

OBERMÜLLER: Yes, but there must be a reason! Can't you at least?—

VOIGT: You'll know soon enough. I'm merely following orders.

OBERMÜLLER: (*strikes the table*): This is monstrous! I will not allow myself simply to be—

VOIGT: Were you in the army?

OBERMÜLLER: Indeed I *am* in the army! I am a lieutenant in the reserves.

VOIGT: Then you must know that all opposition is useless. An order's an order. You will be able to defend yourself later.

OBERMÜLLER: Yes, but I haven't the slightest idea—

VOIGT: Pity. Neither have I. All I have is orders. (*He nods to the two grenadiers who march into the room and take their positions with fixed bayonets at the right and left of the writing table.*)

(OBERMÜLLER *stares at them, and removes his pince-nez. Perspiration is seen on his forehead.*)

(*To the* CORPORAL *standing behind him.*) Find out what the Police Inspector's doing. It's around here somewhere. Room number twelve. (*To* OBERMÜLLER.) Who's in charge of the municipal treasury?

OBERMÜLLER: Herr Rosencrantz, the Municipal Treasurer. But if you don't mind my asking—

VOIGT: Thank you. (*To* KILIAN.) Bring the gentleman here.

KILIAN (*eagerly*): He's waiting in the anteroom, Captain, sir. (*Calls toward the rear.*) Herr Rosencrantz! You may come in!

ROSENCRANTZ (*with a very high stand-up collar, bald head, and dueling scars*): At your service, sir!

VOIGT: Were you in the army?

ROSENCRANTZ: Of course, Captain, sir. Lieutenant in the reserves. —First Nassau Field Artillery Regiment, Number twenty-seven.

VOIGT: Thank you. I regret that I must also place you under arrest and take you to Imperial Headquarters. But you will first balance your books completely and I shall check them over.

ROSENCRANTZ: Very well, Captain, sir. But I'll have to go to the treasury to do so. I'll need a pass for that.

VOIGT: You'll have a guard with you, of course.

OBERMÜLLER (*having pulled himself together again*): Herr Rosencrantz! One moment, if you please! Just what is the meaning of this rather sudden disposition to capitulate? You have no authority to show any balances whatever without my permission! I have not deposed my office *yet!*

ROSENCRANTZ: But when you're under arrest—excuse me, Captain, sir—I thought, at least—

OBERMÜLLER: It's not quite that simple! I demand the appointment of my successor! The municipal treasury cannot without the express consent of the authorities—

VOIGT (*very sharply*): I am the authority in the city of Köpenick! His Excellency the Mayor is nothing more nor less than my prisoner. (*To* ROSENCRANTZ.) You will carry out my instructions!

ROSENCRANTZ (*with a reproachful glance at* OBERMÜLLER): Certainly, Captain, sir!

VOIGT (*calls toward the rear*): One of you men will accompany Herr Rosencrantz to the treasury. I'll allow you ten minutes. Will that suffice?

ROSENCRANTZ: I'll hurry, Captain, sir.

VOIGT: Thank you.

(ROSENCRANTZ *goes off. Meanwhile the* CORPORAL *reappears.*)

Well? What's happened to the Police Inspector?

CORPORAL: He's asleep, Captain, sir.

VOIGT: Asleep? Do you mean in bed?

CORPORAL: No, sir, Captain, he's sitting up, behind his desk. Snoring something awful.

VOIGT: Then wake him. Bring him here at once.

(*The* CORPORAL *goes off.*)

OBERMÜLLER (*now in a state of total consternation, with a trembling voice*): Captain, sir, your actions here will not pass without questions being raised in Parliament. I happen to be a member of the Progressive Party—

VOIGT: That doesn't interest me in the least. I'm merely following orders.

OBERMÜLLER: In that case, Captain, I bow to authority. But I assure you, this matter will be cleared up. Whatever happens here is your own responsibility.

VOIGT: Quite right. My responsibility. Well! It's about time!

POLICE INSPECTOR (*is brought in by the* CORPORAL; *the collar of his uniform is still unbuttoned*): This simply will not do! I refuse to be pushed around at bayonet point!—(*He see* VOIGT *and grows silent.*)

VOIGT: If I may be so bold, sir, just how do you justify sleeping on duty? Is that what the city of Köpenick pays you for?

POLICE INSPECTOR: No, sir, Captain.

VOIGT: I should think not. Now, if you will start by kindly putting your uniform in order—

POLICE INSPECTOR (*his hand first moves to the wrong place, then quickly up to his collar*): Excuse me, Captain!

VOIGT (*more mildly*): After all, we must have order.—(*To a* GRENADIER *in the doorway.*) Yes? What is it?

GRENADIER: Report from the sentry at the main entrance, Captain, sir. At least a thousand people have gathered outside. The sentry asks for reinforcements.

VOIGT: Aha! (*To the* POLICE INSPECTOR.) You! You will hurry down there and restore law and order! After all, you do represent the highest police authority.

POLICE INSPECTOR: Yes, sir, Captain! (*He hurries off.*)

VOIGT (*to* OBERMÜLLER): Can I get you anything? A bit of nourishment, perhaps?

OBERMÜLLER: Thank you, no, but if I may—I'd like to inform my wife of this.

VOIGT: Do you have an official residence?

OBERMÜLLER: Yes, in the neighborhood.

VOIGT (*to* KILIAN): Bring Frau Obermüller to us. But hurry; we won't be here much longer. (*To* OBERMÜLLER.) Until your removal from the premises, you may have free access to your wife. But under guard, of course.

OBERMÜLLER: Thank you, Captain.

(A GRENADIER *appears in the doorway.*)

VOIGT: Well, what now?

GRENADIER: Report from the main post, sir. The municipal councillors have assembled in the anteroom. Their meeting is over and they want to leave.

VOIGT: How many are there?

GRENADIER: Eighteen, Captain, sir.

VOIGT: No one will be allowed to leave. You will kindly repeat my order.

GRENADIER: No one will be allowed to leave, Captain, sir. (*He turns and goes off.*)

POLICE INSPECTOR (*stands directly behind the* GRENADIER, *squeezed in the doorway*): Excuse me, Captain, but they won't let me through—I can't get out to the street—so how can I?—

VOIGT (*calling after the* GRENADIER): You! Come back! Take the Police Inspector with you and see he gets through.

(*The* GRENADIER *goes off with the* POLICE INSPECTOR.)

KILIAN (*in the doorway*): Frau Obermüller will be here at once, sir. She wasn't quite dressed.

VOIGT: Good.—Tell me—who's in charge of the Passport Office?

KILIAN: Excuse me, Captain, sir, but we don't have a Passport Office here. You'll find them only in administrative district centers.

VOIGT (*staring at him for a moment*): Ah, yes, of course, of course.—I'd forgotten all about that.—Well—there's nothing to be done about that now, I suppose. (*He strikes his sword on the ground.*)

FRAU OBERMÜLLER (*rushing in*): For heaven's sake—what's happened! Oh, my poor husband! Oh, Captain— (*Looks helplessly at* VOIGT.)

VOIGT (*saluting very politely*): My dear lady, I do hope you will forgive me, but I have the highly unpleasant duty of delivering your husband to the Imperial Headquarters in Berlin. Any further particulars you may learn from your husband himself.

OBERMÜLLER: I understand absolutely nothing of this—

FRAU OBERMÜLLER (*without listening to him*): But I don't understand—what could they possibly want with him there?

VOIGT: I've told you everything I'm able, dear lady. As far as I know, it's a matter of certain irregularities in the administration.

OBERMÜLLER: I renounce all responsibility—

FRAU OBERMÜLLER: What?! This is terrible! Why, this means he won't be home until evening!

VOIGT (*with a quiet smile*): I rather think so, dear lady.

FRAU OBERMÜLLER: But we're having guests—everything's all prepared—

VOIGT: If I may take the liberty of advising you, dear lady, I suggest you cancel your party. There's still time for your guests to make other arrangements.

FRAU OBERMÜLLER: I'd have to telephone them at once.

VOIGT: Certainly. Whatever you like. The telephone is at your disposal. But for private conversations only, of course.

FRAU OBERMÜLLER: Thank you very much. You're very kind. But this is really too terrible. Can't anything be done?

VOIGT: Unfortunately no, my dear lady. As you know, when an officer receives an order—well, it may go quite against the grain—but that, of course, is why he's a soldier. (*Bows.*)

FRAU OBERMÜLLER: Thank you. (*To* OBERMÜLLER.) You heard what the Captain said. I must call the Junghansens.

OBERMÜLLER: I don't understand.—Yes, of course, call them.

FRAU OBERMÜLLER (*at the telephone*): What shall I say—oh, 518 —I'll just tell them—oh, is Frau Junghans at home? Charlotte, dear, this is Mathilde—yes, thank you, very well—listen, Charlotte, dear, I'm afraid I have to ask a favor of you—no, not the parlormaid—it's that we can't have the party tonight —yes, quite suddenly—I can't explain it to you, there's such a rush—we suddenly have to go off to Berlin—well, I don't know—a few days perhaps—yes, the reserves—all of a sudden —such a surprise—and listen, could you phone Frau Luetgebreune for me, and Frau Koch and Frau Kutzmann—tell them the party's off and that I ask them to—yes, the reserves —oh, perhaps an even longer journey—no, thank you, thank you, anyway—there's nothing to congratulate—good-bye; and thank you again— (*Puts down the receiver.*) She thought you'd been promoted to county council—

VOIGT (*in the meanwhile has paced back and forth with large strides, and during the telephone conversation has taken* KILIAN *aside*): Come with me a moment. (*He goes out with him.*)

(*Except for* MAYOR *and* FRAU OBERMÜLLER, *only the two soldiers with fixed bayonets remain.*)

FRAU OBERMÜLLER: For heaven's sake, tell me what all this means! Don't just sit there like that!

OBERMÜLLER: What else can I do? You can see for yourself. I've tried everything I know. I renounce all responsibility.

FRAU OBERMÜLLER: But you must have some idea. This *can't* make sense, Oscar!

OBERMÜLLER: Sense?! It can be nothing short of slander, that's what! Perhaps it's the proprietor of the steam laundry—oh, but I can't believe that.

FRAU OBERMÜLLER: Didn't the Captain say anything?

OBERMÜLLER: How could he? He's doing his duty. He's following orders.

FRAU OBERMÜLLER (*to the two* SOLDIERS): Who is this captain anyway? Is he a staff captain? Or an A.P.M.?

SOLDIER: I don't know.

FRAU OBERMÜLLER: But you're under his command. You must know where he came from.

SOLDIER: I don't know a thing. We were coming from the swimming school at Plötzensee when this captain stopped us on the street and commandeered us for special duty in Köpenick. That's all I know.

FRAU OBERMÜLLER (*to* OBERMÜLLER): How did he prove his authority to you?

OBERMÜLLER: Authority? He didn't. He's a captain—

FRAU OBERMÜLLER: You allow yourself simply to be arrested by someone without authority you know nothing about? Without official papers? Without a warrant? Suppose it's all a mistake? Suppose he was supposed to arrest someone else?

OBERMÜLLER: That's out of the question. The man knows exactly what he wants.

FRAU OBERMÜLLER: But *you* don't! No, unfortunately! I want you immediately to call the district office in Teltov, or the district council—

OBERMÜLLER: Well, yes, I suppose I could—that is, supposing they all know about it over there—

FRAU OBERMÜLLER: Don't *think* about it, *do* it! (*She picks up the receiver.*)

SOLDIER (*brings his bayonet down on the telephone*): Sorry, I can't allow that.

FRAU OBERMÜLLER: You can't allow what? Did you hear the captain say I could use the telephone?

SOLDIER: That was earlier. But I can't allow this.

OBERMÜLLER: There, you see?

FRAU OBERMÜLLER (*puts down the receiver*): Will you kindly put that bayonet away, it's frightful! I'm not doing anything!

(*The* SOLDIER *grins and puts up his bayonet.* KILIAN *enters with an air of great importance.*)

What is it, Kilian? Where is he? What have you heard?

KILIAN: I can give you no information.

FRAU OBERMÜLLER: What's the meaning of this, Kilian? How dare you speak to me that way! You're forgetting yourself!

KILIAN: I have orders to bring the Mayor and the Municipal

Treasurer to Berlin as prisoners. I'm not allowed to speak to prisoners.

OBERMÜLLER: You have orders to what? (*Sinks back into the chair.*)

VOIGT (*enters*): I've requisitioned two closed carriages. You can get inside them in the courtyard so that no one sees you. The police sergeant here will be in charge of transporting you.

OBERMÜLLER: Captain, sir! May I ask to see some proof of your authority in this matter? I insist on seeing such proof at once!

VOIGT (*knocks with his hand against one of the bayonets*): Doesn't this speak for itself?—I will tolerate no contradiction here! (*More friendly.*) You as a soldier must know that an armed escort means absolute authority.

OBERMÜLLER (*to his wife*): You see? (*He collapses again.*)

FRAU OBERMÜLLER: Captain, I trust you will permit me to accompany my husband on this difficult journey. I mustn't leave him now. I'm certain you understand.

VOIGT: By all means, dear lady. But I must ask you to leave the carriage shortly before we arrive at Imperial Headquarters. My orders are to deliver only your husband. It could cause certain difficulties.

FRAU OBERMÜLLER: Thank you. I'll get ready.

VOIGT (*to* KILIAN): You will kindly accompany the Mayor's wife. (*He bows.*)

(FRAU OBERMÜLLER *nods her head graciously and rushes out, accompanied by* KILIAN.)

VOIGT: Mayor, I'd like to spare you having to ride in the same car with the armed grenadiers. Will you, as an officer, give me your word of honor not to attempt an escape?

OBERMÜLLER: You have my word. I will—

VOIGT: Thank you, that's quite sufficient.

OBERMÜLLER: I shall take the first suitable moment to draw attention to your very considerate behavior, sir.

(VOIGT *salutes. The* POLICE INSPECTOR *enters with a* GRENADIER.)

POLICE INSPECTOR: Captain, sir, order has been restored. My officers are masters of the situation.

VOIGT: Thank you. Anything else?

POLICE INSPECTOR: Yes, begging your pardon, Captain, sir—my duty's over for the day, and, you see, we only have hot water once a week, and my wife has already drawn my bath water by this time. Begging your leave to go home for a bath, sir.

VOIGT: To what? Go home for a bath?

POLICE INSPECTOR: Yes, Captain, sir! I'd like to apply for a bath leave.

VOIGT: Well, if you really need one—(*Claps him on the shoulder.*)—bath leave granted, Inspector. (*Laughs.*)

POLICE INSPECTOR (*earnestly*): Thank you kindly, Captain! (*Goes off.*)

(VOIGT *looks at the soldiers who have also grinned; immediately their faces freeze.*)

ROSENCRANTZ (*enters eagerly*): Beg to report, Captain, the treasury balance has been completed. Here are the ledgers, and here the total amount of cash on hand. (*Places them on the writing table in envelopes and bags with inscriptions on them.*) Four thousand forty-two marks and fifty pfennigs.

VOIGT: Thank you. I'll take charge of the money for the time being. I assume it's all in order. But I'll check it in any case.

GRENADIER (*in the doorway*): Captain, sir, there's someone who wants to see you.

VOIGT (*counting the money*): Bring him in.

COMENIUS (*enters*): Begging your pardon, Captain, sir: Comenius, Councillor Comenius. The fact is we were at a meeting and we've been waiting all this time. I have come as an ambassador for the other municipal councillors—we all have rather pressing engagements outside—and since the matter doesn't concern the community—that is—since it's a matter of personal delinquency on the part of the Mayor—or am I mistaken?

VOIGT (*to* ROSENCRANTZ): Look here, the books show four thousand forty-two marks and *ninety* pfennigs, and you've given me only four thousand forty-two marks and *fifty* pfennigs. How do you account for that?

ROSENCRANTZ: Yes, of course, Captain, sir, you see, in all the haste everything got turned all around and there remained a difference of forty pfennigs.

VOIGT: Very well. After all, I'm not a pedant. But I will, of course, be forced to take note of it, or people may think I personally embezzled forty pfennigs. (*Laughs jovially.*)

ROSENCRANTZ (*laughing with him*): But, Captain, sir!

VOIGT (*to* COMENIUS): Ah, so the worthy councillors have cold feet, eh? Very well, go down and tell them they can leave. The proceedings here are almost at an end. (*To the* CORPORAL.) The councillors are granted permission to leave the building.

COMENIUS: Thank you, Captain, thank you! (*Goes off.*)

KILIAN (*in greatcoat and helmet*): Sir, the carriages have arrived, and the Mayor's wife has already taken her place.

VOIGT: Take the two gentlemen downstairs, then, and drive on. You know where to go. Imperial Headquarters in Berlin.

KILIAN: Very good, sir! The Captain can depend on me. (*To* OBERMÜLLER *and* ROSENCRANTZ.) Forward, march!

(OBERMÜLLER *and* ROSENCRANTZ *are led off.*)

KILIAN'S VOICE (*from outside*): Hurry! Put on your coats! Forward, march!

VOIGT: Well, at least he's enjoying himself. It's not every day he can lead his Mayor off to jail. (*He stuffs the money in his greatcoat pocket, and calls.*) Corporal!

(*The* CORPORAL *comes and stands at attention.*)

The proceedings here in Köpenick have come to an end. In one half hour you will round up the guards, march them to the station, take the train back to Berlin, and report at Imperial Headquarters that you have returned from duty in Köpenick.

CORPORAL: Very good, sir!

VOIGT: Tell your men they did a good job, and that all things turned out for the best.

CORPORAL: Very good, sir!

VOIGT: Here's some money for your train fare. With what's left over, buy every man a beer and a bockwurst at the station.

CORPORAL: Thank you, Captain, sir!

VOIGT: Good-day! (*He salutes with his finger at his cap, and goes off.*)

(*The* SOLDIERS *and the* CORPORAL *stand stiffly at attention.*)

BLACKOUT

SCENE 6

Aschinger's Beer and Snack Bar on New Friedrichstrasse. Early morning. The gas lamp is still burning. The place is being tidied up, with chairs still on the tables. A stove in the corner. Printed signs hang on the wall over the bar, one of which says: "No Credit." Another reads:

"A single beer will never do,
Unless you never have had two.

> *Therefore help your beer go down*
> *With a shot of brandy of renown."*

Empty bottles, unwashed glasses, stale smoke. The night-shift WAITER, *a seedy character in a dirty white jacket, and the* CHARWOMAN *are busily straightening up the place.* WILHELM VOIGT *lies on a small wall bench, behind a number of tables, as though he were dead. He wears his old clothes. All one can see of him are his boots. The* WAITER *climbs up on a chair and puts out the gas lamp. Faint daylight invades the room. The* CHARWOMAN *sweeps up the dirt and cigarette butts.*

WAITER (*still on the chair*): I ain't got any sleep since we started staying open nights around here. Soon as we get rid of the late stragglers we get the early morning cabbies. You'd think we was running a charity here. I don't even remember the last time I got a tip.

CHARWOMAN (*while sweeping, has gone near* VOIGT): What's with him?

WAITER: Sweep him up with the rest of the dirt, the bloody tramp!

CHARWOMAN: Lord, the hangover he's going to have today!

WAITER: Well, he didn't get it here, I'll tell you that much. He's been laying there since yesterday. For a small beer and a half a cutlet he sacked out here and ain't moved since.

CHARWOMAN: Then he must have got bombed before.

WAITER: He didn't look it. He's a tramp. Ought to throw some leftover beer in his kisser.

CHARWOMAN: Ah, let him alone. Maybe he's sick.

WAITER: So why don't he go to the hospital? The first customer comes in here, I want him out.

(*Outside we hear the rolling and clatter of milk wagons. A streetcar passes by.*)

Well, here we go again. The damn sun's enough to make you puke.

(*A* MILKMAN *from the Bolle Dairy enters. He has a heavy red face. With him are two* MILKMAIDS *who enter behind him. They are dressed in blue smocks with the inscription "Fresh milk" embroidered across the breast.*)

MILKMAN: Fritz, my morning usual! Come on, girls, I'll buy you a hot sausage. (*Sings.*)

> "Happy the man
> Who eats what he can
> And drinks what ought to be drunk."

That's my good word for the day. The important thing is a healthy constitution.

(*The* MILKMAIDS *laugh and sit down.*)

WAITER (*has poured the* MILKMAN *a large glass of cognac*): Your morning usual. The girls get a cognac, too?

MILKMAIDS: Oh, no! For heaven's sake!

MILKMAN: What do you mean, "for heaven's sake"? Be glad the good Lord lets cognac grow!

WAITER (*standing by* VOIGT): Hey, you! Get up! You didn't eat anything yet, and you ain't paid yet either! What do you think this is, a flophouse?

MILKMAN: What the hell! It's my dead old uncle they lost in America fifty years ago! He fell out of a mail coach. Morning, unc!

(VOIGT, *still lying down, has scarcely moved. The* MILKMAIDS *laugh.*—VOIGT *sits up as if he were numb.*)

(*Holding his glass out to* VOIGT.) Here! Help put some life into your bones!

(VOIGT *shakes his head.*)

WAITER (*yells at him*): What do you want? You either buy something or get out!

VOIGT: A coffee.

MILKMAN: He's a teetotaler. I smelled that the first thing. He can't be my uncle, I guess. He drunk himself to death.

(*The voice of a* TAXI DRIVER *is heard from outside; he laughs loudly while speaking with someone else. Presently he enters, with a newspaper in his hand.*)

TAXI DRIVER: Hey, look at this! Jesus! What a story! I been laughing so hard my belly's about to pop! (*He falls laughing into a chair.*)

MILKMAN: What's the joke? Your old lady had a kid?

TAXI DRIVER: You mean you haven't heard? Nobody seen the morning paper? It's plastered all over town! They even got out an extra. The crowd's so big in town you can hardly move.

WAITER: All right, all right! I know! Let's see!—What the hell is —the Captain of—

TAXI DRIVER: Köpenick! The Captain of Köpenick! I was born and bred in Berlin, but I never heard of a thing like this! I never laughed so much in my life!

MILKMAN (*has meanwhile read the story, laughs, as the* WAITER, *the* MILKMAIDS, *and the* CHARWOMAN *press around him from behind to look at the newspaper*): I don't surprise easy, but this sure does it! Bravo! Good boy! That's the stuff! Arrested the magistrate and locked them in the cellar! Led the Mayor through the streets in handcuffs—commandeered fifty soldiers from the parade ground, surrounded the whole town—and then turns out to be an impostor!

CHARWOMAN: The nerve of the man!

TAXI DRIVER: Nerve? He must be pretty damn bright, if you ask me! A scholar even, or at least a politician. You wait and see, next thing you know he'll be turning the world upside down. Hey, listen to that! Another Special Edition!

(A NEWSBOY *runs by outside.*)

NEWSBOY (*outside*): Extra! Extra! Read all about the Captain of Köpenick! Extra! Extra! The Captain of Köpenick still at large! Extra! Extra! Read the latest from the Köpenick front! Captain of Köpenick to be promoted to general! Extra! Extra! Mayor's wife charged as accomplice! Read the latest about the Captain of Köpenick. Extra! Extra!

TAXI DRIVER: See you later. I want one of those! (*He rushes out.*)

MILKMAN: Wait, I'll come too! I want one too! Don't let him get away!

(*The* MILKMAIDS *have run into the street, the* WAITER *and the* CHARWOMAN *after them. They run calling after the* NEWSBOY *and disappear.*)

MILKMAN (*claps the newspaper in his hand down on the table in front of* VOIGT): Here, read this, old man! Better than a hot coffee any day! What's the matter, pop, never learn how to laugh? (*Goes off behind the others.*)

(VOIGT *is left alone. He stares at the newspaper, unmoving at first, then suddenly pulls it to him and reads. His jaws begin to move noiselessly; then he speaks in a half-voice, which grows more and more faint.*)

VOIGT: "—and so this mad practical joker, who will undoubtedly cause the world to laugh riotously today, sits safely by, laughing, and enjoying the fruits of his merry robbery—" Is that what they think?—(*He lets his head sink down onto his arms.*)

(*Outside the people come back with their extras. The* TAXI DRIVER *is heard reading through the open door.*)

TAXI DRIVER: Hey, look! A reward! Somebody'll strike it rich! (*He reads, and after each detail a roar of laughter rises.*) "Thin and bony—stoop-shouldered—pale, ugly face—sickly appearance—sunken cheeks—prominent cheekbones—deep-set eyes —crooked, bulbous nose—somewhat bowlegged—hands small and white—" Hey, sounds like the old dead mutt I used to have!

(*Roars of mad laughter from outside.* VOIGT *sits unmoving.*)

BLACKOUT

SCENE 7

The interrogation room in the Police Headquarters in Berlin. It is sparsely furnished with a desk, chairs, and an armchair. The POLICE INSPECTOR *sits in the armchair, the* POLICE COMMISSIONER *beside him at the table.* STUTZ, *the prisoner being questioned, stands in front of them. He is a military-looking swindler with a waxed moustache.*

POLICE COMMISSIONER: So you persist in denying any connection with the Köpenick affair.

STUTZ: I'm not denying anything. I wasn't there.

POLICE COMMISSIONER: Yet you admit you were in Köpenick on the day in question.

STUTZ: Sure. My fiancée lives there.

POLICE COMMISSIONER: Very well. (*With assumed indifference, in order to take him by surprise.*) Naturally you've had the uniform for some time.

STUTZ: Look, Commissioner, let's get this straight. If it really was me—believe me, you'd never have caught me. At least not like that. And *not you.*

POLICE INSPECTOR: Let him go. This isn't getting us anywhere.

POLICE COMMISSIONER (*presses a bell, and a policeman appears*): Take him away.

(*The policeman goes off with* STUTZ.)

POLICE INSPECTOR: Surprise tactics won't work on an old pro like him. Besides, he doesn't even fit the description.

POLICE COMMISSIONER: Exactly why I suspect him. My theory is he did it with makeup. I maintain we must look for our man among ex-soldiers, or even ex-officers who've been dismissed. Nobody else could possibly have carried it off.

POLICE INSPECTOR: I suggest we let the whole thing drop. We'll only make a laughingstock of ourselves.

POLICE COMMISSIONER: Sorry, Inspector, I don't agree. As far as I'm concerned, it's a matter of prestige. If I'm entrusted with a case of this sort, and can't solve it—then why am I the Kaiser's Commissioner of Police?

POLICE INSPECTOR: The Kaiser's not terribly keen on the matter himself. On the contrary. Haven't you read the secret instructions? When they told him about it, he laughed; he was proud of it! "My dear Jagow," he said to the Chief, "what an excellent example of the meaning of discipline! Not another country in the world can equal us in that!"—So you see?

POLICE COMMISSIONER: It's all very well for him to laugh; but if I fail to solve this case, I might as well resign.

(A knock at the door.)

Come in!

POLICE SERGEANT (breathless): We got him! I beg your pardon, sir, but I just got news that—

POLICE COMMISSIONER (has jumped to his feet): Who? The Captain?!

POLICE SERGEANT: Yes, Commissioner, sir. He's been arrested in the Passport Division.

POLICE INSPECTOR: Oh, for God's sake! That makes the fortieth arrest to date!

POLICE SERGEANT: But he's already confessed.

POLICE INSPECTOR: I've got dozens of confessions! (Slams his hand down on a pile of documents.) A few more or less won't make any difference!

POLICE SERGEANT: But he told us where he hid the uniform.

POLICE COMMISSIONER: Damnation! Where is this man?

POLICE SERGEANT: Downstairs in the cross-examination room. Should I bring him up?

POLICE COMMISSIONER: Yes, hurry, hurry!

(The POLICE SERGEANT goes off.)

POLICE INSPECTOR: Just don't get your hopes up. In the Passport Office of all places! Now how could he be so dumb as to—

POLICE COMMISSIONER (pacing back and forth without pause): What have the passport people got to do with it! I won't have it! This is a matter that belongs to our department!

POLICE INSPECTOR: Ah, but nothing will come of it!

(*A knock at the door.*)

POLICE COMMISSIONER (*excitedly*): Come in!

(*The* PASSPORT COMMISSIONER *enters with* WILHELM VOIGT *behind him. He has no handcuffs on, and is flanked by two guards. He stands unconcerned, but quietly and seriously, in the vicinity of the door.*)

PASSPORT COMMISSIONER (*scornfully*): Gentlemen, may I present to you the Captain of Köpenick. You have only to arrest him.

POLICE COMMISSIONER: Him?! So that's what you look like! (*He sits.*)

POLICE INSPECTOR: What makes you think he's the man?

PASSPORT COMMISSIONER: He explained it all himself.

(*The* POLICE INSPECTOR *laughs.*)

POLICE COMMISSIONER: No, no, no! I'd sooner believe it was the other one!

POLICE INSPECTOR: All right, tell us about it.

PASSPORT COMMISSIONER: Well, at 11:30 A.M. this man presented himself at the Passport Office and asked to speak to the commissioner on duty, because he had important information to give. I let him in, asked him what he wanted, and the man made a most remarkable declaration. I took it down in dictation. (*He reads.*) He said he was Wilhelm Voigt, an ex-convict, and had to have a passport. If I'd promise him a passport afterward—he definitely said "afterward"—he agreed to produce the Captain of Köpenick. So I said to myself, there's no harm promising if we can get the man to talk.

POLICE INSPECTOR (*interrupting him*): You had no right to do such a thing! You should have simply arrested him! If the man has any pertinent information, it's his duty to deliver it, without any conditions whatever!

PASSPORT COMMISSIONER: That's right, and I could have died before he'd have opened his mouth, eh? We know all about that approach.

POLICE COMMISSIONER: This is a matter that concerns *our* department! The Passport Office has nothing whatever to do with it!

PASSPORT COMMISSIONER: I beg your pardon! I haven't interfered in your department in the least! You could have arrested him two whole weeks ago! That's how long he's been roaming around Berlin—free!

POLICE INSPECTOR: Come to the point! Come to the point!

PASSPORT COMMISSIONER: Well, as I said, I promised him a passport, because I thought if nobody vouched for him it wouldn't be valid. Then he said: "All right, in that case I'll get the passport later, but you'd better arrest me now, because I'm the man." Those were his very words.

POLICE INSPECTOR: Nonsense! All he wants is to attract attention! He wants a free roof over his head for a day or two during the cold weather.

PASSPORT COMMISSIONER: That's what I thought too. "So you claim to be the Captain of Köpenick," I said to him. "Well then, where's that famous uniform of yours?"—"At the Silesian Railroad Station," he said, "in the Luggage Office," and he gave me a ticket with a number on it. "You'll find it in a big cardboard box." So naturally I sent someone off there at once. (*Sits down, laughs ironically.*) Well, what do you gentlemen think of the matter now?

POLICE INSPECTOR (*in a loud, harsh voice to* VOIGT, *who has stood unobtrusively at the door between the two guards*): Can you prove that you're the Captain of Köpenick?

VOIGT: No, I don't think I can. You gentlemen should be able to do that. I'm not a trained detective like you.

POLICE COMMISSIONER: Shut up and keep quiet!

(*The* PASSPORT COMMISSIONER *laughs.*)

POLICE INSPECTOR: The nerve of the man! Sheer deception! You'll see for yourself when your man gets back from the railroad station. (*The telephone rings. He lifts the receiver.*) Room 1-B. What?! But that's—yes, yes, bring it over at once, by car! (*Puts down the receiver.*) They've found the uniform!—

(*All three stand there silently, looking at one another.*)

PASSPORT COMMISSIONER: I don't suppose *that's* enough proof for you either, eh?

POLICE COMMISSIONER: We must immediately—

POLICE INSPECTOR: Psst! I'll take charge of the questioning myself. (*To the* PASSPORT COMMISSIONER.) Thank you, Commissioner! And now would you be so good as to inform the Chief of the matter?

PASSPORT COMMISSIONER: My pleasure. I'll go up at once and prepare him for the news. (*Starts to go out.*)

POLICE COMMISSIONER: But try not to make it seem all your doing. After all, it was only by the purest chance.

PASSPORT COMMISSIONER: Of course, Commissioner, and I congratulate you on your very unusual stroke of chance! (*Goes out.*)

POLICE INSPECTOR (*has meanwhile gone over to* VOIGT *and signaled the guards to leave*): Well now, my good man, do come a bit closer, won't you? Sit down, and quietly tell us all about it. I suspect you have a great deal to tell. Do you smoke?

VOIGT (*astounded*): No, thank you.

POLICE INSPECTOR (*calling after one of the guards*): Go get a bottle of port from The Last Resort next door! Charge it to my bill! (*Quickly glances at the notes taken by the* PASSPORT COMMISSIONER.) Wilhelm Voigt.—Well, Herr Voigt, your confession does you great credit. Let me assure you of that from the very start. No doubt you were driven to it by a gnawing conscience and a deep sense of repentance.

VOIGT: No, not exactly. I did it for the passport. I couldn't get one in Köpenick, and I had to have one, I just had to.

POLICE INSPECTOR: And you really believe you will be given a passport here and let go?

VOIGT: No, no, I knew beforehand you wouldn't just let me go. But when I get out of jail again, then you *couldn't* deny me the passport. Because they made me a promise, and the promise is public knowledge now.

POLICE INSPECTOR (*jovially*): Dear, dear, dear, but you're a clever fellow! (*In a whisper to the* POLICE COMMISSIONER.) Take this down in shorthand! (*To* VOIGT.) Well now, suppose you explain to me all this business with the passport.

VOIGT: There's nothing to explain. I've got to get a passport sometime so I can get on to a decent life again. I'm sick of all this, you know.

POLICE INSPECTOR: How old are you?

VOIGT: Going on fifty-seven.

POLICE INSPECTOR: I see. And yet you can so calmly contemplate the inevitable thought of imprisonment?

VOIGT: Why not? It'll pass, and anyway I'm used to it. But all this chasing around, playing hide-and-seek, the whole dirty business—I just can't take it anymore. I just can't take it.

POLICE INSPECTOR: But what about the money you took, the four thousand marks? That's quite a pile to run off with!

VOIGT (*reaches into his breast pocket and pulls out a small package*): Here it is. It's not all there, of course. I had to live, and I needed a pair of new boots. Altogether I took eighty-three marks. Here's an account of what I spent.

POLICE INSPECTOR: Good lord, man, you could have traveled a long way on this!

VOIGT: And when it's all spent, I'd be stuck wherever I was. I could have gotten across the border with the money, but I could never have gotten back, and then I'd have to be buried in foreign soil. No, no, that's not for me. First I want a passport, and then I want peace and quiet.

(*The* GUARD *enters with a half-bottle of port.*)

GUARD: Should I uncork it for you, Inspector?

POLICE INSPECTOR: Of course. Our friend Voigt here needs some refreshment after all the excitement.

VOIGT: Oh, I'm not excited. I imagined it all exactly like this. The only thing I'm not used to is you gentlemen being so kind to me.

POLICE INSPECTOR (*jovially*): But, my dear Herr Voigt, it stands to reason! We don't go around biting people here!

VOIGT: I know, I know.

POLICE INSPECTOR: Well then, have a drink!

VOIGT: I never drink on an empty stomach.

POLICE INSPECTOR: Sergeant! Bring a ham sandwich!—You go ahead and drink now, it can't hurt you.

VOIGT: Well, I don't want to be a spoilsport—Prosit, Inspector! (*He drinks.*)

POLICE INSPECTOR: There! That's right!—Tell me now, Herr Voigt, didn't you do *anything* with all that money?

VOIGT: Yes, I stayed in a nice, proper lodging. Except for the first night I spent at Aschinger's. I was so tired, I fell asleep on the spot.

POLICE INSPECTOR: What I meant was, didn't you go on a binge, maybe, or do the town, as they say?

VOIGT: No, I don't like that sort of thing. (*Rather confidentially.*) All I want is my peace, and my freedom—don't you see?— Mmm, this is good. (*Drinks.*)

CHIEF OF POLICE (*enters quickly; he is a heavy, elderly man*): Where is he?! Aha! (*He stares at* VOIGT.)

POLICE INSPECTOR: Yes, sir, that's the man all right! (*With a wink.*) And what a charming gentleman! He's telling us everything quite openly. As you see, I furnished him with some small refreshment.

CHIEF OF POLICE: Quite right! (*To* VOIGT, *who has politely risen.*) No, no, my good man, not at all! Sit down! Sit down! Please!

VOIGT: I will, sir, if you'll take a seat yourself.

CHIEF OF POLICE (*laughing*): Certainly I'll take a seat, and then we can have a nice talk together. Have another drink?

VOIGT: Yes, thank you. This is very nice. I never drink, you know. I'm not used to it.

CHIEF OF POLICE: Of course, of course, but the main thing is you like it.

VOIGT: Prosit, sir! This is very, very nice. (*But he does not laugh; he remains quiet and indifferent.*)

POLICE INSPECTOR (*in a whisper*): We've had everything taken down in shorthand. It's obvious he's a mental case. (*Aloud to* VOIGT.) Well now, my dear Herr Voigt, suppose you tell the Chief of Police here just how you came upon the whole idea.

VOIGT: That's easy. I didn't come upon it; it came upon me, you might say.

CHIEF OF POLICE: But where did you get the idea to dress up as a captain and do such a thing?

VOIGT: Any child in Germany knows that to do what you want all you need is a uniform. I've known that all my life.

CHIEF OF POLICE: But why in Köpenick? How did you happen to hit on Köpenick?

VOIGT: Because it was only one station away. But I made a big mistake there. There's no Passport Office in Köpenick. If I'd thought of that, I'd have gone to the district office in Teltov.

CHIEF OF POLICE: Seems like Teltov had a stroke of good luck that day.

VOIGT: If I had done that, I'd have gotten a passport, and you gentlemen wouldn't be entertaining me here. (*Drinks.*)

CHIEF OF POLICE (*looks at* VOIGT): Good God, what a dunce that Mayor must be!

VOIGT: You mustn't say that, sir. He's not really so stupid. The same could have happened to you. It's all in the nature of things.

CHIEF OF POLICE: Very well, very well. But tell me, where did you pick all this up? All the military language, the commands? It was all so perfect.

VOIGT: No, sir, it wasn't really all that much. In fact a uniform can do it almost all by itself. And besides, in prison at Sonnenburg we spent our free time reading the Field Service Regulations, and the Army Drill Manual. I always took an interest in it.

CHIEF OF POLICE: Then that's all the preparation you had? You simply went out and stopped the first squad of soldiers you came to and led them off to Köpenick?

VOIGT: Not exactly. First I dressed in the uniform—and then I issued myself an order—and then I went off and carried it out.

CHIEF OF POLICE: You certainly were lucky, I must say. Can't deny you that.

VOIGT: There's an element of luck in every military operation, sir. Luck is a commander's main requirement. Napoleon said so himself.

CHIEF OF POLICE: I dare say the world lost a pocket Napoleon in you. (*Pours* VOIGT *another drink.*) Have another drink!

VOIGT: No, no, thank you, I'm beginning to feel it already. But it does taste terribly good. (*He smells it.*) I could almost get used to this.

CHIEF OF POLICE (*laughing*): I'm delighted our good Captain is so pleased with us.

VOIGT: I am, too. I never in my life had such good luck in a public office. They would either lock me up or run me out.

POLICEMAN (*at the door*): The uniform is here, sir.

CHIEF OF POLICE: Bring it in! We must have a look at this! (*While the box is being brought in and unpacked.*) Where did you get it, if I may ask?

VOIGT: From the Jew in Grenadierstrasse who sells old clothes. I bought it with my own money. It belongs to me.

COMMISSIONER: And yet no one came forward with any such information? Despite all our notices? Or did you, in fact, buy it for nothing? (*He makes a motion of grabbing.*)

VOIGT (*with quiet dignity*): My dear sir, I never in my life stole anything from my fellowman. I never ran up against anyone but the government.

CHIEF OF POLICE (*has taken out the uniform and holds up the overcoat*): Aha! So here we have it! A genuine guardsman's overcoat—made by a firm in Potsdam. A lot of years of service went into this coat, from the looks of it.

VOIGT (*raises his glass*): But for all its years, it's still got some service left, eh? (*Drinks to the uniform.*)

CHIEF OF POLICE: Look, why don't you put it on for us? Just the coat will do. The coat and the cap. I'd like to get a look at it once.

VOIGT: Of course, if it'll make you happy. I can put it on again all right. Give it here. (*He takes off his own coat.*)

CHIEF OF POLICE (*in a whisper to the* POLICEMAN): Get a photographer. (*Aloud to* VOIGT.) May I help you there, Captain?

VOIGT: Thank you, no, I'm doing very well. (*He slips into the coat, buttons it, puts on the cap.*)

CHIEF OF POLICE (*can scarcely restrain his laughter*): Why, it's magnificent! (*To the others.*) A sight like that could bring a corpse to attention!

VOIGT (*his hand at his cap in a calm and composed salute*): Thank you. At ease!

(*The* CHIEF OF POLICE, *the* POLICE INSPECTOR, *and the* POLICE COMMISSIONER *burst into a gale of laughter.*)

(*Very seriously.*) Begging your pardon, sir, I'd like to make a request.

CHIEF OF POLICE: By all means! What is it! Tell me!

VOIGT: Do you think I might see myself in a mirror?

CHIEF OF POLICE: You never—why, that's incredible! Didn't you try it on beforehand, and rehearse?

VOIGT: No. The place I changed in was a little cramped—and there wasn't a mirror.

CHIEF OF POLICE: Hurry, bring a mirror! The big one from the dressing room! Prepare yourself for a great shock!

VOIGT: In that case I'd better have a little something. I must prepare myself. (*Takes his glass, fills it with port, and drinks.*)

CHIEF OF POLICE (*wiping his eyes*): Gentlemen—this is the loveliest moment of my thirty years in service.

(*The policeman enters with the mirror.*)

Put it down over there! There you are, Captain! Take a look, and know for once what it means to have respect for yourself!

VOIGT (*steps in front of the mirror, his wineglass still in his hand. He stands with his back to the audience. The CHIEF OF POLICE and the others stand aside and observe him. At first VOIGT stands quite still—then his shoulders begin to twitch, but as yet there is no sound—then his whole figure starts to shake and sway, so that the port spills from the glass in his hand—then he slowly turns around—laughing—laughing harder and harder, laughing with his entire face, with his entire body, with his whole being—laughing until his breath almost stops coming and the tears stream from his eyes. Out of all this laughter a single word gradually begins to emerge—very softly at first and almost inaudibly—then more loudly, more clearly, more distinctly—until finally it explodes in a burst of fresh, mighty, and uncontrollable laughter*): Im-possible!

BLACKOUT

"Come," said the Cock,
"We'll find something better than death!"
THE BROTHERS GRIMM, *The Bremen Town Musicians*

NO MORE PEACE!

by ERNST TOLLER

TRANSLATED BY EDWARD CRANKSHAW AND W. H. AUDEN

CHARACTERS

ST. FRANCIS
NAPOLEON
ANGEL
SAMUEL
NOAH
LABAN
LOT
JACOB
FAT MAN
LITTLE MAN
THIN MAN
DAVID
CAIN
FIRST CHILD
SECOND CHILD
RACHEL
DOCTOR
SARAH
SOCRATES
WARDER

ACT I

SCENE 1

Drawing room on Olympus.

When the curtain rises ST. FRANCIS *and* NAPOLEON *are seated on comfortable clouds before an open fireplace, in which the fire is the sun. In the corner at a switchboard a female* ANGEL. ST. FRANCIS *and* NAPOLEON *are playing dominoes.*

NAPOLEON: A cigarette, my dear Francis?

ST. FRANCIS: Thank you, I don't smoke.

NAPOLEON (*pouring himself out a drink*): Whiskey?

ST. FRANCIS: I don't drink, thank you.

NAPOLEON: The dinner was shocking.

ST. FRANCIS: Well, you know, it's no use asking my opinion. For very many years now, I've lived on manna and rain water. A little of that everyday is all I need.

ANGEL: There's a new cook, Your Majesty.

NAPOLEON: Another Englishman, I'll be bound. We've had roast beef every other day for a week. You know, the Almighty's predilection for the English passes my comprehension.

(*Faint growling of thunder.*)

ST. FRANCIS (*pointing upward*): Softly, my friend. A most capable nation.

NAPOLEON: Capable, but uninspired. I certainly underestimated them!

(*Pause.*)

(*To* ANGEL.) My dear, is there anything on the Northern radio?

ANGEL: A talk by Charles Darwin on "My Earthly Mistakes: Why Man Is Not Descended from the Apes."

NAPOLEON: I've heard that a hundred times already. Anything better on the Southern station?

ANGEL: The heavenly weather forecast.

NAPOLEON: Set fair. Much sunshine. Further outlook very settled. I know.

ANGEL: There's a concert from the central transmitter—an English choir.

NAPOLEON (*to* ST. FRANCIS): Do you mind?

ST. FRANCIS: Not at all.

LOUD SPEAKER:
The heavens are telling Jehovah's glory;

The sounding spheres His power proclaim;
The earth, the oceans, are loud with His story;
Revere, O Man, His Awful Name.

NAPOLEON: I'm afraid it's boring enough up here when one comes to think of it. These panegyrics are apt to get monotonous. . . .

ST. FRANCIS: We live the life of the blessed. We live in peace.

NAPOLEON: Precisely! . . . (*To* ANGEL.) Try something else, child.

(ANGEL *manipulates switchboard; from the loudspeaker issue the strains of the "Internationale."*)

ST. FRANCIS: What a beautiful chorale!

NAPOLEON: What? The "Internationale!" Is this possible? Are the gods going red?

ANGEL: Oh, I'm so sorry, Your Majesty! I got on to Hell by mistake. . . . (*She switches off.*)

ST. FRANCIS: Nevertheless, I found the music very sweet.

NAPOLEON: Have you seen the papers?

ST. FRANCIS: I never read the papers.

NAPOLEON (*to* ANGEL): Have the European evening papers come?

ANGEL: Yes, Your Majesty.

NAPOLEON: What's happening in Paris?

ANGEL: The government has been overthrown.

NAPOLEON: Most unusual! Anything about me?

ANGEL: Your Majesty's name is not mentioned.

NAPOLEON: Hm! The Parisians always were an ungrateful lot!

ST. FRANCIS: You must not forget you have been dead more than a hundred years.

NAPOLEON: What are a hundred years? . . . (*To* ANGEL.) And London?

ANGEL: England is threatened.

NAPOLEON: Who by? America? Germany? Japan?

ANGEL: No. All India. M.C.C. are all out for 17.

NAPOLEON: I'm avenged at last! This is worse for them than if I had conquered India myself. What about Berlin?

ANGEL: The German Government desires nothing so much as peace.

NAPOLEON: Uh! How are the armament shares?

ANGEL: United German Armaments have risen ten points.

NAPOLEON: So . . . ? And the League of Nations?

ANGEL: The League of Nations has inaugurated a new day.

ST. FRANCIS: Who is the saint?

ANGEL: It's in honor of peace. It's to be called Peace Day.

ST. FRANCIS: Amen!

NAPOLEON: That means war just round the corner!

ST. FRANCIS (*up and right*): My dear Napoleon, war has been out-lawed. The governments of the earth have pledged themselves. Their ministers speak of nothing but peace. All the nations are concluding peace pacts. (*Back left.*)

NAPOLEON: What the devil's the use of a peace pact if not to pre-pare for war?

ST. FRANCIS: Ah, you believe only in the evil in man.

NAPOLEON: Well, you believe only in the good in men.

ST. FRANCIS: When I was living on earth men were by no means good. They professed goodness, but their deeds were not good. The rich extolled apostolic poverty while they wallowed in luxury. Rakes and gluttons preached abstinence. Snobs cut themselves off from the sufferings of their fellowmen. If a man with seven cloaks was asked by a beggar for one of them, only one, to warm his shivering limbs, that man would lock his wardrobe and set his dogs upon the beggar. My contem-poraries were lacking in understanding, in the knowledge of goodness; they sowed Satan and corrupted their souls. That was many, many centuries ago. Today mankind is better, more understanding, more humane. God has sent terrible scourges on to the earth to teach men and to lead them to the right path.

NAPOLEON: What do you mean by that?

ST. FRANCIS: Even you, my dear Napoleon, were an ambassador of the Almighty.

NAPOLEON: That's very civil of you, Francis. But I flatter myself that I know something about human nature and don't believe all this chattering about peace.

ST. FRANCIS: Didn't you yourself write in your memoirs that in the end the mind proves stronger than the sword?

NAPOLEON: That was written at the end of my days, at the end of my deeds . . . on St. Helena.

ST. FRANCIS: It has been taken very seriously by your biographers.

NAPOLEON: Am I responsible for my biographers? You know what they are. Napoleon thought this in the morning, that in the afternoon, and something else at night. If I'd had all the thoughts attributed to me by biographers, I should never have got anything done at all. Men of action think infrequently! . . . No, I don't believe in all this talk about peace. I tell you what, would you like to meet a scholar who has made a life study of society and its troubles? You know Marx, of course.

ST. FRANCIS: Which one?

NAPOLEON: Karl Marx. The man who wrote a book.

ST. FRANCIS: What was it called?

NAPOLEON: I don't know. I didn't enjoy it. Actually, of course, Marx is living in Hell, but the Almighty would certainly let him up here for an hour or so.

ST. FRANCIS: I remember—I read that book—what was it called? *Das Kapital.* I did not like it. I really don't think he's quite the man for me. If you don't mind I think he'd better stay where he is.

NAPOLEON: Just as you please. But I promise you that the very people who are boosting peace today will be exalting war tomorrow. You see, if one could *fight* for peace . . .

ST. FRANCIS: Many martyrs have died for peace.

NAPOLEON: Yes, but as martyrs, as sufferers—not as heroes, not as men of action. The martyrs are revered, but the heroes are glorified. Girls dream of heroes, not martyrs. You see, Francis, mankind loves adventure, romantic uncertainty. There is none of that in peace.

(A *sound of distant bells.*)

ST. FRANCIS: Do you hear that?

NAPOLEON: I can't hear anything.

ST. FRANCIS: My ears may be more sensitive to such sounds. All over the earth the bells of peace are ringing.

NAPOLEON: I am still unimpressed.

ST. FRANCIS: You lack faith.

NAPOLEON: I'll make a bet with you.

ST. FRANCIS: I never bet, my dear friend.

NAPOLEON: Nonsense. Pick out the most peaceful town on earth, and I'll send them a telegram saying that war has been declared.

ST. FRANCIS: Not a forged telegram?

NAPOLEON: It wouldn't be the first I've sent, by any means!

ST. FRANCIS: And what would happen? They would pray; they would refuse to fight. Mothers would hide their sons.

NAPOLEON: We shall see! Give me my map and pick a town. Well? London? Paris? Rome . . . No. (*Over the map.*) Some small place . . . What about this? . . . Dunkelstein.

ST. FRANCIS: Dunkelstein?

NAPOLEON: See? It's a little country between France and Spain. You know the sort of place. No income tax, everyone happy, all the European capitalists lock up their money in the Dunkelstein banks. Every other building is a bank. Now, this town, you will agree, must certainly fear war more than anything.

ST. FRANCIS: I'm afraid it must.

NAPOLEON: My dear Francis, you shouldn't speak like that when peace is in question.

ST. FRANCIS (*to* ANGEL): My dear, what is happening in Dunkelstein?

ANGEL: The world lies below you. See? Some sort of demonstration. Listen. A peace celebration.

ST. FRANCIS (*triumphant*): Amen. Very well. I'll take your bet.

NAPOLEON: I'll send that telegram at once!

ST. FRANCIS: But the radio will contradict the lie. The people will laugh at the idea.

NAPOLEON: Who should we get on to?

ANGEL: There's a very nice man in Dunkelstein, Your Majesty. Mr. Laban. Very rich. Practically runs the place.

NAPOLEON: I shall send my telegram to Mr. Laban. Go ahead. And after it's sent, all transmissions to Dunkelstein must be jammed. Let the Central Trouble Station see to it. (*Striking his celebrated pose.*) See to it.

ANGEL: Like this, Your Majesty? (*The* ANGEL *makes a crackling noise like shellfire with her switchboard.*)

NAPOLEON: Excellent. Even I can hear that. It sounds like gunfire.

BLACKOUT

SCENE 2

City Hall in Dunkelstein.

Large hall. On the wall at the rear there is a poster with the inscription: "No More War!" At the front there is the speaker's table. At the rear a buffet laden with delicacies at which SAMUEL *is busy. Enter* NOAH.

NOAH: Where's the fire?

(SAMUEL *goes on working.*)

Hey, Samuel!

SAMUEL: There isn't any fire.

NOAH: Then what are the bells ringing for?

SAMUEL: That's not the fire alarm. Those bells are ringing for peace. . . . You clear out. I am busy.

NOAH: What's all this about peace?

SAMUEL: Don't you read the papers? Don't you know today is Peace Day? In every town in Europe war is being buried with music.

NOAH: And champagne, I see! And you're the undertaker, I suppose?

SAMUEL (*fetching tray*): Don't be funny!

NOAH: Well, mind you don't nail the coffin down before the body is dead!

SAMUEL: Oh, go away! What do you want here, anyway?

NOAH: What do you think old Noah wants? A bit of peace!

SAMUEL: You talk as though peace were something to fill your belly with.

NOAH: That's more than you can say for war! . . .

SAMUEL: Always thinking of your belly—that's you! Have you got a ticket?

NOAH: Ticket? What do I want with a ticket?

SAMUEL: Then you can't hang about in here.

NOAH: Why not?

SAMUEL: Master's orders. Out you go!

NOAH: Oh, it is, is it? Well here I am and here I stay. Old Laban can't bully me! (*He sits down at the table.*)

SAMUEL: Mr. Laban to you! Here, you get off the clean chair! You're dirtier than ever!

NOAH: Right as usual, Samuel. You have to look a bit dirty when you're begging. The customers expect it. Of course if old Laban looked like this he'd scare his customers off for good. Mr. Laban has to dress up a bit. His customers expect it.

SAMUEL: I don't want any lip from you! Get out!

NOAH: Keep your hair on, Samuel! Don't take any notice of old Noah.

SAMUEL: You don't deserve what the gentlemen have been doing for you—working away to bring peace for us all. You just go on making trouble. That's you—always making trouble! When it's war you want peace; when it's peace you want war. And why? Simply because you don't know what you do want!

NOAH: Right as usual, Samuel. But your governor, he always knows what he wants.

SAMUEL: You don't deserve what Mr. Laban's done for you. Working himself ill for you and your like and how he can help you to an honest living. He can't sleep at night for worrying about you. I'd be ashamed of myself!

NOAH: If it would help him to sleep any better you can tell your governor from me that he needn't think anymore about old

Noah. I've got my pride too. So put that in your pipe and smoke it! I'm just not working anymore.

SAMUEL: Ungrateful brute, turning your back on an honest living out of sheer idleness!

NOAH: I'm getting old, I am. I've had to work thirty years and that's long enough for any man. From now on I beg!

SAMUEL: And go about like a dirty guttersnipe.

NOAH: All part of the profession, as I said! Old Laban's in just the same boat. *He* knows!

SAMUEL: If you don't clear out I'll knock your block off, standing there insulting your betters!

NOAH: That's it, Samuel. That's what they pay you for! I like to see a man doing his job properly. Go on. I'll be back for my free beer!

SAMUEL: Scum! That's what you are—scum!

(*Enter the Peace Procession.*)

LABAN: Ladies and gentlemen, I have the honor to introduce to you our distinguished guest, the delegate from the League of Nations, Mr. Lot. He will say a few words to you about the League of Nations.

(*Handclapping.* MR. LOT *bows.*)

LOT: Mr. Chairman, ladies and gentlemen. (*Declaiming.*)

> In the trees man's life began
> Naked through the woods he ran
> Made the lion and tiger yield
> Brandished weapons in the field
> Brandished them above his head
> Struck his human neighbor dead
> Bestial he remained the same
> And the morning never came.
>
> Two thousand Christian years have passed
> Man's a pacifist at last
> Nations, classes, rich and poor
> Look with eyes of hate no more
> White and yellow, black and brown
> To the feast of love sit down
> And the smiling earth may sing
> "War is a forgotten thing."

LABAN: Thank you. My friends and citizens. These are no empty phrases. To lend point to this expression of the brotherhood

of nations, I am this very day giving my daughter in marriage
to a young and very gallant gentleman from Brazil, ladies and
gentlemen, Mr. Jacob. (*To* JACOB.) Say a few words, Jacob,
it's expected of you. (*Enthusiasm.*)

JACOB (*into the microphone*): Mr. President. You must excuse me,
I am afraid I am no speaker.

(*Cries of "No, no."*)

I am a stranger in your beautiful country. I come from distant
Brazil. I am a son of the pampas. I saw the daughter of your
honored fellow citizen and bank manager, Mr. Laban. I fell
in love with her. And now we are to be married and live
happily ever after. All I can say, ladies and gentlemen, is (*Into
microphone.*) long live love! Long live peace!

EVERYBODY: Hurrah!

(*The children's choir, under the direction of* DAVID, *sing the
"Peace Song."*)

PEACE SONG

We are the new battalions,
Humanity's police;
And love is our commander,
And his word is Peace.
With heart and soul
Till we reach our goal,
O'er earth and air and sea.
We will sing this song
As we march along,
Marching on to victory.

Before our friendly handshake
All anger melts away,
United we go forward
Till victory crowns the day.
With heart and soul
Till we reach our goal,
O'er earth and air and sea,
We will sing this song
As we march along,
Marching on to victory.

LABAN: Now, let us outlaw war with all the people of Europe our
witness. Today marks the beginning of a new epoch in the
history of the world. It is the people's day, the day of the

people. The day of peace. Whatever reminds us of war must be sacrificed to peace. Sacrifice! cried the priests of old. And sacrifice, I cry today!

FAT MAN: I sacrifice my service uniform. (*Throws his coat on the table.*)

NOAH (*aside to* SAMUEL): How did he manage to keep his uniform clean like that in the trenches?

SAMUEL: He used to be the War Minister.

NOAH: Oh, that explains a lot.

LITTLE MAN: I sacrifice my war medals.

THIN MAN: I sacrifice my gas mask.

DAVID: I sacrifice my war books praising and glorifying war. They have darkened our thoughts and corrupted our hearts. They were cheap books; they were expensive books!

CAIN: I sacrifice my sword.

LOT: I sacrifice my War Loan.

NOAH (*aside to* SAMUEL): I am almost beginning to believe.

SAMUEL: Believe what?

NOAH: That war is a bad business.

LABAN (*seeing* NOAH): Well, Noah, and what are you going to sacrifice?

SAMUEL: He won't sacrifice anything, Mr. Laban.

LABAN: What?

NOAH: What can I sacrifice, Mr. Laban? When I was in the war I got a bullet in my lung, the doctor stole the bullet to give to his little boy for a souvenir, and before I knew where I was he'd pinched one of my lungs as well.

LABAN: Throw the man out!

(SAMUEL *throws* NOAH *out.*)

A vulgar fellow.

DAVID: And now, it is your turn, children. Come on. You know what to do.

FIRST CHILD: I sacrifice my lead soldiers.

SECOND CHILD: I sacrifice my water pistol.

BOTH CHILDREN: No more war!

ALL: No more war!

LABAN: Then let us swear it!

ALL: We swear!

DAVID: Now run away, children.

FIRST CHILD: I want my soldiers!

SECOND CHILD: I want my water pistol!

DAVID: You will be punished for this!

LABAN: Take them away, Samuel.

(SAMUEL *shoos the children out the exit.*)

Ladies and gentlemen, my friends, let us celebrate. The municipality will pay for the drinks. Will you join me at the buffet?

(DAVID *and* SAMUEL *move table and bench. Dance music. Dancing groups. Some move away from the table upstage toward the buffet.* NOAH *runs on.*)

NOAH: Come on, come on, where's the free drink?
LABAN: Really, this is very embarrassing. Samuel, throw him out. Properly, this time.

(NOAH *is thrown out.*)

RACHEL (*dancing. To* JACOB): Were you very nervous, darling? I thought you spoke beautifully. Much better than the others.
JACOB (*dancing*): I was telling them about you.
FAT MAN (*in another group*): My dear Laban, your speech was wonderful, electric.
LITTLE MAN: The League of Nations delegate was feeble compared with you. What oratory!
FAT MAN: You spoke from the bottom of your heart.
LITTLE MAN: Oratory has nothing to do with brains; it's a matter of *feeling!*
LABAN: You're too kind.
FAT MAN: Indeed no. All the women were in tears.
THIN MAN: You can regard it as a personal triumph.
LITTLE MAN: But, Mr. Laban, I would like to ask you one question. Why did you make a vow? One should never make vows about anything!
LABAN: Peace without a vow? Peace is a serious matter.
LITTLE MAN: That depends on the kind of peace. Everything is relative. Even peace.
FAT MAN: Mr. Laban was certainly not thinking of peace at any price!
LABAN: When may peace be said to cost too much?
THIN MAN: That's a riddle.
FAT MAN: I love riddles.
LABAN: The answer is, when war is cheaper.
     (*Laughter.*)
RACHEL (*in another group*): And will you always speak and think of me?
JACOB: I love you.
RACHEL: Will you go on loving me even when we're married?

JACOB: Nonsense. I'll love you for always.

RACHEL: I feel tonight that if ever you stopped loving me I should die.

(JACOB, *laughing, takes her to the buffet.*)

LABAN (*in the other group*): Speaking as a businessman, peace too has its profits, no less than war.

LITTLE MAN: Sometimes.

LABAN: I am not only talking about international peace.

FAT MAN (*laughing*): We can leave peace of mind to the priests and poets. We're businessmen.

LABAN: No, no, I meant social peace.

LITTLE MAN: Oh, we can keep that all right.

FAT MAN: Yes, but will the workers keep it?

CAIN (*joining them*): Well, gentlemen, I'm against the whole business. I used to be a soldier.

LABAN: If anybody loves peace, Mr. Cain, you ought to.

CAIN: Why? Just because I run a barber's shop? Because my customers are men?

LABAN: Isn't that a good enough reason?

CAIN: Not good enough for me!

LABAN: Ah, you're an idealist, Mr. Cain.

DAVID (*joining them*): What a wonderful day this is! Joy through peace and peace through joy. How did you like my peace song, Mr. Laban? The one the children sang?

LABAN: Very nice. A worthy example of your great talents.

DAVID: Well, you know, what I say is that it isn't everyone who could have written that song, Mr. Laban. Talent isn't enough, you know. Character is what you need. Character. You know, I think I might describe myself as a militant pacifist, don't you?

(A *great commotion at the door.* NOAH *bursts in.*)

SAMUEL: For Gawd's sake clear out of here!

NOAH: I want my free beer!

LABAN: Put the police on him!

SAMUEL: I'll call the police.

NOAH: Free beer!

SAMUEL: You can't come in here dressed like that.

NOAH: There's free beer for everyone.

SAMUEL: For decent people who work for their living and pay their taxes. But not for the likes of you. So out you go. (*Throws him out.*)

CAIN (*dancing to one side with* RACHEL): Rachel, I must speak to you.

RACHEL: Well, why don't you?

CAIN: But I must speak to you alone. Come into the garden.

RACHEL: It's too cold in the garden.

CAIN: I shouldn't have thought . . .

RACHEL: That it's cold? But it is.

CAIN: No, that you would be getting married.

RACHEL: It happens sometimes to girls of my age.

CAIN: I mean that you would marry a foreigner. It has made me very unhappy.

RACHEL: I'm sorry.

CAIN: I'm lonely, and I'm in love.

RACHEL: How nice for you!

CAIN: It would be, but . . . Oh, I could be the happiest man alive . . . But—a Dunkelstein girl married to a foreigner . . . !

RACHEL: How can you talk like that, the day before my wedding?

CAIN: I've loved you for seven years.

RACHEL: And for seven years you've known that I don't love you.

CAIN: What's the matter with me? Oh, I know, I'm only an ordinary hairdresser.

RACHEL: Cain, you know it isn't that. I just couldn't marry you, that's all.

CAIN: Rachel, please.

RACHEL: I'm sorry, Cain, but there's nothing more I can say. So please leave me.

(CAIN *goes. Enter* SAMUEL *waving a telegram, pushing forward through the dancing crowd.*)

SAMUEL: Mr. Laban! Mr. Laban!

LABAN (*hurrying forward*): What is it?

SAMUEL: A telegram, sir.

LABAN (*reading it*): My God!

FAT MAN: What's up?

LABAN: But this is incredible!

LITTLE MAN: Somebody died?

LABAN: Worse than that.

FAT MAN: A slump on the Stock Exchange?

LABAN (*holding up his hand*): Gentlemen! War has been declared!

ALL: War?

LABAN: In the midst of peace!

THIN MAN: What did I tell you.

FAT MAN: You shouldn't have been in such a hurry to make a peace vow.

LITTLE MAN: Just what I always said. War always breaks out in the midst of peace.

FAT MAN: Well, you know, I never trusted this peace. There has been too much about it.

LABAN: But who would have dreamt of it? Nothing's been happening lately.

LITTLE MAN: That's it, you see. When nothing's happening, something goes and happens.

LABAN: Well, we look a nice lot of fools in the middle of a peace celebration.

LITTLE MAN: On the contrary! We have solemnly recorded our peaceful intention. Now for the first time I appreciate the significance of Peace Day.

FAT MAN (*to* LABAN): Who has declared war?

LABAN: It doesn't say.

THIN MAN: Perhaps Spain wants our oil fields.

FAT MAN: More likely we want Spain's ore mines.

LITTLE MAN: Or perhaps nobody wants anything. Perhaps we all have too much already.

FAT MAN: Well, of course, the market's glutted with grain and coal.

LABAN: I suppose I must make this terrible thing known. What will the people say?

LITTLE MAN: You'll find that the first bang is much louder than the voice of the people.

LABAN (*calling*): Samuel.

(SAMUEL *enters.*)

Stop the music.

SAMUEL: Yes, sir. (*He goes off. The music stops. Dancing ceases.*)

FAT MAN: I have important business connections with Singapore. I feel I must leave for Singapore at once.

LITTLE MAN: I must fly immediately to Persia. I am a personal friend of the Shah's, you know.

LABAN: One must do the right thing at the right time.

(*Quartet,* LABAN *and Three Financiers.*)

FINANCIER'S SONG

When it's time for saving, hold; but do not spare your neighbor's gold.

When it's time for hunting, yield to impulse in your neighbor's field.
When it's time for war, rejoice; but say it was your neighbor's choice.
When peace comes, though it's a farce, bear it with patience
   —it will pass.

Chorus:
For snow falls in December,
And roses bloom in May;
And vows will break, remember,
And love is for a day.
"The proper thing at the proper season"
Is the golden rule of reason;
So be clever, then, and never
Give yourself away.

When it's time to watch, then see that other men the watch
   ers be.
When it's time to sleep, then let the rest their interests forget.
When it's time to haste, let yours be sharp and cold without
   remorse.
But when it's time to love, take care and let no feeling
   interfere.

Final Chorus:
Yes, Love was meant for pleasure
And Business meant for gain;
And who will share his treasure
To cure another's pain?
And the dying—leave them lying!—
Will not rise again.

(*After the song the other guests hurry on.*)

LABAN: Ladies and gentlemen, stand firm. The inconceivable has
   happened. War has been declared.
NOAH (*loudly*): No more war!
LOT: That's a catchword for peacetime. As the representative of
   the League of Nations I must leave at once for Geneva. The
   citizens of this city will do their duty. I shall do mine. The
   League of Nations will see to it that this war is the last
   of all wars. Long live the war to end war.

(*March of the men.*)

The Last War

LABAN:

We thought that wars were over, but there's got to be one
more;
Our civilizing mission is to put an end to war.

NOAH:

You'll really stop us, won't you, if you've heard this one
before?

Chorus:
So pack your kit and kiss your girl
And answer Humanity's call.
This is the war to end war—

LABAN:

The last war really!

NOAH:

Or very nearly,

Chorus:
The very last war of all . . .

LABAN:

There'll be peace the whole world over when our peaceful
duty's done
All bloodshed be abolished when our battle has been won.

NOAH:

'Cos there won't be any bleeders left to fire a bleedin' gun.

Chorus:
So pack your kit and kiss your girl
And answer Humanity's call.
This is the war to end war—

LABAN:

This is the last war really!

NOAH:

Or very nearly,

Chorus:
The very last war of all . . .

(*Loud cheering.* LOT *shakes hands with* LABAN. *Exits.*)

LABAN: Ladies and gentlemen, in times of stress Dunkelstein needs
unity of command. The leadership will be undertaken by the
senior officer.

NOAH: Mr. Cain was a sergeant, sir.

LABAN: Thank you. Mr. Cain, I call upon you to assume the dictatorship in Dunkelstein. (*Into the microphone.*) Sergeant Cain is in supreme command. Sergeant Cain is our leader.

(*Loud cheering.*)

RACHEL (*drawing* JACOB *aside*): Our wedding . . . Oh, Jacob!

JACOB: Brazil will keep out of it.

FAT MAN (*drawing* LABAN *aside*): Do you think they will confiscate our money? It's in the Anglobank in China.

DAVID (*hurrying up*): My peace song! My beautiful peace song!

LITTLE MAN: We must all adapt our business to the new conditions. I have been making ploughs. Now I shall make shells.

DAVID: What can I do? I am a poet writing a hymn to peace.

(LABAN *goes to join* CAIN.)

FAT MAN (*to* DAVID): What does it matter? All you have to do is to write war instead of peace wherever it occurs in the verse.

DAVID: That's true enough. But what about the rhythm?

FAT MAN: Well, you can turn it into a march.

DAVID (*brightening*): A march, but of course, how stupid of me. I'll do it at once.

CAIN (*coming forward to the microphone*): Ladies and gentlemen. (*Cheers.*) In these difficult times the leadership has fallen onto my shoulders. We have served peace. But the enemy wants war, and the enemy shall have it.

(*Loud cheers.*)

NOAH: Who is the enemy?

(CAIN *turns to* LABAN. LABAN *shakes his head and points to the telegram.*)

CAIN (*into the microphone*): The enemy is . . . the hereditary enemy of our land.

DAVID: My war song!

(*The band strikes up.* DAVID *leads on the singing children.*)

WAR SONG

We are the new battalions,
    Let nations stand in awe;
For pride is our commander,
    And his word is War.

> With heart and soul
> Till we reach our goal,
> O'er earth and air and sea,
> We will sing this song
> As we march along,
> Marching on to victory.

> Before our iron greeting
> All boasting melts away,
> United we go forward
> Till victory crowns the day.

> With heart and soul
> Till we reach our goal,
> O'er earth and air and sea,
> We will sing this song
> As we march along,
> Marching on to victory.

CAIN: And now, children, you can play with your soldiers again.

(*The children grab the box of soldiers and the water pistol.*)

And the gentlemen who in ignorance of the actual situation sacrificed their treasured souvenirs of war may take them back. . . . To the glory, honor, and victory of Dunkelstein.

(*They crowd around the table.* SAMUEL *distributes swords, etc.*)

And now the medical examination. Fall into line. Doctor, please.

(*Soft musical accompaniment.*)

NOAH (*to* LABAN): Have some strong coffee to make your heart race.
LABAN: Samuel, four black coffees, please.
NOAH: Make it five.

(*Enter* DOCTOR.)

FAT MAN (*before* DOCTOR): I've only got one leg.
DOCTOR: Observer in bombing plane. A-1.
LITTLE MAN (*to* DOCTOR): I'm blind.
DOCTOR (*to* LITTLE MAN): Listening post for enemy air raids. A-1,
(*Declaims.*)

> Halt and maimed and deaf and dumb,
> Listen to the marching drum.

Cough or cold is no excuse,
Narrow chest or feeble mind;
What's the harm in being blind?
Only dead men are no use.
Granddad, father, mother's son,
I will pass you all A-1.

Liar, thief, and murderer, come,
Listen to the marching drum.
Victory in battle wins
Public good from private vice;
Only thought and cowardice
Are the soldier's deadly sins.
Granddad, father, mother's son,
I will pass you all A-1.

FAT MAN: What will become of your jam factory?

LABAN: It will flourish. Jam is a necessity of war. Samuel, send a telegram to the manager! He is to buy up immediately all the stocks of fruit and vegetables in the country!

SAMUEL: Very good, sir.

RACHEL (*enters*): Oh, but what about my wedding?

CAIN: All marriage with foreigners is prohibited!

RACHEL: You forbid my marriage?

CAIN: I? What have I got to do with it?

RACHEL: But that's what you said.

CAIN: I am not myself anymore. Nobody is himself anymore. It is possible that war will be declared against Mr. Jacob's countrymen. In that event this marriage, if it took place, would be high treason.

RACHEL: I will marry whom I choose.

CAIN: In peacetime yes. This is wartime.

RACHEL: I don't give a damn for your war!

CAIN: Mr. Laban, you are her father . . .

LABAN: You must be reasonable, child.

RACHEL: Is it so unreasonable to obey my heart?

LABAN: Even in peacetime it is bad business to follow one's heart. In wartime it's sheer bankruptcy.

RACHEL: And yet, hardly an hour ago, you, you yourself, were eulogizing peace.

LABAN: Not so loud, child.

CAIN: Have some consideration for your father.

RACHEL: Has he any consideration for me? Why should something be wrong now that was right a moment ago? Why should a thing be called faithfulness in one breath and treason in the next?

LABAN: Do you want to ruin us all?

RACHEL: I want my happiness.

LABAN: Oh, if only you were a boy!

RACHEL: Would you have preferred a son?

LABAN: Since you ask me, yes!

RACHEL: And you would let him go to war?

LABAN: I should mourn but I should be proud.

RACHEL: Proud? Why proud?

LABAN: Of being his father.

RACHEL (*calls*): Jacob. We must go away at once. To Australia.

JACOB: To Australia?

RACHEL: Where there is peace. Where we can live in peace together.

JACOB: Be sensible, Rachel.

RACHEL: I won't be sensible. What has this war to do with us?

JACOB: But I am liable for military service. What if Brazil and Dunkelstein go to war?

RACHEL: Dunkelstein! Brazil! Here am I, Rachel. There are you, Jacob. I love you. You love me. What has our love got to do with Dunkelstein? What has our love got to do with Brazil?

JACOB: I have to report to my legation. (*Looks uneasy.*)

RACHEL: I hate you! All of you! All of you! (*To* JACOB.) You too!

(*She goes out.*)

(*The others, except* CAIN, *follow.*)

CAIN (*calling*): Samuel, bring that table.

(SAMUEL *enters.*)

Where is Lance Corporal Noah?

SAMUEL: Outside, sir. He refuses to wear his gas mask.

CAIN: Bring him in.

(NOAH *enters.*)

(*To* NOAH.) You will be my personal servant! You were a lance corporal in the last war?

NOAH: It was a misunderstanding, sir.

CAIN: You will enlist at once!

NOAH: Oh, no I won't, sir.

CAIN: You won't?

NOAH: That's right, sir, I won't.

CAIN: And why not, may I ask?

NOAH: Because I'm scared, sir.

CAIN: Because you're what?

NOAH: Scared, sir, got the wind up.

CAIN: Are you crazy?

NOAH: I can't stand all this shooting, sir. I'm scared of it.

CAIN: Who has been getting at you? The Liberals? The Communists? All Liberals and Communists to be arrested!

NOAH: No, I'm just scared. Always was a nervous sort of bloke.

CAIN: I'll have you put in the cells!

NOAH: Until the end of the war, sir?

CAIN: On bread and water.

NOAH: Ah, now you're trying to bribe me!

CAIN: Get out!

NOAH: But you promised to lock me up, sir.

CAIN: Get out!

(SAMUEL *throws* NOAH *out*.)

NOAH: I'll take it to the courts, I will! I'll sue you for breach of promise! I *will* get locked up!

CAIN (*calling*): David!

DAVID (*entering*): Yes, Mr. Cain?

CAIN: Have you served before?

DAVID: I'm sorry, Mr. Cain.

CAIN: Because you have?

DAVID: Because I haven't, Mr. Cain.

CAIN: Stop saying Mr. Cain. Sir, to me, if you please!

DAVID: Very good, sir.

CAIN: Can you write?

DAVID: But, Mr. Ca . . . sir! You know perfectly well I can!

CAIN: I don't know anything.

DAVID: You really shouldn't drink so much, sir.

CAIN: What?

DAVID: On the first day of war, too!

CAIN: What the devil are you talking about? Who is drunk?

DAVID: Not me, sir.

CAIN: You mean me?

DAVID: Would you ask such a question if you were sober?

CAIN: I'm asking you a military question.

DAVID: Is this a game?

CAIN: Stop this civilian backchat. Answer as a soldier.

DAVID: Private David begs to report that he can write, sir.

CAIN: What have you done? What are you?

DAVID: I'm a schoolmaster.

CAIN: That's nothing.

DAVID: I am the head of a family. I am an honest citizen. I pay my taxes.

CAIN: That's nothing.

DAVID: It counted for a good deal yesterday.

CAIN: Yesterday! You'll find that different things count today. You'll do well to remember that! You've never served as a noncommissioned officer?

DAVID: No, sir.

CAIN: A pity. You are appointed Minister for Propaganda and Enlightenment, and Chief of Counterespionage, do you hear?

DAVID: Thank you.

CAIN: Don't say thank you. Give the true Dunkelstein salute. Like this. (*Raises his arm.*) Hail!

DAVID: I thought that was Roman.

CAIN: It's genuine Dunkelstein.

DAVID: Hail!

CAIN: That's too short. Say, "Hail, Cain!" Good!

(*Bell. Enter* SARAH *with dog.*)

DAVID: It's that Scots woman, it's Rachel Laban's nurse.

CAIN: Keep her out.

SARAH: Dear Mr. Cain. Dear Mr. Cain. I come home. I undress in the dark as you ordered. I tell my Napoleon to lie down. "Lie down, Napoleon" I say, but Napoleon refuses to obey. Napoleon growls; I tie him to the bed. He always sleeps in my bed. . .

CAIN: Napoleon?

SARAH: Napoleon.

CAIN: Who in the world is Napoleon?

SARAH: You don't know Napoleon?

CAIN: I didn't know that your lover's name is Napoleon and much less that you are so violent.

SARAH: How dare you!

CAIN: How old is Napoleon? Is he of military age? Why does he sleep? Why doesn't he protect our country like other young men?

SARAH: Napoleon is no man.

CAIN: Is he a woman?

SARAH: Napoleon is my poodle.

CAIN: Oh, a dog?

SARAH: Napoleon simply wouldn't keep quiet. He went on howling fit to touch a heart of stone and then I ran to the window to call for help. Who do you think I saw?

CAIN: Who?

SARAH: A strange man! A spy!

CAIN: Had you heard any unusual noises up to then?

SARAH: I don't understand.

CAIN: Noises in the air? An airplane?

SARAH: Now you mention it, I had.

CAIN: Good, thank you.

(SARAH *exits with dog.*)

(*To* DAVID.) This spy must be captured. Immediately. Dead or alive.

DAVID: Very good, sir. (*Exit.*)

(SAMUEL *brings in* RACHEL.)

CAIN: Rachel!

(RACHEL *is silent.*)

(*To* SAMUEL.) What is the charge against the prisoner?

SAMUEL: She ran through the streets distributing copies of the New Testament and shouting, "No more war."

CAIN (*to* RACHEL): That is high treason. Do you realize that?

(RACHEL *is silent.*)

(*To* SAMUEL.) Loosen those chains.

(SAMUEL *takes off* RACHEL's *chains.* CAIN *gives a sign and he goes.*

What have you been doing?

RACHEL: I was only shouting what it says on that placard.

CAIN: On the placard? (*Calls.*) Samuel. Take that placard away.

SAMUEL: It only needs turning around, sir. (SAMUEL *goes to placard, turns it around so that the phrase displayed is "Long Live War."*)

RACHEL: God's commandments are not double-tongued.

CAIN: What am I to do with you?

RACHEL: Have me shot, if you've got the courage.

CAIN: Rachel! Stop being foolish.

RACHEL: But I don't suppose you have the courage.

CAIN: You're a child.

RACHEL: As a child I learned a commandment: "Thou shalt not kill."

CAIN: Rachel, let's forget that you said you could not love me. I'm not poor. Rachel, I love you. I oughtn't to love you after all that has happened. But I do. We can say that you had a nerve storm. Rachel, marry me.

RACHEL: A groveling dictator! What a sight! Let go, or I shall scream!

CAIN: You insist on your unhappiness?

RACHEL: Your happiness is other people's misery.

CAIN: Samuel.

(SAMUEL *leads* RACHEL *out at a sign from* CAIN. DAVID *enters.*)

DAVID: I have to report that fifty-seven spies have been arrested, sir.

CAIN: Good. The foreigners?

DAVID: All arrested.

CAIN: Good. Jacob?

DAVID: Arrested.

CAIN: Good.

DAVID: One spy has taken refuge in the cornfields outside the town.

CAIN: Have the fields been searched?

DAVID: I have given orders for them all to be burned. They will be sprayed with gasoline and set on fire.

CAIN: The fire brigade must see that nobody tries to extinguish the flames!

(*Exit* DAVID.)

Dictator's Song

CAIN:

Are you living in the city all your dreary little life,
In a dreary little office, with a dreary little wife?
I will give you flags and banners and processions and a band;
You shall march in step together, you shall feel just grand.

For I am the simple answer
To the man's and maiden's prayer,
I am the spring in the desert,
I am the song in the air,
The clue to history,
I am the Mystery,
I am the Miracle Man.

Are you feeling sick and frightened, though you cannot tell
of what?
Does something hurt you somewhere but you cannot find the
spot?

Are you feeling full of hatred, of resentment and of shame?
I will show you who to punish, I will show you who's to
blame.

> For I am the simple answer
> To the man's and maiden's prayer,
> I am the spring in the desert,
> I am the song in the air,
> The clue to history,
> I am the Mystery,
> I am the Miracle Man.

Or has reading made your head ache, and does thinking give
you pain?
If you'll trust me and obey me, you need never think again.
Is it hard to make decisions, to distinguish right from wrong?
Let me make your choices for you: you'll be free the whole day
long.

> For I am the simple answer
> To the man's and maiden's prayer,
> I am the spring in the desert,
> I am the song in the air,
> The clue to history,
> I am the Mystery,
> I am the Miracle Man.

Is there no one really loves you, are you feeling all alone,
Have you no one you can care for, or can look on as your
own?
Then I will be your father, your lover, child, and friend.
Yes, I will be your favorite, you may love me to the end.

> For I am the simple answer
> To the man's and maiden's prayer,
> I am the spring in the desert,
> I am the song in the air,
> The clue to history,
> I am the Mystery,
> I am the Miracle Man.

I will give you friends to die for, I will give you foes to kill,
I will give you back your honor and your unity of will,
The old heroic virtues and the large triumphal hour,
I will give you back the kingdom and the glory and the
power.

For I am the simple answer
To the man's and maiden's prayer,
I am the spring in the desert,
I am the song in the air,
The clue to history,
I am the Mystery,
I am the Miracle Man.

BLACKOUT

ACT II

SCENE 1

Olympus.

NAPOLEON: Child . . . what's your name? . . . I always forget your name.

ANGEL: Angels like us don't have names, Your Majesty.

NAPOLEON: No names? Don't you mind?

ANGEL: It's the will of God, Your Majesty.

NAPOLEON: And you are happy?

ANGEL: I'm blessed, Your Majesty.

NAPOLEON: Incomprehensible! What is glory without a name?

ANGEL: Glory belongs to God alone, and God is nameless.

NAPOLEON: My dear girl, when there is only one of you, it is easy enough to be nameless.

(*Heavy thunder.*)

ANGEL (*pointing aloft*): Your Majesty.

NAPOLEON: Don't you worry about me. As a boy of ten I used to dream of posterity remembering my name. The history of Europe would be pretty dull without ambition or lust for glory. The Bourbon would still be on the throne of France. The Battle of the Pyramids would never have been won. Jena would be a town chiefly notable as the birthplace of a German poet called Schiller.

ANGEL: And children would never have heard of Waterloo.

NAPOLEON (*indignantly*): You are English?

ANGEL: Nearly all the staff are English, Your Majesty.

NAPOLEON: Mon Dieu!—Non angeli sed angelici—ah?

(*More thunder.*)

I beg your pardon. Tell me, dear, when you were on earth, what did you do?

ANGEL: I've really forgotten. After all, the earth is only a stage on the way.

NAPOLEON: And you're absolutely happy? You desire nothing more?

ANGEL: Well . . . er . . .

NAPOLEON: Aha!

ANGEL: I'm blessed . . . but I am not happy . . . I have one desire.

NAPOLEON: For a name?

ANGEL: I arrived here in the year 1100. In those days, you know, everybody wore very large wings, like these. The new angels all arrive with small, modern wings. If only I too could have small, modern wings I should be absolutely happy. I should ask for nothing more. (*Telephone rings.*) Excuse me.

(*Enter* ST. FRANCIS.)

ST. FRANCIS: Ah, good evening.

NAPOLEON: Good evening, Francis.

ST. FRANCIS: How hot it is! How smoky!

NAPOLEON: The Dunkelsteiners are burning down their cornfields. In my time, it was the enemy who destroyed one's crops. Strategy has changed.

ST. FRANCIS: But this is terrible! To destroy God's bread!

NAPOLEON: That happens often enough in peacetime. Bread is cheap! It is not called God's bread anymore.

ST. FRANCIS: And yet thousands starve every year. (*Looks over edge.*) Do you know, I believe the fire brigade is stopping the people who are extinguishing the flames.

NAPOLEON (*looking too*): There you are. The war's in full swing. They're having a hell of a time.

ST. FRANCIS: Wait. The people will soon come to their senses.

NAPOLEON: Nonsense. You've lost your bet.

ST. FRANCIS: I have committed a more deadly sin. I have unleashed the dark forces of the human soul.

NAPOLEON: And look. The only real pacifist, a girl, is in prison. See?

ST. FRANCIS: Poor child.

NAPOLEON: A simpleminded pacifist. A pacifist for love.

ST. FRANCIS: What do you know of the power of love?

NAPOLEON: They'll shoot Rachel. They'll shoot this man Jacob. They'll shoot all the spies.

ST. FRANCIS: But they are innocent!

NAPOLEON: This is a war, my dear Francis. In war, there is no question of guilt. One shoots as a matter of expedience. Shootings stimulate the morale!

ST. FRANCIS: Then there's only one thing to do. We must contradict your bogus telegram.

NAPOLEON: It doesn't matter a damn that it was bogus. People believe things not because they're true, but because they want to believe them. Truth is a luxury, it is only a handful of discontented intellectuals who fight for truth.

ST. FRANCIS: The number doesn't matter. Whoever is in possession of the truth is invincible. The mind is greater than force.

NAPOLEON: But people *like* force.

ST. FRANCIS: No. People love freedom.

NAPOLEON: Not even the illusion of freedom. They like to feel a strong hand, and they like to leave their politics to their leaders.

ST. FRANCIS: My dear friend, you must not forget that this is an age of democracy.

NAPOLEON: Democracy—pah! The rule of the mediocre! People want heroes, and if they don't have any heroes, they invent them.

ST. FRANCIS: I've heard something of this. Today I believe they call it Fascism.

NAPOLEON: All the great men of history have acted on that theory.

ST. FRANCIS: Who dares say such men are great?

NAPOLEON: The world they live in, and posterity.

ST. FRANCIS: And what is the world they live in?

NAPOLEON: Public opinion.

ST. FRANCIS: Your own public opinion was a newspaper called the *Moniteur*, run by a policeman called Fouché. And what is posterity?

NAPOLEON: History books.

ST. FRANCIS: History books are merely the publicity agents of the conquerors! The defeated are silent. . . . Great men are mankind's misfortune, or so it seems to me.

NAPOLEON: And little men their fortune?

ST. FRANCIS: The poorest of the poor who sow and never reap, what will happen to them?

NAPOLEON: Well, in Dunkelstein, the munitions workers have dared to go on strike. One in every ten has been arrested. They will be court-martialed and shot.

ST. FRANCIS: But no just judge could possibly find them guilty.

NAPOLEON: Justice is a servant of the state. The judges are officials of the state.

ST. FRANCIS: Then something must be done. Immediately! We must send the wisest of all men down to earth. If the people are incapable of recognizing goodness for themselves, he must lead them to it. (*To* ANGEL.) Would you get me Socrates?

ANGEL (*at telephone*): One moment, please.

ST. FRANCIS: Socrates could do it.

NAPOLEON: I doubt it.

ANGEL (*at telephone*): Socrates is here.

(ST. FRANCIS *goes to telephone.*)

NAPOLEON (*to* ANGEL): In Paris, you know, the women have very smart wings. Even if they aren't angels.

ANGEL: You don't say so.

NAPOLEON: Indeed I do. Why, in the old days, I used to know an actress who wore wings of pleated Chinese silk, delicate gold thread embroidery in the middle. Ah . . .

ANGEL: Oh, Your Majesty . . .

ST. FRANCIS (*at telephone*): God be praised! Socrates is ready. The power of his word is greater than the sword. He is coming up on the next elevator.

NAPOLEON: Umph. As far as I can remember they poisoned the old man last time he was on earth.

ST. FRANCIS: They won't this time.

(SOCRATES *arrives, rather breathless.*)

Ah, how do you do, Socrates? So good of you to come.

SOCRATES: Not at all, but I wish the elevators didn't go so fast. I feel that I'm only half here.

ST. FRANCIS: You know Napoleon.

SOCRATES: Certainly, certainly. How do you do?

ST. FRANCIS: We asked you to come and get us out of a little trouble that we've got ourselves into. (*Taking him to the edge.*) You see this little place down here. Dunkelstein it's called . . .

SOCRATES: Dunkelstein, yes . . .

ST. FRANCIS: Well, you see, Napoleon, by way of a joke . . .

NAPOLEON: Nonsense. I did it quite deliberately.

ST. FRANCIS: Well, never mind, anyhow it's done. Napoleon sent a telegram, you see, to say there was a war, and so, you see, there is one.

SOCRATES: Ah, cause and effect.

NAPOLEON: And a very nice one, too.

SOCRATES: Yes, I see. They're shooting each other.

NAPOLEON: Freely and indiscriminately.

ST. FRANCIS: And our idea was that you should go down and reason with them.

NAPOLEON: Which won't do much good.

ST. FRANCIS: But might stop the bloodshed.

SOCRATES: I see. You feel that reason properly applied might stop bloodshed.

ST. FRANCIS: It's a possibility.

SOCRATES: Certainly. I flatter myself that I'm rather good at reasoning.

NAPOLEON: That's why we sent for you.

SOCRATES: It's so very long since I had a chance to try my skill. Everything is so very reasonable up here, don't you think . . . ?

NAPOLEON: Much too reasonable.

SOCRATES: Oh, no, that could never be. Still, I feel it would be an opportunity for me to show what I could do.

ST. FRANCIS: Then you'll go?

SOCRATES: Certainly.

ST. FRANCIS: Thank God, thank God. Take care of yourself.

SOCRATES: I shall be all right if the elevators . . . (*Exit* SOCRATES.)

NAPOLEON (*reading*): What an insult!

ST. FRANCIS: What was that?

NAPOLEON: An insult, I said. This story of a woman and her dog.

ST. FRANCIS: I love animal stories.

NAPOLEON: But this woman called her horrid little dog Napoleon.

ST. FRANCIS: How touching.

NAPOLEON: In my time it was usual to call the eldest son Napoleon.

ST. FRANCIS: What have you against dogs? Aren't they honest and affectionate animals? Deeply devoted to mankind? Why, I often used to wish they'd call the donkey, that gentle, modest creature with the most beautiful eyes in the world—I used to wish they'd call it Francis after me.

BLACKOUT

SCENE 2

Prison cell in Dunkelstein.

JACOB *is striding up and down the cell. Sirens are heard. Cries from outside. "Gas! Gas! Gas! Take cover! Take cover! Lights out! Lights out!" The light in the cell is extinguished, the door is unlocked.*

VOICE: In you go. There's another one to be shot in there! (RACHEL *enters.*)

JACOB: Who is that? (*Silence.*) Stop, or I . . .

RACHEL: Don't shoot, please.

JACOB: It's murder.

RACHEL: It is terrible to die in the dark.

JACOB: The executioner is sympathetic?

RACHEL: I am so young. It is terrible to die so young.

JACOB: Who are you?

RACHEL: I loved a man. The love of a man is a lie. We soar heavenward and fall back into Hell. I loved peace. I believed the men who talked of peace. Peace is the greatest lie of all.

(*The light goes on.*)

JACOB: Rachel!

RACHEL: Don't touch me.

JACOB: I am Jacob.

RACHEL: Jacob is a name for a man. Jacob is a lie.

JACOB: She is out of her mind.

RACHEL: Why didn't I believe in stones, in animals, in flowers? It is good to love flowers. They are what they seem; they seem to be what they are. In the morning when they awake and the silent dew falls on the velvet petals, in the evening when they sleep in glimmering twilight . . . Only man disturbs their peace.

JACOB: Rachel. Rachel, don't you know me?

RACHEL: Tell me that you are a stone and I will love you.

JACOB: Rachel! Rachel!

RACHEL: Oh, Jacob, why have you betrayed me?

JACOB: I have not betrayed you.

RACHEL: What is love that kills when it should warm the heart? You are a man. Put on your uniform and go to war. Shoot! Shoot my father down! Shoot me down! Yesterday it would have been murder; today it is your duty. Go and be a hero, but never again tell a girl that you love her.

JACOB: Oh, why have they sent you here to poison my last hours?

RACHEL: I am what you are, a prisoner.

JACOB: *You* been arrested?

RACHEL: Because I believed in their words. There ought to be a new law; whoever believes words shall be punished with death.

JACOB: They'll keep you here for a few hours and then let you go free.

RACHEL (*with a superior smile*): Yes, Jacob.

(*The door is unbolted, enter a* DOCTOR. *Behind him is* NOAH, *unrecognizable behind his turned-up coat collar.* NOAH *hides himself.*)

DOCTOR: Miss Rachel.

RACHEL: I am ready.

DOCTOR: You were very nervy as a child, weren't you?

RACHEL: Who are you?

DOCTOR: The doctor.

RACHEL: Do those about to die need doctors?

DOCTOR: I have come to examine you.

RACHEL: Does the law insist on that?

DOCTOR: It is a special privilege.

RACHEL: Granted by Mr. Cain?

DOCTOR: Because you are Mr. Laban's daughter.

RACHEL: Is treason no longer treason if one is Laban's daughter?

DOCTOR: Well, it makes a difference.

RACHEL: I understand. You have to certify me mad?

DOCTOR: There can be no pardon without law.

RACHEL: And no law without a lie! Are you to certify Mr. Jacob, too?

DOCTOR: There can be no doubt about Mr. Jacob's sanity.

RACHEL: Then tell Mr. Cain that there can be no doubt about mine either. Nobody knows that better than he.

JACOB: Doctor, she *is* out of her mind.

RACHEL: I am not out of my mind. Go away!

(*Exit* DOCTOR.)

JACOB (*embracing* RACHEL): Rachel!

RACHEL: Is it not better to die than to kill?

JACOB: I was a coward, a coward!

RACHEL: It was dark, and because it was dark you were afraid, and you thought I was the executioner. You were afraid, Jacob. I am glad you were afraid. You must not be afraid of your fear. Isn't it human to be afraid?

JACOB: I was afraid. I thought they were going to shoot me.

RACHEL: But now it is light and you have no fear.

JACOB: Oh, why didn't you save yourself just now? Why must we both die?

RACHEL: Somewhere there must be peace. If not, how could we dream of it? Death is not a lie, Jacob.

JACOB: Rachel!

(NOAH *approaches.*)

NOAH: It's all right. It's only me.

RACHEL: Have you been arrested, too?

NOAH: Not by them.

RACHEL: Who by, then?

NOAH: Well, I arrested myself as you might say. You see, Miss, I ought to be at the front but I didn't want to go. So I hid myself in the cornfields because it was safe there, you see, and warm. Then the fools burned the cornfields. Well, what could I do? What's the safest place in a war? Prison, of course. So I just locked myself up. I am only an old fool. . . . And you two are going to be shot, are you?

RACHEL: Yes, Noah.

NOAH: Ah, death comes early enough without you looking for it. Well, well. They won't keep you here long. They'll take you to the condemned cell. A bad name for a nice warm cell. And from the condemned cell the passage leads to . . . (*Continues in a whispering tone.*) Sshh! Someone's coming. (*Hides himself.* WARDER *enters.*)

WARDER: Jacob! Rachel! You are to be taken to another cell. Is there anything you would particularly like for your last dinner? I can get you roast chicken from the pub across the road. I know the landlady. It's very good, *and* cheap! Come on! (*Takes them out. For a few seconds the cell is empty.*)

NOAH (*sings*):

Noah's Song

"Since Man out of Monkey came,"
  Cried the Cow to the Man-in-the-Moon,
"Equality is not for him;
And since he is half divine,
Ever must his heart incline
To peacocks, jewels, women, wine;
  And who sups with the Devil must have a long spoon."

"Fortune by her fancies led,"
Cried the Cow to the Man-in-the-Moon,
"Brings strange gifts to the marriage bed;
Some get failure, some success,
He that hath, him she will bless,
And he that hath not shall have less;
  And who sups with the Devil must have a long spoon."

"One in rags and vermin must,"
  Cried the Cow to the Man-in-the-Moon,
"Come empty-fisted to the dust;

While another through the land
Rides with rings upon his hand;
For some must kneel and some may stand;
    And who sups with the Devil must have a long spoon."

"Singers are more loved than saints,"
  Cried the Cow to the Man-in-the-Moon,
"And the Good God dislikes complaints;
Who dare grumble if the Law
Spare the rich and take the poor
And two and two add up to four;
    And who sups with the Devil must have a long spoon."

(WARDER *comes back with* SOCRATES.)

WARDER: In you go, Socrates.

SOCRATES: Before you go, my friend, I want to ask you a question. All we know is that we know nothing. Right. Then how do we know that there's a war?

WARDER (*tapping his forehead*): Poor fellow. (WARDER *goes.*)

NOAH (*coming out*): Well, do you know the answer to that one?

SOCRATES: I know that I know nothing.

NOAH: Perhaps that there door knows better. When it opens for us it'll be peace, but while it's locked it's war.

SOCRATES: Very compelling logic, but it won't hold water. A locked door says to itself that it has been locked for one of two reasons (*a*) accidentally, or (*b*) intentionally. Excluding accident for the sake of argument, let us suppose that this door is locked intentionally. The intention behind it may be (*a*) good, or (*b*) bad. The warder who brought me here and locked the door is obeying an order. His intentions are good. The man who gave the order, however, thought that I was a spy. So his intentions were . . . ?

NOAH: Just as good as the other bloke's.

SOCRATES: Oh. So I have no grounds for complaint.

NOAH: All right, but in that case, you'll have to be grateful to the firing squad.

SOCRATES: Don't you think that's going too far?

NOAH: Why? They'll shoot you with the best intentions in the world.

SOCRATES: But, don't you see, they have no *right* to do anything of the kind.

NOAH: Why not? They are only obeying the judge who condemned you, also with the best intentions. You have really no grounds for complaint at all, old man.

SOCRATES: Hm . . . Well, tell me, what are you complaining about?

NOAH: Who says I'm grumbling?

SOCRATES: The majority of criminals regard themselves as innocent.

NOAH: Who says I'm a criminal?

SOCRATES: Well, there you are. You regard yourself as innocent, then?

NOAH: Look here, I'd like to ask you a riddle.

SOCRATES: By all means.

NOAH: When everyone's in clover, everyone has enough to eat.

SOCRATES: Certainly.

NOAH: Well, is everyone in clover in wartime?

SOCRATES: No. So far it has never been known to happen.

NOAH: Then is everyone in clover in peacetime?

SOCRATES: No.

NOAH: Then what is the difference between war and peace?

SOCRATES: Well, *everyone* can't be in clover either in war or in peace.

NOAH: Yet, in both wartime and peace, there's just as much clover growing.

SOCRATES: But your conclusion seems to me to be the contradiction of all reason.

NOAH: Why? What it proves is that some people are in clover in wartime and some in peace. But the some in war and the some in peace are always the same some!

SOCRATES: Well, who are the unlucky ones?

NOAH: All the rest of us. The ones who don't spend their time eating roast beef.

SOCRATES: How do they spend their time?

NOAH: They think.

SOCRATES: How nice! And what are their conclusions?

NOAH: They see that for them even in peace there is always war.

SOCRATES: Very materialistic.

NOAH: But very wise.

SOCRATES: May I ask your name, sir?

NOAH: Certainly. Mr. Noah. And what's yours?

SOCRATES: Mr. Socrates.

NOAH: What? Old Socrates? What are you doing here?

SOCRATES: Well, first they took me for a lunatic, then they decided I was a spy, condemned me to death and here I am.

NOAH: Well, you see where your reason gets you.

SOCRATES: Precisely where yours has got you. Still, I should like to be your pupil. Old Socrates still has something to learn.

DUET (SOCRATES *and* NOAH)

SOCRATES:
> By the Eternal Wisdom moved,
> The stars of heaven turn.

NOAH:
> The Wisdom of this world, my friend,
> Is what you have to learn.

SOCRATES:
> What great philosophers declared
> Now Tom and Dick believe,
> And straight and crooked are the same,
> For all is relative.

NOAH:
> Since bishops told the gaping crowd
> The poor will go above,
> Now Tom and Dick do not expect
> An earthly life of love.

SOCRATES:
> By the Eternal Wisdom moved,
> The stars of heaven turn.

NOAH:
> The Wisdom of this world, my friend,
> Is what we have to learn.

SOCRATES and NOAH:
> The Wisdom of this world, my friend,
> Is what we have to learn.

BLACKOUT

SCENE 3

Olympus. NAPOLEON *with telescope when* ST. FRANCIS *arrives.*

ST. FRANCIS: I've been looking for you all over heaven. Where have you been?

NAPOLEON: Playing darts with the Duke of Wellington. I won.

ST. FRANCIS: Well, the most dreadful things are happening on the earth. Everyone's quite crazy. First they put Socrates in prison. Now they have condemned Rachel and Jacob to death and the poor children are to die in an hour's time.

NAPOLEON: Nasty death, for treason.

ST. FRANCIS: In this case the hero's death, my friend. Still we must do something to stop it. *We* are guilty, we alone. Ah, God, what have I done? Playing with good is bad enough, but I played with evil . . .

NAPOLEON: What are you going to do?

ST. FRANCIS: I don't know. I asked the Almighty's private secretary to arrange an audience for me.

NAPOLEON: Well . . . ?

ST. FRANCIS: He sent word to say that against the stupidity of mankind even the old gods fought in vain. They were numerous. What could be expected of Him?

NAPOLEON: War itself is the only thing to end war. In a mess like this we should call in the ex-soldiers. We have some brilliant strategists here—Alexander, Caesar, Genghis Khan. I suppose that I should take the supreme command.

ST. FRANCIS: I'll have no new war, if you please! All that is needed is the truth. Contradict that telegram of yours at once.

NAPOLEON: I can't do that.

ST. FRANCIS: Why not?

NAPOLEON: It would be the first time in history for an official telegram to be contradicted.

ST. FRANCIS: An official lie, you mean.

NAPOLEON: What're the odds? All that is needed to turn a lie into the truth is to give it official support.

ST. FRANCIS: Napoleon, if you have any friendship for me, telegraph to Dunkelstein the simple, naked, human truth.

NAPOLEON: I warn you . . .

(*Enter* SOCRATES.)

Here comes Socrates.

ST. FRANCIS: My dear Socrates, I am very upset.

SOCRATES: My dear Francis, I am so sorry I could not help you. I was out of practice and not up to the job.

NAPOLEON: In wartime the voice of Reason is the voice of High Treason. I myself, my dear Socrates, would have stood you up against a wall at once. . . . Tell me, why did you vanish from the prison?

SOCRATES: Because I was afraid of having to drink a second cup of hemlock.

NAPOLEON: But when you were condemned to death in Greece so long ago, you were, if you will forgive my saying so, somewhat braver.

SOCRATES: My dear Napoleon, I was not.

NAPOLEON: But for two thousand years the children have been

taught to regard you as one of the finest examples of bravery in the face of death.

SOCRATES: All a myth. Only unimaginative people have no fear. Right up till the last moment I hoped that the Athenians would reprieve me. I played a part. I pretended that I was brave and that I despised death, but only so long as my friends were there. When I was left alone in my cell I fell on my knees and implored the gods to have mercy.

NAPOLEON: That's very interesting.

ST. FRANCIS: But why did you play this part?

SOCRATES: Out of vanity.

NAPOLEON: Why didn't you pray for pardon?

SOCRATES: Vanity.

NAPOLEON: Were you afraid of what the Athenians would have to say about you?

SOCRATES: No, I was afraid of my own wife, Xanthippe. She never would believe that I was wise, would not even believe that I was a man. I wanted to prove to her that I was a man.

NAPOLEON: And did you?

SOCRATES: No. She declared that my death only proved that she'd been right all along. That I had remained an idiot to the last bitter moment. And it was bitter, very bitter—believe me. One month after my death she married a butcher. . . . Now, do you mind if I ask you a question, my dear Napoleon? You said that you would lead your troops to victory or die: yet after the Russian disaster, you fled. Can you tell me why?

NAPOLEON: Out of bravery. A simple soldier has the glorious privilege of dying for his country, a monarch has the more bitter duty of continuing to live.

SOCRATES (*ironically*): I understand.

NAPOLEON (*angrily*): You don't understand anything.

SOCRATES: Perhaps I don't.

ST. FRANCIS: Please, please, my friends, we must have peace in Olympus if nowhere else. Let us consider how we are going to restore peace on earth.

NAPOLEON: Reason has failed to do so at any rate.

SOCRATES: No, it was not Reason's fault, it was mine.

NAPOLEON (*sarcastically*): Perhaps you would like to try again.

SOCRATES: Willingly.

ST. FRANCIS: I should be so grateful to you if you would.

NAPOLEON: Give him another chance.

SOCRATES: I am quite ready to return to Earth.

ST. FRANCIS: But won't he be arrested at once?

NAPOLEON: Naturally he could not return as Socrates. He must go as someone else.

ST. FRANCIS: But as whom?

NAPOLEON: Well . . . as a general, for example.

SOCRATES: Do people believe in the wisdom of generals?

ST. FRANCIS: I've got an idea. How would it do if he were to go as the President of the League of Nations Union? (ST. FRANCIS *sighs*.)

SOCRATES: How would it do if I offered him the Nobel Peace Prize?

NAPOLEON: That's not a bad idea. What opportunities these modern dictators have!

ST. FRANCIS: Do what you feel best, my dear Socrates. You'd better go to the Celestial Tailor and get him to fit you out in tails and a top hat. And fly at once to earth. (*To* ANGEL.) When does the next Air Express leave for Earth?

ANGEL: In twenty minutes or so.

ST. FRANCIS: Then you'll have to hurry.

NAPOLEON: Well, good luck, but I bet you fail again.

SOCRATES: Waterloo to you! (*Exit.*)

NAPOLEON: What will we do if they lock him up again?

ST. FRANCIS: There still remains a telegram telling the truth. (*Exeunt.*)

ANGEL: Long distance, please. Hello, long distance? This is Many Mansions 5563 speaking. I want a personal call to Mr. Laban in the city of Dunkelstein.

(*Business of wings.*)

Hello, long distance? Yes. Mr. Laban, Dunkelstein. What! The lines to D. are cut? Oh, can't you make a special effort for me? Yes, it's Topsy. Oh, and my dear, you know that tall dark angel who was at the party last night—well, he's fallen for you completely. Yes, isn't it? Now be a lamb and put me through. Yes, I'll hold on. Hello, what's that? Who? The Archbishop of Canterbury. Yes, Your Grace—No, Your Grace—if you're wanting fine weather for the weekend you need St. Peter's Department, Pearly Gates 7560. No, Your Grace, I can't. Please clear the line, I'm in the middle of an important long distance call. Thank you—hello, Dunkelstein? Thank Heaven, at last. Mr. Laban? Angel 1100 speaking. You want to save your daughter, don't you, Mr. Laban? Yes, well, I can tell you something—I can tell you something that will save your daughter if you in return, Mr. Laban, will do something, just a little thing, very easy, hardly any trouble to you at all—I can save your daugther, Mr. Laban, if you'll just do something for me. . . .

BLACKOUT

SCENE 4

City Hall in Dunkelstein.

LABAN, FAT MAN, THIN MAN, LITTLE MAN (*singing*):

SPY SONG

Beware of people you meet in the road,
Beware of letters; they may be in code.
Beware of poison in the sugar cube,
Beware of your neighbor in the crowded tube.
Beware of brown eyes, and beware of blue,
Look behind you, behind you; they're watching you,
And keep a sharp pair of eyes in your head.
Look behind the curtain and under your bed.

> Take care, take care!
> Beware, beware!
> You never know,
> You never know.
> Eena, meena, mina, mo,
> You're a Spy, so out you go.

Spies in the bedroom, spies on the roof,
Spies in the bathroom, we've got proof.
Spies on the lawn where the shadows harden,
Spies behind the gooseberries in the kitchen garden.
Spies at the front door, spies at the back,
And hiding in the coat stand underneath a mac.
Spies in the cupboard, under the stairs,
Spies in the cellar, they've been there for years.

> Take care, take care!
> Beware, beware!
> You never know,
> You never know.

Eena, meena, mina, mo,
You're a Spy, so out you go.

Plus fours, shorts, or fishing hats,
Or nurses' uniforms or spats,
Disguised as postmen or as caddies,
Disguised in kilts as hieland laddies.
Gardeners, income tax assessors,
Geological professors,
Disguised as white-haired country rectors,
Disguised as sanitary inspectors.

Take care, take care!
Beware, beware!
You never know,
You never know.
Eena, meena, mina, mo.
You're a Spy, so out you go.

There's a signal in the waving of the guard's green flag,
There's a signal in the dropping of the lady's bag,
Signals in the track that the steamroller leaves,
Signals in the web that the spider weaves,
Signals in the turning of the weathercock,
Signals in the squeaking of the rusty lock,
Signals in the layout of the flowers at Kew,
And signals in the features of the monkeys at the Zoo.

Take care, take care!
Beware, beware!
You never know,
You never know.
Eena, meena, mina, mo.
You're a Spy, so out you go.

(*Exeunt.*)

(*Enter* DAVID *and* CAIN *right.*)

DAVID: You know, I don't believe Socrates is mad at all. We
should lay down our arms, he says, then there would be
peace. A simple recipe!

CAIN: Too simple. A man who prefaces every sentence with the
phrase, "I know that I know nothing," must be a lunatic.

DAVID: I think he's putting it on.

CAIN: Why do you think that?

DAVID: A lunatic usually shows some traces of reason. This Socrates has not spoken one single reasonable sentence.

CAIN: Who do you think the man is?

DAVID: Some spy with a secret mission.

CAIN: Have him shot. . . . Was that spy in the cornfield ever caught?

DAVID: He disappeared without a trace.

CAIN: Go on with the search. Has Noah been found?

DAVID: He's disappeared into the blue, too.

CAIN: Samuel.

(SAMUEL *enters right.*)

Send in the gentleman from the War Ministry.

SAMUEL: Pardon, Excellency, but there's a woman outside who won't go away.

CAIN: Who is she?

SAMUEL: Rachel Laban's nurse.

(SARAH *enters right.*)

SARAH: Where have you hidden my child?

DAVID: That is a secret of state.

SARAH: I wasn't talking to you. Who are you? Aren't you ashamed of yourself, running around like a cat on hot bricks?

DAVID: I'm the Minister for Propaganda and Enlightenment.

SARAH: Would you believe it? A dirty Dominie! Very brave when you are drunk!

DAVID: The Commandant is working, he cannot receive you.

SARAH: Can't receive me? Me?! I've known Mr. Cain since he wore diapers and couldn't speak a word—

SAMUEL: Shall I put her out?

(SARAH *pushes him back.*)

SARAH: Take that for your impudence. (*To* CAIN.) I want to know where you've hidden my Rachel.

CAIN: Rachel is beyond all help, even yours.

SARAH: Beyond my help? If I can't help her who can? I've carried her at my breast. I've played with her, cried with her, I was sick with her when she was sick. I got better when she got better. What have you done with my Rachel, you dirty kidnapper?

(CAIN *is silent.*)

DAVID: She'd talk the hind leg off a donkey.

SARAH: Have you . . . killed her? Then God have mercy on your
soul! Send me to the scaffold, too, for if she's dead there can
be nothing for me but death. My husband was killed in the
last war, and my son. My husband and my son. She was all
I had. (SARAH *weeps*.)

(LABAN *enters and goes to the bench right*.)

CAIN: And here's the broken father! You take him on, David, I
can't stand these scenes.
LABAN: My daughter, my daughter. Mr. Cain, I implore you . . .
You can't kill an innocent child.

(*Telephone*. DAVID *answers*.)

DAVID: Yes—it's for you, Mr. Laban.
LABAN: For me?
DAVID: Yes, a long-distance call.
LABAN: Where from?
DAVID: It sounded like Olympus.
LABAN: Never heard of it. (LABAN *takes telephone*.) Yes? Yes,
Laban speaking. Who? Yes I do, I am in despair. Indeed I
would like to save her. But who is speaking? Angel 1100.
Oh, yes. What? Yes, of course, anything you like, please go
on. You don't say so! No war? A joke? But this is wonder-
ful. . . . What? Not a pure Dunkelsteiner? Well! Now what
can I do for you?—Wings? Yes, I think so, genuine Parisian;
no no, not secondhand, of course not, the very best, small,
smart, and with gold embroidery—I'll have them sent off by
registered mail tomorrow! Thank you very much. Good-bye—
Good-bye . . . Saved! (*To* CAIN.) But you mustn't let me dis-
turb you, my friend! You have important business of war, eh?
Well, you'll soon be through with that. Good-bye, gentlemen.
SARAH: And Rachel? You've nothing to say for that poor child?
LABAN: How can I? This gentleman's time costs money. Come,
Sarah.
SARAH: You heartless wretch! (*Both exit right*.)
CAIN: What on earth was he getting at?
DAVID: He was putting it on, too. Wants to touch your heart
with his manly heroism, so that you'll pardon his daughter.
CAIN: What was that telephone message?
DAVID: Sounded like code.
CAIN: Check it.
DAVID (*into telephone*): Where did that last call come from?
Where? (*To* CAIN.) She says Olympus!
CAIN: Nonsense!

DAVID (*into telephone*): Who? (*To* CAIN.) She says Angel 1100.

CAIN: Code. It's very strange, though; only a few minutes ago all the trunk lines were cut.

DAVID: Do you think Laban's a spy, too?

(CAIN *and* DAVID *stare at each other completely startled. Enter* SAMUEL *right.*)

SAMUEL: Two letters, sir. (*And off.*)

CAIN (*reading letter*): Socrates has disappeared. When they opened the cell it contained nothing but a cloud.

DAVID: What did I tell you? Socrates was putting it on!

CAIN (*reading second letter*): Rachel and Jacob have escaped! From the condemned cell.

DAVID: That was it—a message in code!

CAIN: I'll have you shot if you don't recapture Jacob.

DAVID: Well, they have obviously bribed a warder.

CAIN: Get on with it then, off you go to the prison!

DAVID: Me?

CAIN: Search everywhere . . . How's the agitation against foreigners going?

DAVID: Hot and strong. The Union of Married Women Teachers demands their banishment. The league of ex-postal officials has called a spontaneous protest meeting with the slogan, "Death to all defilers of the race." (*Exit* DAVID.)

(SOCRATES *enters dressed as a gentleman.*)

CAIN: Who are you?

SOCRATES: The Voice of Reason.

CAIN: Ah, the League of Nations delegate!

SOCRATES: Well, one could say the Voice of Reason could be the Voice of the League of Nations.

CAIN: What does the League of Nations want?

SOCRATES: Peace.

CAIN: The League of Nations would do better to work for peace in times of peace.

SOCRATES: If everyone worked for peace in peacetime things would never come to war at all.

CAIN: But now we have war and we shall win.

SOCRATES: Will you win?

CAIN: We have faith in our victory.

SOCRATES: And hasn't the enemy faith in his victory? . . . If no nation had faith in victory they would none of them ever want armies!

CAIN: What precisely is your business here?

SOCRATES: My business has to do with you.

CAIN: Put your proposals briefly and clearly.

SOCRATES: If you made peace, you would be hailed as the savior of the nation.

CAIN: I *am* the savior!

SOCRATES: You should make overtures to the enemy.

CAIN: Will the League of Nations lend me support?

SOCRATES (*after a pause*): With the peace prize.

CAIN: I am to receive the peace prize? Are you bribing me?

SOCRATES: Well—yes!

CAIN: And if I decline?

SOCRATES: Are you so rich?

CAIN: And if I accept?

SOCRATES: Then reason will have won.

CAIN: And my country?

SOCRATES: Your country will lose nothing. It will gain peace.

CAIN: And when must I decide?

SOCRATES: Now.

CAIN: How much is it?

SOCRATES: Thirty thousand dollars.

(CAIN *is silent.*)

Well let us say fifty thousand.

CAIN: You can't bribe me. I accept in the name of the State.

SOCRATES: God be praised!

CAIN: The war is over! There will be a spontaneous demonstration. I will inform the people. No—you'd better tell them.

SOCRATES: Certainly. (*Takes microphone near the window.*) My dear people, what is the matter? Why are you shouting? I don't understand . . .

CAIN: I understand only too well.

SOCRATES: You think the Brazilians are defiling the blood of the Dunkelsteiners. . . . But the Brazilians have just as much right to say that you Dunkelsteiners are defiling the blood of the Brazilians. You think I am a traitor? But perhaps you are traitors? Perhaps we are all traitors? Perhaps we are all betraying each other and ourselves. (*Shouting.*) What do you prove by shouting me down? (*He is hit on the head by a stone, and staggers back.*) . . . No, a stone is no proof either . . .

CAIN: Yet it is a sign of the mood of the people. I do *not* accept your peace prize. . . . The money is confiscated by the State. (*He takes the microphone.*) Fellow countrymen. I acknowledge your spontaneous enthusiasm and salute your struggle for purity of blood, for purity of soil. The defilers of our race shall be punished as they deserve. Dunkelstein for the Dunkelsteiners! (*Cheers.*)

SOCRATES: But reason . . .

CAIN: Reason is an invention of the Brazilians! (*Exit right.*)

SOCRATES' SONG

SOCRATES (*sings*):
> When my body cast a shade
> O Reason was a little light
> On the solitary shed,
> And strict and private was the way
> In its secrecy revealed,
> To the pure initiate,
> While the unregenerate world
> In the night of folly lay.

> "O Holy Light," the wise men cried,
> "In the utter darkness burn!
> Before the mortal worlds were made
> Thou art the light; thou art the way.
> I am thy servant: govern me;
> On my inward darkness shine,
> Straighten my perplexity
> Nor deceive me, nor betray."

> But, O, the Golden Age is ended;
> Electric light is not the same,
> Fools are proud and wise confounded
> So broad and common is the way.
> And men's imaginations see
> Primal darkness overcome,
> For glittering is luxury
> And nights of folly bright as day.

SOCRATES: Poor St. Francis! Napoleon is right. Reason is dead. (*Exit left.*)

(*Enter* CAIN, THIN MAN, FAT MAN, *and* LITTLE MAN.)

CAIN: Hallo, where is he? . . . That League of Nations fellow has disappeared, too. That's one enemy out of the way. Gentlemen, the people have confidence in me. I am the ruler of the country. . . . Has all the gold and silver been confiscated?

FAT MAN: It is all in the strong room of my bank.

CAIN: Even gold fillings must be handed over now.

LITTLE MAN: The dentists are working overtime.

FAT MAN: Bread and meat can be bought by ration cards only.

CAIN: Here is the war map. As soon as the sirens go off, the people will assemble in the bombproof cellars. The town will be hidden in smoke.

THIN MAN: It is already.

FAT MAN: You can't see your hand in front of your nose.

LITTLE MAN: Night over Dunkelstein.

CAIN: All the better! Our air squadrons are now leaving their underground hangars. (*Goes to map on wall.*) Here. They will encircle the enemy somewhere about here and bomb them to bits.

FAT MAN: And send Dunkelstein up in flames.

CAIN: That is war, gentlemen. There will be destruction in any case. Better be destroyed by your own bombs than the enemy's.

(*Noise of airplanes outside.*)

THE THREE: They are coming!

CAIN: Gas masks! (*They put on their gas masks.*)

(DAVID *enters left.*)

Where are they?

DAVID: Outside.

CAIN: Over the city?

DAVID: In the corridor.

CAIN: The enemy in the corridor? (*Screaming.*) Traitor!

DAVID: Who? Me?

CAIN: You! All of you! I am betrayed. My friends have betrayed me.

FAT MAN: You must come to a quick decision.

CAIN: I will . . . I won't . . . I will . . . I won't . . .

DAVID: What are we to do with him?

CAIN: Hang them! Cut off their heads! Shoot them! Quarter them!

DAVID (*shouting off*): Noah to be hanged, beheaded, shot, and quartered.

CAIN: Is it Noah outside?

DAVID: Yes. I found him in the prison.

CAIN: Where is the enemy?

DAVID: The enemy?

CAIN: Yes, the enemy.

DAVID: We don't know. We're still waiting for the fight.

(CAIN *and the other three take off their gas masks.*)

CAIN: Where did you find Noah?

DAVID: In the prison.

CAIN: Where was he arrested?

DAVID: He arrested himself. I discovered him when searching the prison. He had hidden himself in a cell.

CAIN: Bring him in!

(NOAH *enters.*)

NOAH: Everything must be done in order; even death. If I'm to be hanged, why shoot me afterward? If I'm to be shot, why cut off my head? If you cut off my head and then quarter me, you will be dividing me into five, not four.

CAIN: You are a deserter.

NOAH: Right as usual.

CAIN: You are a thief.

NOAH: Wrong for once.

CAIN: You are robbing the State of bread. You smuggled yourself secretly into prison. You have been letting the State feed you for nothing.

NOAH: That's true enough.

CAIN: Punishment for desertion is death. Punishment for theft is prison. You will therefore be imprisoned for a suitable period and then shot.

NOAH: How long have I got to go to prison for?

CAIN: Since you have already spent some time there without any justification, I shall sentence you to—three days.

NOAH: Oh, but just think, Mr. Cain, it was a serious offense. Theft in wartime. I think you could make it a year or three years.

CAIN: One of your days you've already served, so you will be shot in two days' time.

NOAH: If I'd said nothing and taken the punishment, I should have had a day longer to live! A fool I always was . . . (NOAH *is led out.*)

(*Enter* SAMUEL.)

SAMUEL: A telegram for the Government.

CAIN: Give it to me. (*Reading aloud to himself.*) "All operations to cease immediately. War a misunderstanding. Peace on earth." (CAIN *sinks back on to his chair. Buries head in hands.*) Gentlemen, it is the end.

THIN MAN: Of our freedom?

FAT MAN: Of our State?

LITTLE MAN: Of our people?

CAIN: Peace has broken out—in the midst of war!

THIN MAN: A short war.

LITTLE MAN: A sharp one.

FAT MAN: Hurrah!

CAIN: You shout hurrah when your heart should be at half-mast.

DAVID: My lovely "War Song."

FAT MAN (*boxes his ears*): So you'd betrayed war in the same way as you betrayed peace!

DAVID (*boxes the* FAT MAN's *ears*): I didn't want it.

FAT MAN: He hit me.

LITTLE MAN: I saw him.

DAVID (*boxes the* LITTLE MAN's *ears*): And now you've felt it.

THIN MAN: This is going too far.

DAVID (*boxes the* THIN MAN's *ears*): And that's gone too near. (*General scuffle.*)

CAIN: Peace! I demand peace!

THE THREE: It was you who declared war.

DAVID: Back, or I fire. Ow! (*He shoots into the air and the* LITTLE MAN *knocks* DAVID's *revolver out of his hand.*)

FAT MAN: So this is peace.

LITTLE MAN (*knocks* DAVID *down*): Knock out.

CAIN: Samuel, remove the Minister of Propaganda and Enlightenment.

(SAMUEL *leads* DAVID *out right.*)

You wanted to hear my decision. Listen then. I have never loved peace. Now for the first time, I have come to know the true greatness of war. The people are awakened. There is faith, courage, purpose . . . What does this telegram say? Peace . . . Good. We shall declare war again.

LITTLE MAN: Supposing the enemy doesn't want war.

CAIN: We shall force him to submit to our will.

FAT MAN: But whom shall we force? Who is the enemy to be?

CAIN: It's always easy to find an enemy.

THIN MAN: And how do you propose to raise the money?

CAIN: As long as we have paper factories we have money enough and to spare.

FAT MAN: You call that money?

THIN MAN and LITTLE MAN: Bad money.

CAIN: You call yourself patriots and think only of money. Is that how you defend the honor of our country? Don't you realize that our *prestige* demands the continuation of this war? If you leave me in the lurch I shall appeal to the people. And do you know what the people will say? No more peace! . . . I give you three minutes to decide. If you decide wrong I shall have you shot. (*Exit left.*)

FAT MAN: He'll have us all killed.

THIN MAN: A ticklish situation.

LITTLE MAN: Once anybody starts shooting there's no stopping them.

THIN MAN: We must keep cool.

FAT MAN: If we decide for peace we shall probably be shot.

LITTLE MAN: We certainly shall if we decide for war.

FAT MAN: The question is which is dearer, peace or war?

LITTLE MAN: The crops are all burned.

THIN MAN: Bread is scarce.

FAT MAN: We had too much. Now we have too little.

THIN MAN: He's going to appeal to the people.

LITTLE MAN: With a revolver in both hands.

THIN MAN: Anyone who votes for peace will be shot.

FAT MAN: He will not appeal to the people. He won't shoot anybody.

LITTLE MAN: He's got the guns, not us.

(*Enter* LABAN.)

THE THREE (*shouting at* LABAN): Peace has been declared.

LITTLE MAN: But Mr. Cain says he'll declare war again.

LABAN: You must leave this to me.

THIN MAN (*quickly*): Certainly. I'm going to get out at once.

FAT MAN: For myself, I must hurry off to Singapore.

LITTLE MAN: Excuse me, I must fly to Persia and see the Shah.

(*All three make for the exit.*)

LABAN: Don't rush off immediately, gentlemen, I have a plan. Leave me alone with Mr. Cain and wait for me at my office. On my table you will find a paper of the greatest importance. Publish the contents if I do not return within half an hour.

THE THREE: We will. (*The three go off.*)

(*Enter* CAIN *left.*)

CAIN: Well, have they come to a decision?

LABAN: I have made their decision . . .

CAIN: To carry on the war?

(LABAN *bows.*)

I thank you.

LABAN: But there is just one question, one small, insignificant question

CAIN: Ah, who is the enemy? The hereditary enemy, of course.

LABAN (*pointedly*): The people hate all foreigners.

CAIN: And rightly so.

LABAN: Especially the Brazilians.

CAIN: Precisely.

LABAN: Good. Only a native Dunkelsteiner is fit to lead the army.

CAIN: Therefore I shall retain command.

LABAN: I have in my possession a certain piece of paper, quite a small piece of paper, a birth certificate. (*Sharply.*) You are not a Dunkelsteiner at all, Mr. Cain. Your grandmother was a Brazilian.

CAIN: That's a lie.

LABAN: I have the document here.

CAIN: It's a forgery. Show it to me.

LABAN: Here it is.

CAIN: Who gave you this? Socrates? Confess. Can't you see that the Brazilians themselves have forged this document? (*Tears up paper and throws it at* LABAN's *feet.*) There's your precious document!

LABAN: Why go to all that trouble? It was only a copy. The original is locked up in my safe.

CAIN: You shall not leave this building alive. I shall have you shot.

LABAN: Not so fast, not so fast, my dear sir. I think you had better do nothing of the kind. (*Takes out watch.*) If I am not let out of this building within three minutes the town will be plastered with posters exposing you.

(CAIN, *after a moment, takes out revolver and puts it to his head.* LABAN *wrests revolver from him. Long pause.*)

Really, Mr. Cain, apart from the fact that the revolver is not loaded, there's no need to kill yourself. You are young enough to start again. Think what you can do if you go on living. Write your memoirs, fly the Atlantic. The North Pole has been fully explored, but you can try the South Pole. Take an expedition there. We will finance it. You may go now. Goodbye, Mr. Cain. (*At microphone.*) Ladies and gentlemen, this is Laban speaking. I am very glad to be able to announce to you that peace has broken out. Peace on earth! Long live peace!

(A *growing cheering is heard outside. Enter the* LITTLE MAN.)

LITTLE MAN: Peace?

LABAN: Peace!

LITTLE MAN: Peace was unavoidable.

LABAN: Why do you say that? I've always heard war spoken of as unavoidable, not peace.

LITTLE MAN: But peace won't last forever. But there's no need to worry about your jam factory, Mr. Laban. It will prosper again one day.

LABAN: I'm not complaining. Half an hour ago I sold the whole business, lock, stock, and barrel, at a wartime price.

LITTLE MAN: But how did you know?

LABAN: I have my sources.

LITTLE MAN: Where is Cain?

LABAN: Gone to write his memoirs.

LITTLE MAN: Where?

LABAN: To the South Pole, I believe.

FAT MAN (enter left): Oh, Mr. Laban, what has happened to your poor children?

LABAN: My children are quite happy where they are. They managed to escape from prison, went straight to a justice of the peace, and got married.

LITTLE MAN: What do the people say?

LABAN: The people are delighted. They always are when right triumphs over wrong.

FAT MAN: Certainly. The only question is whether they know which is which.

LABAN: Ah, the people know that all right.

SAMUEL (entering): The young couple.

(Enter RACHEL and JACOB, followed by the crowd.)

LABAN: My children!

(Enter the Band. Confusion.)

CRIES: Rachel! Rachel!

RACHEL'S SONG

RACHEL (sings):
    Now the day is done,
    And the fev'rish sorrow
    In the heart of man
    Sleeps until tomorrow.

    Bounded is the sea—
    And the earth is small.
    Man's stupidity
    Has no bounds at all.

Now he strides in folly,
Now stumbles blind and wild,
To terror and illusion,
Obedient as a child.

On wise men now believe,
And then to fools will fly,
And curses where he blessed,
And dreads his destiny.

Yet, if he chose, the earth
And all her fruits were his;
And lucky be the man
Who now unlucky is.

Bounded is the sea—
And the earth is small.
Man's stupidity
Has no bounds at all.

(*Cheers from the crowd.*)

RACHEL: Where is Noah?

LABAN: In prison.

RACHEL: Can't we release him?

LABAN (*to* DAVID): Yes, I think so. Go and release Noah and bring
   him here.

DAVID: Can I bring the children, too? They're so fond of Noah.

LABAN: As long as they don't start singing that "War Song."

DAVID: They shall sing the "Peace Song." (*Exit* DAVID.)

JACOB: You spoke wonderfully.

RACHEL: Everything I said I said for you.

JACOB: And now we've been married two hours.

RACHEL: Just two hours.

JACOB: Will you always love me? Even when we've been married
   two years?

(RACHEL *nods.*)

RACHEL: Forever.

(*Tumult at door.*)

SAMUEL: You can't come in, I tell you. You're dirtier than ever.

NOAH: Right as usual. Is it peace again?

LABAN: Yes, it is peace—don't you know?

(NOAH *goes to placard with the inscription:* "Long Live
War!")

NOAH: How can anyone know? You turn so quickly—and that old placard doesn't know either—look at it.

LABAN: Samuel, take that placard away.

SAMUEL: It only wants turning around. (SAMUEL *turns the placard again showing the inscription: "No More War!"*)

NOAH: It only needs turning around. A ruddy merry-go-round!

THE CHILDREN (*once more sing the "Peace Song"*):

> We are the new battalions,
> Humanity's police;
> And love is our commander,
> And his word is Peace.
> With heart and soul
> Till we reach our goal,
> O'er earth and air and sea,
> We will sing this song
> As we march along,
> Marching on to victory.
>
> Before our friendly handshake
> All anger melts away,
> United we go forward
> Till victory crowns the day.
> With heart and soul
> Till we reach our goal,
> O'er earth and air and sea,
> We will sing this song
> As we march along,
> Marching on to victory.

BLACKOUT

SCENE 5

Olympus.

NAPOLEON: Cigarette?

ST. FRANCIS: Thank you. I don't smoke.

NAPOLEON: Whiskey?

ST. FRANCIS: No, really, thank you. I never drink.

NAPOLEON: You are unhappy, my dear Francis.

ST. FRANCIS: How long is it since you sent the war telegram?

NAPOLEON: For us, the breath of a second. For humanity, the best part of an earthly day.

ST. FRANCIS: To think that a single day can contain so much horror, so much cruelty, so much suffering, such poverty of spirit! I pity mankind.

NAPOLEON: Ah, you see only the suffering. And weren't many of them perfectly happy? Happy to die.

ST. FRANCIS: That, to my mind, is the most dreadful part of it.

NAPOLEON: Well, personally, I call the courage to die, heroism.

ST. FRANCIS: Have so few men the courage to live? Even for peace, you see, they are readier to die than to live.

NAPOLEON: That, my dear old Francis, is because peace is not an ideal which offers a reward for living. There's no place in the sun for the peaceful.

ST. FRANCIS: I wonder if that's true? Perhaps we should meditate deeply upon the nature of peace as it is, and as it might be. Perhaps the peace the statesmen talk so much about is not really the right kind of peace at all.

NAPOLEON: You know, there's a little thing that's worrying me. It's silly, but I can't get it out of my head. How did this man, this banker fellow, find out? And who told him that my telegram was a joke?

ST. FRANCIS: A bitter joke, indeed.

NAPOLEON: But how could he know? How could anybody know? The wireless and the telephone were put out of action. The Dunkelsteiners blew up the railways. And chased off any airplanes that tried to land. (*To* ANGEL.) You're sure you followed my instructions, my dear?

ANGEL (*coming down*): Oh yes, Your Majesty.

NAPOLEON (*pacing up and down*): Then how did Laban know? (NAPOLEON *comes to a standstill face to face with the* ANGEL.) Those are new wings you've got.

(ANGEL *is silent.*)

Small, smart . . . genuine Parisian wings! Where did they come from?

ANGEL: Well, Your Majesty, St. John asked me . . .

(*Thunder.*)

NAPOLEON: Where . . . ?

ANGEL: Well, you see St. Peter said . . .

(*Thunder.*)

NAPOLEON: The truth, please!

ANGEL: Well, really, St. Anthony did say . . .

(*Loud thunder.*)

ST. FRANCIS: Don't lie, child. You have heard the threefold warning.

NAPOLEON: *You* . . . you betrayed my secret.

ANGEL: I did, Your Majesty.

NAPOLEON: You let yourself *be bribed!*

ANGEL: Yes, Your Majesty . . . the old wings didn't suit me at all.

NAPOLEON: Now there you are, you see. When I was on earth I never let a woman into secrets of state.

(*Indignant thunder.*)

Ahem! Still, they are very beautiful wings.

ANGEL: Oh, aren't they, Your Majesty! Now I have no desires at all. I am happy, absolutely happy.

ST. FRANCIS: Dear me. I wonder when mankind will be absolutely happy with no desires at all.

NAPOLEON: Never.

ST. FRANCIS: When, oh when, will peace reign upon earth?

NAPOLEON: My dear Francis, for thousands of years, intelligent men have known that peace is a dream of intellectuals.

ST. FRANCIS: And one day that dream will be fulfilled. Love will be stronger than hatred. The truth will be truer than official lies. And mankind will see the truth and recognize it.

NAPOLEON: I doubt it.

ST. FRANCIS: Peace on earth . . .

NAPOLEON: And when will that day be?

ST. FRANCIS: When the clever stop talking and the wise begin to act.

NAPOLEON: That is a dangerous doctrine.

ST. FRANCIS: Why dangerous?

NAPOLEON: It reminds me of a sentence written by a rebel, "Hitherto philosophers have sought to explain the world. Our task is to change it." For this doctrine he now lies in Hell.

ST. FRANCIS: But surely he was right.

(*Thunder.*)

NAPOLEON: You hear?

ST. FRANCIS (*whispering*): Still—he was right.

CURTAIN

THE LAST DAYS OF MANKIND

(excerpt)

by KARL KRAUS

TRANSLATED BY MAX SPALTER

ACT V

SCENE 54

The CARPER *at his desk.*

THE CARPER (*reading*): "The desire to ascertain the exact length
of time it takes to transform a tree into newsprint led the
owner of a paper mill to conduct an interesting experiment.
At seven thirty-five A.M. he had three trees in the forest next
to his paper mill felled. These trees were then transported
to the wood pulp factory after their bark had been peeled
off. The conversion of the three tree trunks into liquid pulp
was accomplished so swiftly that at nine thirty-nine the first
roll of printing paper had already come out of the machine.
By means of an automobile, this roll was immediately con-
veyed to the printing press of a daily newspaper—a distance
of four kilometers—and at eleven A.M. the paper was already
on sale in the street. Consequently, it took only three hours
and twenty-five minutes to make it possible for the public
to read the latest news upon material derived from trees
upon whose branches that same morning birds had sung their
songs."

(*Outside, the distant cry of a newspaper vendor.*)

It is five o'clock. The answer is there. The echo of my
bloody madness; nothing else resounds from battered creation
except this cry, whereby ten million dying human beings in-
dict me for still living—I who had eyes to see things in such
a way that the world became what I had seen. If it was just
in the eyes of heaven that it happened, it was not in the
least just not to destroy me first! Did I deserve this fulfill-
ment of my deathly fear of life? What is sprouting while I
sleep? Why was I chosen to rehabilitate Thersites and not
chosen to dishonor Achilles? Why did I lack the physical
strength needed to dispose of the sins of this planet with
the stroke of an axe? Why did I lack the intellectual power
to force desecrated mankind to cry out? Why is my counter-
cry not stronger than the tin-plated command which exerts
authority over the souls of this earth? I am preserving documents for a time which will not comprehend them, a time
so distant from today that they will call me a falsifier. But
no, the time to say that will never come. Because that time

357

will simply not be. I have written a tragedy whose perishing
hero is mankind; whose tragic conflict ends as fatally as
that of world and nature. Since this drama has no other hero
but mankind, so it can have no audience! But what does my
tragic hero die of? Was the order of the world stronger than
his personality? No, the order of nature was stronger than
the order of the world. He collapses upon untruth, upon the
unreality which has deprived him of mankind's old signif-
icances and life forms. He perishes because of a circumstance
which affected him as both intoxication and compulsion. Are
there guilty parties? No, otherwise there would be avengers;
otherwise the hero mankind would have resisted the curse of
becoming the slave of his means, the martyr of his necessity. And as the means of life consume the purposes of life,
so they require service on behalf of the means of death—in
order to poison those who survive. If there were guilty parties,
humanity would have resisted the compulsion to become a
hero for such ends! The few who dictated such values would
have been answered by those who were unified to oneness.
But the culprits are not tyrants. Their spirit is shaped by the
mold of the mass. We are all individuals. We all have our
anguish, which means nothing to others. And we are not
inflamed by the contrast posed daily by our sacrifice for the
profits of others, for their gruesome gains. Tyrants yield to
terror. But we would have replaced our tyrants from ourselves. For we are all driven by empty words, and not those
of the ruler but of the machine. Of what use is a revolver
against the machine? Unlike the crossbow employed against
tyrants, the revolver against the machine sets no example.
We are the machine's inventors, and what threatens us is
not the machine gun but the bleak wonder that such a thing
exists. Not its threat but its very being cripples decisiveness.
How could a counter-authority arise to tell us to destroy our
weapons! Can I speak in the auditorium of Europe? So you
must continue to die for something which you call honor
or Bukovina—but about which you know nothing—for it is
really the weapon itself. For what did you die? You would
have saved your necks if all of you had been intelligent
enough to perceive contrasts. What contempt for death!
Why should you be contemptuous of that which you do
not know? Indeed, one is contemptuous of the life which
one does not know. You first become acquainted with it
when the accident of shrapnel does not completely kill you,
or when the commanded beast—which was once a human

being like yourself—foams at the mouth while attacking you; and you realize for a moment that you are standing at a threshold. And at that time, would the order-giving beast dare to say of you that you had contempt for death? And you failed to use that time to cry out to your superior that, not being God's superior, he had no right to destroy what has been created? No, you allowed yourselves to be driven by him—and God—across that threshold where the mystery begins, whose betrayal should be demanded by no earthly state! In pursuit of which everyone dispatches his heroes but no one his spies! If only you had known at the moment of sacrifice of the profits which grew in spite of—no, because of—this sacrifice; in fact, battening on this very sacrifice! Because never before this indecisive war of machines, had there been such godless war profits—and whether you triumph or not, you are losing the war which profits your killers. Your cowardly, technologically advanced killers, who can kill and live only at a distance from the showplace of their deeds. You, too, faithful companion of my word, looking upward with pure belief to the heaven of art, laying your ear upon her heart with quiet knowledge, you, too, had to go over there? I saw you the day you pulled out. Rain and the filth of this fatherland, and its nefarious music constituted your farewell as you were herded into a cattle car! I see your pale face in this orgy of muck and lies, in this dreadful good-bye of a freight station from where human material is sent away by means of decrees which unchain bodies and imprison the spirit and transform condemned life into a nursery where cattle-hands play their games! You did not look like them. How could you have failed to die after having to experience such a going off, in comparison with which Wallenstein's camp appeared like the public room of a palatial hotel! Because machine-man gets dirty before he becomes bloody. So started your journey to Italy, you art scholar. And you, noble poet's heart, who were devoted to the mystery of a vowel in the midst of mortars and murderers—did you spend four years of your youth beneath the earth in order to test your future home? What was there for you to seek? Lice for the fatherland? To wait until the arrival of grenade fragments? To prove that your body was more resistant to the efficiency of the Schneider-Creuzot fortifications than the body of someone from Turin would be resistant to Skoda? Are we traveling salesmen of munitions works, not attesting to the proficiency of their firm by mouth but proving with their bodies the

inferiority of their competition? Where many traveled, there
will be many cripples! May the market outlets be transformed
into battlefields. But that they had the power to force loftier
creatures into the service of depravity—never did the devil
imagine such a confirmation of his dominion. And if it had
been whispered to him the first year of the war—when he
pursued nations with a primer in his hand to make sure they
managed his business with more soul—that in that same year
a petroleum refinery would realize a net profit of 137 percent
from its total share capital; that David Fanto would earn 73
percent; that the banks would clear a net profit of 19.9 million; and that profiteers would be compensated a hundredfold for their depreciation of foreign blood with meat and
sugar and alcohol and fruit and potatoes and butter and
leather and rubber and coal and iron and wool and soap and
oil and ink and weapons—had he known any of this, the devil
himself would have spoken out for the renunciations of peace!
And for that you lay four years in filth and wetness; for that
it became more difficult to reach you with a greeting; for that
the book intended for your consolation was held up. They
wished you to remain among the living, because they had
not yet stolen enough in their stock exchange, had not yet
lied enough in their press, had not yet exploited their official
positions for maximum torment, had not yet proved a sufficient scourge for mankind, had not yet—with all their opportunities and actions—referred sufficiently to the war in
order to justify their impotence and evil lusts and excuse
their criminality. They had not yet waltzed through this
whole tragic carnival in which men died observed by female
war correspondents and in which butchers became philosophers *honoris causa*—they had not yet experienced the final
dance and starvation! How you lay weeks on end beneath
flurries of thrown mines; how you were menaced by ava-
lanches; how you hung suspended on a cable at a height of
3,000 meters between the heavy bombardment of the enemy
and the machine-gun fire of your "own side"—the very mention of this last phrase is equivalent to high treason; how you
were exposed a hundredfold to prolonged torments of delin-
quent types—and often enough without a last meal; how
you had to live through the whole variety of death in the
collision of organism and machine—through high-explosive
mines, barbed-wire entanglements, fortifications and booby
traps, dumdum bullets, bombs, flames, and gas, and all the
hells of barrage-fire—because madness and profiteering had

not yet vented their cowards' anger upon you? And in such abandonment you were supposed to remain "fit for service" because mankind had not yet been afflicted with enough syphilis for the sake of a plundered fantasy? And you outside and we inside—are we to look fixedly into the grave which we had to dig under higher orders—as was the case with Serbian old men for no other reason but that they were Serbs, still alive and hence suspicious! If only one could escape from this adventure unhurt, albeit woebegone, impoverished, and grown old; and if one could get hold of those perennial ringleaders of international crime, in order to pull them one by one toward an acknowledgment of responsibility, to lock them up in their church, and there—as was done with the old Serbs—have each tenth man draw his lot of death! But not to kill them—no, to box their ears! And thus to address them: What, you had no idea, you scamps, that the consequences of a declaration of war encompass among millions of possibilities of shuddering outrage also this: that children are left without milk and horses without oats, and that far from the shooting one can go blind from methyl alcohol—if this suits the war plans of profiteers? You cannot comprehend the misfortune of one hour of suffering by someone imprisoned for many years? Or the groan of yearning and love, which has been dirtied, torn, and murdered? Were you not once capable of imagining what hells are opened in one single minute of a mother's torment as she sits through night and day listening and waiting for a hero's death? And could you not perceive how tragedy became farce, and, through the combination of new disorder and old madness of form, an operetta whose text is as much an insult as its music torture? And you did not perceive that the most trifling of your commands, the most trifling measure of your madness would imprint an inextinguishable stigma upon human dignity? If it were only stupidity which made flight from your area more difficult and let loose against each other your offices for wartime supervision, your passport offices, your offices for passport instructions, your offices for passport stipulations, your offices for border-crossing permits, local commandant, and border-protection commands—all of them entangled with one another. And you overlooked that when you stick everybody into a uniform, they will perpetually continue to salute each other? And you did not notice that these gestures were bound suddenly to become a clutching of the brow indicative of doubts about mutual common sense? And that the head-

shaking of convulsion-afflicted invalids applied to you? And
did you learn nothing from the pastimes of your glory—a
glory destined to fall apart and nonetheless continuing to
bleed the world? How is it that you murdered ones did not
stand up against this order? Against this system of murder and
an economy which condemned all future life to sheer endurance; which smothers all prospects and surrenders the smallest
necessities of happiness to the hate of nations? Senselessly raging in war and groundlessly raging against everyone because
there was a war on! Poverty, hunger, and humiliation piled up
over all who fled and stayed, and all of mankind was in shackles.
And statesmen convoked in precipitous times to check the
bestial drive of mankind were the very ones who unchained
that drive! Cowardly hatred of life—prepared in peacetime to
murder animals and children—took hold of the machine in
order to lay waste to all that grows. Hysteria, under the protection of technology, vanquishes nature; weapons are under
the rule of paper. The rotary press made us invalids before
there were victims of the cannon. Had not all realms of
fantasy been evacuated when that manifesto declared war on
the inhabited earth? At the end was the word. With the
death of the spirit, nothing remained except to give birth to
the deed. Weaklings grew strong to bring us under the wheel
of progress. And that was within her capacity to do, she
alone, who ruined the world with her whoredom! Not that
the press set the machines of death into motion—but that
the press hollowed out our hearts so that we could no more
imagine how that would be—that is the press's war guilt!
And from the lascivious wine of the press's lechery all nations
drank and the kings of the earth made love to her. And
the apocalyptic horseman encouraged her—I saw him rage
through the German Reich long before he went into action.
A decade has passed since I saw his work accomplished.
"With him, it's full speed ahead in all the streets. His moustache extends from sunrise to sundown and from south to
north. 'And the horseman was given power to take peace
from the earth, so that men would slaughter one another.'"
And I saw him as an animal with ten horns and seven heads
and a mouth like that of a lion. "One idolized the animal
and said: Who can match this animal? And who dares to
quarrel with him? He was endowed with a mouth with which
to say great things." And we fell because of him and because
of the whore of Babylon, who persuaded us in all the tongues
of the world that we are all each other's enemies and that

war had to be! And you, the victims, did not revolt against this plan? Did not resist the compulsion to die as well as the last freedom: to become incendiaries? Did not resist the devilry which ordered that the sacrifices for the wool market be carried out beneath the flags of moral pathos! Which attacks God in order to acquire his witnesses to bloody vicissitudes! All sovereign rights and life values were bartered away by materialistic ideas. The child in the womb is forced to feel hate, and the picture of struggling manliness, as well as that of women who nurse and care—their bodies armored, their faces covered by gas masks—will be passed on to the terror of posterity as that of hordes of mythical animals. Believers are shot at by church bells and nothing is regretted at altars made of shrapnel! And is all that glory and fatherland? Yes, you experienced the fatherland before you died for it! You experienced it from the moment when you had to wait for a hero's death in the sweat-and-beer atmosphere of waiting rooms; as they examined human flesh and forced human souls to take the most godless oaths. You were naked—as you should be only before God and a loved one—in front of a commission of slave drivers and pigs! Shame, shame for body and soul should have made you defy the fatherland! We have all seen this fatherland, and the more lucky ones among us who were able to flee saw it still in the figures of insolent border guards. We saw it in all the forms of lust for power pursued by slaves let loose and in the sociability of tip-hungry blackmailers. Only we others did not have to experience it in the figure of the enemy—of the true enemy—who drove you with the machine gun in front of the machine gun. But if we had seen it only in the portraits of these horrible generals, who—instead of women of leisure—advertised themselves in the theatre's yellow press to show that there was not only lots of whoring but murder as well in the world—if we had seen just that, then truly we would have yearned for the hour in which this brothel was closed! And you there—you who were battered and murdered—did not revolt against this activity? You tolerated the freedom-and-pleasure life of press strategists, parasites, and buffoons as a misfortune forced upon you? And realized that they received decorations for your martyrdom? Didn't you spit your glory in their faces? Were you lying in trains for the wounded for the press rats to describe? Did you not break and desert in the holy war in order to liberate us in the rear from the mortal enemy who bombed us daily with falsehoods? And you died for

this business? Did you live through that horror in order to
prolong our own horror, which we gasped through here between profiteering and genuine need, and between the tormenting contrasts of fattened insolence and speechless con-
sumption? Oh, you had less feeling for us than we for you;
every hour of those years which they ripped out of your lives
we wanted to demand back from them a hundredfold; and
always the question directed at you was: How will you look
if you survive all that? When you have escaped from the final
goal of glory, so that the hyenas become travel guides in
order to exploit your graves as curiosities! To fall sick, to become impoverished, to be made wretched, to be afflicted with
lice, to starve and to die for the improvement of the tourist
trade—such is the lot of all of us! They carried your skin to
market—and our own skin they have cut off for their swindles
too. But you have weapons—and did not move into this
hinterland? And you did not return from that field of shame
to the most honorable war—the war to save both us and
you? And you did not stand up as the dead from your fox-
holes to bring that breed to a sense of their responsibility,
to appear to them in sleep with the deformed countenance
which you wore in the hour of dying, with the lusterless eyes
of your heroic waiting time, with the unforgettable mask to
which your youth was condemned by this administration of
madness! Stand up then and confront them as a heroic
death—so that this commanding cowardice of life finally gets
to know the real features of such a death—and may it gaze
into their eyes for a lifetime! Disturb their sleep with your
cries of death! Disturb their sensual pleasures with the ap-
pearances of your suffering! They were able to embrace
women in the night following the day they put you to death!
Save us from them, from a peace which will bring the pes-
tilence of their nearness! Save us from the misfortune of
having to shake hands with returning court-martial judges, and
from having to meet with executioners turned civilians. For the
conscience of this vile cruelty—whose restraints were removed
not by passion but by mechanics—will recover as quickly for
daily work as it did when it was a matter of changing from
the banal to the murderous. Help, you murdered ones! Stand
by me so that I do not have to live among people who, out
of ambition or the urge for self-preservation, gave the order
that hearts should stop beating and mothers' hair go white!
As true as it is that one God lives—this destiny can be
healed only by a miracle! Come back! Ask them what they

have done with you! What they did while you were suffering because of them and what they did before you died because of them! What they did in your Galician winters! What they did that night when telephoning commandants received no answer from your area. Because at the front everything was quiet. And only later did they see how bravely you stood, man next to man presenting arms. Because you did not belong to those who desert, were not among those who retreated, and those who, because they were freezing, had to be warmed up by the machine-gun fire of superiors. You held on to your trenches and did not fall back a single step into the thieves' den of your fatherland. In front of you the enemy, behind you the fatherland, and above you the eternal stars! And you did not take to your heels in suicide. You do not die for the fatherland or because of it; not because of the foe's munition, and not because of your own—you stand and die because of nature. What a picture of endurance! What a Capuchin tomb! Corpses full of fight, protagonists of the Habsburg death-in-life, close your ranks and appear to them in their sleep! Wake up from your frozen state! Step forward! Come forward, you dear confessor of the spirit, and demand your costly head from them! You—where are you who died in the hospital? My last greeting was sent back to me with the information: "Sent away. Whereabouts unknown." Step forward to tell them where you are and how it is there, and that you will never again be willing to let yourself be used! And you there with the face to which you were condemned in your last minute when the commanded beast, foam on its mouth—perhaps formerly a human being like you—plunged into your grave—step forward! It is not your dying but what you were forced to experience which makes a sin of all sleep and all death in bed. Not your death —it is your living experience that I want to avenge upon those who imposed it upon you! I have molded them into shadows, which they are and which they wanted to belie by their appearance! I have stripped off their skin! But as for the thoughts of their stupidity, the emotions of their malice, the frightful rhythm of their nothingness—to these I gave bodies, allowing them to move themselves. Had one preserved the voice of this period on a phonograph, the outer truth would have given the lie to what lay beneath; no ear would recognize either the former or the latter. So does time work to make reality indiscernible and winds up giving amnesty for the greatest crime ever committed under the sun and stars. I saved that reality and my ear discovered the sounds of action, my eyes the gestures of conversation, and my voice—whenever I was simply reiterating—has quoted in such a manner that the keynote was held fast for all time.

> And if the world, which does not yet know, lets me say
> How all this came to pass; then you must hear
> Of deeds, carnal, bloody, unnatural,
> Of chance-ruled courts of justice, blind murder;
> Of deaths effected by force and cunning,
> And unsuccessful plans fallen back
> Upon the discoverer's head: all this I can
> Report truthfully.

And if the times were to stop listening, there would still be a listener above them! I have done nothing but shorten this lethal quantity, which by virtue of its being immeasurable, points to the disparity between time and newspaper. All their blood was only ink—now the writing will be done in blood! This is the world war. This is my manifesto. I have thought it all over carefully. I have taken upon myself the tragedy which falls apart in the scenes of collapsing humanity so that it would be heard by the spirit who is merciful to victims—even if He has renounced for all time any connection with the human ear. May He receive the keynote of this time, the echo of my bloody madness, whereby I, too, share in the guilt for these noises. May He let it count as a redemption!

(From outside, from quite a distance, the call of a newspaper vendor.)